MEEHAN'S
BARTENDER
MANUAL

MEEHAN'S
BARTENDER
MANUAL

JIM MEEHAN

Photography by Doron Gild
Illustrations by Gianmarco Magnani

TEN SPEED PRESS
California | New York

CONTENTS

FOREWORD BY PETER MEEHAN — vii

INTRODUCTION — 1

1 *History* — 7

2 *Bar Design* — 29

3 *Tools & Techniques* — 71

4 *Distillery Tour* — 123

5 *Spirits & Cocktails* — 145

6 *Cocktail Menu* — 395

7 *Service* — 413

8 *Hospitality* — 429

EPILOGUE: BEYOND BARS — 447

BIBLIOGRAPHY — 464

ACKNOWLEDGMENTS — 469

INDEX — 472

MR. MIYAGI: First, wash all the car. Then wax. Wax on . . .

DANIEL: Hey, why do I have to . . . ?

MR. MIYAGI: Ah ah! Remember deal! No questions!

DANIEL: Yeah, but . . .

MR. MIYAGI: Hai! [Makes circular gestures with each hand.]
Wax on, right hand. Wax off, left hand. Wax on, wax off. Breathe in through nose,
out the mouth. Wax on, wax off. Don't forget to breathe, very important.
[Walks away, still making circular motions with hands.]
Wax on . . . wax off. Wax on . . . wax off.

— *The Karate Kid*, 1984

Foreword

BY PETER MEEHAN

Hi. I'm a Meehan whose manual this is not: Jim's little brother.

What you're holding in your hands is like if you took Jim's head—which is big and filled with more than a decade's worth of accumulated heavy-duty, world-class, very Type-A cocktail knowledge—and juiced it like a lime for your Hemingway Daiquiri. It's a lot of time and too many facts condensed into a concise and well-organized opus.

I've suspiciously watched Jim's ascent in the international cocktological community. He and I ended up in the world of food and drink much the way that teachers are said to end up in physical education: what else could we really do? I wrote about what I ate, threw around some curse words, tried to seem authoritative; Jim jumped on the cocktail resurgence train like a hobo, bespoke bindle in hand, right as it really started chugging.

He's always been dandier than I am, so seeing him buy into arm bands and fancy vests and the prissy affectations common to bartenders of the era seemed natural and unimportant at the time. I didn't give a whole lot of credit to his growing stature even as evidence mounted. I remember being surprised when *Bon Appétit* lauded a variation of a Manhattan he'd created, or when people who didn't know we were brothers talked about how they liked drinking at the bar at Gramercy Tavern while it was under his stewardship.

I didn't really pay heed to his skills even after he'd opened PDT, until one night when he came over to my apartment and made drinks with the same bottles and shakers and spoons that I did and they were *so much better* than mine. I was never much for the idea of transubstantiation back in church growing up, but the difference was like that: if my drinks are wine, his are the blood of Christ. I had to admit it, the guy has talent.

I have, fortunately, had the chance to write about (and even write books with) talented chefs. And when I was just getting started, the thing that always struck me was how a chef would walk into his restaurant and immediately clean up an errant piece of paper that had fallen from a straw, or attend to some other detail invisible to the untrained eye. This is the truth of great food-and-drink making: attention to detail and a commitment to doing things right. They are indivisible parts of the overall effort of hospitality and creating deliciousness.

What Jim has set forth in these pages is his attempt to share all of what he knows with us. He wants to crack open our braincases and fill them to the meniscus. The diagrams of bars he admires around the world are his way of saying: this is how I see this space. He notices, I imagine, the softness of the light and the rightness of the music, but what he is really seeing is how it runs, the way some guys might pop the hood of a car and assess the function of the engine. He wants us to have the extrasensory ability to see that, too.

There may be moments between these covers when you feel like you're getting waterboarded with apocrypha, doused into a too-long pour of history and theory. I get that. But I can say, as a shambling and inefficient host, the ability to regurgitate tidbits of the histories of drinks and spirits and great barmen hides my slowness and makes people like my drinks more. Try it. It'll work for you, too.

Since I am a person with a long history of having a short list of good things to say about anything, I want to make sure you take a minute to appreciate how goddamn pretty the cocktail photography is, too. Maybe do this: make a drink out of this book—how about that East India Negroni?—and take a picture of it on your phone. Then flip to page 266 and look at the drink.

That's years of work, right there—that's every detail, every concept of cocktail making put in play. That's all the lessons of this book stirred up into a bracing, bitter, invigorating concoction that you could polish off in less than a minute. That's the magic of a great bartender—the sleight of hand at play, to hide all the work and serve up all the pleasure—and this is the book to teach you how to do it.

Introduction

I first encountered Jerry Thomas's *The Bar-Tenders Guide* at the Pegu Club, Audrey Saunders's iconic New York City bar, which I helped open as a bartender in 2005. Today *The Bar-Tenders Guide* is considered a classic, foundational text, but back then few people had heard of it, and fewer still had held an actual copy in their hands. Looking back, finding this book—which was written nearly one hundred and fifty years prior, in 1862—felt like unearthing an undiscovered book from the Old Testament. For me, it gave new meaning to the work going on around me, under Audrey's direction.

Thomas's book wasn't alone on the shelves behind the Pegu Club bar—there was David Embury's *The Fine Art of Mixing Drinks*, the first theoretical book about mixology, originally published in 1948; a leather-bound edition of Charles H. Baker's 1939 book *The Gentleman's Companion*, which chronicles the food and cocktails that Baker and his band of bon vivants discovered

At Left: Historic Cocktail Books

in their travels; and *The Savoy Cocktail Book* (1930), whose gilded art deco illustrations make it one of the most beautiful cocktail books ever printed. As I paged through Audrey's book collection, the career I'd chosen began to feel more like a vocation. Why else would publishers from a century ago have devoted their resources to printing these beautiful books?

I'd seen photos of many of these books, or skimmed over their titles in the bibliographies of contemporary cocktail guides, but I'd never seen them in person, let alone had the opportunity to page through them behind a bar stocked with so many of the ingredients needed to recreate the recipes. Unlike most rare book collectors, Audrey stored her books behind a bar staffed with an enthusiastic group of readers whose hands were nearly always wet. Her willingness to risk damage so we'd have these resources for inspiration still moves me today.

I began building my own book collection after taking the Beverage Alcohol Resource (BAR) program—a rigorous five-day spirits and mixology course—in 2006. One of the teachers was Brooklyn-based cocktail historian David Wondrich (see page 14). After the class, I asked Dave for a list of the most important cocktail books and he gave me a one-pager of out-of-print books to seek out. From there I turned to Ebay, Bookfinder.com, Abebooks.com, and a cookbook dealer named Bonnie Slotnick.

At times I felt sheepish spending half my week's wages on old bar books. But this was in the early days of the "craft cocktail" revival, when vintage recipes were being promoted by collectors moonlighting as cocktail consultants to new bars and restaurants. In my mind, buying these books was a legitimate investment in my future. Preserving them for posterity made me feel like Noah collecting animals for the ark.

Thankfully, today's bartenders don't need to squander their savings on a rare bar book collection. In 2008, publisher Greg Boehm (see page 9) began reprinting facsimiles of many of the books I've just mentioned (and many more), and now vintage cocktail books are more accessible than ever thanks to online databases such as the Exposition Universelle des Vins et Spiritueux (www.euvs.org).

ON KNOWLEDGE

"Knowledge is a dangerous thing. Let's not forget that this isn't a theoretical job. You can't learn to bartend from a book. You can learn about spirits from a book. You can theoretically say what a highland tequila is going to taste like. But you can't learn about people. You can't fast-track that knowledge. Bartenders who work for six to eight months in a place who say they're not learning anything are missing the point. You may not be learning about the bottles on the backbar, but you're learning how to put the job into action and make people feel good."

ANGUS WINCHESTER

Bar Operator

The challenge today isn't finding information; it's finding *accurate* information. Most contemporary, Internet-based cocktail research is like a game of telephone: it starts where other authors and journalists left off, no longer relying on old bar books and microfiched newspaper articles as primary source materials. Internet search engines don't qualify data, so you have to vet your sources or risk perpetuating a myth, which is nothing new—the origin of iconic recipes, including the Margarita, Manhattan, and Martini, remain unclear thanks to conflicting legend and lore.

When you can find (what authoritative research leads you to believe to be) an original recipe, such as Harry Craddock's Corpse Reviver #2 in the

1930 edition of *The Savoy Cocktail Book*, you may need to research extinct ingredients, such as Kina Lillet, and archaic measurements, such as a "wine glass." Then you need to take what you've learned and decide how to rejigger the recipe to make it taste good today.

But simply reproducing a recipe verbatim from a historical text is not going to tell you the whole story of the drink. Let's say you're looking at the Champagne Cocktail from Jerry Thomas's *The Bar-Tenders Guide*. First, ask yourself: "What would champagne have tasted like after the long hot journey to San Francisco during the gold rush?" The original source of the recipe might not give you the precise answer, but it should open up a new line of inquiry and encourage you to think about the history of wine production, shipping practices, tasting notes from professionals of the time period, and more. All of these details are lost if you just stumble upon the recipe online, in isolation. To fill out the picture, we'll need much more than a search engine to keep track of important events, creations, and their propagators.

Given the sensitive and private nature of the guest/bartender relationship, the history of what happens in bars is largely an oral tradition, transmitted through the hazy fog of a night of drinking. We'll likely never know who stirred the first cocktail of English gin and French vermouth, whether it was served with a twist or olives, and who first called it a Martini. Depending on whom you ask, even recent innovations are shrouded in mystery.

So I believe that bartenders and contemporary cocktail historians must be more transparent about our formulas and practices, in order to preserve them for generations to come. Modern advancements like the dry-shake technique for egg cocktails (see page 98), or recipes for house-made spirits produced using rotary evaporator stills, should be documented and shared, not guarded for competitive gain. What you're reading now is *my* bar manual, inspired by classic operations guides like Charles Mahoney's *Hoffman House Bartender's Guide* and Harry Johnson's *Bartenders' Manual*, the likes of which have not been published for more than a century. Collecting rare antique cocktail books helped me realize that the value of our work at the bar—like the books themselves—could disappear if we don't preserve it.

ABOUT THIS BOOK

In the spirit of Craddock's *The Savoy Cocktail Book,* my first book, *The PDT Cocktail Book,* was a snapshot of what I hope many will fondly recall as a seminal moment in cocktail history. It's a recipe book first and foremost, documenting the popular ingredients and proportions used to make classic and contemporary cocktails at the time of its publication.

In this book, instead of focusing on a particular time and place, I've panned back to address a much more layered subject: bartending itself. I'll begin with a chapter on the history of the American cocktail, from seventeenth- and eighteenth-century punch to the neoclassical cocktails we drink today. From there, I move onto chapters on bar design, tools and techniques, service, and hospitality. This book does include cocktail recipes—one hundred total, which include classics and my own signatures—plus spirits primers to help stock your bar. Each recipe includes information on the origin of the drink, the "logic" behind why it works, and "hacks" for the curious bartender.

Throughout the book you'll find insights from more than fifty friends, colleagues, and mentors who've shaped my views of the craft of bartending. I've included quotes from my former employers, Audrey Saunders and Jimmy Bradley, colleagues like Jeff Bell and Don Lee, icons like Dale DeGroff and David Wondrich, lifelong friends like Brian Bartels and my brother Peter, and spirits producers like Hans Reisetbauer and Beppe Musso. I hope that you'll be as inspired by them as I have been.

I didn't learn how to tend bar from reading books. Tending bar is mastered through thousands of hours spent watching, listening, and learning from your colleagues and guests. That said, I hope this book will foster dialogue about how and why we tend bar. Some of my most respected colleagues and friends (even those featured in the book's portraits) may disagree with the philosophy and practices I've outlined here—so I'm sincerely eager for them to weigh in on the conversation. There are many ways to succeed in the bar business; this is mine.

History

As a bartender, you connect with cocktail history in the first hour of your first day at your first bartending job. It starts with questions like, "Who owns the place? What are they like? Where did you work before? When did we open? Why do we do it this way?" From there, it gets a little more complicated.

Once you've established your bar's narrative, you can start asking questions about the history of the block, the neighborhood, the city, the state, and the country. You can go back thousands of years, if it interests you, to the earliest days of humans gathering to drink alcoholic beverages, or you can focus your attention on a specific strand that captivates you. It is vital for bartenders to remain engaged with our industry's history so they know not only where we stand but why.

Above all else, history makes mixing and drinking cocktails far more interesting. And if you're not interested in mixing drinks, then why would *your* guests be interested in drinking them? A classic rum punch or

Moscow Mule takes on far greater significance when you think about the era in which they became popular: during the age of exploration and at the height of Cold War tensions with Russia, respectively. If you ignore rum's role in global colonization, or the symbolism behind a cocktail prepared with Russia's native spirit (vodka) served in a mug stamped with a bucking mule, then you're missing one of the most interesting parts of the drink.

A second and perhaps more obvious reason to study cocktail history is to learn from the experiences of our predecessors: their pitfalls (think of 1970s-era cocktails like the Harvey Wallbanger, which contributed to cocktail culture hitting rock bottom) and successes. When Hayman's Old Tom Gin was reintroduced to the U.S. market in 2007, bartenders familiar with the history of Old Tom knew that it was different from the gin that they had been working with, so they needed to rejigger their Tom Collins and Martinez recipes to match the original, historic recipes. When David Wondrich revealed that the El Presidente was originally prepared with sweet blanc vermouth instead of dry, he unlocked the drink's potential; his version tastes much better than the ones we'd been pouring before.

Misappropriating history by reenacting instead of interpreting it recently led bartenders to grow handlebar moustaches and dress like cast members of *Boardwalk Empire*. It's important to understand that history is the archive, not the place you're hoping to find or bring back. The only way to stay one step ahead of the curve is to be aware of what's happened in the past, and why it did or did not work then.

Some recipes require a facelift to be transported out of their era. For example, bartender Jeffrey Morgenthaler fortifies his Amaretto Sour with 0.25 ounce of bourbon, bolsters his Grasshopper with the bitterness from 0.25 ounce of Fernet-Branca Menta, and improves his Long Island Iced Tea by omitting tequila and substituting fresh lemon juice for saccharine sour mix. Jeff reclaimed recipes that had been cast from the contemporary bartender's canon by modifying them with popular modern ingredients. His grasp of the past *and* present helped him see something in these drinks that was worth preserving—he knew that with some work, they could be adapted and revived.

ON CONTEMPORARY HISTORY

"In terms of going back to the history of what's actually in the glass, you have to ask: How long have the base spirits been similar to what we're making drinks with now? To me it's only been since the 1940s that the spirits were the same—in both quality and availability. That's one of the reasons that *Bottoms Up* (1951) is one of my favorites. David Embury's *Fine Art of Mixing Drinks*—which was written in 1944/45, just as the war was ending—there's something to be said for using that to understand what's in the glass now."

GREG BOEHM

Publisher

In the chapter ahead, I'll track the history of mixed drinks in America, starting in Europe with punch, then traveling across the Atlantic to colonial America, and on to Cuba, Paris, and other American-cocktail incubators during Prohibition. I'll discuss notable drinks, spirits, and trends across the decades—from juleps to vodka to tiki—and end in the modern era.

Even though most historians credit America for the popularity of cocktails, many of our most influential bartenders were immigrants who mixed concoctions from ingredients sourced from all over the world. This chapter recalls the stories of people—the bartenders and bon vivants—who kept the craft alive in boom times and in times of war, political strife, and ideological turmoil. History is a crowded bar, so keep your eye on the bartender.

PUNCH: THE PROTO-COCKTAIL

Humans have fermented, distilled, and imbibed alcoholic beverages for medicinal purposes and pleasure for over one thousand years, but the ancestors of today's mixed drinks are relatively modern, so I'm going to enter the timeline when punch landed on America's shores. The word *cocktail* had not yet entered the English lexicon (it made its debut in print later, in the nineteenth century).

Tiffany Covered "Roman" Punch Bowl

In his book *Punch: The Delight (and Dangers) of the Flowing Bowl*, David Wondrich traces the first mention of punch to a letter between two English East India Company traders in 1632. The first definition of punch appears six years later, in the journal of a German adventurer named Johan Albert de Mandelslo, who writes about workers in a trading post in Surat along the northwest coast of India imbibing "a kind of drink consisting of aqua vitae, rose-water, juice of citrons and sugar." Accounts from the time confirm that the formula for early punches was aqua vitae (an archaic term for spirits, which in this case was probably palm arrack) watered down with citrus, sugar, and either nutmeg, mace, rose water, or whatever spice was handy. Wondrich calls this formula "the foundation stone upon which all modern mixology rests."

Punch spread around the globe thanks to the British Royal Navy, which is notable, given that the British favored beer and wine over spirits at this time. But the advantage of punch was that, unlike beer and wine, spirits like rum didn't spoil during long sea voyages. As ships returned to England from India, Asia, and the colonies in the Americas—where sugarcane was planted and rum was distilled—they brought punch with them.

Many factors contributed to punch's popularity, ranging from the practical (a pared-down punch was served to sailors to combat scurvy) to the patriotic (as each ingredient was imported from a faroff English colony, punch was a powerful symbol of empire). In America, punch became political when England passed the Molasses Act of 1733 to regulate and tax the flow of molasses, which was used by New England distillers to make rum. In *The Craft of the Cocktail*, DeGroff suggests it was rum, not tea, that precipitated our break from England half a century later.

During punch's reign, the choice of base spirit and the availability of modifiers such as tea, spices, and exotic citrus depended on a variety of factors ranging from trade relations to taxes. Gin was the preferred base spirit for the common tippler: it cost much less than rum, and gained popularity in the eighteenth century (perhaps too much popularity, if you compare Hogarth's famous 1751 print "Gin Lane," depicting the excesses of the time, with the companion print "Beer Street," in which citizens appear healthy and well-behaved).

The recipe for punch started as a simple five-ingredient concoction (popular legend connects the origin of the word *punch* to the Hindi word for "five"): spirit, sweetener, citrus, spice, and a lengthener such as water or tea. From there it evolved to include fancy aromatic sherbets (lemonade-like concentrates of citrus oil, juice, and sugar) and liqueurs that were lengthened with wines and thickened with ambergris (a secretion from sperm whales).

Until the mid-1700s, punch was almost always served in a communal bowl. That changed thanks in part to London's most famous punch maker, James Ashley, who between 1731 and 1776 pioneered serving punch in individual portions. This democratized punch economically and socially, as the imbibers' ability to choose their own drink reflected their newly important sense of individuality. When popular preference shifted from communal bowls to single-serve drinks, recipes were pared down to a single serving; for example, Limmer's Hotel headwaiter John Collins's gin punch was renamed the Tom Collins after the style of gin (Old Tom) it was mixed with. The recipe sailed across the Atlantic to Montreal in the 1860s.

Over time, punch fell from favor but never disappeared. Once it became an individual drink, the formula sired subcategories of mixed drinks such as sours (spirit, citrus, sweetener), daisies (spirit, citrus, liqueur or cordial), and rickeys (spirit, citrus, soda). The bowls were mothballed for special occasions—at least until recent years, as David Wondrich's scholarship has inspired the return of historic pot-stilled spirits like naval rum and reproductions of traditional bowls, ladles, and glasses. The return of classic punch—ladled by the cup or mixed by the bowl—represents the mixed drink's historical arc come full circle.

ON THE ROCKS

While it may not seem like a particularly notable technological advancement today, access to ice changed the course of drink making. Just as James Ashley's decision to serve punch in single-person servings kick-started a wave of cocktail innovation in the eighteenth century, in the first half of the nineteenth century the popularity of mixed drinks took off, thanks in large part to Frederic Tudor. Tudor wasn't a barman, but rather a Boston-based entrepreneur who created the infrastructure to transport ice (which he harvested from Massachusetts ponds) all over the world. Tudor Ice Company's product went from a rare novelty to a barroom staple.

Suddenly, bartenders from New York to New Orleans were crafting elaborate concoctions with ice—and perhaps no drink made better use of the commodity than Richmond, Virginia, bartender John Dabney's Mint Julep. In Robert Moss's *Southern Spirits*, one account described his julep as served in a "giant silver cup topped with a one-foot-tall pyramid of ice, and its sides were encrusted in ice, too, molded into shapes and figures . . . It was a multi-serving drink, and imbibers inserted silver straws through the ice to sip the ice-cold liquor contained within."

If punch was the king of seventeenth- and eighteenth-century mixology, then the julep inherited the crown in the nineteenth. The julep became the world's most talked-about mixed drink, thanks to Dabney and other well-known bartenders, such as Orasmus Willard of New York's City Hotel, whom

Wondrich calls the first celebrity bartender. In *Imbibe!*, Wondrich quotes Englishman Charles Augustus Murray's 1839 travel account, which says that Willard's "name was familiar to every American, and to every foreigner who has visited the States during the last thirty years."

American juleps, particularly fancy renditions prepared with English rum, cognac, and champagne, were America's first notable contribution to the global recipe canon. The julep supplanted English punch, which had reigned "for ten generations as the acme of the mixologist's art" according to *Imbibe!*

THE BIRTH OF MIXOLOGY

Many people assume that the word *mixologist* is a contemporary affectation, but in fact, it dates all the way back to the nineteenth century, when America's cocktail-recipe repertoire ballooned exponentially. This has led many historians to call this era the "golden age" of American mixology. In *The Craft of the Cocktail*, Dale DeGroff attributes the growth of the American bar industry to the confluence of mass European immigration, four decades of tax-free domestic spirits production, and the evolution of public drinking spaces precipitated by legislation that allowed inns to serve alcohol without also offering rooms to let. In cities, restaurants and taverns were bolstered by political parties, which manipulated voting blocks by buying drinks in exchange for votes.

To distribute their largesse, the leaders of the parties chose as their headquarters opulent grand hotels whose lavish build-outs were underwritten by financiers with vast industrial fortunes amassed during the second industrial revolution. Legendary hotel bars such as the Hoffman House in New York City served as the unofficial home of local Tammany Hall officials and the Democratic Party from 1864 until it closed in 1915. The presence of politicians, actors, journalists, and other power brokers in the bar placed bartenders and the craft of the

Imperial Shaker

DAVID WONDRICH

Historian

ON PERSONALITY

"I love writing about drinks because it shows people with personality killing it. Bartending is one of those great humanity jobs that's fun. It's your bar; you can throw people out if they're misbehaving. You can play social engineer. That's the higher order of bartending. That's why I like history, because history shows that in action. An old recipe with a story admits you into that higher order, where you can grasp the true, exceptional nature of these colorful bartenders."

cocktail on a stage where they would flourish like never before. A name for the bartender who specialized in the dispensation of mixed drinks was coined in 1856: *mixologist*.

The recipes and methodology required to carry this mantle were memorialized in a professional bartender's guide—the first of its kind—authored in 1862 by legendary barman Jerry Thomas. Today, much of what we know about Thomas comes from David Wondrich's *Imbibe!*, a comprehensive biography and detailed survey of his recipes. During Thomas's lifetime, his book was updated and reprinted numerous times until his death in 1885, and it was widely copied throughout the world as bar manuals proliferated in the trade.

The quality of bar books between Jerry Thomas's time and Prohibition reflects the evolution of bartending and drink mixing at the time. Well-known bartenders—including Jerry Thomas; William Schmidt, a German contemporary of Thomas who published *The Flowing Bowl* in 1884; Tom Bullock, an African American bartender from St. Louis who published *The Ideal Bartender* in 1914; and Charles Mahoney, an Irishman who wrote *The Hoffman House Bar Guide* in 1906—authored brilliant guides. Their genius was grounded in the understanding that service was just as important as the quality of the cocktails. I only wish that more books of this time had delved into the minutiae of bar operations and that the authors had attributed and annotated their cocktail recipes more thoroughly.

PROHIBITION AND THE BARTENDER DIASPORA

The outbreak of World War I in 1914 and the enactment of Prohibition six years later changed where and how Americans drank—if they drank at all. Puzzlingly, many histories incorrectly extend the golden age of the cocktail into Prohibition, or confuse the two, believing that Prohibition was the best to time to drink in American history. Speakeasies, which openly defied the Eighteenth Amendment, are celebrated, while the violence and widespread corruption on which they depended gets swept under the rug.

Wealthy Americans stockpiled wine and spirits between the enactment of the amendment in 1919 and its enforcement a year later. For those who couldn't afford the luxury, the supply of spirits was spotty, and what you could source depended on where you lived. Cities near the international border, like New York and Detroit, benefited from bootlegging from Europe and Canada, while interior metropolises like Louisville targeted bourbon in bonded warehouses until they were emptied. Cocktails like the Corn Popper (moonshine, cream, egg white, grenadine, soda)—which appears in Judge Jr.'s *Here's How*, published in 1927—shows how the cupboard was emptied to cover up poorly made spirits.

The bartenders who remained in the United States had few fine spirits to work with: American distilleries were commandeered to distill alcohol for the war effort during both World War I and II, and most were closed during Prohibition. In *And a Bottle of Rum*, Wayne Curtis chronicles how enterprising operators smuggled in perfectly good liquor from Canada or the Bahamas from bootleggers, "then cut one bottle of good liquor to make five bottles of bad." If their customers were lucky, the stuff they were blending it with wasn't denatured with toxic chemicals. Tragically, thousands were poisoned and died from unknowingly ingesting such chemicals.

The best bartenders relocated, and many of their patrons followed via cruise liner and airplane. Prohibition was enacted at the dawn of commercial air travel, which it fueled with thirsty customers. The closest place to cop a (legal) world-class cocktail was Cuba, just a couple hundred miles off the coast of Florida, but many bartenders traveled farther afield, to London, Paris, and other European cities.

American-style cocktails were already present in Europe as early as 1850, and gained popularity thanks in part to the publicity they garnered at the World's Fair in Paris in 1867. What's more, European bartenders began writing their own cocktail manuals around the same time Americans did (for example, Englishman William Terrington's *Cooling Cups and Dainty Drinks*, 1869; English-born Parisian Frank Newman's *American Bar*, 1904; and Carl Seutter's *Der Mixologist*, 1909).

American cocktail culture would have perished had its bartenders and customs not been adopted abroad, where Cubans and Europeans already practicing the craft incubated and improved it. Many top bartenders emigrated: Harry McElhone to Paris, Harry Craddock to London, Will Taylor and Eddie Woelke to Cuba. If you look closely at bar books of this era, you'll find innovative new cocktails like the Rose (page 364), Champs-Élysées (page 361), and White Lady (page 234) flourished in Europe, while the simplicity and elegance of cocktails like the Manhattan-inspired El Presidente (page 261) became popular in Cuba.

REPEAL AND STARTING OVER

When Prohibition was repealed in 1933, American cocktail culture didn't suddenly bounce back. On the contrary, there was a backlash against the cocktails of the period—understandably, as many were prepared with juice, cream, and eggs to disguise rotgut spirits. As Ted Haigh notes in *Vintage Spirits and Forgotten Cocktails*, one of the aftershocks of Prohibition was "a shift in who wrote the books. Up to this point, it had always been the bartenders, writing for other bartenders, and to a lesser extent (as the cocktail's popularity grew) for the general public."

But after Prohibition, bartending wasn't the same esteemed profession it had been at the turn of the twentieth century. Publishers were no longer interested in financing book projects authored by bartenders. Most cocktail books written and published in the years following Prohibition were authored by journalists such as Charles H. Baker, H. L. Mencken, and Basil Woon. Technical bar manuals all but disappeared until the twenty-first century.

After Prohibition, bartenders went from being directors to producers, if they were lucky; more often, they had cameos in a narrative dominated by the drinkers. Conservative voices like that of Patrick Gavin Duffy—who in his 1934 *Official Mixer's Manual* suggests that the bartender may "shine in the reflected glories of his patrons" but should not converse with them—were a far cry from folk legends like Jerry Thomas.

Not only did the quality and creativity of published bar books suffer, but the quality of the spirits did, too. After Prohibition, distillers scrambled to replenish their inventories as smaller firms consolidated into larger ones to compete for market dominance.

In *Straight Up or on the Rocks*, William Grimes notes, "In the past, when liquor companies were small and the advertising industry had not mastered the dark art of mass persuasion, the cocktail's laboratory of invention was the local bar. . . . But in the postwar era, the inspiration for new cocktails tended to come from liquor companies keen on boosting sales of a particular product."

In the 1972 edition of *Trader Vic's Bartender Guide*, tiki pioneer Trader Vic laments, "One of the biggest violations of the worthy inventive process is some liquor company who wants you to use its liquor; so it invents a lot of lousy drinks that you can't drink, and puts them into a pamphlet; ultimately those drinks get into some bartender's guide where they really have no place to be." While this practice continues today—spirit companies still use their budget and "bullhorn" to influence consumers with many forms of marketing—I feel hopeful that bartenders have finally reestablished their footing. Contemporary recipes like New York bartender Sam Ross's Penicillin (Islay and blended scotch, lemon juice, ginger, honey) are mixed all over the world, based on their own merit.

COCKTAIL CULTURE IN THE "AGE OF EFFICIENCY"

The invention of products like Seven-Eleven mix undermined the fresh-fruit cocktails served in the pre-Prohibition era. Whereas the technological advancements of the mid-nineteenth century (specifically, the birth of

1930s-Era Waring Blender

the ice industry) improved the craft of the cocktail, in many ways the advancements of the mid-twentieth century did more harm than good. Food and drink were processed and advertised as technological progress to make life easier for the family—and bartender—on the go. DeGroff calls this the beginning of the "Kool-Aid" era of making drinks: add ice, liquor, water, and the mix. Even the classic preparation methods weren't safe. Wayne Curtis notes that misuse of Frederick Osius's Waring blender in place of a shaker "led to the misguided belief that a proper Daiquiri should have the consistency of sherbet."

It only got worse when the U.S. government decommissioned its whiskey distilleries less than a month after Pearl Harbor, in 1942, forcing them to produce industrial alcohol for torpedo fuel. Spirits were rationed and imports declined thanks to well-placed German submarines in the North Atlantic.

Without reinforcements, the whiskey market declined, while rum sales boomed, thanks to lax production restrictions in Puerto Rico. To take advantage of the liquor shortage, unethical distributors forced wholesalers to buy three cases of rum to receive a case of whiskey, which set the stage for sugarcane's somewhat forced return to the mixological spotlight.

Efforts to deplete all the rum needed to acquire whiskey were given a sizable boost by the Andrews Sisters' 1944 smash hit "Rum and Coca-Cola," both at home and abroad, where the spirit and mixer were distributed to the thirsty troops. It also made a noteworthy first appearance in Lucius Beebe's colorful *The Stork Club Bar Book* in 1946, where it was a key ingredient in one of the book's three most popular drinks, the Cuba Libre. (The Moscow Mule and Pimm's Cup also made their first cocktail-book appearances here.)

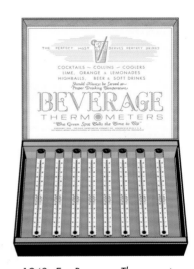

1940s-Era Beverage Thermometers

These cocktails, which are still popular today, all share one characteristic: the mixer is the most flavorful component of the drink. In *And a Bottle of Rum*, Wayne Curtis notes that "more than half of all [American] drinkers didn't like the taste of liquor." This helps explain the popularity of the (blended) Scotch Highball, the Bourbon Highball, and the (vodka) Martini; ad agencies promoted "light," "mild," and "dry" among their merits.

No spirit met the "bland" criteria better than vodka, whose sales went from 40,000 cases in 1950 to 1.1 million in 1954. Once Sean Connery ordered his (vodka) martini "shaken, not stirred" in the critically acclaimed 1964 movie box office smash *Goldfinger*, there was no turning back.

The Opposite of Bland: The Rise of Tiki

The post-Prohibition cocktail trend just chronicled reflects the postwar psyche of Americans who seemed interested in only heavily marketed clear, bland, flavorless drinks that went down easy to get them drunk. Yet there was another American cocktail trend of the time, often overlooked: tiki culture and tropical drinks.

Just off Hollywood Boulevard, Donn Beach (born Ernest Raymond Beaumont Gantt) ran Don the Beachcomber, which served concoctions

Tiki Statue

like the Missionary's Downfall, the Sumatra Kula, and his renowned Zombie. A San Francisco Bay Area bar owner, Victor Bergeron, was so inspired by the Beachcomber that he transformed his Oakland bar into "Trader Vic's," named for his habit of offering guests food and drinks in exchange for decorations for the bar.

The food, drinks, exotic service vessels, casual beachwear, and eclectic tropical décor at these bars helped spawn Polynesian pop culture, which informed the design of motels, drive-in theaters, and resorts, including Beach's own, opened in Hawaii after he returned home from the war. Historian Jeff Berry distinguishes Donn Beach as the superior mixologist and Trader Vic as the better businessman. By the early 1960s, he had twenty-five locations worldwide and multiple book credits, and his Mai Tai had become an international classic.

Both Bergeron and Beach were famed for their hospitality and the quality of their offerings, but it didn't hurt that tropical island tourism began to boom by the 1950s, thanks to Americans' escapist fascination with the Pacific, fanned by soldiers' stories like James Michener's Pulitzer Prize–winning *Tales of the South Pacific*. The Polynesian craze culminated when Hawaii became the fiftieth state in 1959; then tiki cocktail culture faded. The high operational standards of Beach and Bergeron were eventually lost after forty years of prosperity.

In the Caribbean, the Piña Colada made waves at the Caribe Hilton in Puerto Rico, thanks to the 1954 arrival of Coco Lopez—canned coconut cream. In *Potions of the Caribbean*, Jeff Berry compares the Piña Colada to the Cuba Libre, whose "un-rummy" taste is perfect for "What the hell, I'm on vacation!" tippling, and as such became a must for tropical tourists. Ultimately, Berry condemns it for launching the "Crushed Ice Age," in which all cocktails, no matter their original preparation or base spirit, became blender fodder.

The Dark Ages

Most cocktail historians will tell you the cocktail died in the '60s and '70s, a casualty of countercultural drug use, "disco" drinks like the Golden Cadillac (Galliano, crème de cacao, and cream), and the popularity of singles bars. They're not wrong. But as early as the late '50s and early '60s, the craft of the cocktail was disappearing from bars, thanks to a generation of drinkers who preferred two- and three-ingredient drinks like the Highball, Gimlet, and Martini, more often made at home than by a professional in a bar.

It makes sense, then, that one of the only important bar books to emerge from the 1960s and 1970s was Thomas Mario's *Playboy's Host & Bar Book*, published in 1971 and geared entirely toward home enthusiasts. Mario, who began covering food and drink for *Playboy* in 1953, writes off professional bartenders altogether, stating, "In the art of mixing drinks, the author assumes that the accomplished amateur will often outshine his professional counterpart when it comes to originality and enthusiasm."

You don't see much of a defense from Trader Vic, whose revised 1972 edition of his *Bartender's Guide* states that his book "is intended mainly to be a guide for professional bartenders," but "I have

Soda Gun

an idea, however, that more of the bartending I talk about in this book will be done in the home than anywhere else."

If you want to understand why a bar would be the last place you went to for a good drink in the 1970s, page through Jack Tiano's 1981 *The American Bartenders School Guide to Drinks*. The first two and a half pages are both inaccurate ("Mixed drinks did not really gain wide acceptance or popularity until Prohibition in 1922") and patronizing ("In the 1940s, women became even more emancipated—working in war plants, while raising a family"). Then Tiano proclaims that "a large group of American drinkers had developed a liking for sweets from their childhood days and carried this craving into their adult socializing."

This helps explain his enthusiastic celebration of the Harvey Wallbanger (vodka, Galliano, and orange juice) and all the "exotic-flavored liqueurs" of the era, which, he says, were responsible for expanding the bartender's repertoire from only 25 drinks in the 1940s to nearly 150 at the time he penned his manual. He "humbly" pats himself on the back for all his "hard work and sacrifice" since 1969, which led to the founding of thirty-five bartending schools across the nation, where he claims to have trained more than fifty thousand students—distressing indeed, if you assume these bartenders were force-fed Tiano's exotic liqueur–flavored Kool-Aid.

If you look back in cocktail history, you'll find that (respectable) mixology thrives in times of peace and prosperity and sputters in times of war or economic depression. The poor quality of cocktails in the 1960s and '70s should be no surprise, then, when you consider the political turmoil of the Nixon administration and the Vietnam War. Yet there were bright spots: for example, important social progress for women in bars—like the original T.G.I. Fridays on the Upper East Side, where women drank unaccompanied in bars (without social stigma) for the first time in American history. Liberation was also achieved on the other side of the bar, as postwar state laws barring women from tending bar, pushed into legislation by trade unions, were successively repealed by the early 1970s.

"It was what it was. You didn't think about not having tools. You didn't think about anything. You just did what you did, and you made do with what you had. There wasn't a lot of shaking going on. It just was the way it was. Cups over the top of shakers and shaking in the glass— there was a lot of that going on. You didn't even need a spoon."

DALE DEGROFF

Bartender

Another ray of light in a decade characterized by frilly shooters and disco drinks was the work of California bartender Stan Jones, who compiled a massive eponymous *Bar Guide* in 1977 filled with thousands of historic recipes, both good and bad. Holding court like the bartender on the sinking *Titanic*, Jones "laments the ubiquity of lighter and less flavorful spirits, and champions high-quality ingredients, portion control, balance, and the appropriate garnish" in the introduction to his bright orange book, which is among the only valuable relics of the era.

THE CRAFT COCKTAIL REVIVAL

Most mixographers date the contemporary cocktail renaissance back to 1987, and more specifically, to the Rainbow Room and a young actor-turned-barman named Dale DeGroff. The Rainbow Room, opened by legendary restaurateur Joe Baum, was set sixty-five floors above midtown Manhattan's Rockefeller Plaza, where guests' view of the city competed with views of the celebrities, politicians, and socialites who frequented the venue.

DeGroff's opening menu featured twenty-six cocktails, all made with fresh ingredients—a rarity at the time—and emphasized classic recipes that had been forgotten since the 1950s. Over the next twelve years, until the Cipriani Group took over operations in 1999, Dale managed a staff of more than a dozen bartenders and made the Rainbow Room one of the most influential bars in the world. Most bartenders would hang their hats there, but Dale went on to have an even larger impact on the industry as a mentor to other bartenders through his consulting work. Audrey Saunders, Julie Reiner, Sasha Petraske, Dushan Zaric, and Jason Kosmas all credit DeGroff's influence, which only grew with the publication of *The Craft of the Cocktail* in 2001.

Now nearly seventy, Dale maintains a rigorous travel schedule, judging cocktail competitions, promoting his eponymous allspice bitters, supporting the Museum of the American Cocktail as one of its founders, educating bartenders in partnership with B.A.R., and entertaining us as a singer and storyteller with his wife, Jill, an artist who's painted portraits of many important American bartenders.

While DeGroff was working his magic with classic cocktails in the Rainbow Room, vodka occupied the lion's share of shelf space on backbars across the country. "Martinis"—which became the umbrella term for a mixed drinks flavored with fruit juice and any number of other mixers (and, occasionally, vermouth)—epitomized cocktail culture of the 1980s and 1990s, and the most famous example, Toby Cecchini's Cosmopolitan, became an instant classic (not to mention a favorite of Madonna and *Sex and the City*'s Samantha).

But by the 1990s, new brands in other categories began to challenge vodka's heavyweight crown, among them Bombay Sapphire gin and Patron tequila, which entered the market in 1988 and 1989, respectively. When *Cigar Aficionado* magazine launched in 1992, it helped create a cult of connoisseurship that had a ripple effect on handcrafted beverages (including newly popular craft beer and American wine), as retro-styled cigar bars sprang up, featuring classic cocktails and aged spirits to sip while you smoke.

Toby Cecchini

The timing was perfect for the American whiskey industry. Just eight years prior, in 1984, Blanton's launched the first single-barrel bourbon, and other producers followed with small-batch bourbons in 1992, including Basil Hayden's, Booker's, Baker's, and Knob Creek. Scotch distillers launched their single-malts, including Oban, Talisker, Lagavulin, Cragganmore, Dalwhinnie, and Glenkinchie in the U.S. Most bargoers still clung to fruit-flavored Martinis or disco drinks, but brown spirits were creeping back into the public consciousness, and suddenly Americans were open to the idea that a drink didn't have to taste like candy or nothing at all.

By the late 1990s, the message of Dale DeGroff, his disciples, and other leaders in the artisanal food movement—that cocktails tasted better with fresh ingredients—had spread from coast to coast. Bartenders like Tony Abou-Ganim of San Francisco's Starlight Room (and later, all twenty-nine bars of Las Vegas's Bellagio hotel and casino), Dushan Zaric and Jason Kosmas of New York's Pravda and Employee's Only, and Julie Reiner at C3 and Flatiron Lounge set a new standard. What's more, they quieted bar operators (and lazy bartenders) who complained that their recipes were too time-consuming and expensive compared to using soda guns and industrial mixes.

ENTER STAGE LEFT

In 1999, I read about DeGroff and his protégé, Audrey Saunders, and the fabulous (but short-lived) bar they opened on East 49th Street, Blackbird. It became my dream to have a mentor like him. Three years later, I moved to New York City. It was eleven months after 9/11 and the terrorist attacks had ravaged New York's economy, forcing many large clubs and restaurants to close. Paradoxically, the tough times cleared a path for a quality-focused cocktail renaissance led by many of the characters whose voice and portrait are featured ahead.

However, one bartender I could not interview is Sasha Petraske. I never worked for Sasha and won't pretend that we were intimate, but we knew each other and I was close with many members of his staff. One year after I began writing this book, he died tragically at age forty-two. His influence—both directly and through his bars and bartenders—is still felt today, and many (certainly not all) of his values resonate throughout the pages ahead.

After a stint at Von in NoHo (before almost anyone called Bleecker Street west of the Bowery *NoHo*), in December of 1999, Petraske opened Milk & Honey, a tiny bar in an unmarked space on Eldridge Street south of Delancey in Manhattan's Lower East Side. There he featured golden-age cocktails shaken and stirred, with hand-carved blocks of ice. Seats were by reservation only, and when the phone number was leaked in the media, he changed it to ensure that his crowd only grew from within. The only thing more famous than the quality of the drinks was the infamous "Rules" list posted in the bathroom; these were enforced to deter the disruptive and predatory behavior that was common and often encouraged in bars at the time.

Petraske shunned the spotlight, refused to stock vodka (or cranberry juice to make Cosmos), served drinks in classic coupes instead of martini glasses, dressed like he lived in 1920, and cross-trained his entire team to work the floor and tend bar to make sure guests received the same level of service at the bar and tables. He went on to open a second Milk & Honey in London in 2002, Little Branch in the West Village in 2005 (with former head bartender Joseph Schwartz), the Varnish in Los Angeles (with former bartender

Eric Alperin), and Dutch Kills in Long Island City in 2009 (with former bartender Richard Boccato), among many other projects. Ultimately, in 2013, Sasha turned over the Milk & Honey space to longtime bartenders Sam Ross and Michael McIlroy, who reopened it as Attaboy.

Sasha's story is a fitting place to knot this thread. He'll be remembered for many things, including modeling the modern speakeasy on a Tokyo-style bar called Angel's Share, hidden behind an unmarked door on the second floor of a Japanese restaurant in the East Village. Both are operated with a similar service ethos and feature handcrafted cocktails for intimate, civilized groups in a refined setting. What some forget—or will not report—is how socially disruptive this concept was at a time when most bars were still raucous places for singles to cavort, and how he never sacrificed the quality of the drinks, the integrity of his vision, or the well-being of the staff for money at a time when many operators milked their bar like a cash cow.

THE NEXT ROUND

There's never been a better time to be a bartender. Thanks to smoking bans instituted in most major metropolitan areas, bartenders no longer risk their health every time they step behind the stick. Advances in production, packaging, distribution, and storage have improved the quality and safety of our ingredients. But perhaps more important, bartenders have an increased awareness of which methods should be unsentimentally left behind and which should be preserved, unaltered, for posterity.

Here I've chronicled how one of America's most celebrated culinary arts grew up side by side with the country. In this nation of immigrants, many of whom have found work in hospitality soon after their arrival, the cocktail is an amalgam of unique culinary traditions cobbled together in the glass. Like jazz, another American art form built on improvisation, cocktails continue to evolve as new bartenders and ingredients enter the mix. As long as this continues, I have nothing but optimism about the future—especially if those who guide this evolution use history as their muse.

Bar Design

Critical overviews of contemporary bar design are scarce. Most bars are designed by their owners in collaboration with architects and contractors whose work rarely makes it into newspaper features, shelter publications, or architectural journals. The worthwhile ones, such as the overview in *Death & Co* and *The PDT Cocktail Book*, focus on the functionality of the bar (from behind the bar outward) within its four walls, instead of starting in the surrounding neighborhood and working inward. I've dedicated this chapter to examining how a bar's identity should be shaped, both conceptually, in relation to other bars in the neighborhood, and physically, in relation to the structure it occupies. A strong bar concept should serve its neighborhood *and* work within its space. Only after that is accomplished can the operator focus on branding, décor, and interior design.

The assets needed to operate a bar—tables, chairs, mirrors, a physical bar—haven't changed much over the last century. This should come as little surprise, as the primary function of a bar or restaurant—to sate thirst and hunger in a communal setting—hasn't changed either. What has changed, and continues to, is the way in which people interact in bars. Over time, the bar length has contracted to allow for more tables, booths, and stools, which allows guests to sit (whereas historically, bargoers preferred to stand). As the traditional elements the guests interface with evolve, the layout of workstations and machinery behind the bar must also be adapted to accommodate the food and drink fashions of the day.

The industrial designer Dieter Rams once said, "You cannot understand good design if you do not understand people; design is made for people." The most successful hotel, bar, and restaurant operators understand their guests' aspirations, and play to them with thoughtful design and décor.

In this chapter, I'll discuss various commercial bar concepts that each reflect ingenious bar design, as well as a home bar that incorporates elements of home and industrial design on a more intimate scale. I'll explain why each bar works for me and examine how a bar becomes an institution with an identity of its own. Each example has an enduring quality because their founders recognized the importance of letting their creations evolve, based on the input of other stakeholders and the needs of their guests. You can't expect a new bar to be an institution on opening night, but it has a better chance to become one through intuitive design from the outset.

LOCATION

Just as architects must always consider the site for their buildings, bar operators must take location into account when conceiving their bar. This can happen in one of two ways: you either start with a concept and look for the perfect location, or start with the location and figure out what concept will work best there. Successful concepts become destinations that guests go out of their way to visit, but few achieve this status without serving the local clientele's needs first.

Tommy's Menu Board

Surveying the area's nightlife options is the first order of business. The number of bars, population, and tourist traffic help determine the role your bar will play. Besides eating and drinking, people go to bars to watch sporting events and play games; they go on dates, after funerals, and on holidays and dozens of other special occasions. When you're the only bar in town or the sole bar for miles, you need to accommodate a broader array of guests' needs. This is why you see highly specialized concepts—such as a cocktail bar hidden behind a phone booth inside a hot-dog stand—in densely populated cities with lots of bars, and more traditional taverns and neighborhood joints in less-populated towns with fewer nightlife options.

You need to also consider population density, residents' income levels, and their entertainment habits. Residents of well-to-do neighborhoods may

JOHN GLASER

Master Blender

ON FAITH

"An important ingredient in being successful in starting your own business is a high degree of self-confidence and self-belief. It doesn't mean you have to be arrogant. At the end of the day, you have to know you're right or, big picture, on the right path. We all change the course. The Emerson quotation 'The voyage of the best ship is a zigzag line of a hundred tacks' comes to mind. If you believe in what you're doing, it's easier to go out there and convince others."

have higher budgets, but they also tend to go out of town and to entertain at home more often. Older residents don't go out as much as younger ones, and middle-aged locals often look for kid-friendly options. Younger residents may not have the disposable income for high-end dining or drinking; they are more transient and tend to flock to trendy concepts. Tourists and business diners, who are much more likely to splurge on an experience, are key to supplementing the bar's income when the neighbors are away.

Simply measuring the foot traffic in front of a space you're considering can be misleading if you don't consider that traffic's origin and destination. High-end concepts, whose guests allocate more time for their experience, do best when they're near hotels or shopping districts, while more casual concepts tend to succeed near offices (think lunch and happy hour) or around transportation hubs such as train stations or airports, where customers purchase takeout food for their trip. For bars and restaurants with multiple locations, a minimally profitable operation in a high-traffic area near a tourist attraction like a museum can be written off as marketing, as luxury brands do with their boutiques. For small businesses, however, this type of investment usually is not worth the return.

Neighborhoods with a high density of bars have more opportunities for diverse concepts, as long as their audience is open to variety, and other attractions—such as a ballpark or train station—don't have a gravitational pull on their time and attention. Contrary to supply-and-demand logic, choosing a different concept to diversify a neighborhood's offerings may not be the best choice, as many cities develop unofficial districts of certain types of bars—such as clubs, lounges, or sports bars that attract barhoppers who prefer to walk from place to place. To capitalize on a built-in audience, choose the same concept as neighboring bars but stand out by varying your food, drinks, décor, and service protocols.

Bars and restaurants with picturesque views of beaches, mountains, and skylines attract an audience that is there to soak up the scenery regardless of the cuisine. The more remote, the more likely the locals who inhabit the area have sacrificed income for lifestyle, so you'll have a tough time securing a staff focused on operating a bar or restaurant—for high-end venues, service tends to be spotty. In densely populated areas away from sights, food, drink, and service tend to be the primary draw, so operators must work harder to draw guests to their venue. Only the most disciplined operators are able to open profitable fine dining restaurants and high-end bars in high-rent destinations that cater to tourists, who tend to repel serious diners.

Due to the danger of drinking and driving, public transportation available close by is vital to promoting responsible alcoholic beverage sales, unless you're located in an area where most residents walk. Cities like New Orleans, New York City, and San Francisco, which all happen to be dining and drinking capitals, have excellent public transportation options, including trains and streetcars. In cities without these, taxis and affordable car services are essential. Outside of cities, hotels, resorts, and B&Bs are ideal locations for bars, as guests don't have to worry about driving home after a few drinks.

One important decision you'll make is whether to take over a former space that has failed or to renovate an old or new building in which to operate a bar and restaurant. I'm not superstitious, but I do believe some spaces are doomed, so perform the due diligence on a location that has failed before convincing yourself you'll get it right. The advantage of moving into an existing bar or restaurant is that, if the former operator made good decisions, you won't have to install hoods, plumbing, electric, access for those with disabilities, and other fixtures.

You'll still have to make modifications and improvements to succeed where someone else failed. The advantage to renovating a space that has never been a bar or restaurant is that you can decide where to locate everything, from the host stand to the manager's office, instead of having to remodel or make do with another operator's choice. However, in this case, because you're going to sink serious money into a building to operate a bar or restaurant, it's critical to secure a long lease and investment from the landlord.

No one ever told me I was in the real estate business as a bar operator. The most affordable neighborhoods to open bars in are typically being developed by property owners, who lure chefs and bartenders with low rents, support from beleaguered community officials, and hassle-free permitting to build. If longevity is a business goal from the outset and you have the means, buying a building, although much costlier up front, is a much better investment than leasing a space.

A successful bar or restaurant draws a variety of other commercial tenants, which inflates rents and land value over the years. Many bar operators who lease are penalized, once the first lease term is up, with a higher rent and pressure from the neighborhood's new inhabitants to minimize noise and foot traffic around the business.

**ON DRAWING
UP A CONTRACT**

"We've learned how to have really difficult conversations up front so we don't have very difficult years of business together. We're now at a place where I can sit with the people I'm closest to in my life in my lawyer's office and ask the lawyer to draft a contract as if we'll fucking hate each other in five years, and that's the way we do business now. We can laugh about it, and it's uncomfortable for a few minutes, but everyone is protected and feels comfortable, and we sign it and file it away, and we never look at it again. It took years to figure that out."

SUSAN FEDROFF

Bar Operator

CONCEPT

Once you've surveyed the vicinity and chosen a space, you need to come up with a concept, which is really just a technical term for an identity. From the day you open, even when you think, finally, just about everyone knows your business's story, new guests will come in and ask who owns the place, their background, when it opened, and what the signature dishes or drinks are. They want to know the bar's philosophy and how it differentiates itself from other bars and restaurants in the area. Indulge them!

Opening a bar is a labor of love, so if you have a specific passion or area of expertise, share it with others. Your concept could focus on your knowledge of a wine region, beer style, spirit category, or period in cocktail history; it could be reggae music, the 1980s, or an iconic movie. Keep in mind that a clever concept will attract media attention and drive early buzz, but hyper-specialization can undermine the longevity of a business after the first wave of customers visits and the media move on. An earnest, low-concept bar without any kitsch, featuring a broad beverage selection and a well-trained staff, may not make a splash when it first opens, but it won't suffer the trend fatigue that many high-concept bars experience.

Neon Sign, Lost Lake

Before you decide to bring to life an obscure concept such as an ancient Roman feasting hall or a gold rush–era San Francisco saloon, you need to make sure there is enough consumer interest to merit sourcing or fabricating the assets necessary to execute the concept faithfully and profitably. Just because you love pétanque and pastis doesn't mean your American patrons will develop an appreciation for these Provençal pastimes. Willful imagination is a part of concept innovation, but there's a good litmus test for both the potential interest in period recipes and their likely success: the experience of other bars, as well as the willingness of distributors and brands to support your vision.

Case Studies

To position a bar to stand the test of time, you need to have a good instinct for when history is on the verge of repeating itself. A perfect example is the NoMad Hotel, opened by Will Guidara and Daniel Humm in New York City in 2012.

Guidara and Humm felt that the time was right for the NoMad neighborhood of Manhattan, just a ten-minute walk north of the Flatiron Building. It had declined in recent decades, but was historically the epicenter of New York nightlife thanks to grand hotels like the Hoffman House, Delmonico's, and the Albemarle. So Guidara and Humm opened their own grand hotel, featuring a fine dining restaurant, library, and bar.

The concept was so successful, they are now expanding the hotel brand globally.

The timing and execution of the NoMad bar in the neighborhood the owners helped reinvigorate is a good illustration of how architect Ludwig Mies van der Rohe characterizes his creative process. "We must understand the motives and forces of our time and analyze their structure from three points of view: the material, the functional, and the spiritual. We must make clear in what respects our epoch differs from others and in what respects it is similar." The neighborhood was ready for an establishment that was more stately (material); offered a more posh rendezvous than the competition, the nearby Ace Hotel (functional); and was operated with the same level of hospitality as the operator's four-star restaurant a few blocks away (spiritual).

Match Book

Another illustration of Mies van der Rohe's maxim is the Dead Rabbit Grocery and Grog in Lower Manhattan's financial district. The historic 1828 building includes a pub on the first level that serves pints of beer and hearty fare in a room that looks a hundred years old already, with photos of Belfast lining the rafters and sawdust on the floor. Founders Jack McGarry and Sean Muldoon, formerly of the award-winning Merchant Hotel in Belfast, installed an ambitious cocktail bar on the second floor and a private-event space that doubles as an Irish whiskey academy on the third floor. Each of the three concepts showcase the operators' heritage and passions while addressing the neighborhood's entertainment aspirations. The venue is just half a mile from the former turf of the Irish American Dead Rabbit gang, whose gritty determination inspired the founders and serves as the concept's namesake.

NoMad Bar and Library | New York, New York

Bridging the stylistic divide between uptown luxury and downtown chic, Manhattan's centrally-located NoMad Hotel features elements of each in its bars and restaurants. The stately Library, decorated with books hotel guests can peruse or check out to their room, is ideal for meetings and intimate gatherings. Beyond the library's curtained entrance are more convivial dining and drinking options, including the clubby Elephant Bar and theater-like two-story NoMad bar (featured in the floorplan), which is decorated with dozens of contemporary photos of the neighborhood shot by Mackenzie Canlis. The Parlour, Atrium, and second floor of the Nomad Bar are reserved for diners.

NOMAD FLOOR PLAN

1. **28th Street entrance** located around the corner from the NoMad hotel lobby on 6th Avenue

2. **Standing room** with five compact, 42-inch hi-top tables for cocktails and appetizers

3. **Service station** under staircase to second floor with excellent view of tables

4. **Food-service kitchen** for the NoMad Bar barroom and second floor dining room

5. **Four all-gender stalls** with communal powder room

6. **Booths and banquette seating** raised on a platform to improve guest vantage points

7. **Locked cabinet** displays rare bottles served by the pour or in reserve menu cocktails

8. **Passageway** to Elephant Bar, Library, Parlour, and Atrium in the NoMad Hotel

9. **Drink rail** for standing patrons clears a path for servers and preserves privacy in booths

10. **Host stand** where up to 78 guests are greeted and seated on a first-come, first-served basis and up to 65 guests are invited to stand

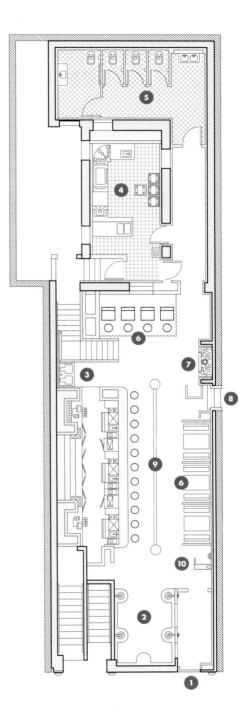

BRANDING

Many operators fail to realize their bar or restaurant isn't just a food and beverage concept in a location; it's a brand. Even if you have no plans to open another outlet, sell merchandise, write a book, or license a product line, you should leave the door open by choosing a unique name that's easy to spell and pronounce in other languages and has an available domain and social media handles. Pay for the domain name even if you don't plan to use it right away, and don't assume that the café in China that's already using that name will be willing to share it. We operate in a global economy.

Business Cards

A business concept needs to speak to the needs of its neighborhood, but if it's going to grow into a brand, it should be able to transcend its place of origin. The NoMad is named after its neighborhood (North of Madison Square Park), which makes it tougher to transplant than the Dead Rabbit, which most people wouldn't associate with its location, even though the namesake gang has roots there. Ideally, the name should evoke a universally positive reaction. The Dead Rabbit was subjected to negative publicity from PETA, who protested the graphic logo of a dead rabbit they shared on social media before they opened.

Many bars and restaurants are named after the owners, which is fine if they plan on being there every day, but becomes a problem when they're no longer involved. My process for naming a concept starts by generating a list of other bars and restaurants that inspire me, then expanding to include car companies, sports teams, fashion labels, and tech companies and analyzing what draws me to them.

The name of your new business should hint at the concept without giving too much away—you'll know you're headed in the right direction when colleagues get excited about it.

A distinctive logo is integral to growing your business into a brand. Once you've come up with a name for your bar or restaurant, allocate resources from the opening budget to a designer or branding agency to help choose the right fonts, color scheme, and iconography to bring the concept to life visually. Saul Bass, who has designed world-famous logos for dozens of companies, including Bell, AT&T, Minolta, and the Girl Scouts, said it perfectly: "Symbolize and summarize."

The logo and fonts for the name should be developed to fit business cards, check presenters, menus, and stationery for the opening and should be memorable enough for merchandise, even if you have no plans to produce any. You don't have to tattoo your logo on your arm, as Jack McGarry (see page 435) did before the Dead Rabbit opened, but it should be stylish, distinctive, and memorable enough for others to do so if they choose.

You can apply your logo to coasters, glassware, swizzles, matchbooks, postcards, mints, toothpicks, or even a fortune-telling fish. But think beyond traditional dry goods and bar paraphernalia. You may not realize it now, but the historic spirits Pimm's #1 Cup and Peychaud's bitters were named after the venues (an oyster house and apothecary, respectively) that served them. The products were so famous and well respected, consumers clamored to take some home and requested them in other bars that willingly stocked them once they became available to the public. McSorley's Old Ale House in New York City is famous for serving just two types of beer—McSorley's Irish Pale Ale and McSorley's Black Lager—which are brewed, bottled, and retailed by Pabst. McSorley's Ale House will hopefully be open forever, but Pimm's and Peychaud's are all that's left from those two nineteenth-century establishments.

Ashtray

The Dead Rabbit Taproom | New York, New York

The photos pinned to the rafters of the first-floor taproom were shared by a magazine based in Belfast, where the owners grew up. The bar is located in a 200-year-old building, and to maximize space in the narrow rectangular room, a 38-foot-long bar counter spans the length of the entire room, save a corner booth in the front where a drawing of barman Henry Besant hangs. A partition in the middle of the bar bisects the space, providing a visual break between the bustling front room and the back, which ends in a low counter where the "grocery store" sells menus, branded merchandise, and provisions such as their house cocktail book and bespoke Irish Coffee blend.

THE DEAD RABBIT TAPROOM
FLOOR PLAN

1 **Water Street entrance** past a small patio, up three stairs, and to the right into the vestibule

2 **Staircase** to the second-floor Parlor Bar and third-floor Occasional Room

3 **Two all-gender bathrooms**

4 **Kitchen** services the entire building using a dumbwaiter to transport food to each floor

5 **Grocery store** with coffee station and space for a DJ to set up on the weekends

6 **Two bar stations** to prepare the 18-cocktail menu for up to 60 guests

7 **Bottled punch station** merchandizes and chills three punches in an iced "Belfast sink"

8 **Table for six** in "Henry's Corner," decorated with traditional Irish musical instruments

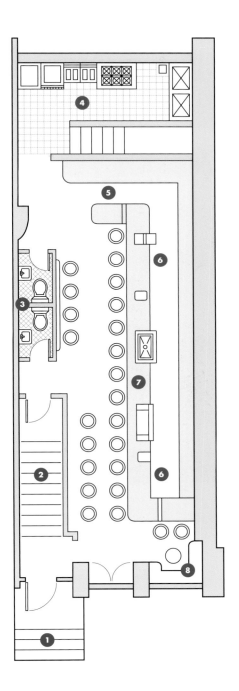

Perhaps the ultimate place to display your branding is the entrance to your business. Outside the bar business, think of the iconic McDonald's golden arches, the Starbuck's mermaid, and the green-red-orange 7-Eleven signs, which are every bit as recognizable as the hamburgers, coffee, and Slurpees they serve—if not more so. Having run a bar that doesn't have a marquee—or any signage, for that matter—for the last decade, I can't overemphasize the power of a memorable entrance and exit. As kitschy and downright silly as entering a bar through an unmarked phone booth in a hot-dog stand is, it's kept PDT at capacity with guests who love surprising their friends who've never been there and aren't expecting it.

INTERIOR DESIGN

Before you do anything else, decide how much space you'll need for a management office, staff lockers, dry and cold food storage, preparation space, and service areas, including the kitchen, bar, and server stations. In high-rent cities like New York and San Francisco, this calculation can be the difference between breaking even and going out of business, so it should be made with the help of an architect and contractor—who will show the owners the most efficient places for plumbing, electric, and ventilation—and staff members, including the chef, head bartender, and general manager, who will have input for how service will flow most efficiently.

Ideally, the front area nearest the windows is set aside for the bar or dining room, with sightlines drawn up for a mixture of secluded nooks for privacy and open space to foster community among more interactive guests. Bathrooms are typically placed out of view in a corner, in the back, or downstairs along with storage, lockers, offices, and prep areas. The bar and host stand go up front near the door, and the kitchen is usually situated at the back of the restaurant, near a rear egress used as a staff thoroughfare and delivery entrance. If your site features spatial obstacles such as central structural columns, offsite bathrooms, or narrow corner spaces walled in by windows, you'll need to get creative with your organization.

Architect and designer Charles Eames defined *design* as "a plan for arranging elements in such a way as best to accomplish a particular purpose." In this respect, design works very similarly to service, as the guests tend to follow the staff's lead behaviorally. A bar and restaurant operator of Eames's mind will have a vision for the type of experience they want to offer and have the bar designed, built, and decorated accordingly. In the same way great managers seem invisible until something goes wrong, utilitarian industrial design, such as the rounded bumper that surrounds most bar tops, goes unnoticed. In addition to providing a comfortable elbow rest, in the event of a spill it prevents any liquid from running off the edge onto your clothes. Thoughtful bar design has the amphibious quality of boat and yacht construction, which is built to keep people dry while surrounded by liquid.

People go to bars and restaurants because they want to be around other people—otherwise, they would eat and drink at home—so sightlines are one of the most important considerations for an architect. It starts at the storefront, where pedestrians walking by see patrons having a good time inside a restaurant and are enticed in to check it out. From there, guests unsure of committing to dinner will wander into the bar to have a closer look.

Most bars are long and straight to accommodate the machinery concealed underneath, so mirrors help guests survey the room without having to turn from side to side and stare. The sightlines of the dining room are designed to accommodate both guests who want privacy during a date or meeting and customers who've come for kinship and engagement. To reiterate, guests go out to be together—even if they don't engage with others during their visit—so an empty bar or dining room is a buzzkill that must be avoided at all costs.

To capture the energy of a room full of people having a good time, larger bars and restaurants should be compartmentalized into chambers of various sizes that can be closed off (with doors, shutters, or planters) or opened up depending on the capacity of the room and the occasion. During the week, these rooms can be rented out for meetings or private functions if amenities such as projectors, screens, and A/V are available and the staff has access to service the room discreetly. Some operators build separate bathrooms and entrances to their private spaces, while others leave them accessible to the public dining room and harness its energy.

In the past, guests were whisked away from the bar into a dining room separated from any view of the barroom, where they were served food from a kitchen hidden behind closed doors. Over time, designers opened things up to the point that many of the best restaurants in the world serve diners at a counter right next to the stove tops or in the kitchen itself. Many guests are taking their meals at the bar now, and those who aren't are still interested in the processes that chefs, bartender, servers, sommeliers, and baristas use to prepare their meal. Cheese and cocktail carts, meat- and fish-cutting trolleys, and open wine tables with decorative decanters are a few ways operators bring the ceremony of service into the dining room—and pique the interest of other guests in the process. Many guests will scan the dining room for appetizing food and drink before ordering, so this is great way to merchandize the menu and make guests feel confident about their decisions.

In addition to sightlines, table placement and size are key, especially in smaller venues. Each table should be large enough for all the plates, glasses, bottles, decorations, and condiments to fit comfortably, but not so large that people feel distant from each other and need to raise their voices. Long stretches of communal table seating—previously reserved for formal dinners and feasts—have become popular again; these may appeal to operators trying to hold down table costs, but the awkwardness of seating perfect strangers next to each other, even with small gaps between tables, typically leads guests to request open seats between parties, which are hard to convince others to fill. Depending on their heft, smaller tables can be removed or combined to create larger tables, which gives operators more options to fill the dining room.

Given the opportunity, most guests would choose to sit in a corner to be closer together and share a view of the room. Unfortunately, most rectangular dining rooms have a limited number of corners, and some seats and tables are truly less desirable than others. Enterprising operators such as Lidkoeb's Rasmus Lomborg sit in every seat in their bar to find the worst places to sit,

ON AMBITION

"I never thought of having to be ambitious. I just wanted to open bars where I'd like to sit at the counter and be served by a bartender. I don't think of *ambition* as having to achieve something other people have already done. Ambition to me is something really different. It's a very personal thing. It's not related to anyone else. It's looking inside and thinking about what I'm yearning for, not what everyone else wants. I think that's when it becomes really good, because that's when it becomes heartfelt and real. That really works for me."

RASMUS LOMBORG

Bar Operator

then work to make them the best possible. Fixes include adding engaging artwork, lighting upgrades, and acoustic tiles; raising the table and chairs onto a platform to improve sightlines; and adding a server so all tables receive more attentive, engaging service. In the same way a bartender recommends and sells a drink, a host "sells" a table by the confidence displayed from the moment a party arrives until they're escorted to the table. When a host seems anxious, guests wonder about the quality of their table, even if it's a good one!

Many operators fail to recognize how poor design contributes to overstaffing. When dining rooms and bars lack service hutches to store napkins, plates, and silverware between courses or POS machines to order from, servers

Lidkoeb | Copenhagen, Denmark

The three-story building where Lidkoeb (pronounced "Lil-coop") is located dates to 1805, when it formerly housed a chemistry laboratory. Huge cast-iron windows and white walls amplify the natural sunlight that beams in from the courtyard during the afternoon, creating an inviting atmosphere during the daylight hours. The booths opposite the bar are raised on a platform to preserve guest sightlines with the bartenders and minimize obstruction from patrons standing behind the stools. Seats around the fireplace and piano encourage guests to venture into the back room, where two larger booths accommodate larger parties of ten to fifteen guests.

LIDKOEB FLOOR PLAN

1 **Entrance** through vestibule, with staircase to lounge upstairs to the right

2 **Two all-gender bathrooms**

3 Five seven-foot **cast-iron window bays** providing expansive views of the courtyard

4 Nineteenth-century Newman Brothers **stand-up piano** for musicians

5 **Low-walled back room** on raised platform for parties of ten or more on each side

6 **Fireplace** to burn wood logs during winter

7 **Centrally located service station** with excellent views of tables

8 **Two bar stations** to prepare a 15-cocktail menu for up to 60 guests

9 6 by 7-foot vintage **wood refrigerator case** to display champagne and other wines

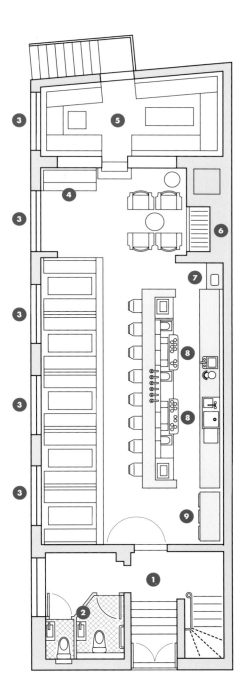

Bar Design

must leave their station to orchestrate their guest's dining experience. Every step a server travels outside of the station compounds over the course of the evening, requiring added staff to compensate. Well-spaced and provisioned service stations with discreet sightlines allow the waiters to remain in their station; this means higher sales and tips for the house and more memorable experiences for the guests.

The bathroom is a microcosm that reflects the care invested in other aspects of the business. Amenities such as accessible, high-powered, water-efficient toilets and hand dryers such as Dyson's compact Airblade will save thousands of dollars—and landfill space—on paper towels over the years. Bathroom lighting should be sufficient to apply makeup or adjust a contact lens, and there should be one faucet and sink for every stall or urinal. Many operators stream the music from the dining room into the bathroom, and some stream something else—like old comedy routines, a favorite of mine. Art or a newspaper to read above the urinals, a hook for your coat in the stall, and a shelf for your drink are nice touches, as is a full-length mirror to make sure everything's tucked in correctly on the way out. Don't skimp on the hand soap!

DÉCOR

When designer Philippe Starck was asked to defend his sculptural metal citrus reamer—which is propped up on three long, spider-like legs that straddle the glass like a headscratcher—he said, "My juicer is not meant to squeeze lemons; it is meant to start conversations." I think Starck's pulling our leg a little here, as his juicer is more than capable of doing both, but it brings up an important distinction between aesthetic and functional design. Form must always follow function, and décor is where designers have an opportunity to make a splash and inspire the dialogue Starck alludes to.

But don't feel compelled to fully decorate your space before opening. Building a restaurant is expensive enough already, so leave some room to acquire new pieces of art, fixtures, and decorations once there's money in the budget to splurge. Some operators display friends' or patrons' art and photos with celebrities or family, and they allow purveyors to provide tasteful posters and point-of-sale such as mirrors, umbrellas, and ice buckets.

Hard benches, uncomfortable chairs, or wobbly bar stools don't reward guests for spending their hard-earned money on a dining or drinking experience. You certainly want guests to be comfortable, so give them a seat with proper cushioning and back support to help them relax during their visit. Well-made furniture is expensive, but unlike the wall moldings, appliances, and other built-ins that operators invest in when they build a bar and restaurant, if things go south they can take furniture to their next venue—or sell it.

Vinyl degrades and tears much more quickly than leather, which burnishes over years of use and is stain- and water-resistant. In venues with hard surfaces such as tile floors, tin ceilings, and brick walls, upholstered surfaces serve as sound dampeners and are much more comfortable than solid wood seats. Chairs should be heavy enough so they don't tip over when a guest who's hung a bag over the back stands up.

Plates, glasses, silverware, and table settings should be in line with the price point of the food and drink. Glasses and plates are the canvas on which bartenders and chefs exhibit their work; even so, these things break, so make sure they're not prohibitively expensive to replace. Linen tablecloths and napkins used to be synonymous with fine dining, but their high cost and environmentally unfriendly maintenance have precipitated a trend toward bare wood tables with aesthetically pleasing placemats. Cloth napkins are still preferable to paper ones, which slip off your lap or end up in unappetizing piles on the table.

What your staff wears—whether a uniform or personal choices—reflects the look and feel of a place as a flag represents its country or a jersey identifies its team. Nike chairman of design John Hoke, whose home bar is featured on pages 68 and 69, declares that "at Nike we design uniforms, which look and feel great for an individual, that aren't just equipment; they're a symbol that represents the character, persona, and purpose of a team." Putting on a uniform—whether provided or owned and chosen for

GARRETT OLIVER

Brewmaster

ON DRESSING UP

"I always respond to people who ask me why I dress up that once I met Angelo Gaja—back in the days when there were no $200 bottles of wine and Angelo's were already $200. He was like seventy years old at the time, wearing a sharkskin suit, crown of gray hair: dude looked like a lion. And somebody asked him, 'Angelo, you're always so finely dressed: why do you dress like that?' He said, 'Well, if you want people to think your wines are delicious, perhaps you should look delicious.' What a badass! I love that guy."

work—should have a transformative effect on its wearer that helps them get into character for the performance ahead.

A well-dressed staff has a tribal quality, like a team or militia, that guests pick up on and venerate. While costly to provide and problematic to tailor to fit all body types, uniforms make it easier for customers to distinguish staff from other guests. Formal bars, restaurants, and clubs should provide their employees with suiting, while more casual concepts can get away with a T-shirt and hat. Given the wear and tear that bar work inflicts on clothing, providing an apron or uniform along with an allowance for dry-cleaning bills and upkeep, such as Gramercy Tavern provided for me when I worked there, should be more common than it is in the industry.

Some of my most memorable meals were at restaurants located on farms, such as Blue Hill Stone Barns in New York, Faviken in Sweden, and Ballymaloe in Ireland, where the operators source as much as they can for dinner from their estate, including flowers and plants to decorate the dining room. Despite my own horticultural ineptitude, I cannot overstate the positive impact flowers, branches, and plants have on your guests and staff.

I worked at a restaurant called Five Points, now operated by the same owners under the name Vic's, when renowned florist Preston Bailey did our arrangements, and at Gramercy Tavern, where Roberta Bendavid and her team cultivated planters and tables of the restaurant like a garden. Greenery is one of the best ways to keep the interior in tune with the seasons, and guests love it. In my opinion, the fragrance of flowers is the only scent you should add to the dining room besides the aroma of food and beverages.

ENVIRONMENT

In a well-designed bar and restaurant, you shouldn't notice the ambient temperature. But it's no small feat to maintain a comfortable temperature when the front door opens and closes all night long and a powerful ventilation system operates in the kitchen. Kitchens with wood-fired grills and ovens are especially challenging when combined with all the heat compressors running to power refrigerators and freezers. Your best options are fresh air, ceiling fans, or air-conditioning (through ducts or blown directly from wall-mounted units and frequently readjusted manually to keep the room cool but not cold). LEED architects and thoughtful contractors can save operators money by routing hot water and heat to warm the building in winter and by installing proper insulation, windows, and a vestibule with proper airflow.

Airkooler Fan

Lighting is another crucial element of bar and restaurant design, as outside glare needs to be kept out during the day and ambient and task lighting provided during the evening. Depending on the venue's exposure and aesthetics, a mixture of blinds, shades, curtains, and umbrellas outside help shade or block out light and cool the room. Natural light can be admitted through skylights in low roof areas; in the evening it must be supplemented, then replaced by warm lighting from above, below, and along the walls. Spotlights should be positioned to highlight art, food, and drink on the table and make menus easier to read. The rest of the room should be lit with a mixture of warm lights—wall sconces and floor and ceiling lamps—that flatter guests' complexions and can be dimmed as needed, using a program set by a lighting designer if the budget allows. Ideally, the lighting should enable guests to take appetizing smartphone photos of their food, drink, and each other without using a flash.

Lamp, Arnaud's French 75 Bar

The variety, genre, and style of music played in a bar is a matter of taste, but should reflect the concept and take guest preferences into account. Take the same care with your music mix as you do with your menu. In other words, entrust it to a human—ideally a DJ or knowledgeable staff member—rather than a streaming service. The volume and tempo of music should be adjusted throughout the night to reflect the pace of service as the room fills up and empties out toward closing. The sound system should be installed by an acoustic engineer, who can choose the right speakers and position them so music casts a veil of privacy around guests' conversations without forcing them to whisper when the room is empty or shout when it's full. Adding acoustic tiles to hard wall surfaces makes it much easier for guests and staff to hear both the music and each other.

Technology changes the way we live and do business, and it should be carefully considered when installing it in bars and restaurants. I used to view Wi-Fi as an amenity for study hall–like coffee shops, but I now

ON LIGHT

"I get excited by light. I get excited by looking at light. Thinking about light. When I see really beautiful light, I'm instantly drawn to it. It can even be dim lighting at a bar, although that's not always right for photography. But sometimes it's right for enjoying the ambience."

DANIEL KRIEGER

Photographer

realize it's necessary for guests from abroad to get online (I know I'm grateful for it when traveling). Security cameras, which I initially regarded as an instrument of the owner's distrust, can actually exonerate bartenders accused of theft and can empower guests who are victims of a crime, so I would no longer work without them.

Turntable

THE PHYSICAL BAR

The physical bar itself should be considered from an aesthetic *and* functional standpoint, taking into account how both guests and bartenders interface with it. The goal is to find the sweet spot that succeeds on both fronts without costly concessions to either.

Take the NoMad bar (see image on page 84), for example. Beneath and behind the regal mahogany bar and in front of the uplit shelves showcasing thousands of dollars' worth of spirits, concealed from guests' view, are service stations, coolers, and machinery. It doesn't matter how much you spend on the façade of your boozy altar; if you do not invest in the functionality of the workstations and quality of bartenders' equipment, you'll never recoup your investment. Just as the bartenders must maintain the guests' area first and work toward their station, the architect and designers must design the bar to accommodate what needs to be served from the interior of the bar out. Let's consider all the elements that contribute to optimum functionality.

The countertop must be wide enough to fit all the plates, glasses, condiments, and utensils a guest needs—everything from a rounded bumper on which guests can rest an elbow, which contains spills to the bar side, to a stainless-steel drip tray, which should be wide enough (at least eight inches) to build cocktails with the smaller shaker tin in front of the larger. Countertops more than thirty-eight inches wide (including the drip tray and bumper) are a challenge for bartenders under six feet tall and impede intimate dialogue with the guests. Countertops less than thirty-two inches (including the drip tray and bumper) are too narrow for a traditional table setting to be laid for diners, so such spacing should be avoided where food is served.

The bar top should be soft enough to prevent glasses from shattering if they tip over, but sturdy enough to stand on if the occasion is ever called for, which is why most are fashioned from wood. Many bars store bitters, syrups, absinthe fountains, and tools along the counter's drip tray, where cocktail ingredients tend to sprawl when undercounter space is used up. While this gives bartenders easy access to their ingredients and something to talk about with their guests, it obstructs the path between plates and glasses, blocks sightlines, and undermines non-cocktail-related dialogue, so I discourage it.

Depending on the height of bar stools, the bar should be around forty-two inches high, so it rests near the waist of a standing guest between five foot nine and six foot two. The countertop should extend between twelve and fifteen inches from the wall of the bar to accommodate guests' legs when they're sitting on a stool between twenty-four and thirty-two inches high, with a cushion no less than twelve inches square and a rung at least eighteen inches below the seat for the guest to rest their feet.

Position coat hooks in between the stools, above the area where guests' knees bend, so they don't bang them when they sit down. A foot rail around the perimeter of the base of the bar, running six to eight inches high, is traditionally installed for standing guests to prop a foot. Architectural details of the outside wall of the bar may be illuminated by a dim rope light recessed into the counter above plugs installed to charge phones and mobile devices.

On the other side of the wall, the countertop should extend at least thirteen inches to recess the ice wells and machinery underneath. Given that the standard ice well is eighteen inches wide and the bottle racks add five to ten inches (depending on whether you install one or two), recessing the equipment maximizes the reach of the bartender who stands in front of it. The ice well should stand at least thirty inches high; ten inches below the countertop (so there's room to scoop) so the bartender doesn't have to bend excessively to retrieve ice from the eighteen-inch-deep well, outfitted with separators to store multiple types of ice and internal bottle wells to keep juices cool.

A rope light on a dimmer switch should be recessed into the bottom of the countertop so bartenders can see everything below and keep their stations clean. Along with the floor, the entire back wall should be tiled or covered in stainless steel to prevent water damage and facilitate cleaning. Rubber floor mats may be laid over the tiled floor to reduce wear and tear on servers' legs and backs and prevent slips, spills, and glass breakage during service.

Bryant's Cocktail Lounge | Milwaukee, Wisconsin

The first floor of this two-story lounge features a well-appointed bar designed with input from its bartenders after a fire damaged the interior in 1971. Its gently curved shape gives patrons the ideal vantage point to view bartenders mixing drinks and other guests enjoying them. Instead of bottles and merchandise, the backbar features glassware, two gold-plated antique National cash registers, a 55-gallon freshwater fish tank, and a McIntosh Stereo System from the 1970s. Over two hundred bottles are stored under the bar counter in a custom three-tier rail that runs the entire length of the bar. Lounge seating is compartment-alized so the bar feels full even if the booths are empty.

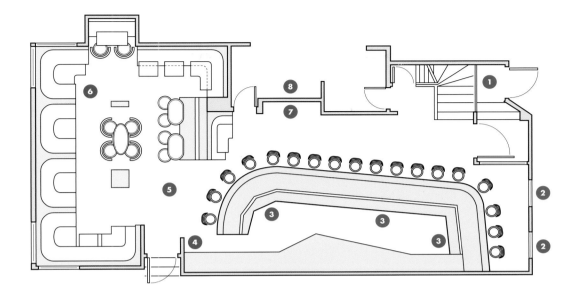

BRYANT'S FLOOR PLAN

① **Entrance** through vestibule, staircase to second-floor seating to the right

② **Shuttered windows** provide natural light during the daytime and privacy for patrons in the bar

③ **Three bar stations** to prepare cocktails for up to 70 guests seated throughout the lounge

④ **Centrally located service station** with sink, refrigeration, and access to cash register

⑤ **Carpeted floor** reinforces lounge feel and dampens sound to improve acoustics

⑥ **Curved booths** with plenty of corner seats offer privacy and expansive views of the room

⑦ **Coat rack** for bulky coats and outerwear

⑧ **Two all-gender bathrooms**

Equipment configuration should take inspiration from cockpit design, with everything needed within arm's reach. Each well should hold enough of each type of ice for two hours' worth of service. Allow space in the speed rack to store all bottles required to prepare the cocktails on the menu, a dipper well to store spoons and strainers, a garbage can and recycling bin recessed under the bar, a sink with a hose connection on the faucet for melting ice at the end of the night, and a sprayer to rinse shakers and mixing glasses between use. A hand-wash sink with soap, a dishwasher, glass chillers for each station, and a beer tap tower should be centrally located for quick access to multiple bartenders.

Curved and horseshoe-shaped bars encourage more interaction between guests, but they require extensive stainless steel customization to recess workstations and machinery underneath to minimize the space between the bartender and the closest edge of the bar.

The backbar should be forty to fifty inches from the inner edge of the countertop; this allow enough space for a barback to slip behind a working bartender to replenish ingredients, bottles, or ice in their well, but not so much that the bartender has to turn around and take more than a step to retrieve bottles from the backbar, enter an order into the POS terminal, or make change from the cash drawer. As in other retail outlets, prime real estate (the backbar) should be merchandised with products for sale. This means storing glassware below counter height in chillers alongside bartender workstations in the front bar or in refrigerators or freezers under the backbar. Install custom cabinetry in a clean, dry space out of guests' sightlines to house china, silverware, backup spirits, bar towels, cocktail napkins, straws, picks, and other dry sundries. Undercounter refrigerators stocked with wine and beer should have glass doors so the guests can peruse their options before ordering.

Cash Register

ON NATURE

"Every second that I'm not thinking how the bar operates—*How can I make it better? How can I make it more efficient?*—I'm experiencing it in everyday life. Everyday life needs to inform our decisions as operators and designers. If I'm not looking at the way leaves grow on trees and birds fly and the way colors look in an aquarium versus the colors on the wall and the way it changes the human condition when you look at these things, I'm not going to be a good operator."

JOHN GERTSEN

Bartender

In addition to a POS terminal (ideally one per bartender) recessed into the countertop so the screen faces the ceiling instead of the guests, a tip jar, and space to store check presenters and office supplies for bills, the countertop and cabinetry above it should be used to display bottles and decorated with a handful of engaging tchotchkes. Position a silent thermal printer above or below the terminal to print checks, and a (noisy) impact printer in the service station so the bartender can hear orders coming in. Most bars display their spirits on stepped, uplit shelves spaced so part of each bottle's label is visible to guests seated at the bar. Bars like Drink in Boston keep their backbar clear by stocking thirty to forty bottles in each well, juices and fortified wines in undercounter fridges, and an expanded selection of high-end spirits in the

Drink | Boston, Massachusetts

Architects Cheryl and Jeffrey Katzes' minimalist design highlights the industrial feel of the Fort Point building—a former wool warehouse—by leaving the massive wood support beams, original stone and brick foundation, and concrete support columns untouched. The quarter-sawn, white-oak bar zigzags around two central columns generating six corners with vantage points of bartenders, other guests, and the sparsely decorated backbar below a bay of windows that overlooks Congress Street. No bottles, merchandizing, or cash registers are displayed. A long glass countertop along wall opposite the bar houses early twentieth-century bug boxes the Katzes sourced after discovering the bartenders used cochineal coloring in their house bitters.

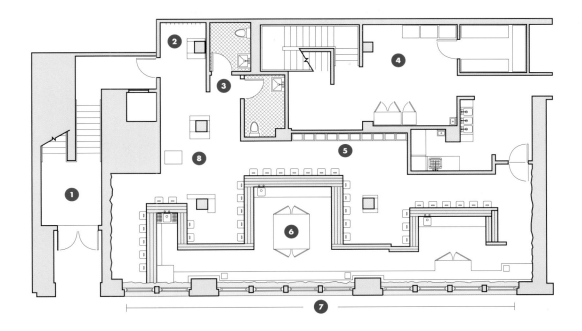

DRINK FLOOR PLAN

1 **Street-level vestibule** with staircase up to Sportello (on the left) and down to Drink (on the right)

2 **Coat rack** for bulky coats and outerwear

3 **Two all-gender bathrooms**

4 **Kitchen** for bar and restaurant prep, dry storage, and pot washing

5 **Glass countertop** for standing guests' drinks above antique insect "curiosity cabinet"

6 **Central island** with herb garden and water bottles on top and undercounter fridge and freezer below

7 **Ten windows** span the back wall, providing natural light and views of Congress Street

8 **Host stand** where up to 72 guests are greeted and seated on a first-come, first-served basis

BO HAGOOD

Furniture Maker

ON GOOD VERSUS GREAT

"When you're budgeting to build
your house, a lot of it comes down to
money. So I like to tell my clients that
the difference between 90 percent
and 100 percent is about 100 percent.
Meaning it's going to cost that much
more time, that much more effort,
that much more planning, and that
much more money to attain that
extra 10 percent. In other words, the
difference between good and great
is tremendous. Out of the general
population in this country, only
1 or 2 percent of people care about
making this commitment or even
notice the results."

bar's center island cabinets. Without the distraction of all the bottles, guests and bartenders can talk about their options, and design and décor are front and center.

Bars with an ambitious cocktail program require a tiled, brightly lit prep area—separated from kitchen prep, if you also serve food—where bar staff can collect ice produced by up to three different machines, squeeze juice, blend purees, simmer syrups, steep infusions, cut garnishes, and more. A long, deep counter with multiple outlets will be necessary to accommodate technology such as a rotary evaporator, an immersion circulator, a dehydrator, and a centrifuge, as well as more standard machinery such as an induction burner, a juicer, a juice extractor, and an industrial food processor.

The prep area should be close to the walk-in refrigerator, the walk-in freezer (where block ice is stored), and the dry goods pantry (where spices are kept). A deep, foot-pedal-operated, double-basin stainless steel sink with an overhead sprayer and plenty of drained counter space on each side enables easy cleaning, rinsing, and drying of fruits, vegetables, and storage containers.

Most bars store dry goods, mixers, spices, and paper goods on stainless steel metro shelves in a pantry positioned between the prep area and a locked liquor room, which ideally is situated in the coolest part of the building or refrigerated to ensure wines and vermouths don't spoil. An additional walk-in refrigerator may be required to store keg beer, wines, and bottled water, depending on the volume of the establishment. Ideally, there's a logical flow to storage and prep areas of the bar, so it's easy to receive orders, put them away, break down and recycle boxes and trash, and transport what's needed for service to the floor.

Finally, there's the management office (which should be lockable). If this space is too nice, the managers won't devote enough time to supervising service on the floor; if it's poorly or inadequately provisioned, managers will do their office work away from the business, which cuts into the time staff have to consult with them.

You can't anticipate everything your staff and guests will require from the physical plant, which is why bar design should be an evolutionary, modular process. No matter what building materials you choose, wear and tear on high-traffic areas and elements such as bathrooms, floors, doors, walls, and chairs will require upkeep and eventual replacement over the years. Renovations to improve the space should be scheduled during yearly maintenance closures. Energy-efficient lights, machinery, and textiles will cost more up front but will save the business thousands over their life span and help preserve the environment for the future. Knowing that the business's identity will always be in a state of flux, it's best to design a bar you can grow into instead of plunging your business into long-term debt designing a room you'll never be able to afford to adapt.

HOME BAR DESIGN

My parents raised me in my maternal grandparents' sprawling Victorian home in River Forest, Illinois. The basement featured a plumbed wet bar with three sinks, plenty of shelving space to store glassware, and a bar to play behind. My grandfather worked in the ticket sellers' union that his father-in-law helped found, and over his lifetime he accumulated hundreds of bottles as gifts from patrons. My paternal grandmother had an even more elaborate bar in her basement.

These bars seemed unremarkable to me at the time but, as I reflect back on them now, they were quite extraordinary, and they must have influenced me subconsciously. Based on the growing interest in cocktails today, I'm confident the home bar is ready for its triumphant return to modern American homes.

For the typical amateur host—at least before they are bitten by the cocktail bug—cocktail ingredients are stored in or around the kitchen: wine and produce in the refrigerator, ice in the freezer, glassware in the cabinets above the countertop, dusty bottles of liquor in the back of an inconveniently located cabinet.

Those who have an aha! moment—likely at a bar or restaurant where a talented bartender serves cocktails prepared with fresh ingredients and premium spirits—may find themselves transformed into a budding enthusiast, and those bottles of liquor will be dusted off and placed on the countertop along with new acquisitions, such as specialized tools, glassware, and recipe books.

Once the kitchen countertop and island become so crowded with bottles and ephemera that cooking becomes inconvenient, sensible enthusiasts scout another location for their home bar. Stationing the bar away from the kitchen is a nice idea, because it means the enthusiast doesn't have to worry about washing dishes and pans to prepare the kitchen for after-dinner drinks.

Sideboards and credenzas near the dining room table are a logical location, but the lack of plumbing and refrigeration limits what you can serve. A bar cart is another option—and unlike the credenza, it elegantly announces "cocktail hour." The cart can be rolled out of sight after drinks are prepared and served, which allows the server to spend time with guests once everyone has a drink.

I worked with furniture maker Bo Hagood (see page 64) to design a custom home bar for Nike design chairman John Hoke's living room; our goal was to employ the principles of professional bar design to create a unit that disappears like a rollaway cart. The coat closet–size bar is concealed by a floor-to-ceiling door that can be opened or closed based on the family's entertainment needs. Tiered shelving maximizes visibility of each spirit, displayed under strategically recessed spotlights.

Bo's cabinetry conceals a refrigerator/freezer unit where glasses, ice, and mixers can be stored. Like most professional bars, the Hoke bar has a mirrored backbar (so you can keep an eye on your guests while you're mixing) and even a concealed tray that can be deployed to butler cocktails to guests. Architectural details, such as the finial brass work that doubles as a touch switch for the lights, echo the same refinement and quality of materials as the mid-century modern furniture that adorns the rest of the living room.

To properly service any more than eight thirsty guests for a cocktail hour, you'll need to either prebatch and bottle the drinks, be a professional bartender with a formidable home bar setup, or hire a pro to set up a bar station and work it for you. I've been vexed to find myself serving cocktails in rented glasses on six-foot-long tables covered in stained white linen in a house with a wine cellar worth more than the sixteen-story building I live in.

I think it's high time for the architects and builders who design today's luxury homes to start allocating resources to home bars similar to what they now devote to "chef's kitchens" and wine cellars. As more assets are developed to increase consumers' knowledge, the craft of the cocktail will once again flourish in homes, as hosts control the music, lighting, soundtrack, décor, and menu, and enjoy the privilege of bartenders, who take great pride in entertaining their guests.

Hoke Home Bar | Portland, Oregon

This home bar features materials commonly found in commercial bars, including brass, walnut, stone, and mirrored glass. The simplicity, proportions, and detailing complement the modern architectural design of the Hokes' home, which is decorated with iconic midcentury furnishings and modern art. Custom fabricated components include a hand-turned brass finial that serves as a light switch, a perforated brass drink rail, and a concealed walnut service tray. The 55-inch-wide by 22-inch-deep bar in the corner of the living room may be concealed behind a massive white door that allows it to blend into the room's white walls inconspicuously.

HOKE HOME BAR CROSS-SECTION

1. **White door** allows the bar to blend into the room's white walls when open or closed

2. **Brass-wrapped display shelving** so backup bottles are visible and easily accessible

3. **Touch-activated finial switch** with 3 brightness settings for overhead and undershelf lighting

4. **Mirrored back wall** allows host to keep an eye on guests while preparing drinks with back turned to the room

5. **Brass drink rail** provides extra counter space for glassware and bottles

6. **Utility drawers** for tools, dry storage, and a garbage can

7. **Leather-backed black walnut tray** with copper handles stowed discreetly for drink service

8. **Subzero fridge/freezer** with icemaker accessible via wood-paneled pullout drawers

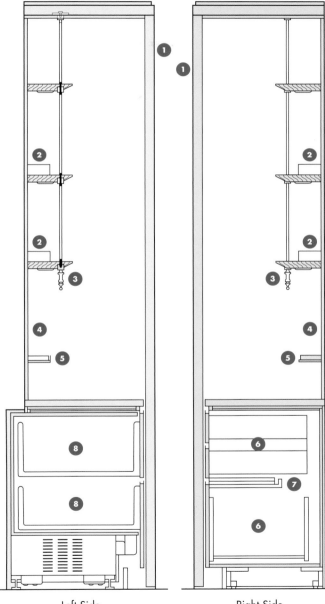

Left Side   Right Side

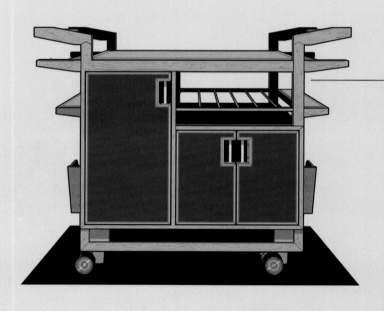

Tools & Techniques

Watching a well-trained team of bartenders serve guests on a busy night is like taking in a dance recital. A great bartender works quickly, without ever looking hurried, moving in the most economical way possible to fill orders. Disciplined bartenders never step into their colleagues' workstations, unless poor bar design demands it, and they are in constant communication with each other, often without words.

Experienced bartenders develop muscle memory that allows them to mix drinks with their heads up. After reaching for a tool or bottle hundreds of times, they can grasp it securely without thinking or looking, assuming it's in its proper place. With practice, they learn how to hold and manipulate bottles of different heights, widths, weights, shapes, and volumes quickly and gracefully.

Most bartending books have a "technique" chapter, broken down by procedure—for example, measuring, pouring, stirring, shaking, straining. However, this assumes that each preparation method happens in isolation, and that a bartender performs each in easy succession.

Of course, in the chaos of a busy bar, this is never the case. When a barrage of drink orders comes in, you have to quickly figure out your plan of attack, and then let that muscle memory kick in. Every action behind the bar should be made after a split-second evaluation of what's the most important thing to do at that particular moment.

And so, this chapter is organized a bit differently, around an unusually complicated drink order, which just happens to require every technique you'll need to prepare the recipes in this book. First, I'll show you, in detail, how we set up for service; then I'll show you how to build the round of drinks, outlining the order of operations and the thought process behind each step.

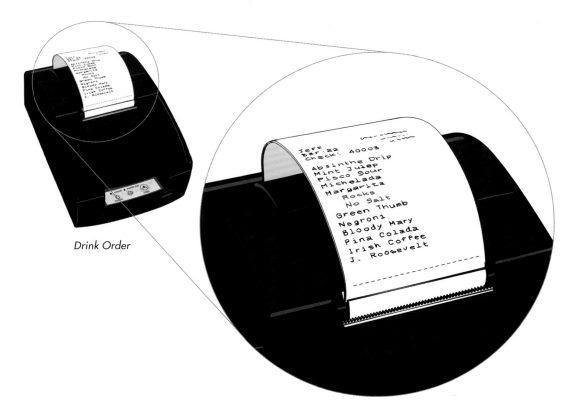

Drink Order

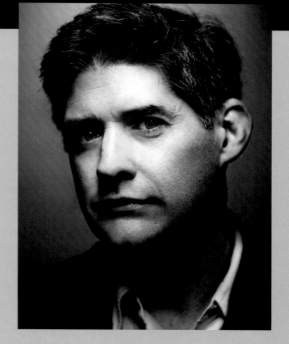

ON BEING A BADASS

"We spend a lot of time working on something, so we don't want to bury it. All of our bartenders like swirling liquid nitrogen around in a glass in our bar. Why? Because our customers like it, and it makes them look like a badass. It's also an excellent way to chill a glass."

DAVE ARNOLD

Bar Operator

The order pictured at left would make most bartenders shudder, but it wouldn't be out of the ordinary for a large party at a well-respected cocktail bar. (If you've ever wondered why many cocktail bars won't seat parties larger than eight, it's because service tends to grind to a halt when orders like this come in.) Batching popular cocktails before service speeds things up, but most bar operators are hesitant to premix ingredients because it detracts from the theater of bartending. If the bar is set up properly and the bartenders split the order diligently, this ticket can be prepared in six minutes or fewer.

SETTING UP FOR SERVICE

Working service in a bar is like painting a room: if you spend hours prepping correctly, all you have to do is apply the paint evenly. Before any order is placed, hours of preparation are needed so each recipe can be executed in a minute or less. This includes transforming fruits and vegetables into garnishes, juice, and purees; producing house-made ingredients such as syrups, tinctures, and infusions; and batching component mixtures or in some cases entire cocktails to expedite service.

This preservice preparation is so involved that some cocktail bars, such as New York City's Dead Rabbit, employ a full-time staff member to do the job. At PDT, porters cut garnishes and prepare juices during the afternoon, and barbacks prepare more involved syrups and infusions during the shift at night, when they aren't on the floor bussing tables and restocking the bar.

House-Made Ingredients

A decade ago, I made many of my own ingredients, such as orgeat; tonic syrup with citrus peel, lemongrass, and cinchona bark; lime cordial; and grenadine. Times have thankfully changed, and now bartenders such as San Francisco's Jennifer Colliau of Small Hand Foods, Charleston's Brooks Reitz of Jack Rudy, and Portland's Daniel Shoemaker and Sean Hoard of the Commissary have started selling high-quality versions of these syrups commercially. This is a boon not only for bars and for enthusiasts who don't have a production staff on the clock, but also for professionals like me, who can now devote this time to other responsibilities.

Scale

In spite of viable commercial alternatives, most serious cocktail bars still make most of their syrups in-house, which allows them to serve

ON MAKING INGREDIENTS

"I felt guilty for having spent
75 percent of my career not knowing
what I was doing. Because I had
looked at this as a means to an end,
I had never focused on translating
what I loved about cooking to the
bar. The first thing a chef taught me
was you can't have good gazpacho
with bad tomatoes. The fact that
I had spent so much of my career not
applying that principle to bartending
bummed me out. There's a part
of me that feels like I'm doing
penance for that."

DANIEL SHOEMAKER

Bar Operator

unique renditions of classic recipes and house creations. For example, the
ginger beer recipe at the Pegu Club (which I've adapted for use in the recipes
in this book and relabeled "ginger wort," as it isn't fermented) is prepared
with ginger, lime, brown sugar, and water, whereas Attaboy prepares ginger
syrup from ginger juice and sugar. Because of this, classics like the Moscow
Mule and Dark and Stormy will taste different at each bar.

I've included ten recipes for homemade mixers in the subrecipe section
of this book (starting on page 390), ranging from simple preparations like
whipping cream to more complex mixtures like Tom and Jerry batter
and horchata. Depending on where you live and the time of year, you can

probably find commercial versions of all of them, but they're typically packaged with stabilizers and preservatives that alter the flavor and body of any cocktail they go into. By preparing your own syrups you'll ensure quality, allow yourself the option to develop a signature style (à la Attaboy and Pegu Club), and minimize waste (particularly at home, where large bottles of syrup will turn before they're depleted).

SIMPLE SYRUP

Every cocktail enthusiast, whether amateur or professional, should know how to make simple syrup (page 391) and have a bottle stored in the fridge for cocktail hour. But do not be fooled by the name—there's a reason that in *The Bar Book*, author Jeffrey Morgenthaler titled his chapter on the subject "Simple Syrups: The Paradox of Simplicity." If you aren't rigorous, your simple syrup may vary from batch to batch, which will affect your recipes once you start mixing. Many bars, especially larger bars in corporate groups, buy commercial sugar syrup. I do not recommend this, as, again, they are filled with stabilizers that affect the taste and texture of a cocktail. If you're not confident in the consistency of your syrups, you can check your results with a brix refractometer (which measures sugar content).

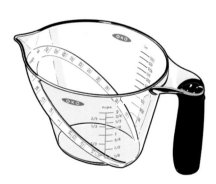

Measuring Cup

Regardless of whether you prepare your simple syrup using one part sugar to one part water, as I do, or a more concentrated "2:1" syrup (two parts sugar to one part water), it's vital that you make your simple syrup with cane sugar—not beet sugar—and that it's granulated and not powdered, which typically has cornstarch added. Many bars measure equal parts sugar and water by volume, but measuring by weight is more accurate and the best way to ensure consistency from batch to batch. After choosing a method, make sure everyone in the bar uses it.

FRESH JUICE

A key decision for any bar is whether to juice lemons and limes before service or to squeeze them to order. Bars that squeeze to order typically employ a handheld press colloquially known as an "elbow," or a larger levered press—I recommend either Ra Chand or Hamilton Beach. Most high-volume cocktail bars juice before service, using the sturdy and reliable Sunkist juicer, which has a covered, engine-powered mechanical reamer. There are more elaborate citrus juicers, such as the Zumex, which slices and presses top-loaded whole fruit, but these take up more space and require more financial capital than most bars and restaurants can afford.

Elbow Juicer

Oil from the peel of the fruit, plus bitterness from the pith, affects the character of the resulting juice. Elbow and Zumex juicers, which press against the peel during the extraction process, yield more oil and bitterness than citrus extracted by hand with a reamer. In my opinion, lemon and lime juice extracted with a reamer (either handheld or mechanical) tastes better a couple of hours after it's been squeezed, when the fruit's flavor begins to shine through sheer acidity. Lemon and lime juice squeezed via an elbow juicer or Zumex taste better à la minute, when the bright, aromatic oils extracted from the peel are still fresh, offsetting the bitterness from the pith.

Each piece of fruit varies slightly in acidity and yields a different quantity of juice. So I find that bottling preservice ensures consistent acidity among all citrus cocktails throughout the course of the evening. If you refrigerate and cover fresh-squeezed citrus right after extraction and throughout the night, it should last about eight hours. As soon as it turns opaque and the acidity changes from piquant to a mouth-puckering tartness, it's likely past its prime. Be wary of packaged "fresh" juice, as it was likely pasteurized and frozen before being thawed and displayed for sale. Store-bought citrus juice is typically sold with pulp, which must be fine-strained before service, which means you may end up discarding up to a quarter of the total volume.

To extract the juice from oranges or grapefruits, you'll need a larger elbow, such as the model pictured on page 77, or larger reamer cones for your mechanical juicer. While most lemons and limes in the United States are similar in flavor and appearance, there is a variety of grapefruits and oranges, so stick to one style, such as Texas's pink Rio Star grapefruits or thin-skinned Valencia oranges. It's fine to mix in other varieties, such as the thick-skinned navel oranges you harvested for their peel, as long as the juice blend is consistent from night to night.

Breville Juice Extractor

The key to a successful fresh-juice program is setting an accurate par for usage so you run out of juice toward the end of each night. All fresh pressed citrus must be used within eight hours of being squeezed, and the bartenders can always squeeze more to order at the end of the night. The bar should record the amount of citrus used each day until you can reliably estimate how much juice to prepare, taking into account weekly and seasonal variance.

Some fruits and vegetables, like celery, can't be squeezed or muddled; others, like pineapple, can be, but are better when separated by an extractor, which minces fruit and vegetables like a food processor and reserves the pulp. To make your own fresh-pressed juice, I recommend Breville's juice extractors for consumers and Ruby's heavy-duty extractor for commercial use. The difference in quality and cost comes down to heft, as more fibrous roots such as ginger, beets, and turmeric require sharp blades and a heavy steel base to stabilize the unit.

Be sure to juice watery vegetables like celery and cucumber or fruits such as watermelon and honeydew right before service, as they oxidize more quickly than citrus or pineapple juice. Avoid extracting to order behind the bar; it is both disruptively loud and time-consuming. After extraction, strain through a fine strainer or let sediments settle before bottling and storing in the refrigerator. Or, if you want to embrace the frothy head of fresh-extracted juice, serve cocktails like the Garibaldi (Campari and fresh orange juice) with a Guinness-like head, as barman Naren Young of Dante does.

Garnishes

Some bars leave a bowl of whole fruit on the bar for bartenders to peel twists and cut wedges, wheels, spears, and other decorative garnishes to order. However, most bar stations don't have the prep space, and many bartenders don't have the time during busy shifts for tasks that can be completed up to three hours before the shift. The downside to preparing fruit and vegetables before service, besides their drying out over a long night, is having to throw out unused garnishes, so be sure to keep a close eye on usage, and prepare only as much as you'll need. You can always cut to order at the end of the night when it slows down.

Food waste is both a financial and a philosophical concern. Never throw away blemished fruits and vegetables that can't be used for garnishing;

WHEN COMMERCIAL IS BETTER

While I'll never refuse a Bloody Mary made from fresh, in-season tomatoes, I've had far too many that taste like consommé. Some ingredients—commercial tomato juice among them—aren't readily interchangeable with fresh ones. I won't even dignify the argument for house-made sauces over brands such as Cholula, HP, and Lea & Perrins in my Bloody Mary and Michelada recipes. When commercial products are an integral part of a cocktail—as with the Bloody Mary and Michelada—swapping them out alters the DNA of the recipe.

save them for juicing and muddling. If you decide to cut your citrus twists before service, reserve the fruit for juicing afterward so nothing is wasted. I find that citrus dries out after removing its peel for twists, so this is a good incentive for cutting your twists before service. Although long, fat swathes of citrus look great in stirred drinks like the Negroni in this order, the larger the peel you cut, the more citrus oil it will add to your drink when you pinch it, so pinch only a portion of the peel.

Store precut garnishes in clean, covered containers, in the refrigerator where possible, or in airtight lidded bowls or pans chilled with ice during service. Herbs should be cleaned and stored in ice water or the refrigerator wherever possible. Following the lead of Sasha Petraske's Milk & Honey bar, many operators store their garnishes in crushed ice on top of the bar, similar to how raw bars display their shellfish. While this a great way to advertise a fresh ingredient–driven cocktail program, it takes up counter space, so undercounter refrigerated drawers, which restaurant kitchens employ, are preferable.

More ornate, sculptural garnishes, such as the horse's neck (a long, spiraling citrus twist with the navel attached on one end), have been popular for decades, and remain an integral part of bartending culture. If you have the knife skills and desire to transform the orange twist for the Negroni into the *Mona Lisa,* go ahead, but don't slow down service, waste fruit, or forget that the oil in the peel is also an ingredient in the recipe. In my opinion, the garnish should fit the rest of the drink aesthetically and philosophically: if it's a simple, workmanlike cocktail, garnish it appropriately. If it's a tiki cocktail that calls for a more elaborate garnish, that's another story. In either case, the garnish should never steal—or be—the "show."

Chef's Knife

Ice

Ice is one of the four main elements of a cocktail, along with glassware, liquid, and garnish (providing the cocktail is prepared or served with ice and has a garnish). Dave Arnold covers the science behind ice masterfully in *Liquid Intelligence*, while Jeffrey Morgenthaler is more philosophical in *The Bar Book*, characterizing it in comparison to cooking: "In the same way a skilled chef uses heat to prepare food, the professional bartender uses ice to prepare cocktails." Why would you obsess over the liquid, source beautiful glassware, hand-cut a garnish, and then use subpar ice? As with a diamond, clarity is the true measure of clean, well-made ice, which will increase the appeal of your cocktails.

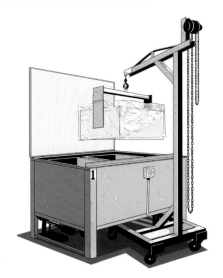

Clinebell Ice Machine

Harvesting ice is the last preservice task you need to perform to prepare the drink order on page 72. For this order, and most others too, you'll need cubed ice, crushed or pebble ice, and larger cubes. Cocktail bars should purchase (or preferably lease, if a reliable service contract is available) an ice machine such as a Kold-Draft or Hoshizaki that makes larger all-purpose 1.25 x 1.25-inch cubes, with a serious ice crusher attached, or supplement it with a Scotsman pebble ice machine. If there's any money left in the budget and space left to store it, get a Clinebell ice machine, which produces clear ice blocks to cut down for cocktails and fine spirits served on the rocks. Many major metropolitan U.S. cities have an ice service that cuts and delivers clear cubes, spears, and spheres for around a dollar a cube, but a Clinebell in a busy cocktail bar will pay for itself within a year.

If you're preparing cocktails at home, or work in a bar or restaurant that can't purchase three ice machines (nearly all of them), you can use silicone molds

"When we're creating something that's permanent—like sculpture or painting—we're always thinking about the end result. We spend a lot of time looking at finished work. For working artists, once we learn something, we never want to see that again; we want to move on, and ice fast-tracks that experience. In the studio, it's all about process for us; outside, it becomes an experience. It's mesmerizing to see people watch it melt away and have that present moment: to be so aware."

SHINTARO OKAMOTO

Ice Sculptor

of all shapes and sizes for cubes, and hearty hammers and canvas sacks to pulverize ice for Mint Juleps and swizzles, and you can freeze your own blocks to carve down with picks, saws, and knives. Ideally, set aside a chest freezer for block ice or store it in zip-locking bags so food odor doesn't contaminate it.

Glassware

Like crystal-clear ice, the visual beauty of mugs, stemware, and cups shapes an imbiber's impression of a cocktail's quality. The quality and character of a bar's glassware selection tend to reflect its values.

Glassmakers such as Riedel, Spiegelau, and Zalto have exploited the beauty of blown-glass decorative decanters for decades and engineered glasses that accentuate the aroma and flavor of many grape varietals and beer styles. In addition to choosing glassware that matches the style of the bar and ethos of the cocktails, consider durability, as glassware breakage can cost a bar hundreds of dollars a night. Develop a par for each type so bartenders never run out of glasses on a busy night.

Size is another consideration. Most recipes are based on standard glassware sizes, such as 5.5-ounce coupes, larger 9-ounce coupes to accommodate extra volume from egg white, 9-ounce absinthe glasses, 12-ounce julep cups, 13-ounce double old-fashioned glasses, 6-ounce Irish coffee glasses, and 12-ounce pilsner glasses. Your guests will expect the glass to be filled to the top, with a little room to spare so it doesn't spill, so be sure to buy the proper size glasses based on your recipes. Larger glasses require larger cocktails, which can lead to unintended overconsumption and drunkenness.

Glassware for Order

Once you've chosen your glassware and bought enough to accommodate the menu and size of your bar, the next step is to store it properly. Glasses should be washed, polished with a clean buffing cloth, then placed in a glass freezer. Frozen glasses become brittle and breakable, so take care when grabbing a chilled glass during service. Pouring an ice-cold drink into a warm glass is pointless, so if no freezer is available it's essential to ice the glass down (see page 99). When making a hot drink, the glass or mug should be warmed with boiling water before the cocktail is poured into it (see "How to Serve Hot Drinks," page 108).

MISE EN PLACE

The bar station should be set up so everything's within arm's reach, to minimize unnecessary movements. Placing tools in the ideal place (what chefs call *mise en place*) will vary from bartender to bartender based on dominant hand and tool preferences, but the goal should be to mirror the setup in each station so if one bartender steps away for a break, the other can step in and make drinks in their absence. The same goes for the bottles; give them labeled positions in the well so anyone unfamiliar with the station knows where everything belongs. And stock backups of every bottle you'll finish during a night in a labeled cabinet nearby.

Cocktail bar setups have become increasingly sophisticated as menus expand. In spite of this trend, I recommend simplifying the bar organization as much as possible. When a bartender cuts him- or herself and needs to go to the hospital, or has some emergency and needs to go home, or quits on the spot (thankfully, in my career this has happened only once), you'll be glad that the

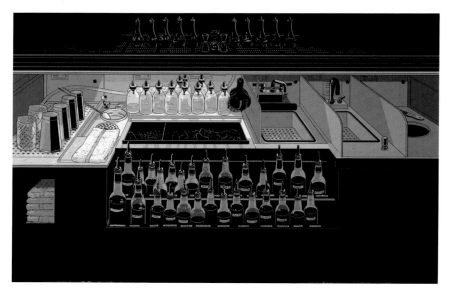

NoMad Bar Station

bar station is not personally customized, so a manager or waiter can step in and keep service humming.

Label *everything* (using a label maker that dispenses clearly written laminated tape)—not only the bottles, but also the places in the well or backup cabinet where they belong.

The typical well (the shelf attached to the ice bin) used to have at least one of each type of base spirit (vodka, gin, rum, tequila, brandy, whiskey) with a few modifiers (triple sec, sweet and dry vermouths, simple syrup). But in cocktail bars where most of the drinks are ordered from the menu, the well should accommodate all the ingredients on the menu; group them so all the bottles necessary to make a single drink are stored next to each other. I tend to put the taller bottles, which tip over easily and catch on your apron, in the middle of the well and the smaller bottles toward the edges.

Ingredients for the most popular cocktails should be grouped on the ends (unless they're in tall bottles) of each well, and each pour spout—should you decide to use pour spouts (see sidebar)—should be faced inward so you can pour with the label facing the guest at all times without needing to spin the bottle to accommodate the pitch of the spout.

SPEED POURERS

Pour spouts, or "speed pourers," actually pour more slowly than pouring without them. The key advantage of speed pourers is that they regulate the pour flow, allowing you to measure by count without a jigger. After working with speed pourers most of my career, I've trained myself to pour without them, which allows me to work more quickly. I view pour spouts as the equivalent of training wheels for a bartender. If you decide to use pourers, know that the rubber stopper around the metal spout breaks down and eventually leaks after a few months of nightly use; have new replacements handy. Remove pour spouts each night and soak in hot, soapy water to rinse off sugary residue that attracts fruit flies.

So that staff can immediately handle a spill on either side of the bar, neatly fold and store wet and dry bar towels in discreet locations out of guests' view all over the bar. (Never hang a towel off your belt or apron, as this is both visually unappealing and unsanitary.) The health code in New York City mandates that wet towels should be stored in buckets of water with an added capful of bleach.

Bar Tools

Like glassware, bar tools are both stylish and functional, and the best aren't cheap. Availability used to be the primary limiting factor, but thanks to companies like Cocktail Kingdom, high-quality bar tools are available by mail all over the world. Unlike top kitchens, where the cooks bring their own tools, most bars cover the cost of tools for their staff. I think this should change, as the profession has reached a point where bartenders should invest in and work with their own tools.

SHAKERS

Choosing the right cocktail shaker used to have more to do with where the drink was being prepared than which shaker was best for the recipe.

Boston Shaker, Parisian Shaker, Cobbler Shaker

European bars tend to use the two-piece Parisian shaker, styled after the three-piece cobbler shaker, which Japanese bars tend to use. Most American bars use the two-piece Boston shaker—either a 28-ounce shaker tin combined with a 16-ounce tempered pint glass or another 18-ounce shaker tin (the latter combination is what bartenders call "metal on metal"). Each shaker has its advantage: the Boston and Parisian have a longer "throw" (distance from one end of the shaker to the other) than the cobbler, which many think is the easiest to use. Cobbler and Parisian shakers require two hands to use, while a Boston, which is what I would use, can be shaken with one hand or both. For the order on page 72 you'll need four shakers, so a good general guideline is to keep four or more on hand in a busy bar.

MIXING GLASSES

You can stir a cocktail in just about anything, and some bars still use the 16-ounce pint glass, which doubles as their mixing glass for their Boston shaker. But most serious cocktail bars stock spouted Japanese mixing pitchers, which are functional, sturdy, and elegant. The high thermal mass (ability to absorb and store heat) of glass mixing pitchers diminishes the chilling power of ice if they're stored at room temperature, so ice them or store them in the glass chiller between uses. Metal tins—especially silver ones— have a low thermal mass, so you can store them at room temperature on the countertop.

Mixing Glass

Choose a smooth-sided mixing glass so the ice doesn't rattle around in the glass; if you don't have a fancy spouted Japanese glass, stir in a shaker tin. Bartender Erik Lorincz collaborated with a Japanese company to create a spouted steel mixing pitcher, which strikes a nice balance between form and function.

BARSPOONS

A well-balanced, gently threaded Japanese barspoon ranging in length from 30 to 40 centimeters is the ideal stirring implement. You'll find a wide variety of barspoons on the market, recognizable by the tooling on the opposite end of the shaft from the bowl. Japanese-style spoons typically have a fork or bulbous bean on the opposite end, English spoons come with pestles for muddling or disks for layering, and inferior American spoons tend to come with a red plastic cap concealing an unfinished, crudely threaded

Barspoons

shaft. I'd forgo the multipurpose options and pick the spoon with the smoothest threading that rests most comfortably in your hand. I've nearly poked my eyes out dozens of times in bars using the forked spoon, so please don't stock that one. Seriously.

STRAINERS

Strainers fall into three general groupings: wire-rimmed Hawthorne strainers, colander-like julep strainers, and conical fine-mesh strainers. There are dozens of styles of Hawthorne strainers to choose from. Look for the quality of the wire spring (gauge and tightness of coil) that wraps around the top of the strainer and a good fit with the shaker tin you're using. The springless julep strainer is uniquely American: most bartenders in other countries don't use one. Look for a good fit with the mixing glass you're using. Bonzer and Yukiwa make great Hawthorne strainers, and Cocktail Kingdom makes the only julep strainer I'd recommend. Fine strainers are typically conical mesh sieves readily available at restaurant supply stores. They are used in conjunction with a Hawthorne strainer when a drink's clarity is paramount.

JIGGERS

There are arguments both for and against measuring your cocktails with a jigger. Having worked for many years with and without one, I'd never

Jiggers

work without one ever again, especially because I no longer work with speed pourers, whose slow and steady stream allows you to measure by counting. Just like shakers and mixing glasses, there are many styles of measures, from the rudimentary conical cups you can find in restaurant supply stores in the United States to the gorgeously machined cylinders they use in the U.K. to the more elegant and functional Japanese-style jiggers, which come in many shapes and volumes.

It's preferable to have jiggers of various volumes, so your pours always fill the cup, instead of having to eyeball a measure within the cup for a smaller pour. I use Cocktail Kingdom's Japanese-style 2-ounce/1-ounce jigger along with their 0.75-ounce/0.5-ounce jigger, and I carefully eyeball 0.25-ounce measures with the 0.5-ounce side of the second jigger, because there isn't a baking spoon or jigger cup of this size. Many bartenders work with a third 1.5-ounce/1-ounce measure, which is great if that's a common measurement in your recipes. Even though I love Oxo's 32-ounce measuring cups, I don't recommend their graduated jigger that many bartenders use as a universal jigger because it requires every measurement to be eyeballed.

Machinery

For the truly dedicated, there is a plethora of even more specialized tools and gizmos that can prepare ever-more complicated drinks. A couple that I've used will suffice for now.

ABSINTHE FOUNTAINS

Traditional absinthe clocks in at between 65 and 72% ABV, so it must be diluted for potability. The water spigots of cheap absinthe fountains tend to leak, so if absinthe is a prominent part of your beverage program, invest in a fountain with well-machined washers that's easy to clean. Many reputable producers provide tastefully branded fountains to distributors to bars in exchange for their patronage, so if the producer or distributor you buy from is willing to furnish one for the bar, I'd strongly consider accepting their offer.

Absinthe Fountain

BLENDERS

The cost of fancy mixing glasses and shakers pales in comparison to that of a high-quality blender, but you get what you pay for. Blenders less than $200 lack the power to pulverize ice into snowy peaks, and they typically leak. It has a steep price tag and formidable size, but Vitamix makes the best blender in the business. The only drawback is the noise they generate, so invest in the models that have a plastic cover to muffle noise, and position them under the bar so they don't block bartenders' and guests' sightlines. If your bar makes a lot of blender drinks, you'll need to invest in multiple blender cups and additional blenders so you don't have to wash cups between use and slow down service.

BUILDING THE ROUND

Now that your station is fully stocked with the tools, ingredients, glassware, and prepared garnishes required to execute all the recipes on your menu and any common requests off of it, I'll walk you through the steps that two bartenders should take to fulfill our model order most efficiently. This chapter is going to assume a degree of familiarity with each drink in the order, so I recommend taking a moment to review the recipe for each as provided in Chapter 5:

Absinthe Drip (PAGE 161)

Mint Julep (PAGE 315)

Pisco Sour (PAGE 353)

Michelada (PAGE 177)

Margarita (PAGE 285)

Green Thumb (PAGE 253)

Negroni (PAGE 235)

Bloody Mary (PAGE 193)

Piña Colada (PAGE 257)

Irish Coffee (PAGE 321)

Jimmie Roosevelt (PAGE 365)

Delegating

In most bars, the service bartender prepares all the drinks for the tables, and the point bartender (or multiple bartenders) serves the guests at the bar. Because bars typically have more tables than places to sit or stand at the bar, guests usually receive their drinks more quickly at the bar, while the service bartender struggles to keep up with the orders for the floor. Given that the majority of sales come from the tables, creating and maintaining a system that is flawed by design is counterintuitive. There's a better way. By rotating the bar staff through each station, instead of always letting the fastest work the service bar and the most gregarious work the point, you can overcome their reluctance to ask for help when it's needed in their station.

I'll assume that you have two bartenders to fill the order on page 72, and so the very first step is for the service bartender to split up the order logically, and delegate some drinks to the other bartender. There are a few different ways you can divvy up an order; for example, you can group the drinks according to preparation method, or each bartender's proximity to the ingredients and machinery required to prepare a recipe. Once the cocktails are split up, the bartenders should work in tandem to finish at the same time, so the drinks go out to the guests when they're appropriately cold (or warm) and perfectly diluted. To accomplish this, the cocktail server needs to be ready to deliver them as soon as the order is ready. Our model order is too large for one tray, so two servers need to butler this to the table.

In my opinion, the most logical way to divide this order is to give the bartender working the point the Green Thumb, Margarita, and Pisco Sour (because they're all shaken) and have the service bartender prepare the Negroni, Mint Julep, Jimmie Roosevelt, and Bloody Mary (because they're not). The other cocktails should be split up based on each bartender's proximity to fixed apparatuses (required for preparation).

Equipment such as the absinthe fountain and beer taps are typically centered on the bar for shared use, so I'd give the point bartender the Absinthe Drip and Michelada, and have the service bartender prepare the Irish Coffee, because coffee is typically served from the wait station. The Piña Colada can be made by whichever bartender is closest to the blender, with the service bartender taking it if both stations have one, because the drink tickets are their primary responsibility.

This means five or six drinks for each bartender, depending on who takes the Piña Colada. If there were more than two bartenders, I would split the order even further.

Deciding the Prep Order

If you're preparing more than two drinks at a time, as we are here, you should prioritize which drinks to prepare first based on whether or not a drink is served on ice, and if so, what type of ice. Cocktails served on the rocks change as the ice melts (see "Dilution," page 101), so this transformation should occur once the drink is in the guest's hands, not while the drink is waiting to be taken to the table. Cocktails served straight up should be poured first, because dilution isn't a concern, and stirred drinks should precede shaken drinks, which will lose their aeration if they sit too long. Cocktails with carbonated ingredients (like the Jimmie Roosevelt, which has champagne) benefit from being prepared last, to maintain their effervescence, whereas strong, sweet cocktails served over a large cube, like the Negroni, should be poured first, as they benefit from added dilution.

There are many ways to prepare the order on page 72, but if I had two bartenders working the bar, I'd have them make the Absinthe Drip and Margarita (point) and the Negroni and Bloody Mary (service) first, followed by the Green Thumb and Pisco Sour (point) and Irish Coffee and Mint Julep (service) second, saving the Michelada (point) and Jimmie Roosevelt and Piña Colada (service) for the third round to ensure that the champagne is fresh and the blended drink doesn't get watered down waiting to go out to the table.

Gather Ingredients and Equipment

To build our round of eleven drinks, the point bartender will need four shakers to prepare the Margarita, Green Thumb, and Pisco Sour; a chilled absinthe glass for the Absinthe Drip; and a chilled highball glass for the Michelada, which should be salted. Our order is for a Margarita rocks, no salt; if the guest asked for their Margarita salted, pull whichever glass is required (coupe or rocks) from the chiller now and salt it. (In the event the guest wasn't asked if they wanted salt for the Margarita, you should salt half the rim now so they have the option to sip with or without.)

In the other bar station, the service bartender will need a blender cup for the Piña Colada, two chilled mixing glasses for the Negroni and Jimmie Roosevelt (unless you stock a bottle of cognac in the freezer for this recipe in particular), and a shaker tin to roll or throw the Bloody Mary. The Mint Julep

---

SPICE RIMS

To apply spice to a glass, rub the outside of the rim with the citrus used in the recipe and then carefully roll the glass in a plate filled with the spice until the entire rim is evenly coated. If you're a perfectionist, you can clean up the edge with a cocktail napkin, but you don't have to be fastidious about the rim for cocktails like the Michelada, as a pinch of salt will actually enhance the flavor of the cocktail.

---

will be built in a chilled julep cup, and boiling hot water should be added to an Irish Coffee glass to preheat it. Add the bitters to the sugar cube for the Jimmie Roosevelt on a cocktail napkin to soak up any excess, and reserve the bitters-soaked cube until you need it.

To ensure that all cold drinks are poured into the coldest possible vessels before service, hold off on removing them from the glass chiller until the rounds are built and the mixing vessels are iced.

Measure and Pour

Measure the shaken drinks into the smaller 18-ounce tin (used in place of the 16-ounce pint glass in most bars in the United States) and position the larger 28-ounce tin behind it to add ice to before shaking. Based on the height of most bar tops, this allows you to see into the shaker tin when you're measuring and to ice all the tins before combining the liquid with ice and shaking. If you mix with tins instead of the pint glass, always build your round in order from left to right (or right to left, if you prefer), as you can't see your progress in the metal tin and it's easier to lose track of where you are with the recipe. Don't add ice to the drinks yet; this way, if you have to step away from your station, you don't risk overdiluting the drinks. (As soon as you add ice, you're on the clock!)

I build cocktails from the smallest ingredient quantity to the largest, and (if two ingredient quantities are the same) from the least costly ingredient to the most expensive. The rationale is, you are constantly interrupted while making drinks behind a bar, so if you lose your train of thought, you know where you are based on what bottle you just put down. Also, if you make a mistake, chances are you'll be dumping sugar and juice down the drain rather than costly spirits. When you're building a round, instead of building each drink one at a time, pour common ingredients at once (for example, pour the simple syrup into the shakers for the Pisco Sour and Green Thumb).

RINSES AND MEASURES SMALLER THAN 0.25 OUNCE

Concentrated ingredients like absinthe or aromatic bitters should be dispensed with a bitters decanter (or, if a rinse is called for, an atomizer to minimize waste). Commercial bitters come with dasher tops, but the size of the aperture varies from brand to brand, so the amount of bitters they dispense changes based on the size of the opening and fill level of the bottle. Cocktail Kingdom makes "dasher darts" that can be screwed onto most commercial bottles, but I prefer to rebottle my bitters into decanters. Other than a dropper bottle, which you'll need for the Pisco Sour garnish, the bitters decanter is the most accurate dispenser for aromatic bitters.

Teaspoons work best for smaller measures, such as the matcha tea in the Green Thumb, along with the spices and sauces in the Bloody Mary and Michelada. Most sauces come with a dasher top that is even less accurate than bitters bottles, so if you'd like to maintain consistency from cocktail to cocktail, measure each ingredient out carefully with clean, dry teaspoons. If you plan on preparing a number of Bloody Marys or Micheladas, batch and bottle the nonperishable sauces and spices to streamline preparation. Measure the capacity of your barspoon so that you can use it to measure sticky, viscous ingredients like apple butter or marmalade from a jam jar.

Matcha Bowl and Whisk

Bitters Decanter

"You can't just leave a tea bag in a pot; you've got to get the ratios and temperatures right. It's like any other recipe. When you make a cake, you don't just put some eggs, flour, and milk in a pan, put it in the oven, spin the dial, and bake it for an unspecified amount of time. It's the same with tea: if you control leaf-to-water ratio, temperature, and infusion time, you can achieve anything. But first take care of those three things."

HENRIETTA LOVELL

Tea Importer

MEASURING TECHNIQUE

Hold the jigger level, a little higher than the opening of your mixing vessel, so after you fill the jigger to the very top, you can gracefully tip it into the mixing vessel. If you're pouring with a speed pourer, you'll have more control of the stream and can pour from a few inches above the jigger for style points. If you're pouring without a speed pourer, it's easiest to rest the lip of the bottle on the edge of the jigger, which will give you more control when you're pouring and stop your hands from shaking if you have stage fright. With or without pour spouts, you'll need to pour right up to the lip of the jigger, which requires a steady hand.

While pouring, I cradle the cap in my palm using my thumb. I grasp the jigger between the index and middle finger of my nondominant hand; then, with my elbow bent at a 45-degree angle and the jigger at about chest level (or slightly above the lip of the mixing glass), I fill the cup of the jigger to the very rim. Then I turn my wrist counterclockwise (leaving the rest of my arm stationary) to transfer the contents neatly into the vessel before replacing the cap, wiping any spills on the bar or bottle with a dry towel, and reaching for the next bottle. Ideally there's a faucet or dipper well with fresh water to rinse your jigger between recipes, and even if there isn't, you'll want to keep three or four sets of jiggers of various measures nearby so rinsing doesn't slow you down.

Once you've learned how to prepare all the drinks with your dominant hand, force yourself to use both hands when mixing and pouring. If the bottles required for a recipe are on your left side, grab the bottle and pour with your left hand into a jigger held with your right hand (and vice versa for bottles on the right). Working ambidextrously is not only faster but will also reduce wear and tear on your joints from twisting and turning unnecessarily hundreds of times each night. If you strain or injure one of your arms, you'll be happy you can prepare cocktails with the other.

Muddling

Muddling is the process of pressing an herb, vegetable, or fruit to release their juice and essential oils. Vegetables or fruits such as the cucumber should be pressed firmly to extract the oil from the peel and pulverize the melony flesh, while the mint leaves (and other delicate herbs) should be pressed gently in an attempt to extract the oils from the leaves without tearing them. Shaking a drink with large ice cubes will also serve some of the same purposes as muddling, so there's no need to belabor muddling in a shaken drink such as the Green Thumb. Muddle the cucumber in the Green Thumb and mint for the Julep after you've added the simple syrup, and before you add anything else, as the sticky syrup will capture the oils released when the cell walls of the herbs and vegetables are broken. More than 1 ounce of sweetener causes many ingredients to float in your mixing vessel, so if a recipe calls for an ounce or more, muddle with a portion of the syrup and then add the rest later.

Muddler

Tasting

The moment after you've added all the ingredients to your mixing vessels, right before you ice them, is the ideal time to taste your drinks (you'll have to envision what they'll taste like after they've been chilled, diluted, or built, which you'll get better at with practice). Plunge a straw (ideally a metal one

---

EGG WHITES

Many bars separate the egg whites and yolks and store the whites in a squeeze bottle so they can easily measure into a jigger. This makes sense, as every egg yields a different amount of white, but egg white doesn't change the flavor of the cocktail, so I've always placed more stock in the theater of separating an egg in front of a guest, which reinforces how fresh it is and the level of care and technique required to prepare the recipe. I always add the egg white to the larger tin instead of the smaller one with the liquid in it, so in the event the yolk joins the white, or pieces from the shell stick to the oozy liquid, I can dump them out and crack another egg without having to remix the drink.

In *The Bar Book*, Jeff Morgenthaler details a few different ways to separate the eggs, including the shell method, in which you rock the egg white out using the shell to retain the yolk; the hand method, in which you split the shell in half and separate the white using a waterfall-like effect; and the tool method, in which you place an egg separator on top of your tin to capture the yolk. Whichever methodology you choose, you should be supremely confident in it before performing it live in front of guests.

Foodborne illness will always be on a guest's mind as you crack a fresh egg into their cocktail, so your handling of the egg will either reassure them that you know what you're doing—or not. Most egg-related contamination comes from the shell, so be sure it's as clean as your hands are.

Before adding ice, shake any cocktails with egg whites *without* ice to emulsify the egg proteins and achieve an airy texture. This can be accomplished with an extra-hard shake with ice, but you risk overdilution if you shake for too long. Simply pour the contents of the smaller tin into the larger one, seal the tin, and shake (see page 101).

that can be washed and reused) into the liquid and cap the top with your index finger, using the straw like a pipette. Tasting every single one of your drinks will slow down service unnecessarily, so taste only to verify the quality of preparations you're unsure of. Straw-tasting cocktails from the mixing vessel after you've iced them but before you strain gives you a better idea of what the guest will taste, but by then it's too late to adjust the proportions. Never straw-taste a cocktail after you've poured it in front of a guest. Once you've poured it, it's their drink, not yours.

Icing

Now you're ready to ice your glasses and mixing vessels. First, pull all the proper glasses out of the freezer and place them in front of the shaker or mixing glass that contains the matching cocktail. I hope you already know this, but all glasses should be gripped from the stem (if it has a stem) or the base (if it has no stem). Your hands (no matter how clean) should never touch any part of the glass the guest's mouth will touch, even after the guest has finished the drink when you're bussing the glass. Given that most commercial glass freezers are stocked from the top down, this can be challenging, but it is essential. I wince every time I see guests (including wine drinkers) hold a stemmed glass by the bowl; their fingers both coat the glass with oily fingerprints and warm the liquid.

For an order of this size, you'll want to be sure all the glasses are prepared (rimmed, rinsed, and chilled or preheated) before you add ice to your mixing glass or shaker so no extra dilution occurs between when you finish shaking or stirring and when you strain the drink. For cocktails served over a large cube or ball of ice, such as the Jimmie Roosevelt, place the ice in the serving glass now, as it will need at least a minute to temper, so it doesn't crack when you pour the liquid over it. Once the frost begins to disappear, it should be fine to pour the liquid into the glass. For drinks prepared with smaller cubes, pour all the drinks into their glasses first, then top with the ice right before service, to minimize dilution.

The next step is to ice the shakers. While larger ice cubes create a more pleasant texture through aeration, as Dave Arnold proved through scientific experiments and wrote about in his book, they require a longer shake to achieve the proper dilution. Smaller ice cubes tend to shatter in the shaker and melt too quickly in your mixing glass, so you have to add more and shake hard or stir fast to get the proper amount of aeration (in a shaken drink), chill, and dilution. Some bartenders layer various-sized pieces of ice in their vessel, using tongs to create the perfect mixture of larger cubes for aeration and chill and smaller cubes for dilution.

I recommend a mixture of one large cube for aeration and a few smaller ones for dilution and chilling. If you have to choose one size, 1.25-inch cubes from a Kold-Draft or Hoshizaki ice machine are preferable.

Twelve to sixteen ounces of ice by volume, or a standard ice-scoop-full, should be enough ice to properly chill and dilute most cocktails, but that will depend on half a dozen factors, including the ambient temperature of the room, mixing vessels, ice, and ingredients, along with the shape, size, and density of the ice used, and your shaking or stirring technique. I typically vary the amount of ice in my shaker or mixing glass based on whether I'm shaking or stirring one or two cocktails at a time. (I'll use more ice when I'm shaking one drink with two hands, as it's easier to keep the tin sealed, and less when I shake two at a time, as it's harder to hold the tins together without their leaking. For stirred drinks, it's the opposite: the more ice you add, the more slowly it dilutes.) As long as you're thinking about what's going on in the vessel when you're shaking or stirring, you can adjust your technique as needed.

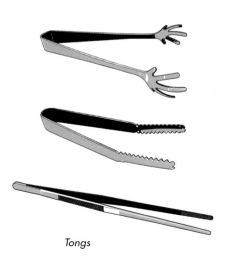

Tongs

The point bartender should start with the Absinthe Drip (page 161). After dripping the water into the glass, plunge the bowl of

the spoon into the glass and give it a stir to help dissolve any residual sugar. It should have a milky, opalescent hue at this stage and be ready to serve with or without the spoon.

Absinthe Spoon

While the fountain's dripping, the point bartender has the luxury of both hands free to shake the Margarita.

Shaking

Thanks to Dave Arnold's research in *Liquid Intelligence*, I don't have to launch into a lengthy primer on the physics and thermodynamics of shaking (which I'm totally unequipped to do anyway), as his experiments (and my experience) show that "from a technical standpoint, your shaking technique doesn't matter at all. . . . As long as you shake between 8 and 12 seconds, your cocktails will be about the same temperature, no matter what you do."

DILUTION

The most important element to consider when you're mixing drinks is dilution. Ultimately, dilution has the potential to alter the flavor of your recipe—the added water brings down the ABV of the mixture, and also reduces the perceptible sweetness of syrups, fortified wines, and liqueurs. In *Liquid Intelligence*, Dave Arnold adds that "our perception of sweetness is radically dulled by cold"; for sweet drinks like the Negroni, this can mean that dilution makes drinks more palatable. Classic recipe ingredients and proportions are fixed, but the amount of dilution you add is up to you. And remember, the colder (or hotter) a drink is, the less you can taste it, so chilling a drink to be as cold as possible isn't necessarily your ultimate goal.

The key consideration is the aeration you're aiming to achieve from shaking, which will depend on the ingredients in the recipe, the ice you use to shake with, and the force with which you shake. More forceful shaking leads to more aeration, and using larger ice cubes facilitates aeration. (So if you're using smaller ice, shake quickly and forcefully to minimize overdilution and maximize aeration.)

For this order, we'll use a Boston shaker, which can be used with one hand (allowing bartenders to shake two drinks at once). Once the larger tin is iced, seal the tins together at a slight angle so you can break them apart after you shake. (If it's not sealed in that way, a vacuum forms when you shake that makes it nearly impossible to pull apart the tins.) If you look straight down from above, the base of the small tin should point to between five and seven o'clock.

Always use both hands to shake a drink if you only have one recipe to prepare, and don't try to shake with two shakers at once until you're confident you can control them gracefully. Once the two tins are joined, grasp the shaker firmly, placing a palm over each end to keep the shaker sealed during the vigorous shaking process. Shake with the larger (bottom) tin facing the guest; this way, if the shaker separates, the leak sprays toward the backbar. You can shake the cocktail over your right shoulder, with your left hand covering the large tin, or over your left shoulder with your right hand covering it.

Once you've mastered the two-handed shaking technique on your dominant side, try to master shaking over the other shoulder to reduce wear and tear on the dominant shoulder.

The Japanese cobbler shaker is manipulated most elegantly with the elbows and wrists, but the Parisian and Boston require more shoulder work, especially if you shake two Bostons at the same time. Bending your knees a little and putting the opposite foot in front of the side of your body that you shake over (like a boxer or batter in baseball) lowers your center of gravity, giving you more stability and power.

Once you've given the shaker a vigorous whip with the larger 28-ounce tin facing out, you can break the seal one of two ways: (1) press the 18-ounce tin on top forward, using your thumb at the six o'clock position with fingers of that hand split between the top and bottom tin at twelve o'clock, or (2) give the larger tin a firm smack, using the palm of one hand with the opposite hand grasping both tins with two fingers on each so they don't fly apart.

The final elements of the bartender's shaking motion that are impossible to quantify are its style, power, elegance, and efficiency. A bartender's shake is the most visible and customizable technique, so it tells you a lot about who they are, how they feel about their job, and the drink itself. Author and former bartender Gary Regan quips that the face a bartender makes while shaking is the same face they make when they're making love! I'm not so sure about that, but I won't order a cocktail from a bartender who shows no passion for their work.

Straining

Once the point bartender has finished shaking the Margarita and popped off the smaller tin, they will place a Hawthorne strainer on top of the larger tin and strain the cocktail into the chilled rocks glass.

The strainer is manipulated using a notch near the handle that slides the strainer back and forward to "open and close the gate," allowing the bartender to strain the drink through either the springs or the metal openings in the strainer itself. Closing the gate (that is, pressing the strainer all the way to the lip of the shaker top) prevents many of the ice shards that broke off the cubes during shaking from getting into the drink.

These little ice shards used to be the hallmark of a good cocktail back when I started bartending, as you have

Julep Strainer

to shake hard (which was rare among lazy bartenders of the past) to break the ice apart, but nowadays most bartenders shake hard and strain all cocktails through a fine strainer (also called "double straining") to remove any pulp, herbs, and ice chips from the final mixture. While the ice shards are pleasant at first, they melt as the drink sits, which can throw the cocktail out of balance. Straining through a fine strainer breaks up the larger bubbles, diminishing the aeration and texture of the cocktail, but given that the Margarita has been ordered on the rocks, the guest probably prefers added dilution, so there's no need to fine-strain.

Throwing and Rolling

Over at the service bar, the Bloody Mary may be either rolled or thrown using a theatrical mixing technique that's an adaptation of Chinese long-pot tea throwing, which has been practiced for centuries. According to *Difford's Guide*, the technique traveled along the spice route from India to Morocco, where the Moors used it to aerate mint and wormwood tea, to Basque country, where it was used to aerate cider, and down to Jerez, Spain, where *venenciadors* (see image on page 158) still use it to long pour sherry. Based on illustrations from nineteenth-century cocktail books, the technique was also used behind the bar in America, and it's ideal for the Bloody Mary, which is soupy when stirred and unpleasantly frothy when shaken. Throwing has become popular again thanks to the bartenders at Boadas in Barcelona, who've been preparing their Martinis this way since the bar opened in 1938.

To throw the Bloody Mary, fine-strain the mixture from the 18-ounce tin into a 28-ounce tin (this removes the gritty spices and pulpy horseradish) and add a scoop of ice. Use a julep or Parisian strainer to hold the ice inside the shaker during the ensuing mixing process. Grab another 28-ounce tin and raise both over your head; slowly tip the shaker, holding the liquid on its side to pour in a steady stream, and catch the liquid in the other shaker as you simultaneously lower that tin as far as you can without spilling.

As long as your top hand is steady and you keep your eyes on the bottom tin, you should be able to "catch" everything without spilling. (I've seen bartenders throw a cocktail from high over their head to a tin suspended at arm's length below their belt while spinning in a circle, but this is ostentatious.) Once the pouring shaker has been emptied of liquid (it will still have ice), bring both shakers back to chest height, transfer the contents back to the pouring shaker, raise them back above your head, and throw again. Repeat this four or five times, then strain the drink into a chilled glass.

If the theatricality of throwing isn't for you, you can roll the Bloody Mary (more my style) by pouring it from one large tin to another five or six times (neatly, with some grace and flair) until you achieve proper dilution, aeration, and temperature. Many bartenders build their Bloody Mary in the glass they serve it in, but I prefer to prepare cocktails (including my Old-Fashioned, which is traditionally built in the glass it's served in) in a separate mixing vessel and strain into a clean, chilled glass.

Stirring

As soon as the Bloody Mary is rolled and strained, the service bartender should ice the mixing glass with the Negroni in it and begin stirring. Seemingly straightforward, stirring is the most difficult technique to master, as it takes quite a while to train your middle finger, index finger, and thumb to grasp the shaft of the spoon near the top like a pencil to rotate the ice around the glass quickly and quietly without creating any air bubbles. Position the back of the bowl of the spoon against the side of the glass so the bowl can cup the ice at the bottom of the glass and move it gently around clockwise.

According to Dave Arnold in *Liquid Intelligence*, "The main variables are the size of the ice cubes you use and how fast and how long you stir. . . . If your ice is on the larger side, you will stir longer or faster to achieve the same result you'll get with smaller ice." Many bartenders ice their mixing glass or stirring vessel and wait until they've prepared other cocktails before beginning to stir, which is fine if they're mixing with larger cubes. Whichever method you use, you can straw taste as you stir to get a sense of how much water the melting ice is incorporating into the cocktail and how cold the mixture is. Temperature is more important if the drink is served straight up, like a Martini, than if it's served over a big cube, like the Negroni, which will benefit from extra dilution and chill as it sits.

In the event the mixing glass isn't heavy enough to stay in place while you stir, hold the very bottom of the glass between your index finger and thumb, to minimize any heat transfer from your fingertips. (One of my favorite mixing glasses is footed, so this isn't a concern.) Regardless of what stirring vessel you choose, you'll need enough ice to penetrate the surface of the liquid, which will vary based on the glass's circumference. One scoop is typically enough.

Hawthorne Strainer

Once the mixture is thoroughly chilled and diluted, strain the cocktail into the chilled glass using a julep strainer (traditionally used in America when straining from a mixing glass), a Parisian strainer, or a Hawthorne strainer. Because the whole purpose of stirring is to minimize aeration during the chilling and dilution process, take deliberate care to pour as close to the prepared glass as possible to prevent air bubbles from forming. It always blows my mind when I see a bartender stir a drink perfectly, then pour it from up to a foot or higher above the glass—stylishly undoing all the proper technique they accomplished beforehand.

At this point, both the service and the point bartender have completed the first round; now they can either butler the first four drinks to the service bar to be garnished by the waiter or, if the waiter is too busy, garnish the drinks themselves. Both bartenders will need to rinse their jiggers, strainers, spoon, and shakers to reset for the second round of cocktails on the ticket.

ROUND TWO

Once their workstations and tools are clean and organized, the point bartender will fill their shakers with a mixture of one large cube for aeration and a few smaller ones for dilution to shake the Green Thumb and Pisco Sour with, while the service bartender fills the julep cup—which already contains the mint, bourbon, and simple syrup—with crushed or pebble ice and reaches for the hot coffee to build the Irish Coffee.

Provided that the Pisco Sour has already been dry shaken (without ice) to emulsify the egg proteins, both cocktails require the same type and length of shake to properly chill, dilute, and aerate them. As long as the bartender is proficient with two shakers, they can shake both at the same time. (In some countries, shaking two drinks at once is frowned on, but wherever time is a constraint, efficiency trumps tradition.) Take special care to seal the shakers, as you'll have only one hand to hold each set together; have two fingers on each tin at the center to ensure that neither side flies off. Do not tap the opposing tins together before you start shaking; this is disruptively loud and showy, and damages the tins.

The muddled cucumber in the Green Thumb will break up even further when shaken, and should be fine-strained. Fine-straining the Pisco Sour is more of a judgment call, but I'd recommend fine-straining most shaken drinks to prevent ice shards from watering them down. I've witnessed

RESETTING YOUR STATION

It's fine for bartenders to set aside tools and mixing vessels to clean once the entire round is complete *if* there's room to bus them out of the way. But if they pile up and clutter the bartender's workspace, then they should be cleaned and reset between each round. One of my first bosses told me, "A clean bar is a happy bar," and by extension, an organized bar is a happy bar, too. Whichever route you choose—cleaning as you go or at the end—be consistent. You'll never build muscle memory behind the bar if you aren't methodical in your ways.

bartenders in busy bars fine-strain two cocktails at the same time. This entails positioning the handle of the fine strainer against the area of the shaker they're pouring from, so the wire basket catches any debris from the lip of the shaker when they pour, using their index finger to manipulate the gate, and holding the strainer on top of the tin—altogether a tricky combination to set up. I'd forgo this technique, and instead position the fine strainer inches above the chilled glass with one hand and use the other to strain each drink through the Hawthorne strainer into the prepared glass.

HOW TO SERVE HOT DRINKS

Most bars heat each hot drink with an espresso machine's steam wand, in a kettle, or in a pan on the stove, which can scorch the liquid if it contains fat. Preparing coffee ahead of time and storing it on a burner plate or in an urn isn't ideal, either, as it will either burn or cool past the acceptable service temperature. Additionally, there's the problem of oxidation: the longer coffee is exposed to air, the less vibrant its flavors. Last but not least, coffee must be brewed at roughly 200°F, but it's too hot to drink at that temperature.

I'd all but given up on the possibility of serving proper Irish Coffees in a busy bar. (San Francisco's Buena Vista Café does it well, but they specialize in Irish Coffees, so they pour through entire pots in large rounds of up to a dozen orders at a time.) Then I saw an immersion circulator behind the bar at the Dead Rabbit in New York (see image opposite). There they bottle the coffee-sugar mixture and store it in hot water, which allows them to keep it at 170°F for lengthy periods without its burning or oxidizing. What's more, the guest can sip their drink as soon as it arrives, instead of having to wait for it to cool down.

And the immersion circulator works for more than just coffee drinks; it is a game changer for hot drinks made with tea, cider, or any other ingredient that could oxidize or be scorched with an espresso wand or in a pan.

Dead Rabbit Irish Coffee Station

For the Irish Coffee, as long as the coffee is presweetened and waiting in the hot water bath heated by the immersion circulator (see sidebar), all the service bartender needs to do at this point is fill the glass nearly to the rim; the whiskey has already been measured and poured into the glass. It's nearly impossible to measure a hot liquid into a steel jigger—and it's somewhat dangerous, because both glass and steel conduct heat quickly—so, provided your glass is 6 ounces, you can just eyeball it and then top with whipped cream. (This is why choosing the proper-size tempered glassware for hot drinks is vital. Alternatively, buy glassware with an easily recognizable fill line, like the top of the handle.)

Swizzling

With the Irish Coffee in hand, it's time to complete the Mint Julep. The best way to achieve the proper dilution and chill in a Mint Julep is using a swizzle stick, which may surprise traditionalists. Fill the julep cup nearly to the top with crushed or pebble ice (pea-sized pebble ice, which can be harvested from a Scotsman ice machine, is preferable to crushed ice, which must be pulverized to order) over the muddled mint, simple syrup, and bourbon mixture, then plunge the swizzle stick, branched end down, *halfway* into the cup (if you sink the swizzle all the way to the bottom and begin swizzling, it will disperse mint throughout the drink). Roll the branch back and forth (gently, so you don't dislodge the mint or aerate the mixture), using the palms of your hands to rotate the pebbles around, which chills and dilutes the mixture.

After 8 to 10 seconds of swizzling, the cup will begin to chill from the bottom up, signaling that the swizzle has done its job. Carefully remove the swizzle without dislodging the mint and ice, then top the cup with a fresh mound of pebble ice and pack it gently with clean

Bois Lélé Swizzle Stick

hands. Before the mound freezes together, plunge a hole into the drink with a straw. Gently brush three or four sprigs of flawless mint leaves against the back of your hand to release their aroma, then plant them through the hole into the cup. Plunge the straw right next to the mint bush so the guest's nose comes close to the mint every time they sip the drink.

As with the first round, once the second round is poured, the cocktails should be placed on the service bar, where the waiter can garnish the drinks while the third round is being prepared, or garnished by the bartender if the waiter isn't present. Time is of the essence for drinks like the Mint Julep, which needs to be garnished with clean hands before the ice bonds together. Artistic garnishes, like the decorative swirl of bitters in the Pisco Sour (see page 353), can be executed by a well-trained waiter, but I wouldn't be surprised to see the bartender make the finishing touches after all the effort that went into preparing it.

ROUND THREE

After the tools and mixing vessels used to prepare the second round have been cleaned and the station is reset, each bartender can begin preparing the third and final round.

Because the point bartender's main focus should be the guests in front of them, they have only one cocktail to prepare for the third round: the Michelada (page 177). Tradition dictates that this should be built in the service vessel, but I sidestep tradition and build it a mixing glass or shaker tin. The Piña Colada and Jimmie Roosevelt, which the service bartender will be preparing simultaneously at the other well, are reserved for the last round to minimize dilution in the blended drink and unnecessary loss of effervescence in the champagne cocktail.

Once you have built the Michelada in a mixing glass, with the rimmed highball glass in front of it, all that's left to do is add the beer, which will come from either a well-chilled bottle or a tap. Pick up the mixing glass by its base with one hand and tilt it to a 45-degree angle before pouring the beer.

To pour a glass of beer, place the glass at a 45-degree angle under the beer faucet or pitch the glass at this angle and carefully pour from the bottle as you slowly return the glass to an upright position. For tap beer, you'll need to pull the handle all the way out when you begin pouring, and gradually close it as the glass fills to form a one-inch head of foam.

Preparing the drink by adding the beer before straining means you lose some carbonation, but it allows you to fine-strain out coarser grains of spice and particulate matter, which helps avoid a soupy Michelada. The Michelada is an unpretentious cocktail that can be prepared half a dozen ways. If you're planning to serve the drink over ice (which I think is optional), you could stir it briefly with ice before straining it over fresh cubes to minimize dilution in the glass when it's poured. Having said this, you have every right to forgo preparing the recipe in the mixing glass if you or your guests prefer it mixed in the glass.

While the point bartender is preparing the Michelada, the service bartender needs to prepare the Piña Colada and Jimmie Roosevelt. To preserve as much of the champagne's carbonation as possible in the Jimmie Roosevelt, prepare the Piña Colada first. Simply add ice to the blender cup, then blend.

Most recipes for blended cocktails won't tell you how much ice is required, even though this is crucial. Add too much ice and you'll get thick-peaked, boozy sorbet; too little, and you'll underdilute. Cubed ice takes too long to blend (which also results in overdilution), so I recommend pebble ice from a Scotsman ice machine or finely cracked ice.

Another common misconception is that you can use the same quantities and proportions of sweet, sour, and strong ingredients in a blended drink as you can for a shaken or stirred one. As I mentioned earlier, dilution from ice lessens the perceived sweetness, so you'll need to adjust accordingly. What's more, if you use traditional recipe quantities in a 6-ounce blended cocktail, the drink will be totally overdiluted (because of the amount of ice), so you'll

BEER TAP TROUBLESHOOTING

Two common issues with tap beer systems are foamy beer and a lack of pressure. If the beer is foamy, chances are the refrigerator where the kegs are stored is too warm, which occurs when the cooler door is propped open for deliveries or a compressor fails. If the cooler is at the correct temperature (between 40° and 45°F), chances are the draft lines between the cooler and tap are not insulated properly.

Beer Taps

Many bars install a glycol system to keep draft lines cool; have this checked when the draft lines are cleaned and the gas tanks replaced. Flat tap beer usually signals it's time to change a keg or to hook up a new tank of gas. When only one beer is pouring flat, it's the keg; when all the beers are a little flat, it's the gas. Tap beer lines and faucets should be cleaned once a month at the very least.

need to increase the ingredient quantities. While the blender is whirring, the service bartender can build the Jimmie Roosevelt.

For recipes like the Michelada or Mint Julep, which have no known author, you have much more leeway to adapt and personalize the original recipe than you do with recipes like the Jimmie Roosevelt, which was created by *Gentleman's Companion* author Charles H. Baker (see "Honoring Tradition," below). So I recommend following the technique laid out in Charles H. Baker's *Gentleman's Companion*: building the Jimmie Roosevelt in the coupe glass in which it is served.

First, add the reserved bitters-soaked sugar cube to the chilled coupe. If you have a bottle of cognac in the freezer (which I recommend if you have a Jimmie Roosevelt on your menu), build the drink with the chilled cognac. If your cognac is stored at room temperature, stir the cognac with ice and strain into the glass (because room-temperature cognac would warm the mixture).

HONORING TRADITION

In *Cocktail Technique*, noted Japanese barman Kazuo Uyeda writes, "Every cocktail was invented by someone, so you have to imagine what it was that the creator wanted to achieve—what he wanted, what he was looking for—by creating this cocktail. Find out where and when the cocktail was created, and think about how much of your own personality you can blend into that."

That said, the most important stakeholder to consider as you decide how to prepare a recipe is the guest. This is not to say that you should alter the way you prepare each cocktail depending on your guests' whims—bar operators go to great lengths to ensure that cocktails are prepared consistently from bartender to bartender—but if a guest specifies the way they'd like their drink to be prepared, you must heed their suggestion.

I defer to *Cocktail Technique* again; Uyeda writes, "No matter how great a cocktail you make is, if the guest doesn't like it, then there's no point. . . . Your most important job as a bartender is to think about how you can make a cocktail that the guest will think is great."

Wine Key

Like beer, champagne should be well chilled (40° to 45°F) before pouring; otherwise, it will be warm and foamy. Avoid opening a warm champagne bottle (or if you must, use extreme caution), as pressure within the bottle increases with temperature. As with beer bottles and kegs, champagne bottles that have been jostled are prone to erupt when opened. It's best to allow carbonated liquids at least a day to settle after delivery or stocking before opening them for service.

GARNISHING

Theatrical garnishes, such as anything set on fire, should be applied right before the drinks are butlered to the table, or presented in front of the guest to ensure they witness the pageantry. Others, like a cocktail pick with cherries or a lime wedge, can be added as soon as the bartender has finished preparing the rest of the drinks for the order.

CHAMPAGNE SERVICE

To open a bottle of champagne, remove the foil and uncoil the wire cage over the cork. Make sure the bottle opening is pointed away from you and your guests, and remove the cage while your thumb is on top of it, so the cork doesn't launch unexpectedly. If you're in a formal setting, cover the cork with a linen napkin and carefully turn it while pushing it in to minimize any noise when it pops loose. Reserve the cork or present it to the guest, wipe any residue from the opening of the bottle, and give the wine a quick sniff to verify it isn't flawed, then pour slowly to minimize any overflowing of foam. If you pour at the proper rate, you should be able to fill a glass with sparkling wine by pouring continuously without stopping to wait for the head to dissipate.

ON PLEASING PEOPLE

"You get this massive adrenaline rush out of pleasing people. There's a huge feedback loop from it. My dopamine rush doesn't come from shopping; it comes from making people laugh, have a great night, and feel cared for."

JACOB BRIARS

Portfolio Ambassador

Too many bars, even those with well-trained waiters, insist that the bartender garnish every drink—even when delegating that task would dramatically speed up service. This is born out of a misguided deference to the bartender, which fosters the same tension some restaurants harbor at the kitchen pass-through, where the cooks agonize over each element of the plate's composition until it's picked up by the servers or runners to go to the tables. I appreciate that bartenders feel proud and therefore protective of the cocktails they craft, but servers are the ambassadors for your creations—and often the outward face of the bar. Allowing them to garnish a cocktail while the bartender prepares the rest of the round is the most efficient way to complete the order.

When affixing each element of a garnish (wedges, wheels, straws, picks, decorations), think about how the guest will experience their cocktail from the front, back, and sides. Generally speaking, garnishes should be planted at the equivalent of two o'clock for right-handed guests or ten o'clock if they're left-handed, so they don't have to turn the glass when they pick it up to sip. (How can you tell a guest's hand preference? Default to right-handed unless you notice that the guest has moved their water glass to the left side, or you notice a watch on their right hand—both indicators they're likely a lefty.) Place a straw near the opposite side of the rim, at seven o'clock or five o'clock.

Make sure you have clean hands when you garnish; at many high-end European bars where the bartenders have been trained by the International Bartenders Association (IBA), garnishes are applied with tongs. Most international health safety laws require garnishes to be covered, and in some cases refrigerated, and plastic straws to be wrapped in paper. I find this wasteful and time-consuming, assuming the staff practices good hygiene. Stainless steel straws are the most environmentally friendly, but require frequent cleaning (and tend to walk out the door along with the menus). Striped paper straws are visually appealing but pricy compared to plastic—and just as wasteful.

A straw should extend no more than two inches from the rim of a glass so the guest can appreciate the cocktail's aroma. This means most bars should stock at least two different lengths of straws: one for cocktails served in rocks glasses, and one for cocktails in collins glasses.

Floating

The Jimmie Roosevelt cocktail is finished with a green Chartreuse float on top of the champagne. The easiest way to float an ingredient is to pour it slowly over the back of a barspoon suspended just above the liquid's surface or down the length of an English-style barspoon with a disk on the end; if the float is less than 0.25 ounce, you can use an atomizer to spritz it over the surface of the drink.

ON TECHNIQUE

"It's like *The Matrix*. It's like Buddhism. It's kung fu. When you get to the top, you realize there are no rules. There is no technique. All techniques are techniques. Everything that you hold as a rule or way of doing something is all situational and depends. The more you know, the more you realize that there are no hard-and-fast ways things have to be. The secret of kung fu is that there is no kung fu. You need to get to a point where you move beyond any specific technique and you see all techniques."

DON LEE

Bartender

Some ingredients float on top of others because they have different specific gravities, like the layers in a pousse-café or Guinness on top of the Bass in a Black and Tan. Others, like the Chartreuse in the Jimmie Roosevelt, are floated for their aromatic qualities; they will eventually integrate into the mixture as you sip the cocktail. Cocktails such as this evolve like an old wine in the glass, as the sugar cube melts and the bitters and Chartreuse mix with the champagne; they should be sipped and savored to witness the transformation.

"I think bartenders should be well
rounded. If you're great at one thing
and terrible at another, that doesn't
make you a good bartender. You
have to be good in general. Treat the
customer well. Make really good
drinks. Take care of running the bar.
Mr. Kishi-San used to say we are
the sheepdog in the bar. The drunk
customers are going right and left,
and we have to lead them. You try to
be good at everything—not perfect.
Some people make really good
drinks, but they do not treat their
guests well."

HIDETSUGU UENO

Bartender

Form and Function

Some garnishes, like paper umbrellas, are decorative; others, like the lime
wedge on a Margarita or Michelada, are more functional. Many guests
assume that any wedge on the rim of a glass should be squeezed into the
drink—as is common for the Gin and Tonic and Cuba Libre—and will do this
without tasting first, which could throw a perfectly mixed cocktail out of
balance. One solution is to float a citrus wheel on the surface of the drink;
this way you get the visual appeal of the garnish without the added acidity.

Cocktails like the Bloody Mary typically come with a cornucopia of
garnishes that may include citrus, pickles, olives, celery, and even bacon.

Elaborate ornamental garnishes go all the way back to early days of the cocktail, when cobblers and juleps were served with every fruit you can imagine, along with herbs, flowers, and more. Many bars, such as Nightjar in London, have become famous for their elaborately garnished drinks. These never cease to amaze me, but in my opinion over-the-top garnishes distract guests from the most important part of a cocktail: the liquid in the glass. Any bar can buy beautiful glasses, clear ice, and fancy garnishes, but only the best serve perfectly balanced cocktails consistently.

Garnishes that sink, such as onions, cherries, and olives, should be attractively skewered on a cocktail pick. Depending on the size of the garnish, either one or three on a pick is the norm, for reasons unknown and unchallenged by me. (The number of olives or cherries on a pick is a superstition observed by most anyone who orders these cocktails.)

Some will tell you to never use inedible garnishes. But there are numerous exceptions I appreciate, such as reserving pineapple leaves to garnish a Piña Colada. Neither aromatic nor edible, the fresh pineapple leaf provides a visual contrast to the milky-white Colada, which can also feature an orange wheel balancing a paper umbrella or a bright-red maraschino cherry. I personally am opposed to the latter—to me, it signals that the bartender views the drink more like an ice cream sundae than a handcrafted cocktail. A fresh pineapple leaf, by contrast, suggests that fresh pineapple juice (which makes or breaks the drink) was used to prepare the cocktail, making me more likely to order one.

Best Practices

Many classic cocktails have a variety of different garnish options—for example, you could garnish the Negroni with an orange wheel or twist. Unless the guest requests a specific garnish, I use the ingredients in the cocktail to inform that decision. As there's no juice in the Negroni, I would apply a twist instead of a wheel. Some bartenders choose to flame the orange twist, which is done by pinching the twist, skin side out, over a lit match (once it's burned through the sulfur tip). This sprays oil through the flame, which ignites before coating the surface of the drink.

Only one classic recipe (the Flame of Love) calls for a flamed citrus twist, which Dale DeGroff popularized in the 1990s. For this reason, and because most bartenders flame their twists with a butane lighter or while the flame is still fueled by the sulfur tip, I avoid flamed twists. The fuel source—sulfur or butane—compromises the citrus oil if executed incorrectly.

A piece of orange peel anywhere between the size of a nickel and a quarter is all you need to garnish a Negroni. Many bars cut long swaths of citrus using a vegetable peeler, which yields a better-looking garnish, but in this case you should not express the oil from the entire peel, which could overwhelm the cocktail. Think of the oil as a measured ingredient.

A spiral twist cut with a channel knife is best for cocktails served in a flute, whose narrow, cylindrical shape helps maintain the garnish's shape. When using a channel knife, be sure to cut the peel over the glass, as most of the oil is released during the cutting process.

SERVICE

Some kitchens serve food as soon as it's ready instead of making the effort to synchronize food preparation so all guests are served what they ordered at the same time. This can work if everything is served "family style" on serving plates that are passed around, or if the guests are ordering a bowl of punch, but if they're ordering individual cocktails, they should receive their first round together instead of piecemeal. It's awkward for the guests to wait until their companions have their drink to take their first sip, and inefficient to send the waiter to a table multiple times to fulfill a single order.

Once all the cocktails are prepared, they should be placed on trays in the order of guest seating, so the server doesn't have to memorize the position numbers or each individual person and their order. The easiest way to accomplish this is to order the cocktails by position number from the POS terminal or write them in order on the guest check so the service ticket reflects the position of the person who ordered the drink. As long as every bartender, server, and manager on the floor knows the position numbers of every table, they can deliver cocktails as soon as they're ready, in the event the server who ordered them is assisting other guests.

FINAL THOUGHTS

Making cocktails is a lot like performing improv: there are rules, you practice, and then on any given night you are thrown into an unscripted situation and hope your training kicks in. And as with improv, bartenders will always beg, borrow, or steal elements from each other, but the key is for them to either make it their own or draw a line and not use it, because it isn't "them." As much as I love watching Japanese bartenders shake with a cobbler shaker, it doesn't feel right in my hands compared to a Boston or Parisian shaker. My jaw drops every time I see the bartenders at the Connaught throw a Bloody Mary tableside in white gloves, but I've never even worn white gloves. Quick flips of the shaker, twists of the muddler, and dramatic pauses while preparing a drink are the sorts of "working flair" I pick up on and appreciate most when I'm watching experienced bartenders carry out their duties. The little things, which most guests don't notice, are how bartenders express themselves through their technique—a window into the person behind the drink. This is why I prefer to sit at the bar if seats are available.

Distillery Tour

Although most consumers select their spirits based primarily on brand recognition, appreciation of the provenance of food and beverage is on the rise thanks to chefs, brewers, and winemakers who've educated the public about the processes and geography that shape their craft. The spirits industry, following in the footsteps of the wine industry, is now inviting consumers to visit production facilities where the craftspeople can be seen at work and the product is available for tasting, the result of which is the creation of a loyal and informed following.

Over the last two decades, I've had the pleasure of touring distilleries around the world, from large, hypermodern facilities to rural, family-owned operations. There is no better way to learn about a spirit than to meet the producers and ask questions on site. Learning how spirits are made will help you choose which products to stock.

At Left: Yamazaki Whisky Barrels

To this end, this chapter offers something of a crash course in how raw materials—be they grapes, agave, grain, or something more exotic—are transformed into a distilled spirit. There are whole books on this subject, so this chapter will favor cultural significance over scientific detail. This centuries-old process can be complex and technical and vary wildly from region to region.

Along the way, I'll take you on several brief "distillery tours" of facilities I've visited around the world. I've included insights on each step of the spirits-making process from representatives of the facilities as well as some of the most knowledgeable experts in the field.

I've juxtaposed modern industrial facilities with artisanal production sites, as there are fine examples at any scale in nearly every category of spirit. Size and quality aren't mutually exclusive, and smaller isn't always better in the liquor business. Corporate distilleries that reinvest profits in tools, machinery, and people create a virtuous cycle between economic growth and innovation that ultimately improves their craft.

Adherence to tradition or pursuit of innovation is likewise a poor gauge for quality. In some categories—tequila, cognac, and Scotch whisky, to name a few—production and labeling is strictly governed by the appellation or powerful trade organizations, which limits opportunities to incorporate new research, technology, and business practices. These products are largely viewed as classics that have stood the test of time in the marketplace; their perceived unchangingness (whether real or imagined) is fundamental to their identity. In other categories—gin being the most radical example during this past decade—innovation is more readily embraced, but innovation alone is no useful measure.

I'll introduce you to traditionalists like Maximino and Faustino Garcia Vasquez, who produce Chichicapa mezcal in the centuries-old way, and innovators like Lance Winters, whose Alameda, California–based St. George Spirits is pushing the boundaries of categories like vodka, gin, whiskey, and even absinthe.

ON STILLS

"It's all about reflux. All about flow and rhythm. How quick? How slow? How hot? How cold? Distillers have a firm understanding of these elements. They understand what's happening in each part of the still. They can see drops of spirit falling back in to be refluxed out in each part of the still. They know what's coming down the purifier pipe. They listen to the steam. So stills become an extension of the person, I think. As a result of that, they begin to learn what tunes can be played on them."

DAVE BROOM

Historian

As we jump from country to country and distillery to distillery, I'll highlight steps in the spirits-making process, like blending and filtering, that get glossed over in many guides. It's worth noting that very few producers have the luxury of controlling the supply chain from the field to the shelf, so you'll rarely see all the steps in one distillery visit.

GROWING THE RAW MATERIALS

Historically, beverage alcohol was produced with whatever source of starch or sugar was most plentiful in a particular region—so, apples were turned into calvados in northern France, grain into whisky in Scotland, and grapes—like those from the nearly ninety-year-old vines at Quinta do Noval (pictured)—become port in Portugal.

Noval Vineyard Grapevine

Generally speaking, grains were the base materials for spirits in colder regions, and fruits or grasses were used in warmer ones. Of course, in the modern era of large-scale commercial farming, this is no longer a hard-and-fast rule. However, many contemporary distillers are returning to their region's roots; for example, NY Distilling Company's founder Allen Katz works with a farmer in the Finger Lakes region of New York State to grow the same heirloom varieties of rye that whiskey distillers used more than a century ago.

His experiments with different varieties not only encourage biodiversity, but also create uniquely flavored whiskeys (something that many people assume is possible only with grape and other fruit-based distillates). The farmers who grow the raw materials he uses to produce his spirits are "unsung heroes in our business and essential partners for anyone who isn't distilling from estate-grown ingredients," says Katz. "We aren't farmers; we're distillers. Without talented, smart farmers to grow our ingredients, we have nothing."

THE HARVEST

The harvester pictured here, called a cosechadora, is used to pick the grapes that will become sherry in the former Domecq Vineyards (now owned by Estevez) in Jerez, Spain. Traditional hand-harvesting is preferable to using modern mechanized harvesters, but the whole story is more complicated. Machines like this cosechadora don't just lower labor costs; according to wine and spirits educator Steve Olson, in hot climates like Jerez their efficiency helps reduce oxidation and prefermentation in the newly picked grapes. Furthermore, according to César Saldaña of the Consejo Regulador (the sherry region's regulating body), the cosechadora can harvest at night when temperatures are much cooler, which is better for the winemaker.

Estevez Vineyard Cosechadora

The value of harvesting technology is undeniable, and should never be rejected based on a rigid adherence to tradition—but we should remember that machines will never be able to decide on their own when, where, and how to harvest. Skilled farmers and well-trained pickers are the heart and soul of great wine and spirits production, whether it's the unsung *jimadors* who harvest agave in Jalisco, or famed distiller Hans Reisetbauer, who decides the perfect moment to pick the fruit in his family's orchards in Austria for his eaux de vie.

TRANSPORTATION: FROM FIELD TO FACILITY

Transport isn't typically discussed in the context of spirits production, but it's a fascinating and vital part of the process. The time between harvesting raw materials—such as berries, grapes, agave, or sugarcane—and their processing and fermentation can be critical; careless and inefficient transport may allow oxidation, mold, or other spoilage to occur, with harmful or devastating effects on the final product. Another logistical challenge for producers to consider is the carbon footprint and cost of inefficient transportation. I marvel at the engineering dedicated to orchestrating these sorts of steps in the process, including safety and quality checks along the way.

This truck pictured below is hauling sugarcane to the mill to be washed, chopped, and pressed for its juice, after which it's transported via an internal pipeline into fermentation tanks at Destiladora de Alcoholes y Rones, where Ron Zacapa and other rum brands are produced in Guatemala.

After distillation, the rum is pumped into tanker trucks that transport it to the aging facility to be matured in a variety of oak barrels. Once the rum is mature, it's pumped into containers and trucked to the bottling facility.

Sugarcane Mill Truck

THE TRANSFORMATION BEGINS

Once the raw agricultural product is farmed and harvested, the next step is for the distiller to convert the base materials into alcohol. This begins with milling in the case of fibrous raw materials such as agave and pressing for more delicate fruits like grapes.

Milling

Maximino Garcia Vasquez (illustrated here in the foreground) and his father Faustino (in the background), mezcal producers in San Baltazar Chichicapa, Mexico, mill roasted Espadin agave using a stone grinding wheel known as a *molino* to prepare agave for fermentation. According to Del Maguey's Gabe Bonfanti, this process has remained in use despite the physical labor because it minimizes stress on the piña fiber from the agave heart, particularly compared to the damage inflicted by a mechanical shredder.

Agave is one of the most difficult of all raw materials to mill, so the "hand of the maker" of each *palenquero* is discernable, according to Del Maguey's Ron Cooper, but the advantages of gentle pressing extend beyond agave. I've tasted whiskey

Chichicapa Palenque Molino

from grain processed with a roller mill and wine from grapes pressed using a pneumatic bladder press, and I'm convinced that gentle milling preserves the vibrancy of the base material in the final product for nearly all spirit categories.

From Mash to Wort

When sugar isn't present in the raw material, as it is with grapes, sugarcane, and agave, fermentation can't take place without the conversion of starch into fermentable sugars through cooking in hot water with enzymes present. For whiskey and beer making, this process is called mashing, and the resulting liquid is called wort.

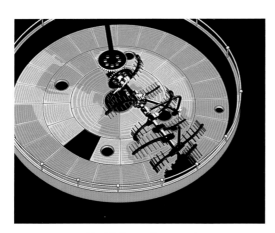

Bruichladdich Distillery Mash Tun

The scotch distiller Bruichladdich's open top, flat-bottomed mash tun shown here dates back to 1881, when the distillery was founded. Modern mash tuns are typically enclosed and use spindlelike rakes to stir the wort before it is pumped out of the tun into the fermentation tank.

The heavy, cast-iron rakes in this mash tun turn the mash evenly and consistently, allowing the hot water to extract the sugar and flavor from the malted barley, which contains natural enzymes required to convert the starch into fermentable sugar.

Water

While not technically a "step" in the process, nothing is more fundamental to the production of spirits than water. Most spirits contain more water then alcohol by volume, so the character of the water used for mashing and fermentation and the cleanliness of the water added after distillation are integral to the final product's quality.

Yamazaki Distillery Water Source

Historically, distilleries were built by waterways with clean water that could be used for mashing, fermentation, heating, condensing, and diluting the final spirit (not to mention cleaning equipment and facilitating shipment). Many breweries, wineries, and distilleries use vast amounts of the hot water generated during production to heat their buildings.

The water source pictured above is from the foot of Mt. Tennōzan, where tea master Sen no Rikyū built a tea house in the sixteenth century to take advantage of its purity and character. This water is pumped into the Yamazaki distillery for use in mashing, fermentation, and distillation of their single-malt whisky.

According to Suntory's former master distiller at Yamazaki, Mike Miyamoto (see page 302), the clean, soft water requires no filtration for mashing and contains minerals that nourish the yeast during fermentation, where the distillate's character is determined. The water is deionized before it's added to the new-make spirit (fresh from the still, undiluted spirit) before entering the cask, a second time when mature whisky is blended with other components, and a third time to adjust the final proof before bottling.

PROPAGATING THE YEAST

After mashing, the wort is transferred to fermentation tanks (pictured on page 134), where yeast, propagated in one of these tanks, is added. Yeast is a living microorganism that feeds on the sugar in the wort, producing alcohol and CO_2 that transforms the starchy liquid into a mildly alcoholic, beerlike mixture called "wash."

Although wild yeast occurs naturally and is present nearly everywhere, to spur fermentation distillers need to propagate enough yeast to impart their desired flavor and characteristics in the finished product. Some producers purchase commercial yeast varieties; others cultivate their own yeast strains. The propagation tank shown here is called a "dona tub" by Kentucky bourbon producers.

Distillers like Maker's Mark use these to grow proprietary yeast strains for use in fermentation. According to Maker's Mark's master distiller Greg Davis, "We use a pure culture from the Samuels family strain to preserve the same flavor profile from batch to batch." Wild Turkey master distiller Eddie Russell says, "Our yeast (used to ferment both bourbon and rye mashes) produces consistent flavors we couldn't achieve with commercial yeasts. It produces spicy, nutty flavors after fermentation, while others yield fruity flavors."

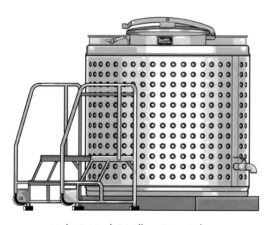

Maker's Mark Distillery Dona Tub

Most distillers stick to the same yeast strain and mash bill (the mixture of grains used to make whiskey) and vary barrel maturation location and duration to produce whiskeys of different characters; Four Roses employs five different strains of yeast to create a variety of bourbons from two mash bills.

FERMENTATION

The two 7,500-gallon fermenters pictured on page 134 are made from red cypress and used at the Woodford Reserve Distillery in Kentucky. According to Woodford's master distiller Chris Morris, "These fermenters represent a combination of tradition and pragmatism, as the distillery has used wooden fermenters since the 1830s, but we ferment a bit differently than our forebears, so we've added cooling coils in the interior of the vats to circulate chilled water when required."

The standard fermentation period in the industry is three days, but in 1979, engineers at Brown Forman experimented with long ferments of five, seven, and nine days at their distillery, and learned that long fermentation at the proper pH, although risky if not conducted properly, can produce a deep level of fruity characteristics from the yeasty esters.

Applying what he learned from these experiments, Chris built smaller fermenters with cooling coils that maintain a low fermentation temperature and developed a proprietary yeast strain that works at a slow pace over six to seven days with a higher proportion of sweet to sour mash.

DISTILLATION

Distillation is the process in which alcohol is concentrated via evaporation (under heat and pressure) with the goal of separating desirable elements as they recondense into liquid. When ethanol (beverage alcohol) is heated, the first and most volatile ester compounds, called "heads," evaporate first. These compounds (think nail polish remover) are undesirable in the finished product, and are separated and redistilled in another run. What follows are the desirable flavor compounds that the distiller wants to capture and recondense into spirit (called the "heart"). Last comes malodorous, fusel-laden "tails" (think rubber and overcooked broccoli), which are also separated and redistilled.

The distiller's art is to separate the desirable flavor compounds from the unpalatable stuff. Knowing when to make the first "cut," to capture desirable

Woodford Reserve Distillery Fermentation Tanks

top notes from the heads (which will become part of the heart), as well as the second, to cut off the earthy tails, is what makes a great distiller. The process is similar to a cook reducing a sauce on the stove, but the goal is to capture specific elements in the steam that evaporates as it simmers instead of concentrating the liquid in the pan.

Suntory's Mike Miyamoto explains: "Larger pot stills with long necks tend to producer lighter, ester-driven spirit due to increased copper contact, while smaller pot sills with shorter necks tend to produce a 'heavy' distillate." Suntory employs eight pairs of pot stills, varying between ten-thousand- and twenty-five-thousand-liter capacity, in seven different shapes and sizes at Yamazaki to produce many different styles of whisky. Natural gas–fired copper pot "wash" stills at the Yamazaki distillery transform the wash into a spirit at 20% to 21% ABV in the first distillation.

OVERSIGHT

Visiting the control room at distilleries such as Cameronbridge in Scotland can make you feel like you've boarded a space ship, as you stare at all the gauges and monitors providing live-stream data from various meters installed at key points throughout the plant, which are all backed up by manual readouts recorded in the distiller's log.

According to former longtime Tanqueray master distiller Tom Nichol (see page 207), "Our computerized system is mainly used as a visual aid, although it does allow you to start pump sequences and control temperature and flow rates once manual settings have been entered."

In addition to all the data, Tom's former control room has a great view of the pots: "I wouldn't like to work in a distillery that you couldn't see what was happening in the still house, as all your senses are required to distill." House Spirits master distiller Christian Krogstad concurs: "A distiller still needs to make decisions based on the readouts and what they hear, see, and taste in the distillery around them. It would be very difficult and dangerous for this to be all analog, requiring that the operators get up on ladders to operate some valves, crawl under tanks to operate others, while simultaneously checking fill heights and temperatures. These monitoring systems allow us to focus on the product instead of having to run all over the place."

Cameronbridge Distillery Tanqueray Gin Still Room

BARREL MATURATION

After distilling, the spirit used to make whiskey, brandy, and other barrel-aged liquors are transferred to oak barrels for maturation. Bourbon producers must use newly charred American oak, while producers in Scotland and Ireland have more cooperage choices, including ex-bourbon barrels and former wine casks (such as sherry butts or port pipes—each barrel size and type has a unique name).

According to Todd Leopold of Denver's Leopold Brothers Distillers, where the thermometer image below was taken, three things occur during maturation: extraction, reduction, and evaporation.

- Extraction refers to the amount of compounds—such as vanillin, tannin, and eugenol—extracted from the barrel, which corresponds to the char level for a new barrel and the number of times a used sherry or bourbon barrel has been refilled.

- Reduction (also known as oxidation) occurs as the spirit's contact with oxygen and the wood barrel transform the aromatic esters in the spirit.

- Evaporation occurs as the liquid in the barrel becomes a gas that diffuses through the wood and escapes into the atmosphere.

Leopold Brothers Distillery Oak Barrel

Distillers can manipulate these three actions by using different size barrels. A sherry butt, for example, holds about 500 liters of whiskey when it's full. Because there's less wood in contact with the distillate than in the much smaller bourbon barrels, there tends to be far less extraction, less evaporation, and more reduction.

So speaking generally, the sherry butt–aged Scotch whisky and Irish whiskey are far less "woody" and more "fruity" (via oxidation) than bourbon. Bourbon, with its much smaller, new 200-liter charred American-oak barrels, tends to have far more flavor extracted from the wood, far less reduction (esters), and more evaporation than scotch.

BLENDING

Consistency is key to building a following for a spirit brand, so with the exception of single-cask products, every producer blends their distillates to achieve a consistent result. While distilling and blending are both art forms, blending accentuates the best characteristics of the distillate's components.

Most master blenders would agree with Lance Winters, the master distiller of California's St. George Spirits (whose blending tank is pictured below): "There are no 'best characteristics' without good distillates." Blending

St. George Distillery Mixing Tank

doesn't just ensure that a brand's product is consistent from year to year; blending diverse distillates can also create depth and complexity.

Lance explains: "We blend nearly everything that gets bottled at the distillery. For white spirits like eau de vie, gin, and vodka, the goal is to make sure that there's as much consistency from batch to batch as we can achieve with spirits distilled from agricultural ingredients. With our barrel-aged spirits, the goal is to get the best out of every batch—accounting for variation if the new blend is an improvement on the previous bottling—and there's a recognizable heartstring between the two."

FILTRATION

Distillers use several methods to filter their spirits before bottling. The polish filtration process uses cellulose sheets of different micron ratings to filter out everything from large organic matter to invisible particles. I photographed the example below, a common plate and frame filter, at the amaro and grappa producer Nonino in Italy.

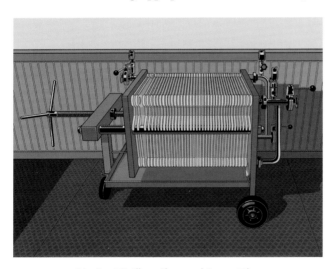

Nonino Distillery Plate and Frame Filter

In addition to polish filtration, many producers chill filter to prevent precipitates in spirits (particularly pot-distilled) that aren't stable at temperatures below 45°F; these precipitates range from a slight haze throughout the liquid to globules that look like cotton balls. The type of raw material, the still variety, the proof of the distillate, and other factors affect the threshold for instability. While unsightly, the precipitates have no effect on the spirit's drinkability, so many whiskey distillers abstain from cold stabilizing and instead bottle in colored glass to conceal the precipitates.

Ransom Spirits master distiller Tad Seestedt favors cold stabilizing down to 50°F to avoid having his spirits cloud over on the shelf, but he stops short of chill filtering, which can strip some of the desirable flavors and aromatics from the spirit, including fatty acids that improve its mouthfeel. Distillers can also use activated carbon, albumin, and other additives, which remove both undesirable and desirable aromatics, flavors, and flaws.

Never one to mince words, Seestedt states that "anyone who claims they don't filter at all is either lying outright, delusional, or completely clueless. The only potential exception is a neutral spirit that's been rectified or distilled to the point where almost no congeners, fatty acids, starches, polysaccharides, or proteins remain."

BOTTLING

According to Wisconsin's Death's Door Spirits founder Brian Ellison, "Investing in bottling equipment is all about control. You can bottle with higher quality standards than a contract bottler whenever you'd like—ramping up or cutting back your inventory based on demand."

Bacardi's chapel-like bottling hall, "Tultitlán," in Mexico City was designed by architect Felix Candela in 1960. I chose the image on page 140 of Krones's state-of-the-art bottling line 2 for the hall, which is situated next to architect Ludwig Mies van der Rohe's office building on the same site, as each underscores the importance that firms like Bacardi place in production.

The room is not just visually stunning and inspiring to work in; Candela's design eliminates the need for column supports for the ceiling, so there's plenty of room for the equipment. Light beams through the windows, so there's no need for electric lights during the day, and the modular design allows the firm to expand the hall organically if they ever need more room.

Bacardi Bottling Hall

The portion of the bottling line pictured above follows bottles of rum from the depalletizer to the labeler, which applies three stickers for the brand and a tax stamp. Roughly a dozen technicians manage the bottling lines, which fill, cap, label, and package a variety of spirits using custom tooling designed for each bottling.

TASTING AND ANALYSIS

Here amid the bottles, notebooks, and pens in Compass Box's London tasting room (see image opposite) are tasting glasses filled with whisky, topped with watch glasses—a circular piece of glass also found in chemistry labs—used to concentrate aromas in each glass. Pipettes are available to add water, which releases aroma and flavor compounds that are easier for some tasters to perceive at a lower proof.

Compass Box Tasting Room

The laboratory bottles filled with whisky represent a fraction of the nearly six thousand casks the firm has maturing at the company warehouse. Company founder John Glaser (see page 32) says, "We keep between five hundred and seven hundred and fifty 'live' samples of casks that are available and ready for us to use in the office and use 'benchmark' bottles to compare against current and proposed bottlings." Cask variation yields different results, even when spirit from the same distillation run is matured in similar barrel types for the same period.

EVALUATING THE PROCESS

While spirits in the same categories may share general production techniques, some elements are more crucial than others in determining the character of the finished product. For instance, using stone fruits such as cherries or plums at the peak of ripeness is crucial to produce eau de vie, but much less important for the grapes used to make cognac and armagnac, where producers transform acidic wines into extraordinary brandies through barrel maturation and blending.

This applies even when we're talking about the same process within a category, such as roasting agave in an oven to convert the sugars for tequila versus a stone pit for mezcal; one process caramelizes the flavors from the plant while the other tastes like you plucked it from the barbecue. To evaluate which processes yields the most delicious results, it's important to evaluate spirits separately within the rubric of their own production spectrum; don't bring your bourbon biases to a Scotch whisky tasting.

Years ago, a colleague professed a newfound appreciation for mezcal before we sat down to taste and evaluate a table full of tequilas, and his (generally negative) feedback on the tequila reflected it. While many modern tequilas are relatively neutral in character compared to older bottlings, as only a few holdouts are still oven roasted, tahona milled, wood fermented, and pot distilled, comparing them to the blast of scorched earth that a sip of mezcal delivers is like comparing apples with oranges instead of comparing Granny Smiths from two different farms or that variety with another, such as the Honeycrisp.

CURB YOUR PREJUDICES

Early in this chapter, I noted that very few producers have the resources and the scale to control every aspect of the distillation process. Most gin and liqueur producers purchase neutral spirit and redistill it with botanicals imported from all over the world, rather than making the spirit from scratch. The most famous French brandy firms age, blend, and bottle new-make spirits they purchase from farmers, rather than producing their own. Many startups from other categories create a formula to be contract distilled, or source and bottle a spirit under their own label until they have enough capital to establish their own production capacity.

Ironically, the type of person who writes off these "sourced spirits" also tends to scoff at the big brands, which often are the only ones able to control their supply chain from start to finish. Before you pass judgment, blame lax labeling laws legislated to empower deceitful brands to mislead consumers, who should be allowed to evaluate their purchases with production information clearly listed on the bottle.

You may also note that I've not included common cosmetic processes in this overview—for example, adding artificial coloring, sweeteners, and stabilizers. This is as intentional as my omission of, say, candy-inspired spirits, fruit- and chocolate-flavored wines, and caffeinated malt beverages— or anything that is intended to mask imperfections or mislead consumers.

I've cultivated strong opinions over many years in the business, based on my experience and conversations with loyal customers, producers, salespeople, and ambassadors. However, setting foot in a distillery is the best litmus test for the credibility of your views.

When you make the pilgrimage, don't assume anything about your tour guide (regardless of their position) and always ask questions (when prompted) if you have them. If your guide doesn't know the answer, he or she should seek it out for you and follow up. Some processes are nearly impossible to explain in lay terms.

Perhaps the most important lesson I've learned during my spirits-education journey—which is far from complete—is to remain willing and open to changing my mind when I'm presented with compelling new data or ideas. Above all else, I try to keep a positive outlook. There are far too many delicious spirits, noble cultural practices, awe-inspiring techniques, and brilliant makers to waste your time dissing the hacks.

In the next chapter, I've included detailed primers on all the major spirits categories: their origins and history, evolution of their production processes, insights from experts, and how to use them in classic cocktail recipes.

Spirits & Cocktails

To understand how cocktails are constructed and the way they "work," you've got to master their base components. Like a jazz musician who memorizes a tune before improvising upon it on stage, a bartender must have a firm grasp of classic recipes' "notes"—the ingredients that define their character—before adapting a recipe for guests *à la minute* during service.

I've included one hundred recipes in this chapter—my "cocktail canon." That number may seem slight when compared to other cocktail books, including one of mine, which contains over three hundred. But when you're trying to establish a foundation for all bartenders, more is not more: it's better to dig deep and master the fundamentals, beginning with the classics.

The recipes in this chapter are classified by their base spirit: aperitifs, vodka, gin and genever, rum and cachaça, tequila and mezcal, whisk(e)y, brandy and eau de vie, and liqueurs. In some cases, my recipe categorization might surprise you—for example, the Michelada (page 177) appears in the aperitif section and the Vesper (page 187) is listed in the vodka section. These choices are intentional.

While the Michelada doesn't descend from the European aperitif's lineage like the Kir (page 165), it's a beloved modern-day "opener" that imbibers—including myself—frequently order upon arriving at a bar. While the Vesper contains more gin than vodka, I believe vodka's role defines the drink, separating it from the gin family of its mother, the Martini.

These considerations are elaborated upon in each recipe, in sections titled "history," "logic," and "hacks." The first is self-explanatory: cocktails should always be connected to the cultural and historical context in which they were created. Logic exposes what programmers would call the recipe's "code," explaining how the proportions and ingredients function. This gives you the data needed to "hack" it, logically, to please the guest with your interpretation.

This chapter also includes primers that delve into the history and production methods of each spirit category. Bartenders today have access to nearly all the historic ingredients they've ever pined for, so the challenge is no longer to figure out what Old Tom gin is and how you can MacGyver what's available behind your bar to mimic its taste; it's which brand of Old Tom gin on your backbar tastes best in a Martinez versus a Tom Collins, and why.

Today, there's such a glut of (mostly good) liqueurs, bitters, fortified wines, and traditional base spirits available that most bars don't have space for all the worthy options. Yet it's not all wine and roses. Interest in classic cocktails has driven many affordable (mature) whiskeys to the brink of extinction, and spirits in other categories may face similar supply issues in the years ahead.

Buyers of fine wine invest in outstanding vintages from noteworthy producers, and spirits buyers should use the same strategy, especially for spirits such as mezcal, since wild varietals like Tobola and Tepeztate may dry up due to high demand. I'm also concerned that climate change is going to affect hallowed production regions before long, and as I reflect upon all the bottles I've poured out, I wish I had squirreled away a few more nuts.

When it comes to spirits, I value *cultural* terroir—the know-how passed down from one generation of producers to the next—over *geographic* terroir. Unlike with wine, distillation and barrel aging obscure the sense of place of the raw ingredients used to make spirits. But there is a human manifestation of terroir: I can taste it in Dan Farber's alembic-distilled brandies from California, which I stock next to cognac, and in many of the malt whiskies of Japan, whose lineage with Scotch whisky is indisputable.

Tradition can also be used to hold back a spirit's identity, as Martin Cate suggests in *Smuggler's Cove*; he makes the case that a category as diverse as rum needs a classification system that allows it to evolve beyond its centuries-old colonial roots. In an interview, I got the same sense from Austrian distiller Hans Reisetbauer, who found no inspiration in traditional fruit brandy production methods in Europe. Perhaps no category faces as much scrutiny of the divide between tradition and innovation as agave spirits like tequila and mezcal—enthusiastic preservationists and corporate technologists share very little common ground.

PDT Cocktails App

Looming over the discussion across all spirit categories is the "craft" spirits revolution that's taken the industry by storm over the past two decades. With dozens of new distilleries producing spirits of all types each year all over the world, it's counterintuitive to silo categories using cultural heritage alone; especially when new distillers produce more stylistically "traditional" spirits.

Denver-based distiller Todd Leopold is an entire time zone away from bourbon's home in Kentucky, yet few producers have greater respect for the time-honored traditions of the category. What he lacks in local tradition in Colorado he makes up for with intellectual rigor, using historic production technology, such as a unique three-chamber still, to leave his mark. He's also one of the few whiskey producers in the world (apart from a handful of distillers in Scotland) kilning and turning his own malted barley by hand.

In his 1919 essay "Tradition and the Individual Talent," the poet and essayist T. S. Eliot writes, "If the only form of tradition, of handing down, consisted in following the ways of the immediate generation before us in a blind or timid adherence to its successes, 'tradition' should positively be discouraged." Unburdened with strict appellation laws and tradition, contemporary distillers like Leopold innovate using historical parameters as guidelines instead of limits, honing a critical sensibility for what to carry forward from history and what to leave behind. The same philosophy is used by bartenders who create modern cocktails from historic templates.

Bartenders and distillers serve as cultural custodians of customs and rituals. For example, most would agree that it's a good thing that you can buy classic Italian bitters like Aperol nearly everywhere to prepare the Spritz, but you shouldn't separate the spirit and recipe from aperitivo culture and Italy altogether. Bartenders and distillers are charged with preserving and promoting cultural heritage and tradition through thoughtful interpretations of historic recipes.

Working this way allows bartenders and distillers to alter tradition ever so slightly as they go—or, in Eliot's words, to realign in such a way that "the relations, proportions, values of each work of art toward the whole are readjusted; and this is conformity between the old and the new." Mixologists now have so many new spirits, they can riff off the classic recipes like the Italian Americano cocktail (Campari, sweet vermouth, soda) with all-American ingredients like Vya Vermouth and Campari analog Bruto Bitters—which allows the recipe to signify in new ways without subverting its heritage.

Eliot's writing remains germane today, given its historical context. When he wrote "Tradition and the Individual Talent," avant-garde art ranging from Igor Stravinsky's controversial *Rite of Spring* (1913) to Marcel Duchamp's "Urinal" (1917) to James Joyce's *Ulysses* (serialized in *The Little Review* from 1918 to 1920) were taking the cultural world by storm. One can only imagine the anxiety Eliot and other artists with classical training and sensibilities must have felt as critical perceptions of their craft were upended.

He insisted that other artists should master their craft and position it within history before abstracting or dismembering it, which resonates strongly with me, having spent many years studying the history of bartending, spirits, and mixed drinks before attempting to create my own traditions. I was trained

BERNADETTE LANGLAIS

Master Distiller

and mentored in an era when bartenders had to be armchair anthropologists;
we didn't have access to the information we have today, so we had to take
initiative.

I'm concerned when I observe others' breezy acceptance of information
of questionable credibility. So much data is readily accessible via a
smartphone with a high-speed Internet connection that it seems to be
rapidly supplanting ongoing study. Channeling Eliot: I believe bartenders
should labor to acquire a sense of tradition before altering it to serve
their purposes. In this chapter, I chronicle my attempts to both honor
and advance tradition, offering my own methodology for you to adapt,
respectfully, as you see fit.

Atlantic
Ocean

*Bay
of
Biscay*

Mediterranean Sea

Adriatic Sea

GERMANY

CZECH REP.

AUSTRIA

★ Paris

FRANCE

● Saumur

● Podensac

● Chambéry
● Cocconato
● Milan
● Padua
● Pessione ● Asti
Pontalier ● ★ Bern
SWITZERLAND
● Marseillan ● Roussillon
● Canelli
ITALY

● Tuir

PORTUGAL

SPAIN

★ Rome

FRANCE

⊙ *Chambéry*
(Dolin vermouth)

⊙ *Marseillan*
(Noilly Prat vermouth)

⊙ *Podensac*
(Lillet)

⊙ *Roussillon*
(Suze)

⊙ *Pontalier*
(Vieux Pontarlier absinthe)

⊙ *Saumur*
(Jade absinthe)

⊙ *Thuir*
(Dubonnet)
(Pernod absinthe)

ITALY

⊙ *Canelli*
(Alessio vermouth)

⊙ *Cocconato*
(Cocchi vermouth)

⊙ *Milan*
(Campari)
(Carpano vermouth)

⊙ *Padua*
(Aperol)

⊙ *Pessione*
(Martini vermouth)

SWITZERLAND

★ *Bern*
(Kina L'Aéro d'Or)

░ *Traditional Production Region*   ⊙ *Distillery Site*   ★ *Capital*

APERITIFS

The word aperitif is derived from the Latin verb *aperire*, "to open"; typically, these spirits and aromatized wines are tart and bright, with a bittersweet quality that stimulates appetite, making them perfect pre-dinner tipples. In *Aperitivo*, author Marisa Huff describes how the aperitivo hour—as it's called in Italy—has evolved into a ritual in Italian cities like Florence, Turin, Milan, and Venice. Aperitivos, she writes, "draw people together to relax in the company of friends over a glass of wine or a cocktail with something to nibble on." Different regions have their own aperitivo traditions: there's the Spritz in Venice, Manzanilla sherry in Cadiz, and pastis in Marseille.

In this section, I'll outline the traditional ingredients of aperitif cocktails: vermouth; quinquinas; bitters and aperitivos; absinthe blanche and verte; sparkling wine; wine, beer, and cider; and fortified wines. I recommend coursing your guest's drinks, starting with dry, lower alcohol options; aperitifs fit the bill perfectly.

Vermouth

The history of modern Italian aperitivos begins at the end of the eighteenth century, when Turin liquorist Antonio Benedetto Carpano trademarked the word *vermouth*, derived from the high German *wermut* ("wormwood"). Instead of selling his proprietary herbal infusion as medicine, he combined it with high-quality Moscato-based wine and sold it to aristocrats in the Sardinian royal court.

As vermouth's popularity spread, port towns like Marseilles, Genoa, and Venice—hubs of the exotic spice trade—developed their own regional formulas. When a border was drawn between modern-day Italy and France in the mid-nineteenth century, the dry white style popularized by Noilly Prat became synonymous with "French vermouth" and the sweet red style made famous by Martini & Rossi became known as "Italian vermouth" in export markets.

Eventually, producers expanded their range; French vermouth producers began making sweet red vermouth, Italian firms formulated their own dry white vermouth, and each released sweeter white vermouth formulas. Today, I employ French "blanc" vermouth (rather than "dry") in nearly all early twentieth–century cocktails that call for French vermouth, as the sweeter Chambéry formula is what would have been used for many cocktails of that era, like the El Presidente (page 261), Algonquin, and Brooklyn (page 325).

Today we have access to a dizzying array of Italian-style vermouths: historic vermouths *alla vaniglias* (featuring vanilla), such as Cocchi Vermouth di Torino; vermouths *con bitters* such as Punt e Mes; and *vermouth chinatos*, popularized in Piedmont, such as Alessio. A contemporary Western style developed by California producers such as Quady in the late 1990s features fewer herbs, resulting in more wine-forward vermouths made with local botanicals.

Noilly Prat Salle des Secrets

Quinquinas

In response to mounting casualties among the French Foreign Legionnaires during the French invasion of Algeria in the 1840s, the French government funded a competition to create a wine-based formula featuring quinine—an unpalatably bitter extract of Peruvian chinchona bark that doctors prescribed to ward off malaria and fever. Joseph Dubonnet and other wine merchants responded by creating vermouth-like formulas dubbed *quinquinas*, flavored with chinchona bark, herbs, and spices. Today, quinquinas are prepared from a red or white wine base that's fortified with neutral spirit, then sweetened and aromatized with bitter herbs and spices. Most are matured in large oak barrels, then bottled between 14% and 17% ABV.

Interest in quinquinas has grown in recent years, thanks to classic cocktail recipes like the Vesper (page 187), which the Hollywood adaptation of the Ian Fleming spy novel *Casino Royale* reintroduced to modern imbibers in 2006. In addition to Lillet, which was reformulated in 1986 (many debate whether or not the formula still contains quinine), other quinquinas include Kina L'Aéro d'Or, Bonal, and Byrrh.

In 2010, pioneering wine and spirits importer Eric Seed began distributing Cocchi's portfolio in the United States, including their delicious white Americano formula, which many still mistakenly categorize as a quinquina. The Americano is actually another subcategory of aromatized wine, named after the French word for bitter—*amer*—that features gentian root as its defining bittering agent. For me, the herbaceousness of the formula makes it a discordant replacement for Lillet in the Vesper, which leads me to wonder, when might Lillet rerelease its original formula?

Bitters and Aperitivos

Following the success of Carpano's wine-based vermouth, Italian bars, cafés, and restaurants began employing their own specialists to create unique housemade bitters. The most famous of these artisans was Gaspare Campari, who created the legendary red bitter, which he popularized by serving it with ice-cold carbonated water from a tap. Thanks to the surging popularity of the Negroni cocktail (page 235) and relatives like the Boulevardier (page 329) and Rosita (page 287), firms such as Luxardo, Contratto, and Martini are now exporting their own red bitters outside of Italy.

A subcategory of these bitters, the aperitivos, includes formulas like Aperol, Contratto, and Select. Typically, aperitivos contain half the alcohol content of bitters like Campari and use less bitter botanicals. Campari bought Aperol in 2004, and, thanks in part to its marketing efforts, the Spritz—a cocktail made by mixing aperitivo liqueur and sparkling wine—has spread all over the world.

Absinthe Blanche and Verte

Absinthe is named after its primary botanical, grande wormwood, or *Artemisia absinthium*, whose medicinal use dates back to ancient Greece. Dr. Pierre Ordinaire developed the first commercial formula, which he began selling as a health tonic in 1792. Like many spirits within the aperitif category, absinthe was prescribed for medicinal purposes, most notably to French soldiers in North Africa, before it gained popularity as a beverage.

Absinthe went on to become the most popular spirit in France, thanks in part to artists and intellectuals like Charles Baudelaire and Henri de Toulouse-Lautrec who championed it—and to the agricultural pest phylloxera, an aphid that wiped out France's vineyards in the latter half of the nineteenth century.

Absinthe is still produced in the areas surrounding the Alps regions of France and Switzerland by macerating botanicals, including wormwood, fennel seeds, and green anise, in a neutral spirit and distilling them in a special pot still, called a *bain marie*, that keeps the herbs and spirit separate from each other to avoid scorching the botanicals.

Traditional alcohol levels for absinthe are 65%, 68%, and 72% ABV, based on the strength of the spirit prior to distillation; the high alcohol level is intended to preserve the essential oils extracted from the herbs during distillation. When bottled clear, it's labeled *absinthe blanche*; a secondary maceration with botanicals is used to create the naturally green-hued *absinthe verte*.

The traditional way to serve absinthe is to dilute it with cold water and stir in a spoonful of sugar. (Contrary to popular legend, absinthe was never meant to be set on fire.) Typically, absinthe is only used in small amounts in cocktails—for example, the Corpse Reviver #2 (page 232) and Sazerac (page 331). Anise, the predominant flavor in absinthe and relatives like pastis and Herbsaint, is a polarizing flavor in America. A little goes a long way, so I recommend springing for one of the high-quality, classic formulas imported by Tempus Fugit Spirits or Ted Breaux's Jade label.

Sparkling Wine

Most bars and restaurants choose the cheapest sparkling wine they stock to prepare popular cocktails like the Mimosa, Bellini, Venetian Spritz (page 167), and French 75 (page 221). I disagree with this tactic, as the character of the wine and mouthfeel of the bubbles affect the cocktail. High-quality sparkling wine can be sourced affordably: you just have to know what you're looking for.

Prosecco, made from the native Italian Glera grape planted throughout Friuli-Venezia Giulia and the Veneto, is the most popular and affordable sparkling wine for cocktails. Look for proseccos from the Valdobbiadene and Conegliano appellations outside Treviso, where the grape and winemaking methods are D.O.C.G. appellation certified.

Champagne, of course, is what first comes to mind when sparkling wine is referenced. When you buy champagne, you're not just paying for the name; the complexity of the wine, finesse of the bubbles, and expense to produce and bottle it figure into the bottom line, as does the name of the brand if they invest in advertising. Its appellation-controlled production follows a labor-intensive process called *méthode champenoise*, in which the wine—typically a blend of Chardonnay, Pinot Noir, and Pinot Meunier from different vintages—is bottled and refermented in racks, top-down at a 45-degree angle so that the lees collect in the neck of the bottle. The lees are removed though a process called disgorging; then sugar may be added, before the cork is inserted and secured with a wire cage and foil.

I asked sommelier Jordan Salcito to select a variety of champagnes for the cocktails that call for it in this chapter, to show how champagne can complement the flavor profile of the other ingredients in each recipe. Most bars don't have the luxury of pouring multiple champagnes by the glass, so look for an all-purpose bottling. I recommend a "brut" (dry), N/V (nonvintage) cuvée (bottling) from a grower-producer (a grape grower who makes their own wine as opposed to a house that sources wines to blend and bottle) that offers a half bottle at a reasonable price so you never have to store an opened bottle overnight.

Wine, Beer, and Cider

Although still wine, beer, and cider play a limited role in the recipes in this chapter, it's just as important for a bar to offer a compelling selection as it is for restaurants. A well-written cocktail menu featuring a carefully curated spirits selection paired with a hastily assembled wine and beer list sends a discordant message to your guests.

I recommend stocking at least three styles of beer: a crisp pilsner or other lager, a malty or hoppy ale, and a rich or dry porter. Rotate seasonal brews on and off the list—for example, a spring maibock, summer saison, fall Oktoberfest, and winter barley wine. I serve cider—typically a complex sparkling apple cider from Normandy—from the fall into the spring. Restaurants and bars featuring cuisine from a region without a dynamic brewing culture may exercise their creative liberty to curate selections beyond those borders.

While most guests are happy with the most popular red or white wine of the moment, consider sourcing lesser-known varietals—such as a French aligoté, which is used in the original Kir recipe (page 165), and is more affordable than most comparable chardonnays.

Allocate time to taste products from smaller suppliers of lesser-known, quality-focused products. Smaller suppliers typically represent lesser-known producers that invest a larger proportion of their resources into production than do bigger brands, which spend more on marketing. If you want to build a reputation as a tastemaker, make it a priority to attend portfolio tastings and take time to build relationships with your salespeople.

Fortified Wines

Sherry, madeira, and port are wines that have been "fortified" with a spirit—often grape spirit—and are steadily gaining favor within the cocktail community. Sherry, a fortified wine produced in southern Spain, is one of the most popular ingredients in cocktails today. This wouldn't be the first

ON INDIVIDUALITY

"To me, wine can't be distilled into one thing. Wine is history, wine is geography, wine is geology, it's anthropology, it's philosophy, and it's sociology. It's all of those things."

JORDAN SALCITO

Sommelier

time, as the Sherry Cobbler was said to be the most popular cocktail of the mid-nineteenth century. (Being among the first cocktails served over ice with a straw may have helped!) Unlike regulatory councils of other fine wine regions that don't market to bartenders, the *consejo regulador* of Jerez has promoted sherry in cocktails for years through programs pioneered by American educators Steve Olson (see page 461) and Andy Seymour.

Sherry—or *jerez* (pronounced "herez"), as it's called there—is produced in three main towns within the Andalusian province of Cádiz: Jerez de la Frontera, Sanlúcar de Barrameda, and El Puerto de Santa María. The mircroclimates of each town help produce a wide array of styles, from the lean, minerally manzanillas and finos, to nutty amontillados and olorosos, to sweet styles made with either Pedro Ximénez or Moscatel

Veneciador

grapes. To maintain a consistent house style and to provide the naturally occurring yeast (flor) with the nutrients it needs to prevent oxidation in the dry white wines, sherries are aged in what's known as a solera system, in which young wines are blended with old wines.

To keep sherry fresh after opening a bottle, store it in the fridge for up to a month. Most bartenders mix sherry like a vermouth when developing cocktails, although there are classics like the Bamboo (page 175) and Sherry Cobbler (page 171) that call for it explicitly. Thanks to its surging popularity in cocktail bars and restaurants, the number of producers and styles of sherry have grown exponentially over the past few years. It's still relatively affordable, especially when compared to other fine wines, although prices will certainly ascend as more consumers recognize its quality.

Madeira is another popular fortified wine named after an island off the coast of Morocco. It comes in four primary styles: the relatively dry Sercial and Verdehlo, and the rich, honeyed Bual and sticky Malmsey, which can age for centuries. Madeira sales never rebounded from the phylloxera infestation that destroyed the island's vineyards in the nineteenth century. Like sherry, there's great value to be discovered in this category.

Perhaps the most celebrated fortified wine is port, which hails from Portugal's ancient stepped hillsides in the Douro valley region, where five

ON THE PUZZLE PIECES

"A product is a big puzzle with thousands of pieces. Each piece is indispensable to complete the puzzle. My team are all part of the puzzle. People, knowledge, technology, and process are the pieces of the puzzle. The role of the master blender is to know all the pieces of the puzzle and guarantee that they're all in the right place to make the picture."

BEPPE MUSSO

Master Blender

varieties of red grapes are used to make a handful of styles ranging from fruit-forward rubies to earthy tawnies and age-worthy late bottled vintages (LBVs). Neutral grape spirit is added before the wine ferments all the way, leaving behind natural residual sugar, which makes port ideal to serve as a dessert wine or to mix in cocktails like the Coffee Cocktail (page 377). Like the wines of so many of Europe's great growing regions, port was cultivated by the Brits and frequently replaced French wines as their tipple of choice when the two countries were at war. Unlike sherry and madeira, port has held its value over time, making the best bottlings prohibitively expensive for use in cocktails.

ABSINTHE DRIP

Origin According to Tempus Fugit's Peter Schaf, the French army commissioned the Pernod Fils distillery to provide absinthe for medicinal purposes to the troops fighting in Algeria in the 1830s. Drinking water was notoriously unclean in desert or tropical zones, so wine, beer, or diluted spirits were often consumed instead. The prescribed dosage increased, and the process became inverted when doctors found the herbal alcohol assuaged the agony of war.

Logic The addition of cold water to absinthe causes a reaction that precipitates the essential oils from the botanicals out of suspension in alcohol, releasing their aroma. The most important consideration is that the water used should be as cold as possible, as ice should never be added directly to the absinthe glass before or after the cold water has been added. Brouilleurs, or "dripping cups" (pictured) were more popular in Spain and the United States (especially New Orleans) than in France, where the fountain reigned supreme. The dripping cup replaces the spoon on top of the glass—a sugar cube is added to the bottom of the cup, which then is filled with cracked ice and placed on the absinthe-dosed glass. Water is poured into the cup,

and the liquid gently streams into the absinthe below.

Hacks The drip can be performed carefully with a handled pitcher or more traditionally with a fountain. Prior to the use of sugar cubes, absinthe was typically sweetened with anisette, or orgeat or gum syrup. Some prefer the drip without sugar, so always ask before adding it.

4.5 oz. ice-cold, filtered water

1.5 oz. Vieux Pontarlier absinthe

1 sugar cube

Garnish: None

Pour the absinthe into a chilled glass. Place a slotted absinthe spoon over the rim of the glass and set a sugar cube in the bowl of the spoon. Using an absinthe fountain or water carafe, slowly drip the water over the sugar cube into the glass. As the dripping water dissolves the sugar cube, watch the "hydrophobic" layer of undiluted absinthe rise to the top of the glass. The drip should be ready when the mixture is completely cloudy. Serve with or without the spoon.

MEEHAN'S BARTENDER MANUAL

CHAMPAGNE COCKTAIL

Origin This recipe appears in the 1862 edition of Jerry Thomas's *The Bar-Tenders Guide*, and dates to at least a decade earlier, where it was enjoyed in moneyed company as a morning drink.

Logic There are those who would scold you for adding bitters, sugar, and a twist to a glass of champagne, and there are those who drink Pétrus with Coke. A bartender's job is to make the best cocktail possible based on the working constraints. When money is no object, make this cocktail with the best champagne you have access to. When cost is a constraint—and it usually is—think twice about making this cocktail without champagne, as so many bars do. I find that the most elegant way to prepare this drink is to dash the Angostura bitters onto a sugar cube on a cocktail napkin (to mop up any excess) and drop it into the glass (with tongs) after you've poured the wine. A disc-shaped lemon twist works if you serve it in a coupe, but it's unwieldy in a flute, where a spiral twist cut with a channel knife works perfectly.

Hacks Ironically, the recipe's titular ingredient—champagne—is typically the first to be swapped out with this cocktail. If you can't or won't spring for champagne, seek out a sparkling wine prepared in the *méthode traditionnelle*. There are many outstanding *méthode traditionnelle* wines that will make most any wine or cocktail aficionado happy.

---

5 oz. Bollinger brut champagne NV
1 Angostura bitters–soaked sugar cube
Garnish: 1 spiral lemon twist

Pour the champagne into a chilled flute, then add the bitters-soaked sugar cube. Garnish with the lemon twist.

KIR

Origin The Kir was named after former Dijon mayor Félix Kir, who served it to visiting dignitaries to promote the region after World War II.

Logic The Kir is a cocktail you won't find in many cocktail books, but the more famous Kir Royale (prepared with champagne) still gets ordered with some frequency, and the recipe is an excellent example of how cocktails can be used to promote a region. Besides mustard, Dijon is famous for its wines and the blackcurrant liqueur crème de cassis. Chardonnay is the noble white grape of Burgundy, but here I use a domestic chardonnay—my favorite New York producer's oak-free Scuttlehole bottling, which provides a clean, crisp canvas to show off the fruit in the cassis. Use only freshly opened wine and store your cassis in the fridge; it oxidizes quickly, so buying it by the half bottle is advised.

Hacks Substitute champagne for still white wine and you have a Kir Royale. Or try aligoté, the other white grape of Burgundy, which was the original wine used for Kir cocktails. Sommelier Jordan Salcito recommends Domaine A. & P. de Villaine aligoté. Aubert and Pamela de Villaine are better known for making wines for Domaine de la Romanée Conti—arguably the most famous estate in Burgundy, if not the world—which should probably remain cassis free.

---

5 oz. Channing Daughters Scuttlehole chardonnay

0.25 oz. Lejay crème de cassis

Garnish: 1 lemon twist

Build in a chilled white wine glass. Garnish with the lemon twist.

VENETIAN SPRITZ

Origin I discovered this recipe on the back label of the first bottle of Aperol I got my hands on in 2003, and kept it on the menu at Pace, the bar I was running, until our contraband stash ran out. Aperol returned to the U.S. market (officially) in 2006.

Logic Talia Baiocchi and Leslie Pariseau's book *Spritz* traces the mixture of sparkling water, wine, and bitters to the 1920s. Many other bitters found their way into the "spritz con l'amaro" up until the 1980s, when many of the smaller (and even some of the bigger) brands fell on hard times and subsequently disappeared. Prosecco was not a part of the formula until the 1990s—before that it was just still white wine, bitters, and soda water. Aperol made the regional tradition a global phenomenon in the 1990s, and its popularity continues to grow thanks to its affordable pour cost, approachable flavor profile, and low alcohol content, which makes one likely to order more than one.

Hacks Select, a bitter released in 1920 on the Venetian island of Murano, is believed to be the first bitter used in the recipe, but it's hard to find outside the Triveneto. When Aperol branded the recipe as their own, they replaced the olive garnish, which is classic in Venice, with a half-orange wheel. If you're feeling traditional, add an olive; Baiocchi prefers her Venetian Spritz with a Castelvetrano.

---

2 oz. Aperol
1 oz. Follador prosecco
1 oz. club soda
Garnish: ½ orange wheel

Build in a chilled rocks glass, then add ice cubes. Garnish with the ½ orange wheel.

TORINO TORINO

Origin This subtle riff on the classic Milano Torino cocktail, created back in the 1860s at Caffè Camparino in Milan, was served to (and renamed by) me on a tour of Martini's vermouth production facilities in 2015.

Logic The Milano Torino—Punt e Mes from Turin and Campari from Milan, served over ice with an orange—is named after the Italian cities where its ingredients originate. Before Italian cuisine became popular in America—thanks to chefs like Mario Batali—only a handful of vermouths, bitters, and amari were exported to the United States. Today, with a dozen suitable sweet vermouths and bitters available to them, many bartenders substitute Punt e Mes and Campari as they do at Martini, which isn't as well known for their delicious bitter—made with natural cochineal coloring, as Campari once was—as they are for their vermouths. Martini master blender Beppe Musso and Bacardi botanist Ivano Tonutti call their shaken Milano Torino the Americano Shakerato, as shaking with ice produces club soda–like dilution and aeration, but I prefer the more cheeky Torino Torino.

Hacks The classic adaptations are adding club soda to produce an Americano, gin to create a Negroni, or prosecco to yield a Spagliato—but don't shake any of them. Piedmont's Contratto makes a delicious vermouth and bitters, so feel free to substitute theirs or other vermouth producers' bitters as they expand into the Milano Torino market.

1.5 oz. Martini Grand Lusso sweet vermouth
1.5 oz. Martini bitter
Garnish: 1 orange wedge

Shake with ice, then fine-strain into a chilled wine glass filled with ice. Garnish with the orange wedge.

SHERRY COBBLER

Origin Jerry Thomas included a recipe for this with a gorgeous image—one of very few—in his 1862 *The Bar-Tenders Guide*, which emphasizes that the " 'cobbler' does not require much skill in compounding, but to make it acceptable to the eye, as well as to the palate, it is necessary to display some taste in ornamenting the glass after the beverage is made."

Logic There are six other cobblers listed after the Sherry Cobbler in Thomas's guide, but the sherry-based version was by the far the most popular of the time. Other than the Champagne Cobbler, which gets lemon and orange peel, all of the cobblers except the Whiskey Cobbler specify slices of orange with seasonal berries, which gives readers a sense that the orange is essential and the berries are something of a novelty. Thomas doesn't specify a type of sherry, which leaves the style open to interpretation. If you use a richer style, such as the cream sherry and East India bottlings I've chosen, you can omit the sugar called for in the original recipe. I've focused on the quality of the sherries over exotic garnishes, but based on Thomas's directions, you can and should go full Nightjar on this one.

Hacks All of Thomas's cobbler recipes call for a straw, which I've omitted in the photo to feature the garnishes, but David Wondrich believes the Sherry Cobbler pioneered the use of straws in cocktails. Some recipes call for the berries to be shaken with the orange instead of being used just for garnish, which will create a much fruitier cobbler than the wine-driven recipe I've posited.

1.75 oz. Lustau Solera Reserva Deluxe "Capataz Andrés" cream sherry

1 oz. Valdespino Deliciosa manzanilla sherry

0.25 oz. Lustau East India Solera sherry

Garnish: ½ orange wheel and seasonal berries: raspberry, blueberry, or blackberry

Shake with ice, then fine-strain into a chilled goblet filled with pebble ice. Garnish with the fruit.

PIMM'S CUP

Origin James Pimm opened a popular oyster bar in London, which he built into a chain of fashionable restaurants throughout the city. His #1 Cup, which was sold in pewter tankards, became so popular he began selling it off-premise in the 1860s.

Logic The Pimm's Cup doesn't appear in a historic cocktail book until Lucius Beebe's *The Stork Club Bar Book* in 1946, which is around the time it was adopted by the Napoleon House in New Orleans. It's best known as the signature cocktail of Wimbledon, where it's served by the pitcher with citrus, cucumber, strawberry, and mint. This recipe incorporates the cucumber into the drink, instead of just serving it as a garnish, and opts for dry ginger ale over the lemonade or bitter lemon soda more common in England. Pimm's is a refreshingly bitter aperitif with 25% ABV, and the perfect base for a summertime refresher.

Hacks This recipe is a variation on New Orleans and London Cups, which were both popular at the time. Today, Letherbee Distillers makes an herbal liqueur similar to Pimm's exclusively for the Chicago bar Pub Royale; unfortunately, it is not yet distributed, but hopefully it will be released publically one day. But until then, Pimm's #1 Cup and a cucumber garnish are absolutely essential to this recipe.

2 oz. Pimm's #1 Cup

1 oz. Q ginger ale, for topping

0.75 oz. lemon juice

0.5 oz. simple syrup (page 391)

3 cucumber slices

Muddle 2 of the cucumber slices and simple syrup, then add the Pimm's and lemon juice. Shake with ice, then fine-strain into a chilled highball glass filled with ice. Top with the ginger ale and garnish with the remaining cucumber wheel.

BAMBOO

Origin In the 1908 edition of *The World's Drinks and How to Mix Them*, Bill Boothby attributes the Bamboo to American barman Louis Eppinger of Yokahama's Grand Hotel. In *Imbibe!*, David Wondrich traces it back even further, to the 1880s, when it started appearing on bar menus all over the United States.

Logic The Bamboo looks and tastes like a cocktail, but has an ABV closer to a glass of wine, making it a perfect aperitif. Boothby's recipe calls for "French vermouth" and "sherry," leaving the door wide open for interpretation of what style to mix with. French vermouth is synonymous with dry bottlings from producers like Dolin and Noilly Prat, but the sweeter blanc formula from Dolin works better in nearly all the recipes of this era that call for French vermouth to be mixed with barrel-aged spirits. For a Manhattan-like Bamboo such as this recipe, pair a dry, barrel-aged oloroso, amontillado, or palo cortado sherry, as I've chosen, with Dolin blanc. For guests who'd prefer something more Martini-like, select a fino or manzanilla sherry and pair it with a dry vermouth. If you choose this option, pare back the Angostura bitters to one dash.

Hacks Substituting sweet vermouth for dry vermouth yields the richer Adonis cocktail. If you're going to garnish the cocktail with an olive as Boothby recommends, let it be one from Spain to reinforce the sherry's origin.

1.5 oz. Dolin blanc vermouth

1.5 oz. Lustau palo cortado sherry

2 dashes Angostura bitters

1 dash Regan's bitters

Garnish: 1 lemon twist

Stir with ice, then strain into a chilled coupe. Garnish with the lemon twist.

NURSE

Origin I dubbed this aperitif the Nurse thanks to its restorative quality for a hangover I woke up with after visiting Noilly Prat's production facility in Marseillan, France, with Ludovic Mizaga and Jacob Briars in 2015.

Logic The wine base of Noilly Prat dry vermouth's original formula is barrel-aged for over two years before the botanicals are added, which yields one of the most complex aromatized wines in the world. I was blown away by Noilly Prat's versatility as a food pairing with the traditional cuisine of the region (oysters and shellfish) when I visited. Instead of serving it with a lemon as they do in Marseillan, I prefer a cucumber slice to enhance the botanicals and lend melony notes.

Hacks The "extra dry" formula of Noilly Prat dry vermouth is made from a wine base that isn't barrel-aged and lacks the nutty, oxidized notes of the original formula. For the photo, we cut the cucumber wheels into crosses to allude to the cocktail's "medicinal value."

3 oz. Noilly Prat dry vermouth
1 oz. club soda
Garnish: 1 cucumber wheel

Build in a chilled wine glass filled with ice. Garnish with the cucumber wheel.

MICHELADA

Origin I won't perpetuate any of the myths concerning the origin of this recipe. The word *michelada* combines *chela* (slang for "beer") with *ada* from *helada* ("cold") with *mi* ("mine"), yielding "my cold beer."

Logic There are many regional variations on this recipe in Mexico, not unlike the subtle distinctions that define American barbecue. The variables include hot sauce, umami sauce (Worcestershire versus Maggi versus HP), and tomato or Clamato juice. The constants are beer (light lager or a malty brew), lime juice, ice, and a salt-rimmed glass—which many call a *chelada*—although the salt is often enhanced with chili, citrus, or dried worms (*sal de gusano*), which is how it was served to me in Oaxaca. There's no need to be finicky about the rim, as any salt that falls into the glass enhances the drink's character.

Hacks Purists who build the recipe in the glass—and anyone concerned with carbonation (as if this would last long enough to go flat)—may gasp, but I prefer to prepare everything in a mixing glass, then fine-strain the liquid of unsightly particulate matter over fresh ice in a rimmed glass. The tequila or mezcal that many sip with this drink also taste good in the glass.

12 oz. Negra Modelo
1.5 oz. lime juice
0.5 oz. Valentina hot sauce
2 barspoons (1 tsp.) HP sauce
1 barspoon (½ tsp.) Maggi seasoning sauce
Sal de gusano and salt, for rimming
Garnish: 1 lime wedge

Build in a mixing glass, then fine-strain into a chilled highball glass filled with ice and rimmed with the *sal de gusano* and salt. Garnish with the lime wedge.

Norwegian Sea

SWEDEN

Gulf
of
Bothnia

Koskenkorva

FINLAND

NORWAY

Helsinki

Stockholm

RUSSIA

Mariefred

ESTONIA

Moscow

Åhus

LATVIA

DENMARK

Baltic Sea

LITHUANIA

North Sea

Kaliningrad

RUSSIA

NETHERLANDS

Bialystok

BELARUS

Warsaw

BELGIUM

GERMANY

Żyrardów

POLAND

UKRAINE

CZECH REP.

SLOVAKIA

AUSTRIA

FINLAND
⊙ *Koskenkorva*
(Finlandia)

POLAND
⊙ *Bialystok*
(Zubrowka)
⊙ *Żyrardów*
(Belvedere)

RUSSIA
⊙ *Kaliningrad*
(Stolichnaya)
★ *Moscow*
(Smirnoff Black)

SWEDEN
⊙ *Åhus*
(Absolut)
⊙ *Mariefred*
(Karlsson's)

⊙ *Traditional Production Region*   ⊙ *Distillery Site*   ★ *Capital*

VODKA

Russia claims to be the birthplace of the spirit, but more evidence points to Poland, where the word *wodka* appears in a manuscript in 1405. The word means "little water" in both languages: *voda* (Russian) and *woda* (Polish) meaning "water," and *ka* used as a diminutive. Monks were among the first to distill vodka infused with herbs and spices, which they dispensed as both internal and topical medicine.

In the sixteenth century, distillation expanded beyond monasteries as the spirit was adopted for recreational use. Distillers used grains such as wheat, barley, oats, and rye as the base of vodkas they flavored with honey, fruit, herbs, and spices. Early styles include Goldwasser, an anise vodka with gold flakes; Krupnik, a spiced vodka sweetened with honey; and Żubrówka, a bison grass vodka that's one of the few classic styles available in the United States today.

Distilleries developed dozens of unique formulations that were imported throughout the Black Sea region and Eastern Europe. In the nineteenth century, vodka distillers began employing continuous distillation technology and innovative filtration methods such as charcoal to purify their distillate. These advances led to more palatable vodkas that didn't need to be sweetened or spiced to mask impurities.

Though the spirit was introduced to most Western imbibers after Prohibition, diplomatic tensions between East and West prevented exports of most traditional vodkas produced behind the Iron Curtain. Some vodkas trickled in after the Communist curtain parted, but disorganized, poorly funded Eastern government monopolies failed to position them in a manner that persuaded Western drinkers that vodka could be as bold and flavorful as the culture from which it originated.

Today, U.S. spirits guidelines define vodka as a "tasteless, colorless, and odorless spirit." EU regulations are equally vague, defining it as "a spirit in which the organoleptic [sensory] qualities of the raw materials are selectively reduced." To the consternation of producers of traditional vodka who value the quality of the raw materials—typically cereal grains like wheat, rye, and barley, or potatoes—EU law permits grapes and beets, while in the United States the source of starch is bound by imagination alone.

With neutrality—explicit in the American definition and implied by the European Union—as vodka's defining characteristic, there are two styles of pure (nonflavored) vodka. The more common Western style, typified by many "super premium" brands, touts distillation, filtration, and water purity for yielding a neutral spirit with little burn or bite. The Eastern style, held over within the vodka belt and embraced by a handful of craft distillers in America today, shows how vodka's raw materials can yield a spirit with pleasing body, subtle character, and a persistent finish.

Vodka didn't appear in Western cocktail books until the late 1920s in Europe and didn't become popular in the United States until well after Prohibition, when the neutral style produced in America took off in recipes like the Moscow Mule. Since then, vodka history has been intertwined with the progression of spirits marketing, from glossy print ad campaigns started by Smirnoff and perfected by Absolut, to placement in movies beginning with Bond, to far-fetched claims of millions of bottles of vodka being "hand-crafted" by a man and his dogs in Texas.

Modern Vodka Production

Any fermentable starch can be used to make vodka, but grains such as rye in Poland, barley in Finland, and wheat in Scandinavia and Russia—as well as potatoes in Poland—are traditional. In areas outside the vodka belt, producers typically choose the cheapest raw materials available, such as corn in the United States, sugar beets in France, and molasses in equatorial islands where sugarcane is plentiful.

Unlike whiskey, mezcal, and pot-stilled rum, whose long fermentations create complex flavors, the conversion process for vodka is conducted quickly, to deter flavorful congeners from forming as the yeast extracts as much alcohol as possible from the starch. Vodka must be distilled to 96% ABV, which would require numerous runs through a pot still, so more efficient column and continuous stills are employed first; then, if the producer chooses, that spirit can be run through a pot still to rectify (i.e., redistill) it.

In countries such as England, producers are required to purchase "neutral grain spirit" (NGS) from an industrial producer—sometimes from the government itself—which they may redistill, dilute, bottle, and market to their own specifications. Former 42 Below vodka brand ambassador Jacob Briars (see page 115) says, "Most vodka in the United States is made from neutral grain spirit from one of four agricultural conglomerates, while in countries like Finland and Poland, the government supplies spirit to the distillers."

This is common for gin and liqueur producers, who use the neutral spirit base as a canvas for other flavors, but more controversial for vodka producers, since so little is done to process the spirit—value brands just add water—before a company puts its name on the label. If you're paying a premium for vodka, it's worth considering distillers who control production from grain to glass—including big brands like Absolut and smaller brands like Woody Creek—over those that just rectify and dilute NGS.

Vodka comes off the still at 96% ABV and goes into the bottle at between 37.5% (lowest ABV permitted by EU law) and 40% in the United States (there are a handful of 50% ABV vodkas), meaning more than half of that bottle is water. Absolut Elyx global brand director Miranda Dickson (see page 185) clarifies, "The use of natural mineral water and arctic melt from icebergs is fairly inconsequential, as water must be demineralized before dilution. The purer the source, the less processing is required, so there's an element of truth in claims that pure water produces better vodka."

Two types of filtration are used in the production process. Western-style vodka is percolated through charcoal or other minerals such as quartz, sand and even diamonds to purify it of flavor and aroma. Polish filtration, in which the vodka is pumped through cotton or cellulose screens of various gauges to remove sediment and solids of any size, helps retain its clarity in the bottle without stripping flavor.

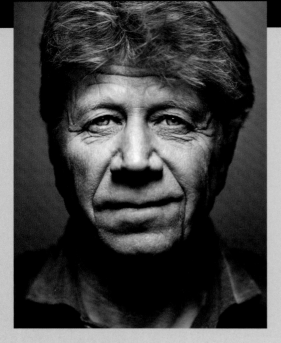

KRISTER ASPLUND

Master Distiller

ON SUSTAINABILITY

"In 1997 we started to put pressure on our suppliers to improve their impact on the environment. We began working actively with the farmers to aim for sustainable farming, without being organic. Organic wouldn't feed the people on Earth. So we have to find an efficient way of sustainable farming. And since then, we've added things. Transport is another area where we're trying to find better methods. For instance, by 2016, since we started three years ago, we've cut the CO_2 emissions from domestic transports by 50 percent. Sustainability has always gone hand in hand with the ambition of everything we do in production."

Additives such as sugar, glycerine for body, and citric acid—a natural preservative with a lemony taste—are permitted by law and used to mask impurities in vodkas distilled from ignoble base materials. Producers aren't required to disclose the presence of additives, which are nearly undetectable when a vodka is mixed with other more flavorful ingredients. If your vodka has lemony notes or the liquid separates into two different wash lines as it cascades back into the bottom of the glass when you swirl it, chances are additives are present.

In 1986, Stolichnaya launched a citrus-flavored vodka, Limonaya, and Absolut introduced a pepper-flavored vodka, Peppar, followed by their own citrus-flavored vodka, Citron, in 1988—and flavored vodkas took off in America. Citrus led to peach, blueberry, raspberry, mango, and currant bottlings in the early '90s, and then things got weird. In the last ten years, bacon, cupcake, whipped cream, energy stimulants, and nearly anything else you can imagine have found their way into flavored vodkas.

Despite vodka's long history of being infused with herbs, spices, and fruits that endowed medicinal qualities and character, some literature suggests Stoli and Absolut invented flavored vodka. This is preposterous, but there's some truth to the nature of the claim, in that these vodkas were among the first to reinforce the troubling notion that "natural" flavor can be manufactured or concentrated by flavor laboratories instead of harvested from the earth.

The TTB permits the use of sugar and artificial flavor in flavored vodka, which need only be 30% ABV instead of the 40% ABV for pure vodka. This opens the door for flavored vodkas that resemble liqueurs, but thankfully there are numerous natural offerings on the market. Żubrówka bison grass vodka (the base of the Tatanka cocktail ahead) is made by macerating the dried grass in pure rye-based vodka for three days to produce an extract that's filtered and added to pure vodka and bottled, with a blade of the grass, at 40% ABV.

In 2002, St. George Spirits' Lance Winters was among the first contemporary distillers to release a naturally flavored vodka line called Hangar One. His experience producing eau de vie helped inform his decision to distill ingredients like citrus peel and to macerate blossoms and leaves, as some gin, liqueur, and vermouth producers incorporate flavor in their products. This led to unusual and delicious flavored vodkas, like the Buddha's Hand vodka I used in the Parkside Fizz cocktail (page 191) before the brand was sold.

Except for stocking a citrus vodka to make Cosmopolitans, most cocktail bars eschew commercially flavored vodkas, preferring spirits that require the alchemy of mixology to make them palatable to general audiences. However, because the flavored vodkas from producers like St. George share similar production methods to those for gin, many work well in gin cocktails like the Southside, the inspiration for the Parkside Fizz.

Contrary to its reputation in some circles, and also because of its problematic legal definition as neutral, no spirit is as challenging to mix with as pure vodka. If the goal of a cocktail is to complement the character of its base spirit—which I agree with—the bartender must choose delicate ingredients that accentuate its subtleties, rather than the traditional battery of flavorful modifiers, including citrus, vermouths, bitters, and liqueurs, that overpower most vodkas.

For example, to accentuate the black pepper notes of Karlsson's vodka, I chose the old-fashioned recipe template (spirit, sugar, bitters, twist) typically reserved to showcase more flavorful, barrel-aged spirits like whiskey and brandy. Sometimes, you must look beyond classic cocktail templates, as I did when I used a yogurt-based mango lassi to complement the vanilla notes of Woody Creek vodka in Cocktail Culture (page 200).

Unless you're a well-versed water sommelier who can connect the minerality of regional bottled waters with vodka (I'm only half kidding here), this approach to cocktail development doesn't apply to neutral vodkas, which serve as a blank canvas to infuse with fresh ingredients—as many bartenders did during the "martini" craze in the 1990s—or as the ideal spirit to spike mixers without affecting their flavor, such as the soupy mix in a Bloody Mary (page 193) or the ginger beer and citrus in a Moscow Mule (page 189).

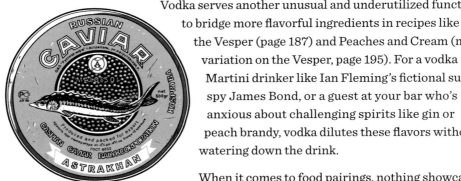

Caviar Tin

Vodka serves another unusual and underutilized function: to bridge more flavorful ingredients in recipes like the Vesper (page 187) and Peaches and Cream (my variation on the Vesper, page 195). For a vodka Martini drinker like Ian Fleming's fictional super spy James Bond, or a guest at your bar who's anxious about challenging spirits like gin or peach brandy, vodka dilutes these flavors without watering down the drink.

When it comes to food pairings, nothing showcases vodka's functionality better than the traditional cuisine of Eastern Europe, where preservation

"Still today, you go into a restaurant in Poland and there's a 375ml or 500ml bottle on the table. So if two people go out to eat a traditional dish like pork knuckle, you'll see them drinking vodka in stemmed glasses—they're not shooting it—and they might have a glass of apple juice or beer on the side if they're thirsty. This is the only way vodka is generally drunk in Eastern Europe . . . That's why their vodka has character and flavor, and people develop an acquired palate for a particular flavor in vodka that pairs with their food, as opposed to a very bland spirit for mixing."

MIRANDA DICKSON

Brand Director

methods such as pickling, smoking, and curing have long been vital to preserve food for the long, harsh winters. Wine and beer lack the power to cleanse the palate between oily, smoked, pickled, and salted foods like beets, herring, caviar, and meat pies served as hors d'oeuvres called *zakuski* in Russia, where vodka is sipped or shot along with a toast between courses.

Tasting products like Polugar—an ancestor of modern vodka revived in Russia—makes me nostalgic for vodka's history and hope that its future can be written *from* history by producers with the courage and vision to reposition its identity to align with its cultural roots. Ironically, Western brands such as Woody Creek, OYO, and Koval are leading this charge, which will hopefully be viewed as a signature achievement of the craft-distilling boom.

VESPER

Origin James Bond orders this dry Martini variation, named after paramour Vesper Lynd, in Ian Fleming's *Casino Royale*, published in 1953.

Logic Few film stars have shaped drinking trends over the years as much as James Bond, whose Vesper serves as a double agent in the "cold war" between vodka and gin Martini drinkers. Typically employed as a neutral base spirit, vodka functions here as a modifier that helps bond the botanicals in the gin with the orange notes and quinine in the Lillet. I agree with Bond's recommendation of a more neutral grain-based vodka—like the winter wheat formula from the 86 Company—over more flavorful potato vodka, and I follow his proportions for gin to vodka (three to one). Doubling the recommended volume of Lillet adds more body to the cocktail, which is accentuated by stirring rather than shaking, as the spy famously prefers.

Hacks In 1986, Kina Lillet was reintroduced as Lillet blanc. The company maintains it wasn't reformulated, but many speculate that the cinchona bark (which makes it a quinquina) was reduced, opening the door for Kina L'Aéro d'Or to be substituted for Lillet in the recipe. I still prefer Lillet for this recipe.

2.25 oz. Plymouth gin

0.75 oz. Aylesbury Duck vodka

0.5 oz. Lillet blanc

Garnish: 1 lemon twist

Stir with ice, then strain into a chilled coupe. Garnish with the lemon twist.

MOSCOW MULE

Origin This cocktail was co-developed by Jack Morgan of the Cock 'n Bull pub in Hollywood and John G. Martin of Heublein, the company that distributed Smirnoff in 1940. It appears in Lucius Beebe's *The Stork Club Bar Book* in 1946, the same year they franchised Cock 'n Bull ginger beer and started promoting the recipe.

Logic Morgan and Martin were having trouble selling their respective products; Martin's girlfriend, Ozaline Schmidt, had inherited a copper factory when her father died, and the company's copper mugs weren't moving. To improve their situation, they developed the recipe for a vodka buck (a highball prepared with ginger ale and lime is called a buck), using each other's products, and named it the Moscow Mule. To promote it, Martin purchased a Polaroid camera, which had just been invented, and went around taking pictures of bartenders with the vodka in one hand and the cocktail in the other. He gave one copy to the bar and used the other copy to entice other bars to serve his recipe. Hollywood celebs started ordering it, and the rest is history. This story behind the recipe is a textbook example of how cocktails are used to deplete inventory and the endurance of recipes thanks to innovative marketing.

Hacks Although I prefer serving the recipe with ginger wort (page 393), commercial ginger beer is traditional, so I've included it in the recipe below. You can substitute your vodka of choice here if you aren't concerned about paying tribute to the original formula. A Moscow Mule poured in a glass instead of a copper mug is a tough sell for me because the copper mug is such an important part of the drink's heritage.

---

4 oz. Fentimans ginger beer
1.5 oz. Smirnoff vodka
0.5 oz. lime juice
Garnish: lime shell, candied ginger

Build in a chilled mule mug, then fill with ice cubes. Garnish with the lime shell and a piece of candied ginger on a pick.

PARKSIDE FIZZ

Origin I created this for Gramercy Tavern's cocktail menu in 2005.

Logic At that time, pioneering distillers such as Lance Winters at St. George and Marko Karakasevic at Charbay were gaining national attention for their naturally flavored vodkas, and greenmarket-driven bars and restaurants such as Gramercy Tavern were their early champions. Lance chose unusual varieties of fruit to flavor his Hangar 1 vodkas, such as makrut lime, mandarin blossoms, and Buddha's Hand, and I loved the challenge of mixing with them for unsuspecting audiences who weren't used to vodka with character. The marzipan notes in an aromatic Lebanese orgeat, which I sourced from a local specialty store called Kalyustan's, tamed the perfumed Buddha's Hand vodka, while the mint added a pleasing herbal dimension. The recipe is a simple twist on the classic Southside Fizz (which appears in *The Artistry of Mixing Drinks*); I named it in honor of the three parks in the neighborhood (Madison Park to the north, Gramercy Park to the east, and Union Square to the south).

Hacks Hangar 1 was acquired and reformulated, and bartenders such as San Francisco's Jen Colliau have gotten into the syrup-making business, which means high-quality orgeat made from blanched almonds is the new gold standard. The DSP CA 162 vodka is the closest thing I've found to the original formula of Hangar 1 Buddha's Hand.

2 oz. DSP CA 162 Buddha's Hand vodka

1 oz. club soda, for topping

0.75 oz. lemon juice

0.5 oz. Small Hand Foods orgeat

8 mint leaves (plus 1 sprig for garnish)

Muddle the mint and orgeat, then add the vodka and juice. Shake with ice, then fine-strain into a chilled rocks glass filled with ice cubes. Top with the club soda. Garnish with the mint sprig.

BLOODY MARY

Origin In 1934, Fernand Petiot of New York's King Cole Bar at the St. Regis Hotel served a spiced tomato juice cocktail to guests from Chicago; they told him it reminded them of a waitress nicknamed Bloody Mary, and the name stuck. Hotel owner Vincent Astor disapproved of the name, so it went on the menu as the Red Snapper.

Logic Like the lime cordial in the Gimlet and tonic water in the Gin and Tonic, the Bloody Mary is the by-product of commercial tomato juice, canned by College Inn Food Products in 1928. By 1936, influential bartenders such as Frank Meier of the Ritz Hotel in Paris endorsed the product, stating in *The Artistry of Mixing Drinks* (page 42): "It is advantageous to procure it in that form [canned] instead of from fresh tomatoes, which in most countries can be obtained only at particular seasons." This holds true today, as the viscosity of commercial tomato juice is vital to the texture of the drink, which is achieved through rolling or throwing the cocktail—never shaking. Bloody Mary mix tastes better when it's allowed to marry for a few hours before service, so it should be batched in the morning for afternoon brunch service or the prior evening for breakfast.

Hacks I'm wary of bartenders who spend more time garnishing a drink than preparing it. Rather than diverting attention from the liquid with a gaudy garnish, I focus my attention on the spices, hot sauce, and tomato juice brand. I prefer to fine-strain my Bloody Mary to remove any gritty spices and pulpy horseradish.

---

4 oz. tomato juice

1.5 oz. Belvedere vodka

0.25 oz. lemon juice

0.25 oz. lime juice

0.25 oz. Lea & Perrins Worcestershire sauce

1/2 tsp. Gold's horseradish

1/2 tsp. La Boîte Bloody Mary spice mix

1/4 tsp. Cholula hot sauce

Garnish: 1 celery stalk

Build in a shaker, then fill with ice cubes. Roll, then fine-strain into a chilled pint glass filled with ice. Garnish with the celery stalk.

PEACHES AND CREAM

Origin I created this for the PDT cocktail menu in the spring of 2013.

Logic Angus Winchester flew me to Copenhagen in 2009 to help him launch a cocktail program at the luxurious Nimb Hotel by the Tivoli Gardens. In a preopening meeting, Chef Thomas Herman, who ran a fine dining restaurant in the hotel at that time, shared some pickled baby peaches with us and suggested we serve them as bar snacks. Bright and briny, they would, I imagined, be perfect in place of an olive as a garnish for a Martini. Years later, when I was finally able to get my hands on enough of them to put on the menu at PDT, I came up with this Martini variation to show them off. The name, which refers to the ingredients, is the sixth track on Beck's 1999 album *Midnight Vultures*. I love incorporating pop culture into geeky cocktail recipes to give them some levity.

Hacks I chose Absolut's high-end Elyx bottling to pay tribute to the Scandinavian chef who introduced me to pickled baby peaches, but most well-made grain-based vodka will do. Once you've located the rare pickled peaches, finding a barrel-aged peach eau de vie (not a liqueur labeled "peach brandy") will be your next-toughest task. Peach Street Distillers' release was one of the first authentic offerings in over a century. In the likely event you can't source the peaches, substitute a small olive such as a Lucques.

---

2 oz. Absolut Elyx vodka

0.5 oz. Lustau Solera Reserva "Capataz Andrés" Deluxe cream sherry

0.5 oz. Peach Street Distillers peach brandy

0.5 oz. Lillet blanc

Garnish: 1 pickled baby peach

Stir with ice, then strain into a chilled coupe. Garnish with the peach.

GOLD COAST

Origin I created this vodka old-fashioned, featuring classic Swedish ingredients, in the winter of 2009 after visiting the Bjäre peninsula in southern Sweden, where the potatoes used to distill Karlsson's vodka are grown.

Logic Before Karlsson's, most vodka brands I was familiar with emphasized their neutrality instead of their character. After visiting the fields and learning about the different potato varieties (including tasting vintage bottlings made from multiple single potato varieties), I was inspired to create an old-fashioned cocktail (which most mixologists prepare with pot-distilled or barrel-aged spirits) sweetened and spiced with the flavors of Sweden. Instead of sugar and spice, I used a splash of citrus and arrack-based liqueur called Swedish punsch with dill and black pepper, common ingredients in Swedish cuisine. Applying pepper with an atomizer instead of muddling peppercorns allowed me to maintain the clarity of the cocktail, which should be served over a clear cube.

Hacks You can make black pepper tincture by infusing peppercorns in high-proof vodka and fine-straining the mixture instead of sourcing the black pepper essence. Kronan Swedish punsch, which is widely distributed in the United States, is more flavorful than Carlshamns, so cut the quantity in half.

---

2 oz. Karlsson's Gold vodka

0.5 oz. Carlshamns Flaggpunsch

1 sprig fresh dill (plus 1 for garnish)

Garnish: Aftel black pepper essence

Muddle the dill and Flaggpunsch, then add the vodka. Stir with ice, then fine-strain over one large ice cube in a chilled rocks glass. Garnish with 2 spritzes of black pepper essence and a sprig of dill.

TATANKA

Origin According to *Difford's Guide*, the Tatanka, which means "buffalo" in Lakota (a Native American language), became popular after the movie *Dances with Wolves* was released in 1990.

Logic The original recipe calls for bison grass vodka, "Żubrówka" in Polish, to be mixed into a highball lengthened with apple juice. Mixing a drink with apple juice seems odd now, but makes more sense when you look back at recipes from this time period, such as Dick Bradsell's Treacle cocktail, which calls for dark rum to be mixed with maple syrup and bitters. Instead of drowning the fragrant vodka in cloyingly sweet apple juice, I've remade the original recipe into a Stone Fence analog with a dry Norman sparkling cider, whose earthy aromatics pair perfectly with the grassy vodka. A Polish friend supplied me with blades of dried bison grass to reinforce the herbal, nutty quality of the vodka and break up the drink's appearance visually as a garnish.

Hacks If you choose to honor the original recipe, I'd recommend serving it with freshly extracted green apple juice with an apple slice floating in the frothy head. A slice of apple—fan a few out if you're feeling fancy—will work in place of the bison grass.

3 oz. Dupont sparkling apple cider
2 oz. Żubrówka bison grass vodka
Garnish: Bison grass

Build in a chilled collins glass filled with ice cubes. Garnish with a few blades of bison grass.

CZECHMATE

Origin I created this to serve during a seminar in Prague with London bartender Ben Reed in the spring of 2015.

Logic On behalf of Absolut Elyx, Aleš Půta, who owns the Hemingway Bar in Prague, invited me to the Czech Republic to speak to local bartenders about the New York bar scene alongside bartender and author Ben Reed, who represented London. He asked each of us to serve a cocktail after the session, so I created a twist on the King Carl Collins—a recipe I'd created in Sweden and named after their reigning monarch, using the collins as a template to showcase the brand's Swedish heritage. In Stockholm, I had served it with champagne and Swedish punsch; in Prague, I mixed it with a local lager and Becherovka, a cinnamon-forward herbal liqueur. When combined with subtly flavored mixers, vodka stands up on its own in a cocktail. Otherwise, it's used to bridge ingredients, as it does in the Vesper, or as a canvas to layer flavor on, as I've used it here.

Hacks A vodka from the Czech Republic would be the ideal substitution for Absolut Elyx to unify all the alcoholic ingredients under one flag. Extra credit for serving it with chess-related accoutrements.

1.5 oz. Absolut Elyx vodka

1.5 oz. Czechvar pilsner

1 oz. lemon juice

0.5 oz. Becherovka liqueur

0.5 oz. simple syrup (page 391)

Garnish: 1 lemon wedge

Shake the vodka, liqueur, juice, and syrup with ice, then fine-strain into a chilled pilsner glass filled with ice. Top with the pilsner. Garnish with the lemon wedge.

COCKTAIL CULTURE

Origin I created this cocktail in the spring of 2014 to serve at the Food and Wine Classic in Aspen, Colorado.

Logic After visiting Woody Creek's distillery in Aspen in 2013, I incorporated their aromatic potato vodka into an Indian lassi for an event held the following year during the Food and Wine Classic. The yeasty, vanilla notes of the vodka pair perfectly with the creamy, Colorado-based yogurt, which is rarely incorporated into cocktails. Most imbibers are familiar with citric acid in their drinks, but lactic acid from dairy, acetic acid from vinegar, and malic acid from apples can also be used to balance sweetness. "Culture" is a double entendre referring to the popularity of craft beer and spirits in Colorado and the use of yogurt in the recipe.

Hacks Although this recipe was designed for Woody Creek vodka, many full-bodied vodkas (ideally rye or potato based) can be substituted. Noosa makes a passion fruit yogurt that could be used in lieu of the puree. High-quality vanilla extract is essential; a little goes a long way in the glass.

1.75 oz. Woody Creek vodka
0.75 oz. Noosa honey yogurt
0.5 oz. Boiron passion fruit puree
0.25 oz. vanilla syrup (page 392)
Bourbon vanilla extract
Garnish: None

Shake with ice and fine-strain into a chilled coupe. Spray 2 spritzes of the vanilla extract over the surface.

COSMOPOLITAN

Origin Toby Cecchini created this cocktail in the fall of 1988 at the Odeon in New York City.

Logic Toby's coworker at the Odeon told him about a cocktail her San Francisco friends ordered called the Cosmopolitan, prepared with vodka, Rose's lime cordial, and grenadine, shaken and served "up" in a martini glass. He liked the name, but after mixing one he hated the way it tasted. So he recast it as a daisy with a splash of Ocean Spray cranberry juice cocktail in place of grenadine, and the newly released Absolut Citron as the base. The staff fell in love with it and began recommending it to bar regulars, including Lou Reed, Keith Haring, KRS-One, Sam Shepard, Johnny Depp, and Madonna. Its frequent appearances in *Sex and the City* from the second season on cemented its place in late-twentieth-century pop culture and beyond.

Hacks Toby prepares his Cosmo with equal parts lime, cranberry juice, and Cointreau with a lemon twist, but I prefer to accentuate the orange in the Cointreau over the lemon in the vodka. Fresh cranberry juice is far too tart to pour unsweetened, which is why I've added the simple syrup.

2 oz. Absolut Citron
0.75 oz. Cointreau
0.75 oz. lime juice
0.5 oz. cranberry juice (unsweetened)
0.25 oz. simple syrup (page 391)
Garnish: 1 orange twist

Shake with ice, then fine-strain into a chilled coupe. Garnish with the orange twist.

SCOTLAND

NORWAY

SWEDEN

Windygates
Girvan · Edinburgh

IRELAND

DENMARK

North Sea

Celtic
Sea

ENGLAND

NETHERLANDS

Berlin

POLAND

Witham
Plymouth · London · Zoetermeer · Amsterdam
· Dordrecht

English Channel

Brussels

BELGIUM

GERMANY

CZECH REP.

Bay
of
Biscay

FRANCE

Loßburg

Axberg · Vienna

AUSTRIA

SWITZERLAND

ITALY

AUSTRIA
- ⊙ *Axberg*
  (Blue gin)

ENGLAND
- ★ *London*
  (Fords gin)
  (Beefeater gin)
- ⊙ *Plymouth*
  (Plymouth gin)
- ⊙ *Witham*
  (Hayman's Old Tom gin)

GERMANY
- ⊙ *Loßburg*
  (Monkey 47 gin)

SCOTLAND
- ⊙ *Windygates*
  (Tanqueray gin)
- ⊙ *Girvan*
  (Hendrick's gin)

NETHERLANDS
- ⊙ *Zoetermeer*
  (Bols genever)
- ⊙ *Dordrecht*
  (Rutte genever)

⋮ *Traditional Production Region*   ⊙ *Distillery Site*   ★ *Capital*

GIN AND GENEVER

Of all base spirits—vodka, gin, rum, tequila, whiskey, and brandy—gin is rarely ordered neat or on the rocks, making it the only base spirit served exclusively in mixed drinks. The finest marques in other categories are typically reserved for neat pours or a few ice cubes, whereas few bartenders would withhold a fine gin from the mixing glass. Like the aperitifs and liqueurs that bookend this chapter, dry gin's botanicals shine brighter when they're combined with other ingredients.

The word *gin* is an Anglicization of *genever*, which is how the Dutch pronounced the old French word *genevre*, derived from *juniperus*, the Latin word for juniper. Through the etymology of the word, you can neatly trace the ancestry of dry gin back through Dutch genever to Brussels (hence the French), where it was first distilled with juniper berries, its namesake botanical.

Juniper Branch

Gin's history and early applications are steeped in the medicinal history of alcohol. Spirits historian Dave Broom (see page 125) traces juniper all the way back to ancient Egypt in *Gin: The Manual*, citing the Ebers Papyrus (c. 1550 BCE) as listing juniper as a cure for jaundice. In 1269, the first reference to juniper combined with alcohol appears in *Der Naturen Bloemein*, in which Belgian author Jacob van Maerlant characterized juniper berries "cooked in wine" as medicine.

Wine remained the base for spirits distilled with juniper until the sixteenth century, when a succession of poor grape harvests in the Spanish-occupied Low Countries, present-day Netherlands and Belgium, prompted distillers to substitute sour beer, rye, and malted barley for it just before wine imports were cut off during the Eighty Years' War beginning in 1568. By this time, its purpose had shifted, as the English, who joined the Dutch in their rebellion against the Spanish, noted when they coined the term "Dutch courage" for genever after watching soldiers drink it before going into battle.

Even before the Spanish banned grain distillation in the Low Countries in 1601, distillers had begun to flee. One notable example was the Bersius family, who had landed in Cologne before settling in Amsterdam (which was not Spanish occupied), where they began making liqueurs under the name Bols in 1575. Their timing was fortuitous, as in 1602 the Dutch East India Company was founded, which brought shiploads of exotic spices and fruits to Amsterdam. Lucas Bols became a shareholder in 1700, which was convenient for a producer who needed spices to make liqueurs and genever (from 1664) and the infrastructure to distribute them.

Spices flowed into Amsterdam, which gained a reputation for its liqueurs, while grains entered the port of Schiedam, which became known for its Korenbrandwijn (grain brandy). Unlike previous wine-based juniper spirits, genever evolved from the grain-based spirit—distilled from rye, corn, and wheat—called malt wine. Spices, including juniper, were added to make the single-malt-like spirit—genever—more palatable to the upper class, whose political representatives deprived them of French brandy during frequent outbreaks of war.

In 1688, the Dutch Protestant William of Orange replaced James II as king of England and declared war on Catholic France. In 1690, his parliament legislated lower duties on domestic spirits made from corn and banned French brandy imports. The new law left a loophole open for anyone to distill or compound spirits—and just about everyone did, which more than doubled gin production over the following two decades. A "gin craze" took hold of England, and public drunkenness reached epic heights until the Gin Act, prohibiting distillers from selling to unlicensed merchants, passed in 1751, closing scrupulous shops as well.

According to David Wondrich in *Bar Smarts*, once home distilling and compounding was beaten back in parliament, ornate gin palaces were erected in London that encouraged a more civilized—and taxable—setting to sip the national tipple. Genever-based gin punch "became one of the

ON RESOURCEFULNESS

"In Northern Europe, we have grain, so we distill grain. Whereas in the Caribbean, they have sugarcane, so they distill sugarcane. Germany, England, and Holland all distill grain. It started off in Holland, where there was a lot of wine trading. If the wine went sour, you could distill it and not have to throw it away. They say the Dutch are real tight. They didn't want to throw anything away, so they distilled it and called it *brandewijn*, which means 'burned wine.' They realized they could do the same thing with their beer, and called it *corenwijn. Coren* is another word for 'grain' (not corn), so it's called grain wine."

MYRIAM HENDRICKX

Master Distiller

sporting drinks of the upper class at home, while for the protectors of the Empire in the far-flung tropical regions of India and Africa, gin and quinine-water became the tonic drink (as in, medicinal) of choice."

The combination of new legislation and poor grain harvests between 1757 and 1763 made gin prohibitively expensive to produce, which enticed wealthy entrepreneurs into the business—including the Gordons, Booths, Boords, and Curries, who collectively brought an air of gentility to the category. After the 1780s, distillers such as James Stein in Fife, Scotland, and the Coates family in Plymouth, England, began distilling gin outside of London, which lent geographic diversity and new production insights to the English gin category.

Genever historian Philip Duff claims that "the rich, whisky-like malt wine proved too much of a challenge for the inexperienced London distillers, so genever was reduced to some grain alcohol with botanicals, often just soaked instead of being redistilled." The situation began to be rectified— pun intended—in 1827, when Scotsman Robert Stein installed his new continuous still at the Kilbagie Distillery. His design was improved by Irishman Aeneas Coffey in 1830, and soon a cleaner base spirit for gin led to a whole new role for juniper and the other botanicals.

Early nineteenth–century English gins were sweetened by retailers, who bought them from rectifiers, who distilled the spirits with botanicals. According to David Wondrich's research, Hodges, a pioneering London distillery in Holborn, was the first to market and sell their gin unsweetened in 1826. After years of English distillers using sugar to mask the quality of the base spirit—middling attempts to reproduce malty genever, according to Duff— botanicals were emerging as the star, thanks to a cleaner, drier platform.

From here on, gin evolved from a soldier's spirit, used to fortify military medicine, such as Angostura bitters (to make the Pink Gin), Rose's lime cordial (to make a Gimlet, page 219), and quinine (to make a Gin and Tonic, page 217), into a spirit worthy of an officer or a gentleman in a club, in fancy American-style cocktails imported from England's former colony. Early nineteenth–century cocktails in America were made with Holland-style gin until Old Tom and London's dry gin began to appear in recipes printed around the turn of the twentieth century.

Bolstered by new distillation technology that made gin among the cheapest (and fastest) spirits to produce, English gin producers were joined by distillers in America and elsewhere, who began to chip away at "Holland's" market share as palates shifted to the lighter English style. As punch—whose quality depends on aromatic, pot-distilled base spirits like malty genever— waned in popularity, individual cocktails mixed with vermouth and bitters, which share many of the same botanical as English gin, became fashionable.

As French brandy distillers were devastated by phylloxera at the end of the nineteenth century, gin producers, whose grain base was unaffected by

ON BEING HUMBLE

"You have to have enough passion
to carry it through to do a good
job. Basically, don't take shortcuts,
stick to what you know, and if
you don't know it, ask somebody
who does know it. And don't be so
far above yourself. There's always
people below you who come
up with a suggestion that works.
So accept that fact."

TOM NICHOL

Master Distiller

the infestation, expanded their market share. Gin was widely embraced by
American bartenders, who continued to receive English gin shipments sent
to bootleggers in Canada and the Bahamas, who then distributed it through
the mob. During Prohibition, America's own gin craze swept the nation,
as desperate drinkers resorted to toxic "bathtub" gin compounded with
industrial alcohol and juniper essence.

During the 1940s and '50s, fruity Prohibition-era gin-based cocktails—which
buried the taste of the base spirit with cream and eggs—were discarded in favor of
simple, austere classics like the Martini. My favorite characterization of the era
is from Bernard DeVoto's paean to the Martini, *The Hour*, in which he dismisses
all drink options beyond a "a slug of whiskey" and the dry gin Martini. In his

New York Times review of a reprint of *The Hour*, William Grimes sarcastically notes, "The first, of course, is not even a mixed drink. The second he surrounds with more caveats and fine-print instructions than a car-repair manual."

DeVoto's brand of mixological conservatism didn't last long once well-financed vodka companies' marketing messaging began to penetrate the American consumer psyche through innovative advertising and public relations. By 1954, vodka was selling over one million cases a year, and in 1967 it surpassed gin sales in the United States. Using gin's signature drink—the Martini—Smirnoff touted the flavorlessness of vodka as a positive attribute in the drink that "leaves you breathless." It was a consequential indictment of juniper that shaped the gin industry's marketing strategy for decades to come.

Absolut vodka's innovative U.S. importer Michel Roux brought his Midas touch—along with the vodka marketing playbook—to the gin category when he launched a super-premium line extension of Bombay gin called Sapphire in 1987. Using a historic Carter Head still, which suspends the botanicals in a basket above the spirit in a pot still, allowing only vapor to come into contact—Bombay created a more approachable gin that vodka drinkers embraced once they saw its eye-catching blue bottle, which stood out like a beacon on the backbar.

By the year 2000, Bombay Sapphire was selling a million cases a year, but its success had little effect on the rest of the category, as it was marketed like a super-premium vodka. This was also the year Scotland's William Grant launched a "peculiar gin" distilled with roses and cucumbers called Hendrick's, in an iconic old-timey apothecary bottle with a premium cork closure.

Neither Hendrick's nor Bombay Sapphire were a traditional juniper-forward London dry–style gin like Tanqueray or Beefeater, which remained unpopular until 2004, when Simon Ford (see page 457), a charismatic English brand ambassador representing a little-known historic gin brand called Plymouth, arrived in New York and began educating bartenders about the history and application of gin in tastings across the entire category, instead of just promoting his own brand.

Both Ford and Charlotte Voisey (see page 451), a Hendrick's gin ambassador who moved to New York City from London in 2006, were instrumental in getting bartenders to mix with gin, along with Audrey Saunders (see page 452), whose gin-focused cocktail program at the Pegu Club began to turn the tide with consumers. Nearly twenty years after Bombay Sapphire was launched, Saunders convinced bartenders and her guests that classic gin's juniper notes were something to celebrate, not sidestep.

The category grew exponentially in the decade that followed, thanks in part to innovative "new Western" gins known for their use of local botanicals— for example, Aviation, which launched in 2006. These were soon followed by reissues of historic formulas to re-create classic cocktails, such as Hayman's Old Tom gin in 2007, Plymouth sloe gin in 2008, and Plymouth navy-strength in 2012. In 2008, Bols launched a malt-wine-heavy formula of genever in a smoked glass bottle molded in the shape of their ceramic corenwijn bottles, bringing the category's history full circle.

Genever

Genever must include juniper, by law, but the berry isn't required to play a dominant role in the flavor profile as it is with gin. This leaves room for other botanicals and malt wine—distilled in pot stills from a mixed mash bill of rye, wheat, corn, and malted barley—to factor into the flavor profile. Many producers keep the components—neutral spirit, malt wine, and the botanical distillate—separate, then blend and age them before bottling, depending on the marque and house style.

In the 1950s, a new, drier style with less malt wine, labeled *jonge*, was released to compete with vodka, as the malty, aged *oude* genevers and corenwijn were falling out of favor. The difference between the two styles' character and applications are broad, which has precipitated what I believe to be an identity crisis that's still working its way out in the market today. Brands like Bols have returned to higher proportions of malt wine in their genever, while others, such as Rutte, rely more heavily on botanicals.

Rutte Genever Recipe

The aromatic pot-stilled malt wine works well in cocktails typically reserved for whiskey (especially Irish whiskey, whose cereal notes are front and center), such as the Improved Old-Fashioned, traditional punch, and recipes that descend from it, like the Tom Collins. Unaged bottlings with larger percentages of malt wine, such as Bols, mix unpalatably in cocktails with vermouth and bittersweet liqueurs, whose botanicals are better paired with marques containing less, such as Rutte's Old Simon.

Dry Gin

Most of the cocktail recipes here are prepared with London dry gin, which is produced by redistilling high-strength, neutral alcohol—typically sourced grain neutral spirit—and botanicals, including juniper, in a pot still to a minimum strength of 70% ABV. Neutral spirit of the same type may be added after distillation, but no coloring or sweetening is permitted. Some

Tanqueray #10 Still

producers distill botanicals separately and mix them together, but most distill them together in one shot, dilute it to around 44% ABV, and bottle it without manipulation afterward.

London dry is an EU-recognized style of gin with no geographic designation, so it can be made anywhere in the world. Production guidelines are much more flexible if the product is labeled a "distilled gin," which allows for artificial flavors, colors, and sweeteners to be added. "American gin" permits adding botanical flavor (compounding) without distillation, as long as juniper is the dominant flavor of the resulting product and it's bottled at a minimum of 40% ABV.

The type of high-strength neutral base spirits (such as wheat, grape, or corn) and type of still (common ones are pot stills akin to those used to make whiskey and Carter Head stills) employed to extract the botanical's precious oils have become more diverse as new technologies, such as vacuum distillation and super critical fluid extraction, have entered the industry. Seemingly inconsequential procedures—such as whether the botanicals are steeped or suspended above the boil and how fast the distillation run is conducted—have a marked influence on the final product.

Beefeater Gin Botanical Scale

Gin botanicals, such as juniper, coriander, cardamom, orris and angelica root, citrus peel, cubeb berries, and more—these are organic ingredients whose character changes from season to season, which requires master distillers to adapt their recipe to account for crop variations. In this, historic brands, including Beefeater, Plymouth, Tanqueray, and Bombay, have an advantage over new distillers, thanks to longstanding relationships with botanical suppliers and centuries of distilling experience.

If you find yourself getting bogged down with the production process and botanical formulas when considering which gins to stock at your bar, mix your candidates into classic cocktails, such as a Martini or Negroni, and with tonic water to see how they taste. Nontraditional botanicals like raspberries and elderflower may sound appealing, but they tend to mix discordantly in historic recipes.

For guests hesitating to try a gin cocktail, modern bottlings like Bombay Sapphire and Tanqueray #10 place more approachable botanicals such as citrus on the same footing as juniper and mix well in classic cocktails like the limey Gimlet. More idiosyncratic bottlings with unusual botanicals, like Hendrick's and Monkey 47, tend to mix better in recipes outside the classic cocktail cannon that incorporate ingredients sourced from the region they're produced in, such as my After Nine cocktail (page 386).

ON CONSISTENCY

"If you're a brand, you need to be consistent. Making new gins is relatively easy. It's easy to do something differently. What's difficult is to keep something consistently the same. You make the same gin, so when you use it in a cocktail, you know exactly what you're getting, by running the stills in the same way, by making the cut at the same place that works: particularly into the tails near the end of the run. There's no piece of equipment that's giving us advice on that other than the distiller's nose."

DESMOND PAYNE

Master Distiller

Most modern reissues of historic styles of gin are interpretive, as the character of the remaining samples has diminished a great deal after more than a century. With no clear consensus on what they should taste like today, there's plenty of room for interpretation by the bartender, who should use the creative liberty to create new recipes, like my Hans Solo (page 236), and rejigger old ones, as I have in the Last Word recipe (page 227), prescribed with navy-strength gin.

MARTINI

Origin Several recipes incorporating various proportions of dry gin, dry vermouth, and orange bitters appear around the turn of the century under many titles, making the Martini's origin difficult to pin down. Frank Newman lists a "Dry Martini" prepared with Martini dry vermouth in his 1904 French bar guide, *American Bar*, which leads me to believe the reputation of the vermouth brand had something to do with the name's sticking.

Logic Before the word *cocktail* became the umbrella term for mixed drinks a decade ago, "martini" referred to a mixed drink served up in a V-shaped glass. Over the course of the last century, the recipe has vacillated between gin and vodka mixed with varying measures of dry vermouth, served with olives, a lemon twist, or both. The words "wet" (perceptible vermouth) and "dry" (little to no vermouth) refer to the amount of vermouth the guest would like in the drink, with "dirty" called for if they'd like olive brine added. The Martini has been shaken, stirred, and poured undiluted from a freezer into a glass sprayed with vermouth by devotees of the drink over many generations, so there's a wide range of options to consider.

Given free rein, focus on pairing a gin and vermouth with complementary botanicals, and dial back the vermouth in your vodka Martini so the mouthfeel of the base spirit is perceptible. Choosing the right proportions of gin and vermouth, incorporating enough dilution through stirring, and serving it at the proper temperature (arctic) all distinguish a great Martini from a merely good one.

Hacks Most people who order Martinis make them at home or know exactly how they'd like theirs prepared, so focus your creativity elsewhere. For a nice touch, serve the drink in a smaller glass, with the balance in an iced carafe on the side and a small plate for the olives.

2.25 oz. Fords gin

0.75 oz. Dolin dry vermouth

Lemon peel

Garnish: 1 olive

Stir with ice, then strain into a chilled coupe. Twist a lemon peel over the surface and garnish with the olive.

GIN AND TONIC

Origin Quinine, an extract from cinchona bark, was taken as an antimalarial throughout the British colonies from the 1820s onward. To make it more palatable, it was incorporated into fortified wines and tonic waters that English soldiers spiked with gin. In *Straight Up or on the Rocks*, William Grimes credits Canada Dry's bottled tonic, served at the 1939 World's Fair in New York, with popularizing the drink in America.

Logic In 2004, Brian Van Flandern garnered national media attention for the cinchona bark–based syrup he developed to serve in his Gin and Tonic at Thomas Keller's new flagship Manhattan restaurant, Per Se. Brian's syrup led other bartenders down the path, including Brooks Reitz, Tom Richter, and Jennifer Colliau, who've all created commercial tonic syrups to be combined with soda or incorporated as a cordial in other cocktails. After experimenting with my own at Gramercy Tavern, I now prefer the mouthfeel of modern tonic waters like Q over compounding my own with soda water and syrup. Finding the right proportion of gin to tonic and serving them in the proper manner—either poured for the guest or served alongside the prepared glass—are key to this seemingly simple two-ingredient recipe.

Hacks Many bars, especially in Spain, stock multiple brands of tonic water for bartenders to pair with gins distilled with complementary botanicals, which are served with a variety of synergistic garnishes in bulbous wine glasses.

---

4 oz. East Imperial Burma tonic water
2 oz. Plymouth gin
Garnish: 1 lime wedge

Build in a chilled collins glass, then fill with ice. Garnish with the lime wedge.

GIMLET

Origin *To Have and Have Another* author Philip Greene credits Hemingway's go-to safari cocktail to Royal Navy surgeon Sir Thomas Gimlette, "who encouraged men at sea to mix lime juice with their gin rations, circa 1880."

Logic One need look no further than the back label of a bottle of Rose's lime cordial—which drowns lime juice from concentrate in a wash of high-fructose corn syrup, sodium metabisulfite, and FD&C Blue No. 1—to understand why the Gimlet has declined in popularity. I'd wager Lauchlin Rose's original formula, patented in 1867, was made with natural ingredients, which is why I've chosen to prepare my own in its place. Given the recipe's naval heritage, a navy-strength bottling of gin is an excellent choice to substitute in my recipe, which features a gin distilled with fresh lime peels. The first printed recipe for the Gimlet, in Harry McElhone's 1922 *ABC of Mixing Cocktails*, calls for the cocktail to be prepared with equal parts gin and lime cordial, which is way too sweet for contemporary imbibers.

Hacks The most popular hack is the addition of lime juice to balance the sweetness of the cordial, which would certainly satisfy one of Sir Gimlette's scurvy-ridden sailors, but it raises the question of whether the cocktail is then a Gimlet anymore. You're welcome to try the recipe with Rose's as it was intended, but I have a hard time stomaching the stuff.

2 oz. Tanqueray No. Ten gin
0.5 oz. lime cordial (page 393)
Garnish: 1 lime wheel

Stir with ice, then strain into a chilled coupe. Garnish with the lime wheel.

FRENCH 75

Origin The French 75 recipe that appears in Judge Jr.'s 1927 *Here's How* is a refined version of the "75" cocktail from Robert Vermeire's 1922 *Cocktails—How to Mix Them*. Vermeire's version is prepared with gin, calvados, lemon juice, and grenadine. He states, "It has been called after the famous light field gun, and was introduced by Henry of Henry's bar fame in Paris."

Logic The recipe in *Here's How* calls for the drink to be built with cracked ice in a tall glass and states that "if you use club soda instead of champagne, you have a Tom Collins." Ice cubes break up the champagne bubbles, so most bartenders serve this drink up in a coupe or a flute. Regardless of how you serve it, it's important to mind the proportions of each ingredient. If you want the gin to shine, don't just fill the glass up with champagne after you've poured the shaken ingredients into the glass. It should be served with champagne—not cheap sparkling wine—and sommelier Jordan Salcito recommends the 100 percent Pinot Noir (Blanc de Noir) Savart l'Ouverture to stand up to the citrus.

Hacks Dale DeGroff specified the French 75 with brandy in *The Craft of the Cocktail* and Plymouth gin or cognac in *The Essential Cocktail*, which opens the door for a legitimate modern version made with either. While history is on the side of gin, the house French 75 at the bar of the same name in New Orleans is made with cognac, so there's plenty of modern precedent for whichever version you prefer.

---

1 oz. Tanqueray gin

1 oz. Savart l'Ouverture champagne

0.5 oz. lemon juice

0.5 oz. simple syrup (page 391)

Garnish: None

Shake the gin, lemon juice, and simple syrup with ice, then fine-strain into a chilled fizz glass. Top with the champagne.

AVIATION

Origin This recipe's first printing is in Hugo Ensslin's 1916 *Recipes for Mixed Drinks*.

Logic The Aviation was unearthed by Paul Harrington and Laura Moorhead, who wrote about it in 1998 in *Cocktail: The Drinks Bible for the 21st Century*. The influence of this book, which was one of the first to examine the anthropological significance of cocktails, cannot be overstated during this pivotal moment in American gastronomy. Unlike popular drinks of this time, classic cocktails such as the Aviation shared philosophical and gustatory affinities with New American Cooking, which was reshaping the fine dining landscape from San Francisco to New York City. Inspired by American chefs, who were exploring new culinary traditions, bartenders began researching their history, which led them back to books like Harry Craddock's *Savoy Cocktail Book*, where Harrington's version of the Aviation (without violette) originates. Years later, David Wondrich found the first printing (with violette) in Ensslin's recipe book—one of the last published before Prohibition.

Hacks Like so many "lost" ingredients that were distributed after demand for pre-Prohibition cocktails surged, I have to credit Craddock, who published it without crème de violette: the cocktail tastes like soap if you're not judicious with the quantity. That said, the name likely obliquely references the color of the sky, so you lose that connection when you omit it.

2 oz. Tanqueray gin
0.75 oz. lemon juice
0.5 oz. Luxardo maraschino liqueur
0.25 oz. Rothman & Winter crème de violette
Garnish: None

Shake with ice, then fine-strain into a chilled coupe.

20th CENTURY

Origin Very few people would know about this recipe from W. J. Tarling's ultra-rare 1937 *Café Royal Cocktail Book* if it weren't for Ted Haigh, who gushed about it in *Vintage Spirits and Forgotten Cocktails* in 2004. Tarling chronicled cocktails from the U.K. Bartenders Guild (UKBG), including this one, attributed to C. A. Tuck. Tuck went on to publish his own recipe book, *Cocktails and Mixed Drinks*, in 1967, after seventeen years as the head bartender at London's Piccadilly Hotel.

Logic Haigh attributes the title and inspiration of the recipe to the Twentieth Century Limited train, which was widely known as "the world's greatest train." He imagined most Londoners would have seen the 1934 film *Twentieth Century* starring John Barrymore and Carole Lombard right before the actual train's locomotive was famously remodeled and christened the Commodore Vanderbilt in 1935. The publicity about the line continued pouring in when New York Central Railroad hired legendary industrial designer Henry Dreyfuss to create a new locomotive, called the J-3, to pull the Twentieth Century train. It was completed in 1938, a year after the cocktail appears in Tarling's book, but

Haigh believes the fanfare leading up to the launch fertilized the ground for Tuck's imagination. *À la* Dreyfuss, Tuck modernized his colleague Harry Craddock's Corpse Reviver #2 recipe (page 232) by substituting crème de cacao for Cointreau and doing away with the absinthe, which was banned by this time.

Hacks Bold gins like Tanqueray stand up to the crème de cacao, which should be procured from one of the better French liqueur lines, such as Brizard, Giffard, or Cartron. Dial back the crème de cacao to account for the sweetness of Kina L'Aéro d'Or if you prefer a more flavorful quinquina than Lillet.

1.5 oz. Tanqueray gin

0.75 oz. Marie Brizard crème de cacao (white)

0.75 oz. Lillet blanc

0.75 oz. lemon juice

Garnish: None

Shake with ice, then fine-strain into a chilled coupe.

LAST WORD

Origin In *Imbibe!*, David Wondrich traces this cocktail, which appears in Ted Saucier's 1951 *Bottoms Up*, back to vaudevillian Frank Fogarty's trip to the Detroit Athletic Club in 1915.

Logic Seattle bartender Murray Stenson put this on the cocktail menu at Seattle's Zig Zag Café in 2002. At that time, his bar was one of the few places in the country that stocked obscure historic liqueurs and bitters used to prepare pre-Prohibition classics from old tomes. Thanks to pioneering bloggers, including Robert Hess (drinkboy.com), Paul Clarke (cocktailchronicles.com), and Jamie Boudreau (spiritsandcocktails.com), his recipes traveled. Nicknamed "Mur the Blur" for being one of the city's fastest bartenders, Stenson, amazingly, became known for this four-ingredient cocktail requiring precise proportions to balance the bold flavors. He told me that they put the cocktail on the menu after a neighboring bar cribbed their entire list. One way to distinguish your offerings from other bars' is to stock different spirits.

Hacks Green Chartreuse, for which there is no substitute, is one of the most powerfully flavored spirits behind the bar. I'd recommend pairing it with a bold gin, such as a navy-strength bottling, or upping the gin quantity to stand out.

0.75 oz. Perry's Tot "navy-strength" gin

0.75 oz. Luxardo maraschino liqueur

0.75 oz. green Chartreuse

0.75 oz. lime juice

Garnish: None

Shake with ice, then fine-strain into a chilled coupe.

RAMOS GIN FIZZ

Origin According to *Imbibe!*, Henry Charles Ramos—known as Carl—first served the Fizz at the Imperial Cabinet Saloon in 1888, then moved his business to the Stag Saloon, across from the St. Charles Hotel, in 1907. The drink was so popular that Ramos employed more than a dozen barbacks to keep up with demand.

Logic Many guests expect you to shake this cocktail for up to twelve minutes, which popular legend stipulates is necessary to achieve its mythical ethereal texture. Bartender Don Lee, who helped style all the cocktail photos in this book, recommends separating the shaking for chilling from the shaking to create the foam. "The CO_2 from the soda water will create more than enough foam. Rather than adding the soda water at the end, which leads to a mushroom cloud–like unstructured shape, you can shape the foam by pouring the shaken cocktail over the soda in the bottom of the glass and letting it rest to allow the excess liquid to drain off the foam, which helps it settle into a more stable shape."

Hacks Before you lose track of the goal (a delicious drink) by focusing all your attention on technique, I'd address this cocktail's Achilles' heel: the orange flower water. Most commercial brands taste soapy and synthetic in comparison to the hydrosols my friend Atef Boulaabi sells at SOS Chefs in New York City.

---

2 oz. Beefeater gin

1.5 oz. club soda

0.75 oz. heavy cream

0.75 oz. simple syrup (page 391)

0.5 oz. lime juice

0.5 oz. lemon juice

5 drops orange flower water

1 egg white

Garnish: None

Pour the club soda into a chilled collins glass. Dry shake the rest of the ingredients, then shake with two 1.25-inch ice cubes until they disintegrate, then pour unstrained on top of the club soda. Let the head settle when it reaches the rim of the glass for 2 minutes or so, then slowly pour the rest through the center of the head to create a soufflé-like head of foam.

MARTINEZ

Origin The recipe appears after Manhattan Cocktail #1 and #2 in O. H. Byron's 1884 *The Modern Bartenders' Guide,* with no ingredients, just the statement: "Same as Manhattan, only you substitute gin for whiskey." It's often credited as the predecessor of the dry Martini cocktail, but Byron's annotation suggests other ancestry.

Logic As the legend of the Aviation grew in the early years of the cocktail renaissance, the scarcity of maraschino liqueur made the Martinez another grail drink. In 2006, a recipe for the Martinez was included in *The Museum of the American Cocktail Pocket Recipe Guide,* with speculation it was the Martini's precursor. In 2007, Hayman's released a historic Old Tom gin, which Eric Seed imported to the United States in 2008, thus beginning the race to re-create the Martinez. In 2009, Ransom released a barrel-aged Old Tom gin with guidance from David Wondrich; it gives bartenders a more robust gin to employ in a recipe originally formulated for whiskey.

Hacks Authentic Boker's bitters are still hard to come by, but there are reliable recipes online if you're committed to re-creating the original. If not, substitute a dash of cardamom-heavy Regan's bitters and a dash of Angostura. Some recipes call for a lemon twist, but as with a Manhattan, I prefer the roundness that orange contributes.

1.5 oz. Hayman's Old Tom gin

1.5 oz. Martini Rosso vermouth

0.25 oz. Luxardo maraschino liqueur

2 dashes Boker's bitters

Garnish: 1 orange twist

Stir with ice, then strain into a chilled coupe. Garnish with the orange twist.

CORPSE REVIVER #2

Origin This recipe's first appearance is in Harry Craddock's 1930 *The Savoy Cocktail Book.*

Logic Craddock humorously warns, "Four of these taken in swift succession will unrevive the corpse again." The unusually named recipe follows the formula for Corpse Reviver #1, which prescribes grape and apple brandy mixed with sweet vermouth, to be "taken before 11 a.m., or whenever steam or energy are needed." With no rhyme or reason linking each recipe's ingredients and proportions, we're left with the notion that a Corpse Reviver is not a family of cocktails linked by similar ingredients and preparation methods; rather, it's any drink you consume in the morning when you're hungover. Unlike many of the other recipe proportions in this nearly century-old book, this one works beautifully as written.

Hacks For a lean, bone-dry version of the drink, mix it with Lillet blanc, the modern descendant of Kina. Or stick with Tempus Fugit's Kina L'Aéro d'Or, which yields a more boldly flavored rendition of the drink, thanks to its bitter herbal profile and residual sweetness.

0.75 oz. Fords gin

0.75 oz. Cointreau

0.75 oz. Tempus Fugit Kina L'Aéro d'Or

0.75 oz. lemon juice

Vieux Pontarlier absinthe, for rinsing

Garnish: None

Shake with ice, then fine-strain into a chilled absinthe-rinsed coupe.

OLD FRIEND

Origin I created this cocktail for the fall 2012 cocktail menu at Chef's Club in Aspen, Colorado.

Logic Ephemeral ingredients and limited-edition spirits have always found their way into my recipes. As I look back at my career, I wish I had created more cocktails like this approachable gin sour! Its color, character, pour cost, name, and low proof all position it to appeal to everyone, from first-time gin drinkers to the bar's accountant, and every one of these ingredients is easy to source. A distant cousin of the whiskey-based Old Pal cocktail (with Campari as the only direct relative), this recipe brings bold flavors into agreement, forging an intimate bond with its imbiber—hence its name.

Hacks Beefeater works beautifully, but most London dry gins will mix well here too. White, yellow, and Ruby Red grapefruit all work; just be sure to monitor the acidity, as sweetness may vary depending on the variety. Luxardo, Martini, and Contratto bitters could stand in for Campari if need be. I've yet to taste an elderflower liqueur quite like St-Germain, so be sure to have a bottle on hand.

1.5 oz. Beefeater gin
0.75 oz. grapefruit juice
0.5 oz. Campari
0.25 oz. St-Germain
Garnish: 1 lemon twist

Shake with ice, then fine-strain into a chilled coupe. Garnish with the lemon twist.

WHITE LADY

Origin The gin-based White Lady appears in Harry Craddock's 1930 *The Savoy Cocktail Book*.

Logic Craddock's White Lady was prepared without egg white, as is the signature version of Bar High Five owner Hidetsugu Ueno (see page 118), who recently switched the gin in his recipe from Beefeater to Tanqueray. Harmonizing the citrus in gin (a variety of peels combined with other botanicals), Cointreau (sweet and bitter orange peels), and lemon juice is much easier with egg white, which helps smooth out the mixture by lending a pleasing texture. As early as 1946, the recipe appears with egg white in Lucius Beebe's *The Stork Club Bar Book*. Cointreau is drier than other triple secs on the market and packs a punch, at 40% ABV, so if you forgo the egg white, try adding 0.25 ounce of simple syrup to balance the acidity of the lemon juice.

2 oz. Beefeater gin

1 oz. lemon juice

0.75 oz. Cointreau

1 egg white

Garnish: None

Dry shake, then shake with ice and fine-strain into a chilled egg coupe.

Hacks Cocktails prepared with egg white tend to have a musty aroma, so a twist of lemon or orange peel over the surface is a nice touch. McElhone's White Lady, printed in his *ABC of Mixing Drinks* (1922) and *Barflies and Cocktails* (1927), contained brandy, crème de menthe, and Cointreau.

NEGRONI

Origin Barman Fosco Scarselli of Caffe Casoni in Florence served Count Camillo Negroni his first Americano with gin in place of soda sometime between 1917 and 1920, which he thereafter called his "usual."

Logic According to Luca Picchi in *Negroni Cocktail*, "Camillo chose gin, which would have substantially increased the alcohol content, without, however, changing the color and would have added a pleasant, dry, clean sensation to the drink, while enhancing it with the extraordinary and unmistakable bitter flavor of juniper." When mixing the Negroni, you must always keep the strength, sweetness, and integration of all the botanicals in mind. Serving it over ice dilutes the mixture, mitigating the sweetness and alcoholic strength of the cocktail. Choose a higher (at least 46% ABV) proof gin like Beefeater, whose orange notes complement the Campari if you serve it in equal parts.

Hacks I often mix this drink with more gin than sweet vermouth and bitters for guests who prefer strong, dry drinks and serve it straight up instead of on the rocks so I can control the dilution. Feel free to experiment with other gin, sweet vermouth, and bitter brands.

1.25 oz. Beefeater gin
1.25 oz. Campari
1.25 oz. Martini Rosso vermouth
Garnish: 1 orange twist

Stir with ice, then strain into a chilled rocks glass filled with ice. Garnish with the orange twist.

HANS SOLO

Origin I created this in the fall of 2013 upon receipt of PDT's allocation of a proprietary bottling of Hans Reisetbauer's Blue gin, aged for six years in an Austrian wine barrel.

Logic I've always been an outspoken fan of Hans Reisetbauer's spirits, which prompted him to afford me the opportunity to serve his first barrel-aged Blue gin at PDT. After tasting the cask-strength gin at different proofs, we agreed on the ideal strength (52% ABV), and he bottled it with my name on the bottle. To pay tribute to his gesture, I created a singular serve whose title alludes to a more famous Han. Using the Prince of Wales cocktail as my template (cognac, champagne, madeira, curaçao, and bitters), I came up with this riff—not knowing that Jean-Marc Roulot and Hans are good friends.

Hacks Hans has barreled more gin, and he will release it in due time. Other than the madeira, which can always be older, and the cuvée of champagne, which you're welcome to splurge on, this one's meant to be a mixture of two—or three, if you count Roulot—good friends' finest offerings.

1 oz. Reisetbauer barrel-aged blue gin

1 oz. Robert Moncuit Grand Cru brut champagne

0.75 oz. Blandy's 5-year Sercial madeira

0.25 oz. Domaine Roulot L'Abricot du Roulot liqueur

1 dash Tempus Fugit Abbott's bitters

Garnish: None

Stir the gin, madeira, liqueur, and bitters with ice, then strain into a chilled coupe. Top with the champagne.

HANKY PANKY

Origin Ada Coleman, the Savoy Hotel's head bartender from 1903 to 1926, created this cocktail for actor Charles Hawtrey, who exclaimed, "By Jove! That is the real hanky panky" when she served it to him.

Logic The original recipe in *The Savoy Cocktail Book* prescribes equal parts dry gin and Italian vermouth with just a couple of dashes of Fernet-Branca, and for the cocktail to be shaken instead of stirred. I've rejiggered this recipe with 0.5 ounce more gin and upped the Fernet-Branca quantity so it functions more like Campari in a Negroni instead of Angostura bitters in a Manhattan. The recipe is a little too rich when mixed with a sweet vermouth like Carpano Antica Formula, so I've opted for Cocchi's vermouth di Torino.

Hacks There are countless combinations of gins, sweet vermouths, and fernets that can be used in place of the brands I've chosen. The original proportions are more appropriate as an aperitif, and the fernet could be upped even more if this were requested as a digestif.

2 oz. Tanqueray gin

1.5 oz. Cocchi vermouth di Torino

0.25 oz. Fernet-Branca

Garnish: 1 orange twist

Stir with ice, then strain into a chilled coupe. Garnish with the orange twist.

RUM AND CACHAÇA

Rum is a by-product of sugar production: it is distilled from sugarcane syrup or molasses in nearly every tropical and subtropical cane-growing country in the world. In Brazil and the French departments (territories) in the Caribbean, such as Martinique, fresh sugarcane (as opposed to the syrup) is pressed to produce cachaça and rhum agricole. Rum is one of the most diverse categories of spirits: it can be clear, amber-hued, or black, and its flavor spectrum ranges from nearly neutral to heady, high-proof drams.

Unlike many spirits, the color of a rum tells you very little about its age, as caramel coloring is often added to young "gold" rums as well as mature rums that rely on it to maintain a consistent appearance from batch to batch. Dark rums are colored (and sweetened) with molasses, whose inky color and bold character obscure age. Ironically, most white rums are barrel-aged to add body and character, then filtered with active charcoal to remove the color.

The history of rum is inextricably tied to the slave trade. When early European explorers like Columbus failed to find a shortcut to the Far East, they quickly switched their sights to plundering minerals and other natural resources in the West Indies and Brazil. There, the rich volcanic soil was perfect for growing sugarcane—the oil of its age. Boats carrying Africans enslaved by ruthless merchants would sail to the West Indies, exchange the slaves for molasses, and then sail to America to trade for rum, which they'd bring back to Europe to trade for more slaves.

This hideous exchange became known as the Triangle Trade. The Spanish, Dutch, Portuguese, French, and English were all guilty of perpetuating the crime for over three hundred years until the war of 1812, when the English began emancipating their slaves. Sadly, the legacy of slavery persists today in poor cane-growing countries, where producers perpetuate its effects through low wages and deplorable working conditions for workers. One can't cover rum's history without acknowledging the legacy of human slavery—a stain that will never come out.

Bundaberg Molasses Well

Commercial molasses-based rum production in the West Indies originated in Barbados towards the end of the seventeenth century. The early, crudely produced rums were unremarkable tastewise, but in the following century, numerous tracts were published by planters to spread information about production practices to improve its character.

Jamaican planters were the first to distinguish their rums from the rest of the English colonies by mastering the art of long fermentations with dunder reserved from the still after distillation. This practice produced fruity esters in funky, sulfurous rums prized for their "hogo"; an Anglicization of the French *haut goût*—the "high taste" of meat hung to dry-age before roasting.

In 1687, the English Royal Navy began issuing each crew member half a pint of this type of rum daily in place of beer, which spoiled over the course of the long hot journeys aboard the ship. Despite being served at 58% ABV—"navy-strength"—the sailors consumed their ration uncut until 1740, when Admiral Edward Vernon ordered it to be diluted and served with sugar and lime juice on the side to combat scurvy. Vernon habitually wore a rugged grogram cloak, earning him the affectionate nicknames "Old Grogram" or "Old Grog,"

"My uncle was the first one to tell me that your job was not just for us, it's for all of the producers of Martinique as well. He said, 'You will be successful if you make Martinique rhum the cognac of the Caribbean. This will work only if you put Martinique on the map; it will stay on the map only if Martinique rhums succeed, because we have nothing else.'"

BEN JONES

Brand Director

and the sailors applied the name to Vernon's mixture, grog, one of the earliest rum cocktails on record.

Rhum Agricole

In the early nineteenth century, when France switched to government-subsidized sugar beet sugar during the Napoleonic wars, cane sugar prices collapsed. This left many smaller sugar producers in Martinique (and elsewhere) with no market for their sugar, and less molasses to make industrial rum. This led growers to produce rum directly from sugarcane, as Rhum JM founder Jean-Marie Martin began doing in 1845.

Sugarcane Harvest

In 1996, rhum agricole from Martinique achieved *appellation d'origine contrôlée* (AOC) ("appellation of controlled origin"), a French certification granted to certain French agricultural products from specified geographical locations.

AOC rhum agricole is produced from sugarcane grown in one of twenty-three designated municipalities on Martinique from fresh-pressed juice with no syrup or molasses added. It must be column distilled between 65% and 75% ABV and bottled no lower than 40% ABV. Unaged rhum blanc rests for three months before bottling, straw-colored rhum paille matures in oak barrels for no less than a year, and rhum vieux ages for a minimum of three years in barrels no larger than 650 liters.

Rhum agricole is unusual in the world of spirits because it is one of the few categories that is capable of expressing terroir: the different volcanic soils and oceanic microclimates create flavors that really shine through in certain bottlings. The fiery (typically 50% to 55% ABV) rhum blanc is a taste worth acquiring: ideally through the island's signature Ti' Punch, which agricole importer Ed Hamilton taught me how to make in 2005. After visiting the island with Benjamin Jones of Rhum Clement, I learned that it was okay to make the cocktail with older rhums, and I have never looked back.

Ron: The Rum of Cuba

By the mid-nineteenth century, there were over a thousand distilleries on the island of Cuba. As relative latecomers to the industry, Cubans had access to production technology that wasn't available when other islands entered the market. Consequently, Cuba is known for its column-distilled, more modern style of rum.

Prior to the nineteenth century, Cuba exported most of its molasses to be made into rum elsewhere (particularly to distilleries in New England). But when the Spanish government realized the profit that could be made by distilling it, they offered a grant to develop new technology to improve Cuban rum.

Cruzan Colum Still

The most famous innovator was a Catalan immigrant named Facundo Bacardí Massó who took over a distillery in Santiago de Cuba in 1862. He began using a quick-fermenting yeast to yield a light rum that he filtered through charcoal, as vodka producers had been doing since the end of the eighteenth century. In addition to popularizing charcoal filtration of rum, Cubans aged rum in American white oak barrels, which improved the character of the rum even further.

Cuban rum took off during Prohibition, when American tourists fell in love with cocktails such as the Daiquiri (page 262), Mojito (page 249), and El Presidente (page 261). Today, the Cuban style made famous by Bacardi yields light, white rums that gain texture through aging before they're filtered of their color, as well as rich, barrel-aged rums with brandy-like qualities.

"Terroir is hard to describe, but it's clear in my mind. It's geology, climate, and know-how. You cannot rule out know-how in terroir. You don't just go back to nature and purity; what about the producer? Art is the product of humans. That's humans interacting with their environment. Terroir is a human thing. It's not only the rain and the subsoil: it's what you do with that. If you think it's just the soil, then you drink a piece of chalk."

ALEXANDRE GABRIEL

Master Blender

The Future of Rum

Today, many brands throughout the Caribbean are discontinuing their flavored rum lines and lowering their added sugar content in favor of premium rums that showcase each island's rum-making heritage. With talk of new production standards—including more universally recognized labeling laws, which give consumers more information about where their rum comes from and how it's made—the category is poised for progress in the years ahead.

Cachaça

There are accounts of sugarcane distilling in Brazil from as early as the 1500s, a century before records of rum in the Caribbean. Cachaça, literally "burning water," is produced in Brazil, which is the world's largest sugarcane grower.

While production is concentrated in the hands of a few large companies who make fiery unaged "industrial" cachaça from molasses, thousands of small producers make "artisanal" cachaça from fresh-cut sugarcane. By law, these cachaças must be distilled no higher than 54% ABV—typically in copper alembics—and bottled between 38% and 48% ABV to ensure they retain the aroma and character of the sugarcane. Any bottling that contains more than six grams of sugar per liter must be labeled "sweetened cachaça."

Artisanal cachaça is typically rested in neutral casks or stainless steel tanks, which impart no color, and labeled *classica*, *tradicional*, or *prata*. Cachaças matured in wood barrels, which gain color and character from the wood, are labeled *ouro*, *envelhecida*, or *premium* if aged for a year in barrels no larger than 700 liters, and *extra-premium* after three years. Former bourbon barrels and cognac casks are used, but many producers use a variety of native Brazilian woods that (unfortunately) bars them from being imported to the United States.

Most guests' first encounter with cachaça is in a Caipirinha (page 255) made with a pungent, hangover-inducing industrial bottling. The second most likely application, the Batida, is typically blended with sweetened condensed milk and fresh tropical fruit. Cachaça ("ka-sha-sa"), Caipirinha ("kai-peer-een-ya"), and Batida ("ba-chee-da") are nearly always mispronounced on the first attempt by English-speaking customers, which bartenders should anticipate and offer preemptive prompts and apologetic corrections.

GREEN TEA PUNCH

Origin I created this to ladle out at Banks Rum's stand at Bar Convent Berlin in the fall of 2010.

Logic David Wondrich's book *Punch*, published the month I created this recipe, popularized punch at large mixology events where preparing individual portions *à la minute* was nearly impossible. Classic punches comprise five ingredients: spirit, sugar, citrus, spice, and a more substantial portion of a liquid such as tea or wine. In this punch, the grassy sencha tea reinforces the herbal notes in the rum, while the mint brightens everything up. Dave makes the best punches I've ever tasted, and one of the hallmarks of his preparation is dilution: they go down like lemonade instead of a classic sour, which ensures the bowl's role as a hive of social activity at his parties.

Hacks If you don't have an elegant punch bowl with cups and a nice big (ideally clear) block of ice to keep the liquid cold, you could serve it from a pitcher. Make sure you pull the ice block out of the freezer 45 minutes before service to ensure it tempers; otherwise, it will fissure when you submerge it in the punch. I garnish each serving with freshly ground nutmeg if I'm ladling it out myself.

MAKES 80 OZ.

25.5 oz. Banks 5-Island rum

11 oz. brewed sencha tea (4 g. tea brewed with 12 oz. water for 5 minutes and then strained)

11 oz. brewed mint tisane (3 g. leaves brewed with 12 oz. water for 1.5 minutes and then strained)

8 oz. lime juice

1 cup (220 g.) evaporated cane sugar

Garnish: Grated nutmeg

Combine the brewed teas and stir in the sugar until it dissolves. Add 4 cups of pebble ice to chill the mixture. Add the rum and lime juice. Chill the mixture before service then serve in a punch bowl over one large block of ice. Ladle into small cups filled with ice and garnish with nutmeg.

MOJITO

Origin The Mojito appears as the "Rum Mojo" in a rare 1929 Cuban bar guide by Juan A. Lasa called *Libro de Cocktail* and a decade later in Charles H. Baker's *The Gentleman's Companion* as "Sloppy Joe's Mojito," prepared with Bacardi Oro rum and served with a spiral lime peel.

Logic The cocktail returned to prominence in 2002, when Pierce Brosnan (playing James Bond) encountered Halle Berry (playing Jinx) for the first time in *Die Another Day*; he offered her a sip of his Mojito after she emerged from the Cuban surf. Most American bartenders, having never been to Havana and without access to instructional videos in the early days of the Internet, had no idea how to prepare the drink properly, let alone use the proper tools and ingredients. To this day, you'll see untrained bartenders mutilate the mint in the bottom of a glass like they're churning butter, along with half a dozen other mixological indiscretions that led to the drink's falling from favor as fast as it rose. Avoid the pomp and circumstance reserved for relatives like the Mint Julep; shake the mint leaves with the rum, lime, and simple syrup and fine-strain the leaves so they don't muddy up the cocktail's appearance.

Hacks The Cubans bruise the entire mint sprig (gently with a large muddler) with granulated sugar and lime juice in the bottom of a collins glass, then build the rest of the ingredients on top of it. I prefer the clean appearance and streamlined preparation of my recipe, but I respect the tradition. Gold rum, as Baker's recipe calls for, is a nice touch.

---

2 oz. Caña Brava 3-year-old rum

1 oz. club soda

1 oz. simple syrup (page 391)

0.75 oz. lime juice

8 mint leaves (plus 1 mint sprig for garnish)

Muddle the mint and simple syrup, then add the rum and lime juice. Shake and fine-strain into a chilled collins glass filled with ice. Top with the club soda. Garnish with the mint sprig.

HEMINGWAY DAIQUIRI

Origin Constantino Ribalaigua published his Daiquiri #4 as the "E. Hemiway Special" in the 1937 edition of La Florida's house cocktail book. According to Philip Greene, who wrote a whole book on Hemingway's favorite cocktails, by 1947 the drink had doubled in size, gotten more grapefruit juice, and become known as the Papa Doble.

Logic Bartenders like Ribalaigua used the blender like an artist's paintbrush after they mastered the art of chilling, diluting, and aerating a drink with the innovative new machine. In *Islands in the Stream*, Hemingway describes Daiquiris "that had no taste of alcohol and felt, as you drank them, the way downhill glacier skiing feels running through powder snow . . ." You'll need to consider the sweetness of the grapefruit juice (based on the type you use), as the maraschino must balance the acidity without overwhelming the rum's character. Use crushed or pebble ice for blender drinks, and measure the quantity of ice you're adding per drink by using measured scoops or a blender cup with measurements on the side.

Hacks I also serve this shaken, using 2 ounces rum, 0.75 ounce lime juice, 0.5 ounce maraschino liqueur, and 0.5 ounce grapefruit juice. Before the drink became known as Hemingway's Daiquiri, Ribalaigua called this his Daiquiri #4, which he served with 0.25 ounce of simple syrup. If this recipe is too dry for you, add the simple syrup and call for it accordingly.

3.5 oz. Bacardi Heritage white rum

2 oz. grapefruit juice

1.5 oz. Luxardo maraschino liqueur

1 oz. lime juice

28 oz. by volume pebble ice

Garnish: 1 lime wheel

Build in a blender cup and blend until smooth. Pour into a chilled coupe. Garnish with the lime wheel.

GREEN THUMB

Origin I created this cocktail in the spring of 2013 for a PDT pop up at the Park Hyatt New York Bar in Tokyo.

Logic Whenever PDT popped up in other countries, I worked with my team to create new cocktails that showcased the fruits, vegetables, spices, wines, and spirits of our host nation, as we do for the menu in New York City, which features ingredients from all over the northeastern United States. Thankfully, PDT is only a few blocks away from an amazing Japanese grocery store called Sunrise Mart, where Jeff Bell, John deBary, and I sourced almost all the traditional ingredients we needed to create a Tokyo-style PDT cocktail menu. For this recipe, matcha tea's grassy quality reinforces the earthiness of the rum and celery. St-Germain adds brightness, while the cucumber functions as an aromatic garnish—the peel is bitter and vegetal, while the meat is melony and aromatic. The name parallels the challenge of mixing all the green ingredients into harmony with the talents of a green-thumbed gardener.

Hacks Most Cuban-style white rums will work well in this recipe, which was originally served with Brugal Especial Extra Dry. If you don't have an extractor to juice the celery, you could muddle a 3-inch rib, but it will require some elbow grease. Be sure to measure the matcha with a measuring spoon, as a little goes a long way.

2 oz. Caña Brava 3-year-old rum

0.5 oz. lime juice

0.25 oz. St-Germain

0.25 oz. celery juice

0.25 oz. simple syrup (page 391)

$1/8$ tsp matcha tea powder

1 cucumber wheel (plus 1 for garnish)

Muddle the cucumber wheel and syrup, then add everything else. Dry shake to incorporate the tea, then shake with ice and fine-strain into a chilled coupe. Garnish with the second cucumber wheel.

CAIPIRINHA

Origin The Portuguese word *caipirinha* translates as "little peasant girl" and has been traced back to 1856 by cachaça expert Felipe Jannuzzi. He found a reference to the recipe uncovered by a historian in a document written by civil engineers during a cholera epidemic in the cachaça production region of Paraty.

Logic According to Portland bartender Andrew Bohrer, the defining characteristic of a traditional Brazilian Caipirinha is that it must be prepared in the glass. He clarifies that when he's in Brazil, he prefers it prepared in the glass, but at home, he's come to expect the drink to be shaken and poured unstrained after muddling. It's a little more complex than the debate over whether to prepare an Old-Fashioned with a sugar cube or syrup, because shaking helps integrate the sugar, which is vital for extracting the oil from the lime peel, but the side effects are aeration and dilution. Instead of assuming how the guest would prefer it to be prepared, give them their options. Industrial cachaça is permitted, but Jannuzzi (and I) prefer unaged artisanal cachaça or bottlings aged in neutral Brazilian woods. Serve it with a metal straw or swizzle for the guest to muddle the limes and stir.

Hacks If you prepare the Caipirinha with vodka in place of cachaça, it's called a Caipiroska. The rum-based version is called a Caipirissima. If you substitute other herbs or fruits for Persian lime, it's called a Caipifruta. Many bartenders prepare the recipe with simple syrup in place of superfine sugar to ensure that all the sugar dissolves, which is logical but deviates from the spirit of the drink.

---

2 oz. Leblon cachaça

1 Persian (also know as Tahiti) lime

2 barspoons (1 tsp.) superfine sugar

Garnish: None

Slice the ends off the Persian lime and halve from end to end. Slice away the pith from the central column, then quarter each half. Add the lime to a rocks glass with the peels facing the bottom of the glass, then add the sugar. Gently muddle to extract the oil from the peel and juice from the meat. Add the cachaça and ice, then stir to integrate the mixture.

PIÑA COLADA

Origin In *Potions of the Caribbean*, tiki archeologist Jeff Berry traces this recipe back to 1954, when Caribe Hilton bar manager Ricardo Garcia substituted the newly available Coco Lopez for house-made coconut cream in their legendary welcome cocktail, which became known as the Piña Colada.

Logic An expertly prepared blended drink is the cocktail world's equivalent of a great pastry chef's ice cream, whose texture is as remarkable as its flavor. Mastering the physics and thermodynamics of the blended drink requires the same attention to detail as the shaking or stirring that only transforms the liquid in a cocktail. To achieve the proper dilution, chill, and texture, ice must be measured like an ingredient, as adding too little yields an improperly balanced slushy consistency and adding too much leads to a frosty, sorbet-like mixture better served with a spoon. You'll never achieve this texture with full-size ice cubes, so add crushed or pebble ice to the whirring blender until it produces what Jeff Morgenthaler calls "a central vortex, with distinct curves of drink flowing into it, almost like pillows of drink folding into each other" in *The Bar Book*.

Hacks Most Piña Coladas are prepared with canned pineapple juice and Coco Lopez coconut cream, which looks and tastes like suntan lotion. Many would wield my Bloody Mary logic (supporting commercial mixers) against me here, but the only way I'll take this drink is with handmade coconut cream or sorbet and fresh pineapple juice. A more flavorful rum doesn't improve the drink.

---

4 oz. Bacardi Heritage white rum

3 oz. pineapple juice

3 oz. coconut sorbet

1 oz. lime juice

18 oz. by volume pebble ice

Garnish: 1 pineapple leaf

Build in a blender cup and blend until smooth. Pour into a chilled hurricane glass. Garnish with the pineapple leaf.

TI' PUNCH

Origin In *Potions of the Caribbean*, Jeff Berry traces the first mention of "yon Ti' Punch" in English back to travel writer Lafcadio Hearn's 1890 account of his time in Martinique, *Two Years in the West Indies*.

Logic Rum importer Ed Hamilton popularized this recipe in New York City by enticing bars to serve it with authentic swizzle sticks—*le boi lélé*—that he hand-carried between flights to and from the island. The *ti* is the Creole contraction of the French "petit"—as in a small punch—which most locals drink with the grassy 100-proof white rhum. The key point that differentiates Ed's Ti' Punch from any other cocktail I know of is the lime "cheek": a disk of lime cut with equal parts peel and flesh, that you squeeze into the glass to express the oil and juice before adding the other ingredients. As for technique, there's no need to thrash the mixture with the swizzle stick; a slow and steady swirling motion is all that's needed to chill and integrate the mixture.

Hacks In 2008, I visited Martinique, and when I ordered my first Ti' Punch I was served a room-temperature glass of agricole rhum on a saucer with half a lime wheel, a packet of sugar, and an espresso spoon to stir them together. The experience—like many others over my travels—reinforces that the origin of a great recipe should be respected, but the execution may be improved by bartenders elsewhere. I suggest serving it with Neisson's Réserve Spéciale in place of the higher-octane traditional rhum blanc.

---

2 oz. Neisson Réserve Spéciale rhum agricole

1 barspoon (½ tsp.) Petite Canne sugarcane syrup

1 lime disk (silver dollar–size twist cut straight off the side of a lime to retain flesh with the peel)

Garnish: None

Squeeze the lime disk on both sides (to express the oil from the peel and juice from the flesh) into a chilled rocks glass, then add to the glass. Add remaining ingredients and top with pebble ice. Swizzle, then top with more pebble ice and swizzle again.

EL PRESIDENTE

Origin Fernando Castellon discovered the first printing of the recipe in John B. Escalante's 1915 *Manuel del Cantinero*, in Cuba's Biblioteca Nacional. In *Imbibe!*, David Wondrich attributes the recipe (once thought to be American Eddie Woelke's) to Constantino Ribalaigua of Bar La Florida in Cuba, who claimed authorship in an interview in 1937.

Logic Constantino's recipe omits the bitters and grenadine, which have become standard, and calls for equal measures of vermouth and rum, which yields the rum canon's equivalent of a Fitty-Fitty Martini. A few years back, Wondrich discovered that the French vermouth being mixed in Cuba at this time was the sweeter Chambéry style; if you were previously preparing this drink with dry vermouth, you'll find that the blanc formula will elevate this recipe to new heights. Even if you mix the drink with white rum, as the original recipe calls for, the barspoon of grenadine will have little effect on the cocktail's final hue. Given that Cuban-style white rums are traditionally aged and charcoal filtered of their color, I've taken the liberty of recommending an aged rum for this recipe.

Hacks At equal parts vermouth and rum, this is an incredibly quaffable stirred drink, but there's room to ratchet it up a notch by upping the rum to 2 ounces and paring back the vermouth to 1 ounce. Cuban rum is still hard to come by in the United States, so substitute Bacardi 8 for the Havana Club in my recipe, or for Constantino's version, go with a flavorful white rum like Banks 5-Island and omit the bitters and grenadine.

1.5 oz. Havana Club Añejo 7 Años rum
1.5 oz. Alessio vermouth bianco
0.25 oz. Pierre Ferrand dry curaçao
1 barspoon (½ tsp.) Jack Rudy grenadine
1 dash Angostura bitters
Garnish: 1 orange twist

Stir with ice, then strain into a chilled coupe. Garnish with the orange twist.

DAIQUIRI

Origin The earliest printed recipe appears in Jacques Straub's 1914 recipe guide *Drinks*, although the combination of rum, lime, and sugar came long before Western bar guides began documenting these formulae.

Logic Sadly, nowadays most Daiquiris are served from huge alcoholic slush dispensers, so the first order of business is to clarify which "Daiquiri" is being requested. It's seemingly straightforward, yet every guest has his or her own rum preference and palate. The ABV, character, and sweetness (in some cases) of the rum require different quantities of lime, which may vary in acidity if you juice each lime to order, and sugar, which varies in molasses content. Rich syrups prepared from unrefined sugars such as Demerara add perceptible flavor and viscosity when mixed with a higher ratio of sugar to water, but require a longer shake to achieve proper dilution.

Hacks Many prefer to shake with a bar-spoon of superfine sugar instead of syrup, which adds an extra level of complication (dissolving all the sugar) to one of the canon's most nuanced recipes. During its heyday, the Daiquiri was prepared in a blender, which requires entirely different ratios of each ingredient to balance.

2 oz. Bacardi Heritage white rum
0.75 oz. lime juice
0.75 oz. simple syrup (page 391)
Garnish: 1 lime wheel

Shake with ice, then fine-strain into a chilled coupe. Garnish with the lime wheel.

FIVE ISLAND FLAMINGO

Origin I created this recipe for Banks 5-Island white rum in the summer of 2010.

Logic One of my primary responsibilities as the first bartender ambassador for Banks rum was to create memorable, easy-to-prepare cocktails to help promote it to consumers in bars. Using iconic highballs paired with emerging mixers that drove sales and built awareness for the brands that marketed them—such as the Cuba Libre (Coca-Cola and Bacardi) and Moscow Mule (Cock 'n Bull ginger beer and Smirnoff)—for inspiration, I chose Ting pink grapefruit soda from Jamaica to pair with the 5-Island rum, which has a prominent Jamaican rum component in the blend. I dubbed it the Flamingo for its pink hue and flung it from the nest in hopes it would fly.

Hacks The success of the aforementioned highballs had a lot to do with the popularity of the mixers, which depend on good distribution. While the rum has spread its wings all over the world, Ting remains tough to find, so you'll probably have to use another brand of pink grapefruit soda to prepare this recipe.

3 oz. Ting pink grapefruit soda
2 oz. Banks 5-Island white rum
0.75 oz. lime juice
Garnish: 1 lime wedge

Build in a chilled collins glass, then fill with ice. Garnish with the lime wedge.

MAI TAI

Origin When Trader Vic served this for friends visiting from Tahiti in 1944, they took a sip and declared it *"Maita'i roe a'e"* ("out of this world—the best" in Tahitian).

Logic His guests' characterization of the creation should come as no surprise, as Vic's original recipe was prepared with seventeen-year-old Wray & Nephew rum as the base spirit, which must have been divine. After supplies of the rum dwindled to a point where he could no longer list it on the menu, Vic developed a rum blend to mimic its flavor, using younger Jamaican and Martinique rums.

Hacks In his book, Cate likens the dome-shaped shell of the lime squeezed to prepare the drink alongside the mint sprig to "a little tropical island with a palm tree on it." My version, sans the shell, relies on orgeat prepared from blanched almonds—instead of almond flavor—to achieve the desired "nutty and snappy" flavor Vic was looking for when he sought a replacement for old Wray & Nephew.

1 oz. Clément Premiére Canne rhum

1 oz. Appleton Estate Reserve rum

0.75 oz. lime juice

0.75 oz. Small Hand Foods orgeat

0.5 oz. Pierre Ferrand dry curaçao

Garnish: 1 mint sprig

Shake with ice, then strain into a chilled rocks glass filled with pebble ice. Garnish with the mint sprig.

AIRMAIL

Origin David Wondrich reintroduced this recipe in his first cocktail book, *Esquire Drinks*, in 2002. The original appears in a Bacardi rum pamphlet from the 1930s titled "Bacardi and Its Many Uses."

Logic The cocktail reappears in W. C. Whitfield's *Here's How* in 1941, approximately thirty years after the first commercial deliveries of mail via airplanes commenced on a small scale worldwide. This regal rum-based collins is a delivery vehicle itself, composed of rum from Cuba, champagne from France, and lime from the tropics. The transportive quality of cocktails like this one remains one of their most enduring attributes. Be wary of the style of champagne you mix with, as off-dry bottlings contribute considerable sweetness to balance with the rest of the recipe.

Hacks Choosing a wildflower honey that complements the rum is a nice touch. The original recipe calls for it to be prepared with Bacardi Gold rum in a highball glass filled with ice, no garnish. Follow this formula if there's no occasion to dress it up.

1.5 oz. Bollinger brut champagne NV

1 oz. Bacardi 8-year rum

0.5 oz. lime juice

0.5 oz. honey syrup (page 392)

Garnish: None

Shake the rum, juice, and syrup with ice, then fine-strain into a chilled goblet. Top with the champagne.

EAST INDIA NEGRONI

Origin I created this rum-based riff on the Negroni in the fall of 2009.

Logic Rum typically stars in Cuban and Tiki cocktails, so I chose the Negroni as my inspiration to open bartenders' minds to rum's versatility. East India sherry is a blend of oloroso and Pedro Ximénez sherries that are aged in a hot, humid bodega in a special solera that mimics the conditions the wine would have undergone during transatlantic journeys of the eighteenth century. Cook's ship would have stocked sherries like this one, which stands in for sweet vermouth quite admirably.

Hacks Its title makes East India sherry the key ingredient here. If you're going to sub the rum, I'd choose an English-style rum with some barrel age, such as Appleton Reserve or Mount Gay Black Barrel. Martini, Luxardo, and Contratto bitters mix well, but you'll have an easier time sourcing Campari.

2 oz. Banks 5-Island rum

0.75 oz. Lustau East India Solera sherry

0.75 oz. Campari

Garnish: 1 orange twist

Stir with ice, then strain into a chilled rocks glass filled with one large ice cube. Garnish with the orange twist.

PLÁTANOS EN MOLE OLD-FASHIONED

Origin This cocktail was inspired by a dessert I was served in Guatemala during a trip to tour Zacapa's rum production facilities. I created it to serve at the StarChefs.com International Chefs Congress in the summer of 2010.

Logic I always pay close attention to flavor combinations when I dine out, even more so when I'm abroad. Chefs and sommeliers use the phrase "If it grows with it, it goes with it": for centuries, pairings like Muscadet and oysters, Barolo and wild boar, or sherry and Jamón Ibérico have had a cultural and historical connection beyond the table. For this reason, I dine at restaurants that feature traditional cuisine to discover new flavors, and see how they pair with spirits. In this case, the earthy chocolate-and-cinnamon-spiced mole bitters was a revelation with Zacapa's rum.

Hacks This band is tough to break up. I'd choose a rich rum if I were going to switch anything, and retain Bittermens' Xocolatl mole bitters. I source the chile (the same used for the Mezcal Mule) at Zaragoza, a local Mexican specialty store in the East Village.

2 oz. Zacapa 23 rum

0.25 oz. Giffard Banane du Bresil

12 drops (⅛ tsp.) Bittermens Xocolatl mole bitters

Garnish: Pinch of ground chile

Stir with ice, then strain over one large ice sphere into a chilled rocks glass. Garnish with the chile.

UNITED STATES

MEXICO

Gulf
of
Mexico

Arandas

Tequila

Amatitán
Guadalajara

Atotonilco el Alto

Santiago Matatlan

Mexico City

Santa Catarina Minas

San Luis del Río

Pacific
Ocean

BELIZE

GUATEMALA

HONDURAS

NICARAGUA

MEXICO

⦿ **Amatitán**
(Partida tequila)

⦿ **Arandas**
(El Tesoro tequila)
(Siembra Azul tequila)
(L&J tequila)

⦿ **Atotonilco el Alto**
(Siete Leguas Tequila)

⦿ **Santiago Matatlan**
(Sombra mezcal)

⦿ **Tequila**
(Casa Dragones tequila)

⦿ **Santa Catarina Minas**
(Del Maguey Minero mezcal)

⦿ **San Luis del Río**
(Del Maguey Vida mezcal)

Traditional Production Region   ⦿ Distillery Site   ★ Capital

TEQUILA AND MEZCAL

Agave, from the Greek word for "royalty," *agavacea*, refers to a family of succulents of which the most famous—*Agave tequilana* Weber var. *azul*—is the sole variety used to make tequila. Tequila is named after a small town in the state of Jalisco that was known for its mezcal in the late eighteenth century. Tequila is to mezcal what cognac is to brandy: the most famous appellation-regulated agave spirit, which is only permitted to be distilled in the states of Jalisco, Guanajuato, Tamaulipas, Nayarit, and Michoacan.

While mezcal, from the Náhuatl word *mexcalmetl* for "cooked agave," refers to the entire agave spirits category, it's typically reserved for the agave spirits produced in Oaxaca and eight other Mexican states recognized by the Denominación de Origen, including Guerrero, Durango, San Luis Potosí, Zacatecas, Guanajuato, Michoacan, Tamaulipas, and Puebla. Unlike tequila, it's made from over thirty varieties of agave, including but not limited to Espadin, Barril, Cupreata, Arroqueño, Papalome, Tepeztate, Tobaziche, and Tobala, which can be processed individually or together in a blend.

Other agave-based spirits from Mexico include bacanora, raicilla, sotol, tuxca, and comiteco, which are exported to the United States in only limited quantities. Most countries with appellation of origin laws recognize Mexico's Denominación de Origen for agave spirits, but the United States— its largest export market—does not. The lack of protection promotes rather than discourages counterfeiting in the United States and forces producers who ship mixto tequila (a best-selling style, 51 percent agave sugar and 49 percent from other sources such as molasses, with added caramel) to rely on faith instead of laws to prevent adulteration.

According to Lucinda Hutson's *Viva Tequila*, archeological work from historians like Miguel Claudio Jimenez Vizcarra suggest that agave spirits were being made just outside of Tequila, in volcanic terraces in the town of Amatitan, using clay pot stills, which geographer Henry J. Bruman posits could have been brought by Filipino sailors before the Spanish. This technology is still being used to produce agave-based spirits in parts of central and southern Mexico where communities were geographically isolated from the Spanish.

The Spanish brought their distillation technology with them when Cortez landed in 1519. Before then, the Aztecs drank an agave-based beverage called pulque, produced by fermenting aguamiel (agave sap), extracted from six different species of agave that aren't used to make tequila or mezcal. The sour, viscous liquid is not fit for distillation, and it nearly disappeared when beer was introduced as an alternative in the early twentieth century.

The first commercial license to distill in the town of Tequila in Jalisco was granted in 1795 to José Maria Guadalupe de Cuervo, whose descendants have built the brand into the king of the category. In 1858, a farmer named Don Cenobio Sauza moved to Tequila and began working with the Cuervos before acquiring his own distillery in 1873. In addition to becoming the first distiller to export mezcal to the United States, Sauza was among the first credited with extolling the virtues of blue Weber agave in tequila.

According to David Wondrich's research, Sauza won a gold medal at the 1893 World's Columbian Exposition in Chicago for their "mezcal brandy" and another at the 1910 San Antonio International Fair, but neither had much effect on American consumers until Prohibition, when many would settle for whatever they could get their hands on. Sauza began labeling their tequila "Mexican Whiskey—Positively Old" to appeal to their whiskey-deprived neighbors to the north.

Among those flocking south of the border for legal alcohol were Hollywood celebs, who made the Tequila Sunrise—a signature cocktail of Tijuana's famed Agua Caliente racetrack and resort—America's first popular tequila drink. Finishing a close second was the tequila daisy, which is what bartenders of the 1930s would have called a tequila sour sweetened with grenadine or orange curaçao. The Spanish word for "daisy" happens to be *margarita*, and that was the name that eventually stuck in bars all over America.

Despite the popularity of the Tequila Sunrise and Margarita, tequila appeared in very few important cocktail books until the 1937 *Café Royal*

Cocktail Book, published in London, which contains ten tequila recipes, including a tequila daisy dubbed the Picador. The first major cocktail book to carve out a full chapter for tequila drinks was the 1972 revised edition of *Trader Vic's Bartender's Guide*, which placed tequila ahead of vodka as the frontier spirit of mixology for the time.

In 1949, the first Mexican standard of identity for tequila stated that the spirit had to be made from 100 percent blue Weber agave grown in Jalisco. A series of agave shortages, stemming from blight and poor planning, prompted producers to decrease the amount to 70 percent by the mid-1960s. In 1970, just four years before the appellation of origin went into effect, they lowered the minimum to 51 percent; the rest could be blended with spirits distilled from "other sugars" such as sugarcane or corn.

The resulting mixto tequila was the only type you could find in American bars—unless you count bootlegged Herradura, which was a favorite among Hollywood actors like Bing Crosby—until the 1980s, when Bob Denton and Marilyn Smith, who'd worked in various roles throughout the spirits industry, discovered Caliente blanco tequila at the Tijuana racetrack. They were so enamored with the tequila, they flew to Tamaulipas to meet with distiller Guillermo Gonzales about importing it to the United States. There they discovered his four-year-old Chinaco tequila and negotiated a deal to export them both.

Chinaco was not only the first 100 percent agave tequila imported to the United States, in 1983, but also the first super-premium añejo botting, which Denton and Smith served in snifters like fine brandy. The Hollywood crowd lapped it up, and soon demand outstripped supply. Before other circumstances forced Gonzales to close his distillery, Denton and Smith began searching for another producer for the Chinaco label, which led them to the Camarena famiy of La Alteña distillery in the highland town of Arandas.

Don Felipe Camerena refused their request to supply tequila for Chinaco, but compromised by accepting their offer to create a new tequila, called El Tesoro de Don Felipe, using estate-grown agaves and traditional production methods. Bottles trickled north at the end of the 1980s, beginning with a blanco that Denton and Smith labeled "silver," followed by distinctive barrel-aged bottlings the couple were known for.

Soon after, architect Martin Crowley and entrepreneur John Paul Jones DeJoria created a brand called Patrón using tequila sourced from the Siete Leguas distillery in Atotonilco. Patrón took off, thanks in part to John Paul's marketing acumen and experience selling door to door as a salesman, but many attribute the brand's success to the producers' eschewing its provenance as a tequila, instead advertising it as the world's greatest premium spirit.

In the 1990s, Ron Cooper (see page 277), an artist in residence in Oaxaca, became so enamored with the local mezcal that he ventured out into the remote villages to meet its producers. Their uncompromising, traditional production practices reminded him of the conviction he and his colleagues were bound by in his own field. Cooper coined the term *single-village mezcal* to describe his favorite producers' mezcals, and he began importing them to the United States—mostly for friends and fellow artists—under the Del Maguey label.

Sommeliers familiar with the concept of terroir were among the first to embrace Cooper's mezcals, which benefited from the halo effect of tequila brands like Chinaco, El Tesoro, and Patrón, which were vaulting agave spirits to new heights. Despite the early support, the going wasn't always smooth; Del Maguey had to rebuild the category's reputation, which suffered the stigma of cheap bottlings containing a worm (actually a moth larva called a *gusano*) plucked from the agave and deposited in the bottle, purportedly to prove its "deadly" strength.

At over $50 a bottle, single-village mezcals like Cooper's might never have taken off if it weren't for New York City bartenders like Phil Ward, whose Oaxaca Old-Fashioned cocktail, prepared with reposado ("rested") tequila spiked with Del Maguey mezcal, became so popular at Death & Co in 2007 that he opened an agave-focused cocktail bar called Mayahuel down the street. Fulfilling the same function for artisanal mezcal as the Tommy's Margarita (page 283) has for 100 percent agave tequila, Phil and other bartenders' mezcal cocktails paved the way for artisanal mezcal to become one of the most popular spirits in the contemporary bartenders' repertoire.

Tequila: The Source

The town of Tequila lies just north of Guadalajara in a high valley at the foot of a volcanic mountain, 4,000 feet above sea level. To the east, the highlands, Los Altos, rise another 3,000 feet above the valley; at nearly 7,000 feet elevation, hot days and cool nights yield agaves larger and sweeter than those harvested in the valley. (Unless a tequila specifies it's made from estate-grown agave, chances are it was made from agave sourced from both the highlands and the valley.)

All agave is hand-harvested by highly skilled *jimadors*, who use a shovel-like tool called a *coa* to expertly shear off the sword-like *pencas* (leaves), exposing the *piña* (heart), which looks like a pineapple. This must be dug out of the earth and loaded onto a truck. Blue Weber agaves ripen over a period of six to twelve years, depending on where they're grown, and range from 60 to 150 pounds when fully mature. Each plant ripens at a different pace, which *jimadors* gauge by sight after years of work in the fields.

Once the agaves are trimmed and harvested, they're transported via truck to a distillery to be cooked, converting the complex sucrose in the fibers into two fermentable sugars: glucose and fructose. Larger *piñas* are halved or quartered, before being cooked in a stone oven called an *horno* (my preferred process), an autoclave (industrial pressure cooker), or a diffuser that employs chemicals in a steam-based conversion process.

After roasting for up to twenty-four hours in the *horno* and cooling for another day, the *piñas* are removed and placed in a pit to be either crushed by a stone mill called a *tahona* or pulverized using a powerful roller mill to extract all the juice from the roasted fibers. The resulting mash is transferred (with or without fibers) to a steel or wood vat, where water and yeast are added to start fermentation. Up to ten days later, a mash of 4% to 6% ABV is ready for distillation.

Jimador

Traditional tequilas are double pot-distilled to a relatively low proof (from 40% to 70% ABV), resulting in a spirit that retains the character of the agave. Despite this, only a handful of tequilas—including El Tesoro, Siete Leguas, Astral, and Siembra Azul—still employ long ferments and distill in traditional stills *with* the agave fibers. It's a shame that after waiting over six years for the agaves to ripen, most producers rush them through the distillery to convert their sugar into alcohol.

With the exception of tequilas like El Tesoro, which is distilled to proof, most blancos are diluted and bottled unaged after distillation at a minimum of 40% ABV in the United States. Tequila aged from two to twelve months in oak containers of all sizes is labeled reposado. Tequila aged for a minimum of one year in oak barrels (typically former bourbon barrels) no larger than 600 liters is labeled añejo. In 2006, a new category, extra añejo, was established; it requires that the youngest tequila in a blend be aged a minimum of three years in barrels no larger than 600 liters. Because of the hot days and cool nights of the Mexican desert, tequila matures quickly.

There are two types of tequila, yet I've only just described the process for making 100 percent agave tequila, as it's the only style of tequila that most reputable cocktail bars mix with. As noted earlier, the best-selling mixto style of tequila allows up to 49 percent of fermentable sugars to come from sources other than agave, such as molasses; these are labeled "Gold" or "Joven Abocado" (young and adulterated).

Tequila production is regulated by the Consejo Regulador del Tequila (CRT), which assigns a Norma Oficial Mexicana (NOM; Official Mexican Standard) number to each distillery in addition to monitoring production, testing for safety, and maintaining the category's production guidelines. Though the organization has many virtues, larger producers have a disproportionate say in the council's legislative efforts, which undermines its ability to protect the quality of tequila from opportunistic profiteering.

Many tequila brands in the United States are contract distilled by producers that supply upward of a dozen different labels. While most are forgettable, a handful of contract-distilled tequilas are produced and marketed using innovative techniques that highlight tradition in tequila, including Corazon, Astral, and Siembra Azul. Others, such as Casa Dragones, are pushing tequila's reputation into a thoroughly modern niche of the market that projects aspirations for Mexico's future beyond its heralded past.

Mezcal

Most mezcal is produced in the southwestern state of Oaxaca ("wa-HA-kah"), more than 5,000 feet above sea level, around the same elevation as the highlands of Jalisco. The rugged terrain is home to sixteen ethnolinguistic groups, with thousands of subcultures, according to Chantal Martineau, who interviewed Zapotecs and Mixtecs who speak dozens of different dialects in her book *How the Gringo Stole Tequila*. The cultural diversity of the state is manifested in its mezcals, produced from nearly thirty different agaves in rustic *palenques* (mezcal distilleries) scattered throughout the region's remote nooks and crannies.

Santa Catarina Minas Horno

Many of the procedures used to make mezcal in Oaxaca's *palenques*—including hand-harvesting the agaves, as is still done for tequila—would have been used a century ago, which is just fine with the *mezcaleros* I've met. Besides the expanded variety of agaves permitted for mezcal—Espadin being the most prevalent—the biggest difference between tequila and mezcal is the method by which the *piñas* are cooked.

For tequila, the *piñas* are steamed in autoclaves or roasted in brick *hornos*, whereas for mezcal, they're roasted in deep earthen pits lined with stones heated by burning wood, then covered with straw mats and left underground for days or weeks, allowing the heat to convert their sucrose into fructose and glucose. This process imbues the agave with an earthy, smoky quality similar to that of the peated malt used to make some Scotch whiskies.

The roasted agave cools for a week—allowing fermentation to begin—before it's transferred to stone pits to be crushed to a pulp with a molina pulled by a donkey or by hand, using large wooden bats to extract the aguamiel. From here, it's carried in buckets to wooden vats for fermentation via

natural yeasts native to the *palenque*. Depending on ambient temperatures, fermentation takes anywhere from five days to a month.

Once the aguamiel reaches around 5% ABV, the solids and fibers are transferred to a copper or ceramic still, which holds an average of 25 gallons. Over the next ten to twelve hours the mixture is slowly heated by wood fire, vaporized, and condensed using cool spring or river water under vigilant supervision. The first run, called *ordinario*, is redistilled for another ten to twelve hours, and the final strength of the spirit collected is typically between 50% and 60% ABV. For traditional mezcal, no water is added before bottling, and barrel aging is rare for single-village mezcal.

RICHARD BETTS

Sommelier

ON DATA VERSUS DOGMA

"I'd like to see the wine and spirits industry be more thoughtful, and one way we can do this is by asking ourselves if we're discussing data or dogma. Regrettably, a great deal of energy is spent spewing nonsense to be heard or to distinguish oneself. This is purely ego-driven and doesn't advance real knowledge or ask meaningful questions. Instead of making definitive pronouncements, we'd be better served by discussing what we know as well as what we don't know, so we can get on with the task of investigating and learning. This quest for real knowledge and education is meaningful: it creates transparency and can make us better on so many levels."

Like tequila producers, mezcal distillers are subject to the NOM, which went into effect in 2005 when the Consejo Mexicano Regulador de la Calidad del Mezcal (mezcal regulatory council, known as Comercom) opened. All certified mezcal carries a NOM number, must be bottled at its point of origin, and may not be shipped out of the country in bulk, as is permitted with mixto tequila. Mezcals produced with nonagave-based sugars are permitted, and many are bottled with the larvae of a moth (the aforementioned *gusano*) that lives on the agave plant, either on its leaves or in its roots.

Faustino Vasquez and Assistant

Unlike tequila, whose producers and contractors export (and profit from) their own spirit, most mezcal distributed beyond the villages is purchased and bottled by foreigners like Cooper. For nearly twenty years, Ron was one of the only *négociants*—as French wine merchants who source and bottle grower wines are called—but since Ward and others found an application to grow single-village mezcal's sales, at least a dozen others have joined him, flooding the market with single-village mezcals. I hope the new *négociants* remain as generous and forward thinking as Cooper.

PALOMA

Origin One legend of this recipe's origin points to a pamphlet, "Popular Cocktails of the Rio Grande"—which doesn't turn up in any collections or databases—and to the legendary Don Javier Delgado Corona of La Capilla Bar in the town of Tequila, who's famous for creating a similar cocktail called La Batanga (prepared with cola)—but who has denied authorship.

Logic My first exposure to this recipe was in David Wondrich's artsy flip book *Killer Cocktails* from 2005, around the time bartenders throughout the United States started incorporating tequila cocktails other than the Margarita onto their menus. Neither the combination of ingredients nor the name appears in any recipe guides before this, despite Squirt's being imported to Mexico in 1955 and the maker's claim, on their website, that it became popular as a mixer in cocktails like the Paloma in the 1950s. According to Wondrich, "In the 1940s, you start seeing references in Mexico to '*changuirongo*,' which is simply tequila cut with soda—any kind, from ginger ale to Coke to whatever." He sent me a Squirt advertisement from 1977 that proclaims, "Squirt makes your favorite tequila zippy, zesty, and a little bit zany" with no mention of this being a Paloma.

Hacks The original recipe is garnished with a lime, but a grapefruit wedge is a logical substitution. Compound spice rims—incorporating citrus, chile, or *sal gusano*—are all within scope, as is adding a little fresh grapefruit juice to the mixture. Preparing the recipe with juice in place of the soda yields a similar cocktail called the Cantarito. Blanco tequilas make delicious Palomas, and the grapefruit soda is up to you. Look for the cane sugar–sweetened Mexican Squirt or a fruity alternative from Ting or Jarritos.

---

3 oz. Squirt
2 oz. Siete Leguas reposado tequila
0.5 oz. lime juice
Garnish: grapefruit wedge

Build in a chilled kosher salt–rimmed tumbler, then add ice. Garnish with the $1/2$ grapefruit wheel.

TOMMY'S MARGARITA

Origin Between 1987 and 1988, Julio Bermejo (see page 455), the second-generation owner of Tommy's Mexican Restaurant in San Francisco, created this modern Margarita variation that substitutes agave nectar for triple sec. The recipe became famous thanks to London bartenders Dre Masso and Henry Besant, who put it on cocktail menus all over the world.

Logic According to Bermejo, when this recipe was created, Margaritas were distinguished by the quality of the orange liqueur (Cointreau and Grand Marnier battled for market dominance) instead of the tequila, as most bars stocked only low-quality mixto bottlings. Herradura was one of the only 100 percent agave tequilas distributed in the United States then, with miniscule quantities of Chinaco, Caliente, and El Tesoro trickling into the market. After discovering agave syrup in a local health food store, Bermejo mixed it into a syrup to enhance the agave character of his Margarita instead of sweetening it with orange liqueur. Since he began serving them this way, only 100 percent agave tequila from Mexican-owned and -operated companies have been served in the eponymous house Margarita.

Hacks If you don't specify which tequila you'd like your Margarita to be made with at Tommy's, they'll squeeze a lime into a blender cup and add 2 ounces of reposado tequila, 1 ounce of proprietary agave syrup, and ice, then shake it in the blender cup before pouring it unstrained into a heavy glass goblet. No salt, straw, garnish, or orange liqueur stands in the way of appreciating the tequila.

---

2 oz. L&J reposado tequila

1 oz. lime juice

1 oz. agave syrup (page 392)

Garnish: None

Shake with ice, then pour unstrained into a chilled rocks glass.

MARGARITA

Origin This recipe appears as the Picador Cocktail in W. J. Tarling's 1937 *Café Royal Cocktail Book.*

Logic By definition, a daisy is a sour sweetened with curaçao or grenadine. *Margarita* is Spanish for "daisy." As for the recipe and preparation, there are as many Margarita recipes as cold remedies out there, and everyone thinks they're an expert. I always ask the guest whether they want it straight up or on the rocks; with salt, without, or with a half salt rim; and their tequila preference (brand and maturity). Be aware that as with the Daiquiri, some people expect their Margarita to come in fruit flavors from a blender. I would stick to 100 percent agave tequilas, kosher salt for the rim of the glass, and Cointreau as your triple sec. If you substitute agave syrup for triple sec in the recipe, be sure to clarify that it's a Tommy's Margarita.

Hacks A Margarita with Grand Marnier is called a Cadillac Margarita, which is tasty; adding a splash of mezcal is a nice touch if requested. For years I spent an inordinate amount of time fastidiously applying salt rims to the outside of the glasses I served Margaritas in before it hit me that salt (in small quantities)

magnifies flavor! A little salt in the glass improves the drink, so save the detailing for glassware polishing duties.

_____

2 oz. El Tesoro Platinum tequila
0.75 oz. Cointreau
0.75 oz. lime juice
0.25 oz. agave syrup (page 392)
Garnish: 1 lime wedge

Shake with ice, then fine-strain into a chilled, half kosher salt–rimmed coupe. Garnish with the lime wedge.

ROSITA

Origin I discovered this recipe in the 2006 edition of *The Museum of the American Cocktail Pocket Recipe Guide,* which was my go-to (pre-smartphone) as a bartender at Gramercy Tavern and the Pegu Club. Later, I traced it back to Greg Boehm's 1974 edition of *Mr. Boston Official Bartender's Guide*.

Logic The name means "little rose" in Spanish, which undoubtedly refers to the crimson hue the Campari imparts to it. The original recipe calls for it to be prepared with equal parts tequila, Campari, and a split measure of dry and sweet vermouth, which yields more of a Negroni-esque Rosita. Seventeen years later, it appeared in the same proportion and prep with a dash of bitters added in Gary Regan's *The Bartender's Bible*. Fifteen years after that, the pocket guide adapts the recipe to the proportions I've adopted here and modernizes preparation from stirring over crushed ice in the glass to chilling and diluting in a mixing glass so it can be served over fresh ice. The original recipes don't specify a type of tequila, leaving the choice up to you.

Hacks All three earlier recipes call for the drink to be garnished with a lemon twist and served on the rocks, but I prefer to serve it straight up and garnish it with an orange twist like a Manhattan. One logical variation would be to prepare it with blanco tequila using the original recipe—which has no dash of bitters—and serve it on the rocks like a Negroni. You have history on your side if you prefer a lemon twist.

1.5 oz. Partida reposado tequila

0.5 oz. Martini Rosso vermouth

0.5 oz. Dolin dry vermouth

0.5 oz. Campari

1 dash Angostura bitters

Garnish: 1 orange twist

Stir with ice, then strain into a chilled coupe. Garnish with the orange twist.

21st CENTURY

2 oz. Siete Leguas blanco tequila

0.75 oz. Marie Brizard crème de cacao (white)

0.75 oz. lemon juice

Pernod, for rinsing

Garnish: None

Shake the tequila, crème de cacao, and lemon juice with ice, then fine-strain into a chilled, Pernod-rinsed coupe.

Origin I created this for the menu at the Pegu Club with the guidance of Audrey Saunders in 2007.

Logic The innovative nature of Tuck's 20th Century cocktail (page 225) epitomized this period in the twentieth century, and at the turn of the twenty-first, I wanted to stake my claim to its predecessor. These years were the equivalent of the gold rush in modern mixology, and tequila was one of the final frontiers. At that time, there were only a handful of classic tequila cocktails, despite its being one of the most popular spirits in the country thanks to the Margarita, and I knew it paired well with chocolate. The absinthe ban was lifted in 2007, so many recipes incorporated a rinse or a dash to see if it would help. Pernod—the pastis, not the absinthe— reinforces the vegetal notes in the tequila.

Hacks This recipe works well with most 100 percent agave blanco tequilas. The key ingredient adaptation to be aware of is the white crème de cacao. Giffard, Brizard, and Cartron all mix nicely, but vary in chocolate character, so be sure to taste and adjust accordingly.

WITCH'S KISS

Origin I created this for the PDT cocktail menu in the fall of 2008.

Logic One of my favorite vendors at the Tompkins Square Park Sunday Greenmarket down the street from PDT was Red Jacket Orchards, which sold an apple butter that reminded me of childhood trips to Michigan, where we spread it on our toast for breakfast. While tequila shines brightest in a summer Margarita, the aged bottlings mix beautifully with fall fruits and vegetables such as apples, pears, pumpkin, and squash. Using the Margarita recipe as my template, I substituted apple butter and Strega, which means "witch" in Italian, for Cointreau and lemon juice for lime. The name alludes to the Widow's Kiss cocktail, which combines Strega's French sibling, yellow Chartreuse, and Bénédictine with apple brandy.

Hacks When a barback mistakenly infused a whole case of tequila with cinnamon, I figured it wouldn't hurt to try it in this recipe. I've served it with cinnamon-infused tequila ever since. Just add a three-inch stick to a bottle for twenty-four hours, then remove it.

2 oz. Siete Leguas reposado tequila

0.75 oz. lemon juice

0.5 oz. Strega

1 barspoon (½ tsp.) agave syrup (page 392)

1 barspoon (½ tsp.) Red Jacket apple butter

Garnish: 1 lemon twist

Shake with ice, then fine-strain into a chilled coupe. Garnish with the lemon twist.

EL DIABLO

Origin Greg Boehm found a Ronrico rum pamphlet from the late 1930s that includes a recipe for the El Diablo, which appears later in Marco and Hyman's book *The How and the When.* In 1947, Trader Vic published a variation on it called the Mexican El Diablo, with tequila in place of Ronrico rum.

Logic In addition to pioneering recipes with rum, Trader Vic was the first to include an entire chapter of tequila cocktails in a cocktail book, in the revised 1972 edition of his bartender's guide. This recipe is a hybrid of the Buck or Mule, the name given to the vodka-based version, and the Tequila Sunrise, which was prepared with cassis, lime, and soda at the Biltmore Hotel in Phoenix from the 1930s onward, before grenadine and orange juice became standard.

Hacks Carbonated commercial ginger beer can be used to lengthen this cocktail into a highball if desired, but the ginger wort gives it the spice many tequila lovers crave. Time spent in wood softens and rounds the bite of blanco tequila, which works just fine if a reposado bottling is unavailable.

2 oz. Siembra Azul reposado tequila

1 oz. ginger wort (page 393)

0.75 oz. lemon juice

0.5 oz. Giffard crème de cassis

Garnish: 1 lemon wheel, 1 piece of candied ginger, 1 blackberry

Shake with ice, then strain into a chilled rocks glass filled with ice cubes. Garnish with the candied ginger picked to the lemon wheel and blackberry.

MEZCAL MULE

Origin I created this for Sombra mezcal founder Richard Betts in the winter of 2008.

Logic At the time, I was fascinated with the way peated whisky and mezcal added a smoky quality to drinks, and used the recipe to explore as many flavors as I could. Passion fruit's heady perfume notes are reminiscent of the wild aromas of the crushed agave during natural, open-vat fermentation. The cucumber reinforces the vegetal character, while the lime and ginger add acidity and spice. A pinch of Mexican chile, which is commonly added to slices of jicama and oranges served as snacks in *mezcalerias*, adds heat and an earthy quality that balances the smoke. When mixed correctly, it's strong, sweet, sour, smoky, vegetal, hot, and even a little floral, thanks to the aromatic cucumber garnish.

Hacks Originally, Richard was sourcing mezcal from Ron Cooper's *palenque* in San Luis Del Río. When Richard switched *palenques*, and Ron started producing Vida there, I switched to Vida because I prefer this drink with San Luis Del Rio mezcal. This recipe is a high-wire act with little room for substitutions.

1.5 oz. Del Maguey Vida mezcal

1 oz. ginger wort (page 393)

0.75 oz. lime juice

0.75 oz. Boiron passion fruit puree

0.5 oz. agave syrup (page 392)

3 cucumber slices (plus 1 for garnish)

Garnish: Candied ginger, pinch of ground chile

Muddle the cucumber slices and agave syrup, then add the remaining ingredients. Shake with ice, then fine-strain into a chilled rocks glass filled with ice. Garnish with the candied ginger picked to the cucumber slice, and a pinch of ground chile.

SAN MIGUEL

Origin I created this for Casa Dragones in the spring of 2014 when they launched their blanco tequila.

Logic The first thing I do after choosing a base spirit to create a cocktail is nose and taste it to identify which notes I can reinforce through other ingredients. I smelled grapefruit, so I chose grapefruit oil from the peel, and I used celery bitters to add fresh herbal notes that complement the vegetal notes of the tequila. The grapefruit oil overwhelms the tequila's aroma when you twist it over the surface, so I twist it into the glass before pouring the liquid, as you would apply an absinthe rinse. I wanted to reinforce the clarity of the cocktail, which remains clear after adding everything, so the twist is not included as a garnish.

Hacks You could use another tequila, but San Miguel is the brand home of Casa Dragones. Miracle Mile celery bitters was the only brand on the market at the time I created this that tastes like fresh celery, not celery seed, so substitute accordingly.

2 oz. Casa Dragones blanco tequila

1 barspoon (½ tsp.) agave syrup (page 392)

2 dashes Miracle Mile celery bitters

1 grapefruit twist

Garnish: None

Pinch the grapefruit twist into a chilled rocks glass, then discard it and add a large ice sphere. Stir with ice, then strain into the prepared glass.

MECHUGA

Origin I came up with this for Misty Kalkofen, who asked me to create a cocktail with one of Del Maguey's single-village mezcals in the summer of 2015.

Logic Minero mezcal is distilled in the village of Santa Catarina Minas by Florencio Carlos Sarmiento, who also produces the prized pechuga mezcal for Del Maguey. To mimic the third distillation of minero used to make pechuga—in which apples, plums, plantains, almonds, and pineapple are added to the pot and a chicken breast is suspended below the condenser—I added damson plum–infused gin for fruit, and spice and sherry to impart an umami quality. A clove-studded orange peel is used to make Café Brulot in New Orleans; its festive appearance and aroma are perfect for this cocktail. The name *mechuga* is a mashup of "my" and "pechuga."

Hacks This recipe will work with most single-village mezcals, but the ingredient logic and meaning behind the name break down. Feel free to substitute other palo cortado sherries and Abbott's bitters formulas. At 33% ABV, Averell Damson gin liqueur strikes a balance in strength and sweetness between a gin and a liqueur.

2 oz. Del Maguey Minero mezcal

1 oz. Averell Damson gin liqueur

0.75 oz. Lustau Palo Cortado Península sherry

1 dash Tempus Fugit Abbott's bitters

Garnish: 1 clove-studded orange twist

Stir with ice, then strain into a chilled rocks glass filled with two ice spheres. Garnish with the orange twist.

North
Atlantic
Ocean

Kirkwall

SCOTLAND

Carbost

Keith

Dufftown

Aberfeldy

NORTHERN
IRELAND

Bruichladdich

Crieff

Bushmills

Campbeltown

★ *Edinburgh*

North Sea

Dundalk

Dublin ★

Irish Sea

IRELAND

Cork

ENGLAND

Celtic Sea

English Channel

BELGIUM

FRANCE

IRELAND
- ⊙ *Cork*
  (Jameson)
  (Powers)
  (Redbreast)
- ⊙ *Dundalk*
  (Tyrconnell)

NORTHERN IRELAND
- ⊙ *Bushmills*
  (Bushmills)

SCOTLAND
- ⊙ *Aberfeldy*
  (Dewars)
- ⊙ *Bruichladdich*
  (Bruichladdich)
- ⊙ *Campbeltown*
  (Springbank)
- ⊙ *Carbost*
  (Talisker)

- ⊙ *Crieff*
  (Famous Grouse)
- ⊙ *Dufftown*
  (Balvenie)
- ⊙ *Keith*
  (Strathisla)
- ⊙ *Kirkwall*
  (Highland Park)

⋮⋮ *Traditional Production Region*   ⊙ *Distillery Site*   ★ *Capital*

WHISK(E)Y

A confluence of the popularity of classic cocktails (whiskey-based cocktails are outnumbered only by gin), the craft distilling renaissance (led by whiskey makers), and food advocacy that encourages buying local have bolstered whiskey sales over the past decade. The category hasn't seen sales like this since the 1970s.

Whiskey requires a minimum of a couple years of aging to make it palatable, and from six to twelve years to realize its potential. Sourcing mature whiskey wasn't a problem when it wasn't selling, but now that it is, many producers who built their reputation with age statements have removed them in the hopes they can convince consumers to pay the same price for younger whiskey based on their brand's prestige alone.

The word *whiskey* (spelled "whisky" when referring to Canadian, Scottish, and Japanese bottlings) descends from the Gaelic *uisge beatha* for aqua vitae. According to historian Dave Broom, whiskey distillation is described as early as the fourteenth century, in Chaucer's *The Canterbury Tales*. Although it isn't called "whiskey" by name, Broom notes that the canon's yeoman describes "Cucurbites and alambikes" (distilling vessels and alembics), plus ingredients including "oille of tartre," "alum glas," "berme," and even "wort," the beerlike precursor to whiskey.

Political turmoil led thousands of Irish and Scots to emmigrate to North America in the eighteenth century, bringing their whiskey-distilling acumen to a brave, rum-soaked new world. Early American whiskeys, many distilled by Dutch and German immigrants, were produced from rye, a hearty grain planted to replenish nutrients in tobacco fields. This began to shift when the U.S. government offered incentives to plant corn. In 1776, the governor of the state of Virginia (which extended all the way into Kentucky at that time) offered settlers free land in exchange for clearing it to grow corn.

Following America's first tax on domestic spirit production in 1791, which led to the Whiskey Rebellion in western Pennsylvania in 1794, whiskey distillers ventured farther into the frontier to evade the taxman and Washington's army.

The water beneath the fertile land beyond the Appalachians (and beyond the taxman's reach) in Kentucky passes through a limestone shelf that filters impurities, adds calcium, and gives it a pH that facilitates fermentation. Plentiful access to pristine water is a common characteristic of the remote, bucolic regions where many whiskeys originate. These narratives, however, typically suppress the attraction of rugged terrain for moonshiners seeking a place to conceal a still under the taxman's nose.

Eventually, technology trumped tax evasion as the key promoter of growth in the global whiskey industry. Some advances were made through diligent trial and error, such as Scottish immigrant Dr. James Crow's sour mash method, in which he held back spent mash (which still contains live yeast) to deter unwanted bacterial growth and maintain a healthy pH for the following batch.

Another innovation, which wasn't adopted outside Tennessee, occurred in the mid-1800s when Jack Daniel's founder Alfred Eaton began filtering new-make through sugar maple charcoal to strip it of congeners before aging. This became Tennessee whiskey's signature distinction from bourbon.

The most prized attribute of bourbon whiskey—charred oak's contribution to its character—was brought to the attention of distillers by customers in New Orleans who began asking for the whiskey from Kentucky's Bourbon County by name.

By the time the corn was harvested at the end of the summer, mashed, fermented, and distilled, the rivers had frozen over, forcing distillers to wait until spring to ship the barrels, which had been charred on the interior to remove any odors from the previous contents. When the whiskey arrived in New Orleans via the Ohio River, it had taken on pleasing characteristics from the charred oak barrel.

Brewer Thomas Molson installed Canada's first known whisky still in 1801, followed from the 1820s onwards by millers such as Gooderham & Worts, Henry Corby, and Joseph Seagram, who distilled whisky to profit from surplus grain grown on their sizable agricultural holdings. Detroit grocer Hiram Walker built his distillery in Windsor, Ontario in 1858.

In 1887, barrel aging was first codified by Canada, who implemented a one-year minimum age for all whiskies, raised to two years in 1890, which eventually led the rest of the industry to fall in line. In 1915, the UK passed the Scotch and Irish Whisky Immature Spirits Act, requiring all whiskies to be aged for a minimum of three years, with an addendum that Scotch whisky may be aged only in Scotland.

As important as barrel aging is to the quality of whiskey, the most pivotal technological breakthrough came in 1827, when Scottish distiller Robert Stein invented the patent still, which Irish excise collector (here we go again with the taxman!) Aeneas Coffey refined and patented in 1830.

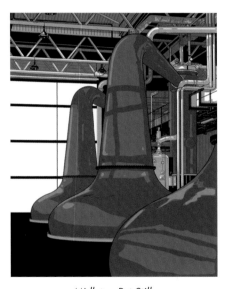

The new Coffey still could be run continuously to produce a lighter style of whiskey at a higher proof than pot stills. It was immediately embraced by producers of vodka, gin, and rum, but many Irish whiskey distillers rejected it for whiskey production. With the largest pot stills in the industry, the Irish were already producing light, clean spirit (with character) and preferred the taste.

At this time, most whisky in the UK was sold unaged, straight from the still to middlemen who distributed it, such as

Midleton Pot Stills

Scotsman Andrew Usher, the Edinburgh agent for Glenlivet, who created the first blended malt whisky (with multiple single-malts) in 1853. In 1860, blending pot-stilled malt whisky with column-distilled grain whisky was legalized, and merchants such as the Chivas Brothers, John Walker, William Teacher, and John Dewar transformed the Scotch whisky industry into a global leader driven by brand names instead of the places the whiskies were distilled.

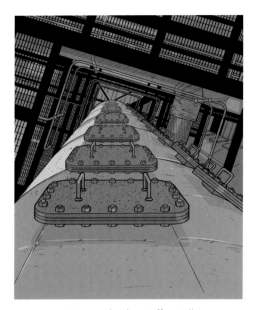

Cameronbridge Coffey Still

Many Irish and American distillers weren't sure what to make of nearly flavorless grain spirit—distilled just below vodka's proof—being used to make whiskey, and they stuck to their production practices. According to *Spirits Distilled*, Scottish, Irish, and American whiskey distillers appealed to a royal commission, "but only in America did a law, the 1909 Bottled in Bond Act, oblige clear differentiation between straight and blended whiskeys." Canada was an early adopter, but most Irish distillers held out until the 1930s.

Prohibition was another speed bump for the Irish, who (mostly) took the high ground against bootleggers compared to Scottish distillers, who built their market share in America during this time. When Prohibition was repealed, Canada and Scotland had a huge leg up on Kentucky bourbon producers, who had no aged stocks to draw from.

On the other side of the world, Japan's whisky industry took its first steps in 1923, when Masataka Taketsuru, who came from a sake brewing family, returned home from an apprenticeship in Scotland to help Shinjiro Torii open the Yamazaki Distillery in Kyoto. They launched their first whisky in 1929, after which Taketsuru left the company to found his own company— Dai Nippon Kaku, "The Great Japanese Juice Company"—on the island of Hokkaido, where he began producing apple juice and wine. He released his first whisky in 1940 and changed the company name to Nikka Whisky in 1952.

Irish Whiskey

Irish malt whiskey—including pure pot-stilled whiskey produced from a mash of malted and unmalted barley—is either double or triple distilled in huge pot stills that yield a lighter distillate than most squat stills in Scotland. Corn-based grain whiskeys are column distilled to a high proof and reserved for blends, which must be aged for a minimum of three years in wood barrels: bourbon, sherry, and other wine casks are used. Any age on the bottle represents the youngest whiskey in the bottle.

By 1978 there were only two distilleries in Ireland: Midleton in County Cork and Bushmills in County Antrim. Both were owned by Irish Distillers Ltd [IDL]. A decade later, John Teeling opened Cooley. Today, however, Ireland is home to upwards of twenty new plants of differing sizes, including new Teeling distilleries in Dublin and Dundalk, Tullamore, Slane Castle, West Cork, and Dingle.

Midleton Distillery Cooper Ger Buckley's Work Bench

Scotch Whisky

Blended Scotch whisky is produced in Scotland from column-distilled grain whisky from a mash bill of corn or wheat that's blended with up to 40 percent pot-distilled malt whisky. There are currently eight grain distilleries and over one hundred malt distilleries in Scotland that trade freely with each other, giving blenders a huge variety of whiskies to choose from. All Scotch must be aged for a minimum of three years, and any age statement refers to the youngest whisky in the blend.

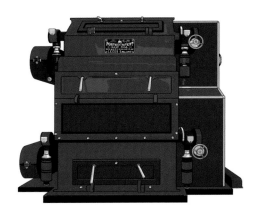

Talisker Roller Mill

Single-malt Scotch whisky must be produced in a single distillery from 100 percent malted barley that may be dried by peat. The smoky quality of the peat is preserved when the distiller double or triple pot distills to no higher than 70% ABV. The shape and size of the stills and the length and inclination of the pot's lyne arm have a significant influence on the character of the new-make, which must be aged for a minimum of three years, although twelve is more common. Malt whiskies from two or more distilleries are called blended malts and follow the same guidelines.

Single-malts weren't marketed beyond Britain until the 1960s, so any classic cocktails calling for Scotch most likely were mixed with a blend. Premium bottlings, which contain higher proportions of malt whisky, are aged twelve years or more. Price is typically a limiting factor when it comes to Scotch whisky, so look beyond the big brand names for lesser-known bottles from independent bottlers like Compass Box, Gordon MacPhail, or Murray McDavid. While most production has been industrialized, distillers like Balvenie, Springbank, and Bruichladdich still use traditional production practices (and more people) to make their whiskies.

American Whiskey

The term *bourbon* refers to a style of whiskey that can be made only in America; the best bottlings are still produced near its namesake county in Kentucky, which is the only state that can be listed on a bourbon label. A mash bill of at least 51 percent corn is supplemented with wheat or rye, depending on the distiller's preference, and malted barley for fermentation using distinctive proprietary yeast strains. Additives for color or sweetness are forbidden.

"Straight" bourbon, rye, corn, and Tennessee whiskeys must be distilled under 80% ABV and bottled no lower than 40% ABV by law, although most hover closer to 50% ABV. Straight rye whiskey follows straight bourbon production guidelines, except the mash bill must contain at least 51 percent rye. Tennessee whiskey production is nearly identical to bourbon production, save for the Lincoln County process, in which the new-make spirit must be filtered through charred sugar maple charcoal to strip impurities (flavor!) before it enters the barrel.

(I tend to avoid powerful vermouths and liqueurs that bury the subtleties of Tennessee whiskey in cocktails.)

Straight whiskeys from Kentucky and Tennessee must be matured in brand-new 200-liter charred oak barrels for at least two years in warehouses whose exposure to the elements—cold winters and hot summers—maximizes flavor extraction from the

Brown-Forman Cooperage Barrel Charring

wood. Originally, tax on whiskeys "bottled in bond" wouldn't be paid until the whiskey was released from the bond warehouse, but today, this term refers to a four-year-old whiskey produced in a single distillery that's bottled at 50% ABV.

MIKE MIYAMOTO

Master Distiller

"These days, I have a feeling that our whisky has a tendency to mix with other things. Japanese culture accommodates European, Western, Chinese, and Indian culture into it. We learned how to make whisky from Scotland, but now we make Japanese-style whisky. Japanese whisky seems to be united with other things. Japanese people always try to be friendly with other people. We are very peaceful, friendly, and modest, and look up to our neighbors. As a whisky, we don't want to conquer the world. We'd rather see it taken gently and nicely by other people."

Bonded ryes such as Rittenhouse and bourbons such as Old Grand-Dad are beloved by bartenders for their robust character that shines through other mixers in cocktails.

Bars typically differentiate "wheated" whiskeys, such as Maker's Mark, which use wheat as the primary small grain to complement the corn in the mash bill, from those that use rye, which adds more spice. Proof is another qualitative factor, as an 80 proof whiskey (the legal minimum) lacks the power of a bonded bottling like Old Grand-Dad or a cask strength whiskey like Booker's. Age is less important for straight American whiskeys, because Kentucky and Tennessee whiskey are matured in new oak barrels in environments in which huge temperature and humidity fluctuations facilitate maximum flavor extraction.

Canadian Whisky

Canadian whisky is produced from new-make spirit based on corn, barley, wheat, or rye saccherified by barley or rye malt; distilled in pot or column stills; and aged separately for a minimum of three years in barrels no larger than 700 liters; they are then blended and bottled. A maximum of 9.09 percent of the blend may consist of additives, including other spirits such as brandy or wine. With such laissez-faire regulations, the quality of the final product depends on the integrity and ambition of the master blender.

Grain Harvester

Canadian whiskies are colloquially known as rye, despite most having very little rye whisky in the blend. A handful of bold, flavorful whiskies—particularly ryes—formerly destined for blending with light grain whisky have been released uncut, such as Lot 40, which I use in the Toronto cocktail (page 335). Demand for rye whiskey caught many Kentucky producers off guard when classic cocktails took off, so a handful of American bottlers—such as Whistle Pig and Lock, Stock and Barrel—source rye from Canada, where there's no shortage of mature whisky.

Japanese Whisky

Suntory and Nikka are the two largest producers of Japanese whisky, which has become one of the most celebrated whisky regions in the world since 2001, when their single-malts and blends began beating Scotch whiskies in international whisky competitions. Unlike the Scots, Japanese distillers don't trade whiskies, so each house produces a variety of whiskies from imported malt (peated and unpeated) and corn distilled in pot and column

Hakushu Rickhouse

stills of different still shapes, sizes, and styles. The new-make is aged in a variety of casks—including Japanese Mizunara oak—in aging facilities across the islands.

Japanese whisky expert Stefan Van Eycken points out that although traditional Scottish whisky production methods are used for inspiration, rather than priding themselves on consistency from year to year as the Scots do, the Japanese value the concept of *kaizen*—"continuous improvement." Government production guidelines are even more lax than in Canada, so making great whisky is a free-will pursuit, not a mandate imposed by strict guidelines. Japanese whisky prices have skyrocketed in recent years, pushing mature malts and blends out of budget for use in cocktails.

A Word about Craft Whiskeys

Some of you may be wondering: where's the craft whiskey overview? The short answer is, there's not a whole lot to be said just yet. Besides a handful of whiskey distillers beginning with Anchor in 1993, most new whiskey brands are less than a decade old, which is the inverse of dog years when we're evaluating a whiskey company's body of work. It gets even more complicated when you try to figure in companies like Whistle Pig, Bulleit, High West, and Angel's Envy, which sourced whiskey and bottled it under their own label while they were building their own distilleries or waiting for new-make to mature.

It will take decades to reconcile the differences between sourced whiskey and the new-make that these companies distill and mature and to draw any definitive conclusions. Producers such as New York's Hudson have worked around traditional maturation timelines using small oak barrels to maximize the spirit's contact area with wood; others, such as Death's Door,

"When you say 'craft,' I think of courage. And I think of the period from 1950 to 2000 when there was only one craft bourbon distillery in the country, and that was us. That was either genuinely stupid, or a good idea, but the timing was terrible. Or it really was Dad's hobby, and he didn't care as long as the whiskey tasted good. And I think it was the latter."

BILL SAMUELS

Company Director

have released unaged whiskey in the hope consumers would subsidize their production costs. Despite innovation being driven by craft producers, it's too early to tell which production practices will endure.

Ultimately, the most important element for quality whiskey production is time. Hiram Walker master blender Don Livermore found an 1895 interview with Hiram Walker in which he claimed he would have never built his distillery—which is now the largest in North America—knowing he had to age whisky for a minimum of two years; "the capital required for the raw materials and production equipment was too much to invest up front." It's a cautionary tale for aspiring producers, and a reminder that good whiskey comes to those who wait.

HIGHBALL

Origin The origin of the highball and the meaning behind the word likely lead back to Ireland or Scotland. Instead of perpetuating any myths, I'll direct your attention to the 1940s, when Scotch whisky and soda—the Highball—began evolving into a category of mixed drinks.

Logic In the 1948 edition of *The Fine Art of Mixing Drinks*, Embury defines a highball as "any tall iced drink (6 ounces or more) consisting of a base liquid (alcoholic or nonalcoholic) in combination with a carbonated beverage and with or without auxiliary coloring and flavoring agents, but definitely without lemon or lime juice. If citrus juices are used the drink becomes a Buck or a Collins or a Rickey and is no longer a Highball." He goes on to say that while you can use cola or ginger ale, plain soda water is expected in a highball. Around this time, Suntory began using the highball to promote their whisky in Japan, and the serve remains popular today. In Japan's best bars, the highball is served, with a variety of Japanese whisky brands and supercharged sparkling water sourced from mountain streams, in paper-thin hand-turned glasses, chilled by large crystal-clear cubes.

Hacks The highball has become so popular in Japan, you can buy it in cans from vending machines. Suntory created a machine that dispenses them super-chilled with pleasant pinpoint-size bubbles for select *izakayas* (Japanese pubs). Most prepare their highball with blended whisky, but I prefer mine with a single-malt. Be restrained if you're inclined to garnish a Japanese whisky highball: use a mint leaf or slice of lemon at most. When prepared with still water in place of sparkling, it's called a Mizu-wari.

> 3 oz. club soda
> 2 oz. Yamazaki 12-year Japanese whisky
> Garnish: None

Build in a highball glass filled with large cubes.

ROSY CHEEKS

Origin I created this recipe for a holiday entertaining article for *Playboy* editor Hugh Garvey in the winter of 2012.

Logic Hugh asked me for a festive punch recipe his readers could prepare and serve during the holidays. The photo department requested that it be red, and as with most recipes printed in national magazines, the ingredients had to be easy to source. Plymouth's sloe gin, a sloe berry–infused gin-based liqueur, provides the color, while champagne signals celebration and balances the liqueur's sweetness. Tempus Fugit released their decadent chocolate liqueur in 2012, which reinforces the cacao notes in the pure pot-stilled Irish whiskey and breeds familiarity among casual imbibers. Holiday cocktail parties aren't the right venue to trot out your most challenging cocktails, so it's important to focus on approachable flavors. If you serve this as a punch, be sure to hold off on adding the champagne until guests arrive, to preserve its effervescence.

Hacks Each of these ingredients is the Cadillac in its category. Holiday parties are the perfect time to splurge, and, in this case, you get what you pay for, so substitute with caution. There's nothing explicitly seasonal about this recipe, so I serve it year-round.

---

2 oz. Robert Moncuit Blanc de Blancs champagne

0.75 oz. Redbreast 12-year Irish whiskey

0.5 oz. Plymouth sloe gin

0.5 oz. Tempus Fugit crème de cacao (dark)

0.5 oz. lemon juice

Garnish: 1 lemon wheel

Stir the whiskey, sloe gin, crème de cacao, and juice with ice, then fine-strain into a chilled wine glass filled with one large ice cube. Top with the champagne. Garnish with the lemon wheel.

STONE FENCE

Origin In *Imbibe!*, Wondrich traces the recipe back to its role in the victory at Fort Ticonderoga during the Revolutionary War in 1775, where it was served as a "savage mixture" of New England rum and hard cider. Nearly a century later, it appears in Jerry Thomas's 1862 *The Bar-Tenders Guide* as a bourbon cooler lengthened with unfiltered cider.

Logic Between the days of the Revolutionary War and Thomas's time, bourbon whiskey made headway in America as cider fell from favor. Ever the diplomat, Wondrich gives Thomas points for his "suave and smooth" version, but takes him to task for it being a "feeble" relative of the "liquid courage" that inspired our liberators a century before. Given the recipe's flexibility, it all depends on your perception of the fence. Thomas's is genteel, with the recipe manifesting as something you'd sip on a Southern veranda while looking out at the stone fence surrounding your property, whereas the rum-based version conjures images of a band of soldiers in a colonial tavern plotting to ascend a fortress's stone wall. Thankfully, hard cider from heirloom apples has made a comeback along with

hogo-rich pot-stilled rums, so you have plenty of alternatives to the elegant bourbon-based cooler if you're feeling bellicose.

Hacks I added maple syrup for depth of flavor in Thomas's recipe, and I restrained myself from adding Angostura bitters, but that doesn't mean you should show similar discipline. If you do add bitters, and substitute rich rum for bourbon, you'll be making a long version of Dick Bradsell's classic Treacle cocktail.

---

3 oz. unfiltered hard apple cider

2 oz. Old Grand-Dad bonded bourbon whiskey

0.25 oz. Grade A dark amber maple syrup

Garnish: 1 apple fan

Build in a chilled collins glass then fill with ice. Garnish with the apple fan.

BROWN DERBY

Origin Dale DeGroff included this recipe, first published in *Hollywood Cocktails* by Buzza & Cardozo in 1933, in *The Craft of the Cocktail*, where he credits it to a celebrity haunt in Hollywood called the Vendôme Club, which served the cocktail in honor of their neighbors in the dome-shaped Brown Derby restaurant on Wilshire Boulevard.

Logic *Southern Spirits* author Robert Moss did some investigating and found evidence suggesting that George Buzza did not find this drink at the Brown Derby or the Vendôme Club. "The very first entry (the Absinthe cocktail) and the very last (the Zazarac) are lifted directly from *The Savoy Cocktail Book*, and so are dozens upon dozens of the ones in between—word for word, from the ingredients lists to the instructions." Moss says. He believes Buzza renamed Craddock's De Rigueur cocktail—which was pilfered from Judge Jr.'s *Here's How*—the Brown Derby. The earliest version called for scotch, but Craddock and Buzza left it open for interpretation, so I side with Dale and mix it with bourbon.

Hacks This recipe will work with a variety of whiskies, including single-malt scotch, straight rye, or bourbon. Its quality hinges on varying the proportions of grapefruit juice and honey to suit your guest's palate. Ruby Red grapefruit juice is much sweeter than yellow grapefruit juice, and much less aromatic than elusive white grapefruit juice, which pairs nicely with wildflower honey. Substitute lemon juice for grapefruit juice in a bourbon version and you have a Gold Rush cocktail; swap raspberry cordial for honey syrup in a rye version to make a Blinker cocktail.

---

2 oz. Maker's Mark bourbon whisky
1 oz. grapefruit juice
0.75 oz. honey syrup (page 392)
Garnish: None

Shake with ice, then fine-strain into a chilled coupe.

MINT JULEP

Origin Juleps (unlike this one) date back to the fourteenth century. The ones we're interested in date back to the eighteenth century, when mint was added to the classic Sling (spirit, sugar, water).

Logic Ice transformed this mixture into an institution in the early part of the nineteenth century, and has been part of its downfall in the twenty-first. Traditional ice cubes melt too slowly to properly dilute a Julep, and they lack the surface area to chill it rapidly enough to maintain its integrity while you're sipping it. The ideal ice to serve a Julep with is pulverized with a mallet and either frozen again or added to an ice-cold julep cup during preparation. Pebble ice from a Scotsman machine isn't as cold, but its uniform-size "pebbles" dilute and chill more evenly and don't stick to the cup like crushed ice does. Higher-proof bourbon is recommended to withstand dilution, and only the most beautiful mint will do. A stainless steel straw is a nice touch.

Hacks Nineteenth-century Juleps, such as those published in Jerry Thomas's *The Bar-Tenders Guide*, were prepared with decadent wines, French brandies, aged genevers, and rich Jamaican rums and garnished with fruit and berries in addition to the mint. They're all still fair game as substitutes. I'd forgo the fruit and pat a little powdered sugar onto the mint leaves if ornamentation is appropriate.

2.5 oz. Booker's bourbon whiskey

0.5 oz. simple syrup (page 391)

8 mint leaves (plus 3 mint sprigs for garnish)

In a chilled julep cup, muddle the mint and simple syrup, then add the bourbon and top with pebble ice. Swizzle, then top with more pebble ice. Garnish with a bouquet of mint sprigs.

BLOOD AND SAND

Origin This cocktail was named after the silent film of the same name, which premiered at the Rialto Theater in Los Angeles in 1922. The recipe first appears in Harry Craddock's *The Savoy Cocktail Book* in 1930.

Logic Rudolph Valentino plays the role of star-crossed matador whose love life affects his good judgment in the bullring, which becomes his undoing. The original recipe calls for equal parts of each ingredient, which yields an insipid mixture, in my opinion. Increasing the percentage of scotch, and choosing a blend or malt with enough character to cut through the other ingredients, is recommended. Orange juice is the kiss of death for most cocktails, and the method of extraction is part of it. A reamer or Sunkist juicer is the best method to prevent the bitter pith from affecting the flavor.

Hacks Blood orange juice would be a nice touch, given the symbolism of the name, but you'd have to pare back the sweet vermouth and cherry liqueur to mitigate its sweetness. Cherry Heering, your other source of metaphorical blood, works well here, but it's worth experimenting with Cazottes or Luxardo Sangue Morlacco, which have brighter cherry fruit flavor. A twist of orange is a nice touch, and brandied cherries will work, too.

1.5 oz. Johnnie Walker Black blended Scotch whisky

0.75 oz. orange juice

0.5 oz. Carpano Antica Formula vermouth

0.5 oz. Cherry Heering

Garnish: None

Shake with ice, then fine-strain into a chilled coupe.

HOT WHISKEY

Origin This recipe is a hybrid of Jerry Thomas's Irish Whiskey Punch—prepared with "pure Irish whiskey," hot water, and lemon oleo saccharum—and his Whiskey Skin, served with whiskey, hot water, and lemon peel with no sugar, from the 1862 *The Bar-Tenders Guide*. David Wondrich dates the first mention of the hot toddy (which is what we'd call this drink today) back to the 1750s, and celebrated it as "a fixture of American tippling for a century or more" in *Imbibe!.*

Logic When I visited Ireland for the first time in 1997, I saw a patron sipping this toddy the locals called "hot whiskey" in a pub in Galway on a chilly rainy day, and I ordered one without hesitation. As a native Midwesterner weaned as a bartender in Wisconsin, I was no stranger to hot toddies, but I'd never tasted one served with a clove-studded lemon wedge, which serves the same steam- and heat-mitigating function as the creamy head on an Irish Coffee. Since alcohol boils at a lower temperature than water, if you combine boiling hot water with alcohol, heady fumes will evaporate from the glass, repelling all but the most intrepid imbibers. The lemon floats to the surface,

blocking the steam from billowing up, and the heat from the water enhances the cloves' aromatics.

Hacks I prefer a pure pot-stilled Irish whiskey in this drink, but some of the more flavorful blends work well, too. Just about any pot-stilled spirit mixes well as a toddy; you're welcome to sweeten with sugar or agave or maple syrup and use tea in place of hot water, if you please. Toddies from Thomas's time were garnished with nutmeg, but clove and cinnamon are superb substitutes.

---

4 oz. hot water

1.5 oz. Powers Irish whiskey

1 oz. honey syrup (page 392)

Garnish: 1 lemon wedge studded with 3 cloves

Build in a preheated tempered mug. Garnish with the lemon wedge.

IRISH COFFEE

Origin The Irish Coffee was invented by Joe Sheridan for a convoy of Americans whose flight was grounded due to inclement weather at Foynes air base in 1942. The recipe's reputation grew thanks to travel writer Stanton Delaplane, who sampled Sheridan's handiwork later at Shannon airport and imported it to San Francisco's The Buena Vista in 1952, where it's still served today.

Logic Most bartenders serve this recipe with light, blended Irish whiskey, whose nuances are buried by the coffee, which oxidizes and burns when it's heated over a boilerplate. To solve the problem, at the Dead Rabbit they brew a robust blend of coffee, bottle it with the sugar, and store it sealed in a hot water bath (see page 109) to maintain the proper temperature and prevent it from oxidizing or being scorched. For service, they pour the whiskey and sweetened coffee into the glass, then float heavy cream that's whipped until it's still wet enough to pour, but thick enough to float on top of the coffee. The cream lends a rich, velvety texture that cools the coffee to a temperature you can savor and prevents the more volatile alcohol from evaporating off.

Hacks The recipe is traditionally served in a footed 6-ounce glass, which requires you to reduce the coffee to 3 ounces and the whiskey to 1.25 ounces, so there's enough room for the whipped cream. Feel free to grate a little nutmeg over the freshly whipped cream, as they used to at the Dead Rabbit.

4 oz. brewed coffee

1.5 oz. Redbreast 12-year Irish whiskey

0.5 oz. simple syrup (page 391)

Freshly whipped cream (page 393), for topping

Garnish: None

Build the coffee, whiskey, and simple syrup in a preheated tempered mug. Top with whipped cream.

BOBBY BURNS

Origin The recipe appears as the "Baby Burns" in the 1900 edition of the Bishop & Babcock Company's recipe guide *Fancy Drinks*, which alternates between tavern fixture pricing and recipes every other page.

Logic It reappears as the "Robert" Burns with Irish whiskey (!), sweet vermouth, and absinthe in both *Jack's Manual* in 1910 and *Drinks* in 1914 and then resurfaces as the more colloquial "Bobby" Burns with the original recipe in *Recipes for Mixed Drinks* in 1917. In *The Fine Art of Mixing Drinks* in 1948, David Embury muddied the water even further when he listed the "Bobbie" (yet another Bob) Burns with Drambuie (because it has a Scotch whisky base) instead of Bénédictine and added a dash of bitters. Despite being named after Scotland's poet laureate Robert Burns, it's clearly not nationalistic or locavore in conception (in the way the Rusty Nail is) if you consider the sweet vermouth's provenance and role in the recipe. The Bobby Burns's relationship to the Rob Roy parallels the relationship between the Brooklyn and the Manhattan, where the liqueur modifier(s) replaces the aromatic bitters' role as a binding agent that enhances the blend of vermouth and whisk(e)y.

Hacks The recipe was originally garnished with a lemon twist, but Dale DeGroff began serving it with Scottish shortbread cookies on the side for Bobby Burns Day (January 25) at the Rainbow Room in the mid-1990s, and the tradition continues. Based on the checkered history of the drink, there are many legitimate hacks, but I'd focus on finding harmony among the scotch, sweet vermouth, and Bénédictine.

---

2 oz. Compass Box Oak Cross blended malt Scotch whisky

0.75 oz. Martini Rosso vermouth

0.25 oz. Bénédictine

Scottish shortbread cookies (preferably Walker's), for serving

Stir with ice, then strain into a chilled coupe. Serve with the cookies on the side.

BROOKLYN

Origin The cocktail appears in Jack Grohusko's 1908 *Jack's Manual* with sweet vermouth instead of dry vermouth.

Logic The Brooklyn is included in the 2004 edition of Ted Haigh's *Vintage Spirits and Forgotten Cocktails*, which bartenders of the time used to generate a wish list of "lost" spirits such as Amer Picon, which still isn't shipped to the United States. The original recipe in *Jack's Manual* calls for sweet vermouth, which was replaced by dry vermouth for posterity in Jacques Straub's 1914 *Drinks*. I find that Manhattan-style recipes calling for dry vermouth from this time period—such as the El Presidente, Algonquin, and Blackthorn—taste better when made with sweeter Chambéry blanc vermouth, which was popular at the time. The oxidized notes of dry vermouths like Noilly Prat don't pair well with fruit modifiers such as cherries, pineapple, and sloe berries (a relative of the plum).

Hacks Amer Picon has been reformulated into a lower-proof bitter, so the bright-orange-flavored Bigallet China-China or Amaro Cora works well in its place. This formula spawned Milk & Honey barman Enzo Errico's Red Hook cocktail as well as half a dozen other well-known riffs named after Brooklyn neighborhoods.

2 oz. Rittenhouse bonded rye whiskey

0.75 oz. Dolin blanc vermouth

0.25 oz. Luxardo maraschino liqueur

0.25 oz. Bigallet China-China Amer liqueur

Garnish: None

Stir with ice, then strain into a chilled coupe.

MANHATTAN

Origin According to *Imbibe!*, this cocktail had already gained widespread popularity by the time it appeared in O. H. Byron's *The Modern Bartenders' Guide* in 1884. While it can't be concluded beyond a shadow of a doubt, it likely hails from New York City's Manhattan Club.

Logic Byron lists two Manhattan recipes that both call for gum syrup and Angostura bitters; #1 specifies French vermouth and #2 calls for Italian vermouth supplemented with curaçao, and neither specifies a garnish. Many of the early recipes for the Manhattan were adaptations of the Improved Whiskey Cocktail (prepared with gum syrup, curaçao, absinthe, or maraschino), with vermouth being the innovative point of differentiation. With dozens of options for each ingredient, the priority should be to find a vermouth whose botanicals complement the character of the whiskey, with the bitters there to integrate the mixture. Most of the early recipes didn't specify rye whiskey, so don't allow a history-minded bartender to con you out of a good bourbon Manhattan.

Hacks Employees Only has always served their house Manhattan with 0.5 ounce of curaçao, which is a delicious homage to the early recipes. While cherries are common and expected, an orange twist is a nice touch and should be substituted if the bar doesn't have real cherries. Save the neon-red cherries dyed with red #3 coloring for the napkin next to your ice cream sundae.

---

2 oz. **Buffalo Trace bourbon whiskey**

1 oz. **Martini Rosso vermouth**

2 dashes **Angostura bitters**

Garnish: **3 brandied cherries**

Stir with ice, then strain into a chilled coupe. Garnish with the cherries on a pick.

BOULEVARDIER

Origin This recipe was published alongside dozens of Harry McElhone's most loyal patrons' personal recipes in *Barflies and Cocktails* in 1927.

Logic According to McElhone, "Now is the time for all good barflies to come to the aid of the party, since Erskine Gwynne crashed in with his Boulevardier Cocktail: ⅓ Campari, ⅓ Italian vermouth, ⅓ bourbon whiskey." Gwynne was an American expat in Paris who founded a literary magazine called the *Boulevardier* the same year *Barflies* was published. The presence of an entire section in a cocktail book devoted to a bar's guests' favorite cocktails, including recipes they came up with, was unprecedented. The recipe appears in McElhone's *Harry's ABC of Mixing Cocktails* with Canadian Club— what bartenders probably poured when a guest ordered a drink with rye whiskey at that time.

Hacks I prefer it with two parts rye whiskey, but you could serve it with equal parts bourbon, as Gwynne preferred it, or Canadian Club, as Harry's served back in the day. This recipe will work with a host of whiskeys, vermouths, and bitters; the botanicals in vermouth di Torino work well with the American barrel-aged whiskey. Substitute dry vermouth for sweet and you have an Old Pal cocktail.

---

2 oz. Wild Turkey 101 proof rye whiskey

1 oz. Cocchi vermouth di Torino

1 oz. Campari

Garnish: 1 orange twist

Stir with ice, then strain into a chilled rocks glass filled with one large ice sphere. Garnish with the orange twist.

SAZERAC

Origin According to *Imbibe!*, the Sazerac was popularized by William H. Wilkinson around the turn of the twentieth century at the Sazerac House Bar owned by Thomas H. Handy & Co., "who also dealt in liquors and made Handy's Bitters from the formula they had purchased from A. A. Peychaud."

Logic This preparation is a perfect example of how a bartender layers flavor in a glass spatially, as a chef arranges components of a dish and sauce on a plate. By rinsing the glass with absinthe instead of dashing it in with the bitters, its aroma envelops the glass and integrates with the cocktail once they come into contact. The interior of the glass receives a second coat of aromatic "paint" from the lemon oil sprayed from the pinched twist, which coats the surface of the liquid and intermingles with the absinthe above the cocktail's wash line. The lemon oil masks the ABV of the cocktail beneath it just long enough for the imbiber to acclimate him- or herself to the beguilingly complex mixture, whose ingredients continue to marry with each sip. Many guests are finicky about the preparation of their Sazerac, so always ask whether they want Angostura bitters or just Peychaud's, and see whether they prefer it to be sweetened with a sugar cube or syrup.

Hacks Before absinthe was legalized in 2007, Sazeracs were prepared with New Orleans' own Herbsaint, which stands in admirably for the green fairy. Offering to prepare the cocktail with cognac in place of rye whiskey, or as its partner, to honor the city's French heritage is typically met with Francophilic glee.

---

2 oz. Sazerac rye whiskey

1 Demerara sugar cube

3 dashes Peychaud's bitters

2 dashes Angostura bitters

Jade Nouvelle Orleans absinthe, for rinsing

Lemon peel

Garnish: None

Muddle the sugar and bitters, then add the whiskey. Stir with ice and strain into a chilled rocks glass rinsed with the absinthe. Pinch a lemon peel over the surface and discard.

OLD-FASHIONED WHISKEY COCKTAIL

Origin The cocktail was first defined on May 6, 1806, in *The Balance and Columbian Repository* as "a stimulating liquor, composed of spirits of any kind, sugar, water and bitters." By the time it showed up in a professional bar manual for the first time in Theodore Proulx's 1888 *The Bartender's Manual*, it was already "old-fashioned."

Logic David Wondrich traces the first appearance back to 1833 with either rum, genever, or brandy as the spirit base, as whiskey was too coarse for company at that time. Nowadays, it's best to ask whether your guest wants their Old-Fashioned prepared as listed here, or with oranges and cherries. If they ask for the latter, they'll be expecting you to muddle half an orange wheel with a couple of cherries in addition to the sugar cube and bitters, which I'd advise you to prepare in a mixing glass and strain before service. It can be prepared in the glass with the ice it's served with, or in a mixing glass from which the chilled and diluted liquid is strained and served over fresh ice. Some prepare it with a sugar cube, others use syrup; a variety of citrus peels are used.

Hacks Nothing is sacred here except the simplicity of the formula. The base can be split between two or more categories; a variety of sugars can be substituted; and lemon, lime, orange, and grapefruit work well, depending on the base spirit you're working with. Given the simplicity of the drink, here's where you want to trot out your best glassware and fancy ice. This recipe didn't become the mother of all cocktails without being procreative, so reserve the snobbery for another recipe.

---

2 oz. Wild Turkey 101 proof rye whiskey

1 sugar cube

2 dashes Angostura bitters

Garnish: Lemon and orange twists

Muddle the sugar and bitters, then add the whiskey. Stir with ice and strain over one large ice sphere in a chilled rocks glass. Garnish with the lemon and orange twists.

TORONTO

Origin A recipe for the Fernet Cocktail calling for equal parts fernet and either cognac or rye whiskey was first printed in Robert Vermeire's 1922 *Cocktails: How to Mix Them* with the addendum that "this cocktail is much appreciated by the Canadians of Toronto."

Logic A similar formula, called the King Cole Cocktail, appears in Hugo Ensslin's 1916 *Recipes for Mixed Drinks*, with bourbon instead of rye and garnished with orange and pineapple. Harry Craddock, who cribbed dozens of cocktails from Ensslin's guide, offered it with rye whiskey or Canadian Club: both King Coles used fernet in place of Angostura bitters, using Old-Fashioned cocktail proportions. In the 1948 edition of *The Fine Art of Mixing Drinks,* David Embury stiffens it up with more whiskey and settles on calling it the Toronto instead of the Fernet, Canadian, or King Cole. He prepares it with Canadian whisky sans Angostura with an orange twist à la Craddock instead of the lemon twist à la Vermeire. Given the potency of Fernet-Branca and the subtlety of most Canadian whiskies, a little goes a long way. Corby's Lot 40 Canadian rye, which is distilled in pot stills from a 100 percent rye-based mash bill, has

the brawn to stand up to the bitters. I'd recommend a Kentucky straight rye such as Wild Turkey or Rittenhouse if you can't source a straight rye from Canada.

Hacks Canadian expat Jamie Boudreau serves his with a flamed orange twist. In addition to the variety of rye whiskeys to experiment with, there are a number of new fernets in the American market, including Leatherbee from Chicago and Contratto from Italy. I'm still open to the lemon twist.

2 oz. Lot No. 40 Canadian rye whisky

0.25 oz. Fernet-Branca

0.25 oz. Demerara syrup (page 391)

2 dashes Angostura bitters

Garnish: 1 orange twist

Stir with ice, then strain into a chilled coupe. Garnish with the orange twist.

BROWN BOMBER

Origin I created this for the PDT cocktail menu in the spring of 2008.

Logic Suze wasn't imported to the U.S. market until early 2012, but thanks to the popularity of Wayne Collins's White Negroni (Plymouth gin, Lillet blanc, Suze), we always kept a bottle on hand and asked our international guests to bring more when they visited. Gin and Tennessee whiskey are both dry, high-proof, flavorful base spirits that pair beautifully with the Lillet and Suze, so I swapped them out and renamed the drink. The name plays off the cocktail's strength (epitomized by boxer Joe Louis)—"getting bombed," a term for drinking too much—and its amber hue.

Hacks This will mix nicely with most Kentucky straight bourbon whiskeys in place of Dickel #12. I'd stick with Lillet, as Cocchi Americano rarely works well in its place, and Kina L'éro d'Or is too sweet here. Avèze Gentiane can be substituted for Suze if need be.

2 oz. George Dickel No. 12 Tennessee whisky

0.75 oz. Lillet blanc

0.5 oz. Suze Saveur D'Autrefois

Garnish: 1 lemon twist

Stir with ice, then strain into a chilled coupe. Garnish with the lemon twist.

PURPLE RAIN

Origin I created this cocktail in the fall of 2013, to serve before a dinner at McCrady's, hosted by chef Sean Brock, on behalf of a culinary festival called Cook It Raw in Charleston, South Carolina.

Logic The premise behind Cook It Raw is for chefs from all over the world to learn about the culinary traditions of the region where the event is hosted, and to apply them in their own style when they cook for the local community. So, I created this bourbon sour to honor the heritage of McCrady's, which was built by a madeira importer in the late 1700s, and to complement its head bartender Ryan Casey's bright green cocktail offering for the evening. The name "Purple Rain"—an allusion to the legendary Prince tune—plays off the violet-hued Crème Yvette and rainwater madeira (a historic style made from a base of Verdelho with two old lots of Tinta Negra Mole), which adds acidity to balance the sweetness.

Hacks Rainwater madeira is the key to the cocktail's logic, so leave it be. Crème Yvette is more balanced than crème de violette, but the latter could be substituted if necessary. I'd stick to a wheated bourbon like Maker's or W. L. Weller, and always steer clear of canned pineapple juice.

1.5 oz. Maker's Mark bourbon whisky
0.75 oz. Rare Wine Co. rainwater madeira
0.5 oz. Crème Yvette
0.5 oz. lemon juice
0.5 oz. pineapple juice
Garnish: 1 brandied cherry

Shake with ice and fine-strain into a chilled coupe. Garnish with the brandied cherry.

CAMERON'S KICK

Origin The recipe appears in the 1922 edition of Harry McElhone's *ABC of Mixing Cocktails* with the annotation "Orgeat Syrup is manufactured with almonds" underneath instead of a clue as to who Cameron is, where the recipe was created, or by whom—lore included for many of the book's other recipes.

Logic The use of orgeat as the sole sweetener and the split base of Irish and Scotch whisk(e)ys are unusual and memorable, as it is more common to see split bases of spirits in different categories from this time. The kick in the cocktail definitely comes from the whisk(e)ys, and the types you choose will have a huge impact on the cocktail's character. We can assume the recipe was made with lighter, blended whisk(e)ys when it first appeared in McElhone's guide, but choosing an older blend, blended malt, single-malt, pure pot still, or peated whisk(e)y will create different kicks.

Hacks The explanation clearly states that the orgeat must be from almonds, so an artificially flavored almond syrup will not suffice as a substitute here. The original recipe doesn't call for a garnish, but a lemon twist is a nice touch.

1 oz. Dewar's White Label blended Scotch whisky

1 oz. Bushmills Original Irish whiskey

0.75 oz. lemon juice

0.5 oz. Small Hand Foods orgeat

Garnish: None

Shake with ice, then fine-strain into a chilled coupe.

FOR PEAT'S SAKE

Origin Jeff Bell and I created this cocktail for the PDT fall menu in 2011.

Logic Our process began with a constraint every bar manager faces periodically: an abundance of product coupled with the need to deplete it to keep inventory value in check. Pernod absinthe was the surplus spirit in this case, which requires powerful partners to pair it with and a recipe to give them all an opportunity to shine. We chose the Last Word as our template; substituted one of the peatiest malts on the market for gin, which was overpowered by the absinthe; and added celery juice in place of lime to marry the briny scotch with all the herbal components. Using equal parts of each ingredient was unpalatable, so we tinkered with the proportions.

Hacks Luxardo maraschino and green Chartreuse have few peers, but you're welcome to tinker with the absinthe brand, proportions, and choice of peated malt based on your guest's preference—the original version of this drink was prepared with Ardbeg 10-year. Scylla and Charybdis come to mind as you meddle with scotch and absinthe options. As for the name, if you can come up with a better pun, go for it; it was really for the inventory's sake.

1.5 oz. celery juice

1 oz. Bruichladdich Octomore Scotch whisky

0.5 oz. green Chartreuse

0.5 oz. Luxardo maraschino liqueur

0.25 oz. Pernod absinthe

Garnish: None

Shake with ice, then fine-strain into a chilled coupe.

GEORGE WASHINGTON

Origin I created this for the menu at PDT in the summer of 2013.

Logic Every once in a while, a product comes along that blows your mind. Nicolas Palazzi, an independent bottler and U.S. spirits importer, introduced me to Cazottes Wild Cherry liqueur, and I begged him for as much as he could sell me. Based on their miniscule production of only six hundred bottles a year, that amounted to twelve 375ml bottles, which I wanted to showcase in a cocktail. Instead of using a recipe that calls for cherry liqueur, such as the Blood and Sand, I chose my colleague Michael Klein's Tompkins Square cocktail: a variation on the Vieux Carré that substitutes kirschwasser for cognac. I loved the way cherry worked in the recipe, and I rejiggered it with applejack as a co-base and the cherry liqueur in place of Bénédictine.

Hacks I've tried this with pure apple brandy and prefer it with applejack. Most bonded ryes from Kentucky would work in place of Wild Turkey, although I prefer Turkey. St. Elizabeth Allspice Dram works, but Bitter Truth is, ironically, less bitter. The likelihood of sourcing Cazottes is slim in most markets, so look for Luxardo's lesser-known Sangue Morlacco cherry liqueur.

1 oz. Laird's applejack

1 oz. Wild Turkey 101 proof rye whiskey

0.75 oz. Cocchi vermouth di Torino

0.75 oz. Cazottes Wild Sour Cherry liqueur

Bitter Truth Pimento Dram allspice liqueur, for rinsing

Garnish: 3 brandied cherries

Stir the applejack, whiskey, vermouth, and cherry liqueur with ice, then strain over one large ice cube into a chilled rocks glass rinsed with the Bitter Truth. Garnish with the brandied cherries on a pick.

DUBOUDREAU COCKTAIL

Origin I created this for the PDT cocktail menu in the spring of 2009.

Logic One of the most memorable cocktails I collected as the deputy editor of the *Food & Wine Cocktails* 2008 edition was Jamie Boudreau's Cooper's Cocktail, a bittersweet cocktail named after St-Germain founder Rob Cooper, prepared with rye whiskey, St-Germain, and Fernet-Branca and served up with an orange twist. I loved the flavors, but found that the fernet and St-Germain overpowered the whiskey, so I rejiggered it into a Brooklyn cocktail variation with Dubonnet in place of vermouth. This gave me an opportunity to put my high school French to use: *DuBoudreau* means "of Boudreau."

Hacks This should work with most bonded rye whiskeys. Sweet vermouth, sherry, madeira, or other kinas are worth experimenting with, or conduct a comparative tasting between French Dubonnet and American Dubonnet; the former isn't imported to the U.S. market. If you replace the Branca, stick to St-Germain and a dry fernet.

2 oz. Rittenhouse bonded rye whiskey

0.75 oz. Dubonnet Rouge

0.25 oz. Fernet-Branca

0.25 oz. St-Germain

Garnish: 1 lemon twist

Stir with ice, then strain into a chilled coupe. Garnish with the lemon twist.

IRELAND

UNITED
KINGDOM

North Sea

Baltic Sea

POLAND

Berlin ★

GERMANY

BELGIUM

CZECH REP.

CALVADOS A.O.C.

English Channel

Paris ★

SLOVAKIA

Eigeltingen ⊙

Axberg ⊙

Vienna ★

FRANCE

Fritzens ⊙

AUSTRIA

Bay
of
Biscay

COGNAC
A.O.C.

Cognac ⊙
Jarnac ⊙

SWITZERLAND

HUNGARY

ARMAGNAC
A.O.C.

SLOVENIA

CROATIA

BOSNIA
& HER.

Adriatic Sea

ITALY

SPAIN

Mediterranean Sea

AUSTRIA

⊙ *Axberg*
(Reisetbauer eau de vie)

⊙ *Fritzens*
(Rochelt eau de vie)

FRANCE

⊙ *Cognac*
(Martell cognac)
(Pierre Ferrand cognac)
(Rémy Martin cognac)

⊙ *Jarnac*
(Hine cognac)
(Louis Royer cognac)

GERMANY

⊙ *Eigeltingen*
(Stählemühle eau de vie)

⠿ *Traditional Production Region*   ⊙ Distillery Site   ★ Capital

BRANDY AND EAU DE VIE

The word *brandy* is derived from the Dutch word *brandewijn*, literally "burned wine," which refers to the wine's distillation into eau de vie. Some of the world's most famous brandies come from the town of Cognac, whose position on the Charente River near the port of La Rochelle provided easy access for Dutch trading ships in the sixteenth century.

Today, brandy is produced all over the world, but the world's most prized bottlings—barrel-aged cognacs and armagnacs from wine, calvados from cider, and clear eau de vie and schnapps from ripe berries and tree fruit—are all produced in the European Union.

The Romans planted fruit trees and made wine and cider from apples, pears, and grapes in France as early as the fourth century. According to Mark Ridgwell's *Spirits Distilled*, the wines and ciders from this region didn't become popular until the Middle Ages, after the Norman king Henry II married Eleanor of Aquitaine in 1152. Over the next three hundred years, the English developed an unquenchable thirst for French wines and ciders.

This thirst soon extended to French spirits, as distillation spread from Northern Africa to Spain, then up into the rest of Europe during the Middle Ages. Thanks to their proximity to Spain, winemakers in Gascony were among the first to benefit from distilling knowledge, followed by winemakers in the Charente and cider producers in Normandy. A 1558 journal entry from a Norman nobleman, Gilles de Gouberville, mentions production of *eau de vie de cidre*.

Around this time, the Spanish Armada occupied the South American port of Pisco (in what became Peru), where they planted wine grapes including Torrontel and different strains of Muscat in the arid tropical valleys. According to an article by Éva Pelczer, the region's wine grew so popular that the Spanish crown banned exports to squelch competition with domestic production in 1641. With no export market for their wines, South American farmers began distilling it for sailors heading up and down the coast.

In North America, settlers planted apple trees in cooler climates where crops used to brew beer wouldn't grow, and by the 1670s, hard cider was the most abundant fermented beverage in the northeast. Before distillation became common, applejack was produced by skimming the ice off the top of cider barrels left outside during the cold winters, concentrating the alcohol.

Back in France, Dutch importers, who favored the wines of the maritime province of Charente, started distilling wine to prevent acidification on their ships and became known as *winjbranders* ("wine burners"). By 1630, Charente winemakers began distilling twice, which reduced the yield, lowered shipping costs, and improved the character of the eau de vie.

According to cognac historian Jacques Blanc, in 1638 the English author and merchant Lewes Roberts called the Charente eau de vie "cogniacke," and five years later Philippe Augier founded a company called Cognac Augier. After

Maison Ferrand Charente Still

war interrupted Dutch trading from 1701 to 1713, merchants from other countries took an interest in this region, including Jean Martell from Jersey, Richard Hennessy from Ireland, and Thomas Hine from England.

Around 1817, cognac merchants began classifying their barrel-aged brandies as VOP (Very Old Pale) and VSOP (Very Special Old Pale). By the mid-1800s, cognac producers began to package and ship their brandy in bottles, which helped foster the growth of glass factories, printers, and cork manufacturers throughout France. Compare this with the apple brandies of calvados, which were distributed to Paris by cask well into the middle of the twentieth century.

North of France, Empress Maria Theresa, who ruled the Hapsburg Empire in the middle of the eighteenth century, introduced a grant permitting any household to make up to 200 liters of distilled spirits annually, with a special clause for land-owning farmers to distill up to 300 liters. In addition to increasing the monarch's revenue on fruit distillates, the empress fostered a free market that began to recognize quality.

Between 1875 and 1880, disaster struck French winemakers when the agricultural pest phylloxera began feeding on their grapevines' roots. By 1893, only 10 percent of France's grapevines were unaffected. During this time, cider production in Normandy more than tripled and took wine's place at the French table. It took nearly a generation for the vineyards to recover, and although the wine and brandy industry is not as large as it once was, the product is better thanks to rigorous production guidelines.

In the early 1980s the first wave of craft distillers in America started a brandy revolution, spurred by Hubert Germain Robin and Ansley Coale, who combined historic French distillation, aging, and blending methods in conjunction with innovative American winemaking. Their predecessors include Dan Farber of Osocalis, Lance Winters of St. George, and Steve McCarthy of Clear Creek, who've helped balance the quality of brandy and eau de vie on both sides of the Atlantic ever since.

Cognac

The most famous of all brandies is produced in the Charente province of France by over two thousand independent distillers who grow grapes, make wine, and mostly contract distill their eau de vie for large *négociants* such as Hennessy, Martell, and Courvosier, who age, blend, and bottle. Independent producers, such as Pierre Ferrand, Frapin, Guillon Painturaud, and Paul Beau, have their own labels but lack the distribution and marketing budgets of the larger *négociants*.

The Ugni Blanc, Colombard, Folle Blanche, Montils, and Folignan grapes grown in the region's mild marine climate and chalky soil produce wines with high acid and low alcohol, ideal for distillation, which is carried out in direct-fired Charentais pot stills. These yield two types of eau de vie: *brouillis* (25% to 27% ABV) on the first run and *bonne chauffe* on the second distillation (around 71% ABV).

The eau de vie is aged in 350-liter casks made from French oak. According to Osocalis founder Dan Farber, "The wide-grained Limosin *Quercus robur* has the most robust tannins, adding structure to the brandy, while Tronçais *Quercus petraea* is tighter grained, yielding more perfume." The barrels rest in ancient cellars for long-term aging of up to eighty years before being transferred to wicker-covered glass carboys, called *bonbonnes*, stored in a locked chamber in the cellar called a *paradis*.

Maison Ferrand Cognac Paradis

More than the makers of any other brandy, cognac producers have separated themselves from the pack by uniting under strict regulations and collective marketing.

ON MATURITY

"As the greatest of the great brown brandies will live in barrel for the time scale of a human life, so do they pass through life cycles from birth to childhood, teenage years, adulthood, middle age, and elderly distinction. It is in these contexts that one must reflect on and judge the characteristics of an aged brandy. Clearly one cannot expect a refined conversation with a child any more than one would expect childlike energy from a respected elder. Yet in both cases there is beauty and inspiration to be found, albeit different in nature."

DAN FARBER

Master Blender

In 1936, the French established quality standards for cognac, specifying official grapes for winemaking, geographic vineyard designations, and specifics for distillation and aging. In 1946, the Interprofessional Bureau of Cognac (BNIC) was founded; it serves as the governing and marketing wing of the industry.

Cognac producers blend young brandies with small amounts of much older brandies and dilute to 40% ABV before bottling. Adding sugar is permitted, which contributes residual sweetness in certain blends. VS and three-star cognacs are a minimum of two years old, VSOP blends are a minimum of four years old, and XO blends are a minimum of six years old, but all are typically much older by average age of the blended spirits. Vintage and cask-strength cognacs are quite rare.

Pisco

Pisco, the spirit of Peru and Chile, originates from the Quechua word for "little bird," once used to describe the subtropical desert between the foothills of the Andes and the Pacific coast of Peru. Peruvian pisco may be made from eight aromatic and nonaromatic grape varietals, including Quebranta, Molar, Italia, Moscatel, and Torontel.

After a week to ten days of natural fermentation, the grape musts are pot distilled between 38% and 48% ABV. After distillation, the spirit is rested in neutral clay, steel, or glass vessels—no coloring, sweeteners, barrel aging, or dilution is permitted—for a minimum of three months; then it's bottled at proof.

Peruvian pisco is made in three styles: *puro*, from a single grape variety; *acholado,* from a mix of grapes; and *mosto verde*, from partially fermented musts, requiring much more fruit to distill. In my experience, blends containing nonaromatic grapes such as Quebranta are necessary to balance the floral varieties and lend structure in cocktails like the Pisco Sour (page 353) and Pisco Punch (page 355).

Apple Brandy

Three styles of AOC calvados are produced in the northeast portion of Normandy, centered around the city of Caen. The apples used for cider production are from four different types that are blended, pressed, and fermented together into a low-ABV cider with no added sugar. Natural fermentation is carried out for up to a month; then the cider is stored in barrels before distillation.

AOC calvados can be pot or column distilled and must be aged for at least two years. Calvados Pays d'Auge is distilled from ciders containing no more than 30 percent pears, distilled twice in an alembic pot, and aged for at least two years in oak casks. Calvados Domfrontais is distilled from ciders that must contain no less than 30 percent pears distilled once in a continuous column and aged for at least three years. While some new wood is used, most calvados is aged in old oak casks, which promotes earthy, rancio notes in the brandy.

The earthy notes of calvados, which wasn't widely distributed in the United States until the 1970s, clashes with the clean fruit flavors of classic cocktails like the Jack Rose (page 359) and Pink Lady. For these recipes and many more, American bartenders have historically relied instead on blended applejack.

The only U.S. apple brandy brand available up until very recently was Laird's, which presses Red and Golden Delicious, Jonathan, Gala, Fuji, Stayman, and Winesap apples and ferment them using a proprietary yeast strain for one to two weeks, depending on the weather. The cider is distilled in a hybrid pot still with rectifying column to 80% ABV and aged in second-fill former bourbon barrels.

Their applejack is a blend of 35 percent apple brandy aged three to four years and 65 percent neutral spirit with added caramel for color only. American bartenders have recently fallen in love with their straight apple brandy, bottled with pure apple brandy aged three to seven years at 50% ABV. In the past it was bottled in bond, but demand forced them to add brandies younger than four years old, the minimum to label it as bottled in bond.

Eau de Vie

Eau de vie—French for "water of life"—is the term for grape-based distillate before it's barrel-aged to become brandy, and for full-strength fruit distillates made from berries and tree and stone fruits. In the alpine regions of the Black Forest in southern Germany, Alsace, Switzerland, Austria, and northeast Italy, it's sometimes called schnapps; in Hungary they call it *palinka*.

Most eau de vie is produced on small farms and distilleries from common fruits, such as plum, pear, raspberry, and cherry, along with unusual fruits, such as quince, rowan berry, and currants, which taste better in a spirit than as a snack.

In Austria, Hans Reisetbauer distills an average of 50 pounds of hand-picked fruit from his family orchard in Axberg to produce 1 liter of eau de vie. He's so particular about the minerality of the water he mashes with that he ships it in from an alpine pasture in Mühlviertel. After the sugars are converted, he distills in a copper pot and collects only the heart cut.

Unlike barrel-aged spirits, the goal of eau de vie is to capture the essence of the fruit at its peak ripeness with no sugar supplement. After distillation, the eau de vie is rested in neutral glass or steel vessels for a minimum of six months, although many producers rest them for a decade or more before bottling.

Due to the prohibitive cost of producing eau de vie, it's among the most expensive spirits to pour. Thankfully, as little as 0.25 ounce of eau de vie from a producer like Reisetbauer shines through other spirits as a fresh fruit accent in a cocktail. Domestic producers, including Oregon's Clear Creek and California's St. George, produce laudable eau de vie at a lower price point.

Unlike gin, whiskey, and rum, which have a long history of being mixed, in modern times there is what some would call an "open relationship" between brandy and cocktails. Besides VS cognac, Peruvian pisco, and American applejack, many of the brandies just discussed are too expensive for most bars to mix with profitably. Cost is not the only barrier; the top armagnac, calvados, Spanish brandy, and eau de vie brands are difficult to source outside cosmopolitan cities.

Reisetbauer Tasting Thief

I hope to see this change in the years ahead, as cooperation from the producers and regulatory councils help bartenders learn to appreciate and mix cocktails with these fine brandies. Pioneering San Francisco bartender Thad Vogler, who works in the cradle of American brandy production, sources calvados and armagnac directly for use in his cocktail programs at Trou Normand and Bar Agricole. Thanks to Thad and others—like Sullivan Doh, who spotlights French spirits at Le Syndicat in Paris—the future is promising.

ON GETTING STARTED

"In 1994 I came home to my wife and said, 'We will start distilling,' and she said, 'Are you crazy? You have no idea.' And I said, 'I have no idea.' And then I bought all the books, and I read nine thousand pages in three months. Bought my first distillery. I got it on the sixteenth of September. I never saw a distillery before. I started with 800 kilos of Pear Williams from fifteen old trees. This was my first mash. It was only fourteen days' fermentation, and the guys asked me if I already distilled it. The guys said it was impossible, because it needed months. I said there was no sugar inside, and if there's no sugar inside it must be ready. They said I was crazy, and I said they were assholes."

HANS REISETBAUER

Master Distiller

PISCO SOUR

Origin Victor Morris, who opened an American bar in Lima in 1916, made this drink famous; however, a 1903 pamphlet, "Nueva Manual de Cocina a la Criolla" by S. E. Ledesma, includes the first printed Pisco Sour recipe titled "cocktail." We can thank Fernando Castellon (via Wondrich in *Imbibe!*) for letting the truth get in the way of a good story here.

Logic Pisco's character depends on the grape varietal or blend it's distilled from, so once you've offered your guest their options, the primary tasks at hand are to balance the cocktail, properly emulsify the egg white, and decorate the frothy head elegantly. A standard shake will suffice after dry shaking, and you can fine-strain without compromising the texture. Decant your bitters into a dropper bottle so you have pinpoint control of the shape and size of your bitters decoration. As long as the head is thick like a Guinness, the bitters will remain on top of the liquid and not affect the taste of the drink underneath. Besides decoration, the bitters' purpose is to cover up the earthy aroma of the egg white.

Hacks "Lime" in spanish is *limon*, so you'll often see Pisco Sours prepared with lemon juice, which works well, too. When I visited Peru in 2009, all of my Pisco Sours were prepared in a blender with (too much) gum syrup, and aromatized with Peruvian Amargo Chuncho bitters, which are a nice touch.

---

2 oz. La Diablada pisco

0.75 oz. lime juice

0.75 oz. simple syrup (page 391)

1 egg white

Garnish: Angostura bitters

Dry shake, then shake with ice and fine-strain into a chilled coupe. Garnish with drops of Angostura swirled with a straw.

PISCO PUNCH

Origin Pisco Punch became legendary thanks to Scottish barman Duncan Nicol, who purchased San Francisco's historic Bank Exchange Saloon—with its house punch recipe—in 1893 and kept it a secret, despite fanfare and public prying, until his dying day in 1926.

Logic The recipe here was adapted from a recipe David Wondrich uncovered from one of Nicol's former bar managers in the *California Historical Quarterly* from 1973, and printed in *Imbibe!* The appeal of the lost recipe was not only the fact that his version was the most popular; there was also widespread speculation that it was prepared with a secret ingredient. In *Drinking the Devil's Acre*, author and pisco producer Duggan McDonnell confides that initially "many thought that the magic ingredient in the punch was merely gum arabic," which was brought back by San Francisco bartender Jen Colliau, who now bottles it under her Small Hand Foods label. But there was also speculation that Nicol's secret ingredient was cocaine, which may explain why he permitted only two portions per patron.

Hacks Unsatisfied with pineapple gum as the secret ingredient, Duggan McDonnell makes a cogent argument for the cocaine to have manifested in the form of Vin Mariani, a Bordeaux-based fortified wine aromatized with coca leaves. Using Rudyard Kipling's description of a red drink as further evidence, McDonnell prepares his Pisco Punch with the addition of a Bordeaux-based quinquina, Lillet rouge—a delicious hack, and a cogent application of mixography.

---

2 oz. Campo de Encanto pisco

1 oz. Small Hand Foods pineapple gum syrup

0.75 oz. lemon juice

0.5 oz. pineapple juice

Garnish: 1 pineapple spear

Stir with ice, then strain into a chilled highball glass. Garnish with the pineapple spear.

SIDECAR

Origin This recipe appears as the "Side-Car" in Robert Vermeire's *Cocktails: How to Mix Them* in 1922. The directions state, "This cocktail is very popular in France. It was first introduced in London by MacGarry, the celebrated bar-tender of Buck's Club."

Logic Vermeire's recipe calls for equal parts of each ingredient and no simple syrup or sugar rim. My recipe, by contrast, calls for simple syrup but omits the sugar rim. Nowadays, the evocatively titled Sidecar— which we've yet to find the inspiration for—is prepared as a daisy instead of the more baroque Brandy Crusta, the source of the sugar rim and recipe. The trick with daisies, including the Margarita and the White Lady, is balancing the acidity of the citrus with Cointreau, which isn't sweet enough to temper the bite of the juice when they're mixed in equal proportions. Instead of substituting an inferior orange liqueur or rimming the glass with sugar, add simple syrup to bring everything into balance without raising the ABV of the mixture (Cointreau is 80 proof) or overpowering the cognac with more orange flavor.

Hacks The recipe doesn't call for a garnish, but a lemon or orange twist is a nice touch to accentuate the lemon juice or orange liqueur. I'd substitute armagnac or one of the more venerable alembic brandies from California, such as Osocalis or Germain-Robin, before searching for a substitute for the triple sec.

2 oz. Rémy Martin VSOP cognac
0.75 oz. lemon juice
0.5 oz. Cointreau
0.25 oz. simple syrup (page 391)
Garnish: None

Shake with ice, then fine-strain into a chilled coupe.

JACK ROSE

Origin The origin of the name is unclear, but the first Jack Rose was printed in *Jack's Manual* in 1910, which called for it to be prepared with "cider brandy" and lemon, lime, and orange juices; sweetened with raspberry syrup and superfine sugar; served on the rocks; and topped with soda. Four years later it was pared back to applejack, lime juice, and grenadine in Jacques Straub's *Drinks*, which still stands today.

Logic Applejack remains something of a novelty, but Ted Haigh stumped for it in the influential 2004 edition of *Vintage Spirits and Forgotten Cocktails*, in which the Jack Rose is the second printed recipe. In 2005, Audrey Saunders (see page 452) convinced Lisa Laird (see page 405), the ninth-generation family operator of Laird & Company, to distribute her apple brandy in New York City so she could feature it at the Pegu Club. Following Audrey's lead, applejack and its more robust, uncut 100 proof apple brandy took off in cocktail menus across the city and beyond. Another element of this cocktail's renaissance was Haigh's insistence that it be prepared with pomegranate-based grenadine instead of prevalent brands, which contain no fruit juice. By 2005, POM Wonderful pomegranate juice (founded in 2002) was widely distributed, so many bartenders began making their own grenadine with it.

Hacks Applejack, calvados, and pure apple brandy yield a Jack Rose cocktail with a different apple character. Calvados is more earthy and complex, the 100 proof pure apple brandy is more clean and bright, and applejack buckles under the citrus and pomegranate. The original recipe calls for lime juice.

---

2 oz. Laird's apple brandy
0.75 oz. lemon juice
0.75 oz. Jack Rudy grenadine
Garnish: None

Shake with ice, then fine-strain into a chilled coupe.

CHAMPS-ÉLYSÉES

Origin Martin Doudoroff traced this recipe back to thriller author Nina Toye and food writer A. H. Adair's recipe guide *Drinks—Long and Short*, published in London in 1925.

Logic I encountered this recipe in a reprint of *The Savoy Cocktail Book* and put it on the menu at Gramercy Tavern in 2006 when there were still "new" drinks left to "discover" in old cocktail books. After David Wondrich exposed Harry Craddock for cribbing 146 recipes from Hugo Ensslin's *Recipes for Mixed Drinks* in his introduction to the Cocktail Kingdom reprint of the obscure guide in 2009, I began to suspect the Champs-Élysées wasn't Craddock's cocktail either. In 2014, Martin Doudoroff began working on an ambitious index—in the form of an app—of the origins of thousands of recipes. He uncovered six recipes from *The Savoy Cocktail Book*—all scaled up to serve six portions, including the Champs-Élysées—in *Drinks—Long and Short*, which Craddock printed verbatim. Sadly, Toye and Adair don't list the cocktail's origin or creator, nor does their recipe clarify whether to mix it with green or yellow Chartreuse. For this reason, you are welcome to experiment with both.

Hacks The version I served on the menu at Gramercy Tavern was sweetened with Darjeeling tea syrup and the older VEP bottling of green Chartreuse, which sent its pour cost through the roof. When price (and profit) are no object, I prepare it as I imagine it would be served on Paris's luxurious Champs-Élysées: with XO cognac and VEP green Chartreuse.

---

2 oz. Pierre Ferrand 1840 cognac

0.75 oz. lemon juice

0.5 oz. green Chartreuse

0.25 oz. simple syrup (page 391)

1 dash Angostura bitters

Garnish: None

Shake with ice, then fine-strain into a chilled coupe.

NEWARK

Origin John Deragon and I created this cocktail for the PDT menu in the fall of 2007.

Logic Brooklyn cocktail variations were all the rage when we came up with this. Enzo's Red Hook, Mickey's Greenpoint, Audrey's Little Italy, Chad's Bensonhurst, and Julie's Slope were being mixed all over Manhattan, and John and I wanted to throw our hat into the ring. With nary a neighborhood left to choose from, we pondered our options along with the dwindling supply of rye whiskey, which was being held back by our suppliers thanks to overwhelming demand for classic whiskey cocktails in the city. As Manhattanites are forced to do, we looked across the river for inspiration, and came up with this New Jersey apple brandy–based twist, which substituted Fernet-Branca for Amer Picon, which is neither imported to the United States nor formulated the same as it was back in the day, and we subbed sweet vermouth for dry. Boozy and bitter, it was, we felt, worthy enough to be Newark's namesake.

Hacks Look for Laird's 100 proof apple brandy (ideally the older bonded formula) to provide a sturdy backbone to balance the other powerful flavors in the recipe. A well-made calvados would work, but you lose the Jersey connection. Vya is more wine focused than most vermouths, but Cocchi's vermouth di Torino would work well here, too.

2 oz. **Laird's apple brandy**
1 oz. **Vya sweet vermouth**
0.25 oz. **Fernet-Branca**
0.25 oz. **Luxardo maraschino liqueur**
Garnish: None

Stir with ice, then strain into a chilled coupe.

ROSE

Origin In his *ABC of Mixing Cocktails*, Harry McElhone attributes this recipe to Johnny Mitta of Paris's Chatham Bar.

Logic The original recipe calls for Sirop de Groseille, a red currant syrup, which would limit the window in which you could prepare this recipe to just a few weeks in the summer when the currants are ripe. Ted Haigh canonized this obscure cocktail in the 2004 edition of *Vintage Spirits and Forgotten Cocktails*, where he called for it to be prepared with dry French vermouth and raspberry syrup—an ingenious hack. The floral quality of the raspberry syrup brightens up the earth notes in the cherry eau de vie. I've found the sweet blanc vermouth from Chambéry is the key to balancing this recipe, as more botanically driven dry vermouths are tailored for gin drinks.

Hacks Hans Reisetbauer's wild cherry eau de vie yields an ethereal Rose. Before Small Hand Foods raspberry gum syrup was released, I used to prepare this with a barspoon of Bon Maman raspberry preserves, and fine-strained the mixture. Don't ruin this with cheap cherries; seek out brandied Morello cherries, or *griottines*, as they're called in France.

2 oz. Dolin Blanc vermouth

1 oz. Reisetbauer wild cherry eau de vie

0.25 oz. Small Hand Foods raspberry gum syrup

Garnish: 1 brandied cherry

Stir with ice, then fine-strain into a chilled coupe. Garnish with the cherry.

JIMMIE ROOSEVELT

Origin Charles Baker published this recipe, with a great story about it, in *The Gentleman's Companion* in 1939.

Logic Audrey Saunders included this cocktail on the opening menu at the Pegu Club, and I've always loved the way it evolves in the glass. If you serve it in a coupe and float the Chartreuse, the herbal liqueur dominates the aromatics as the bubbles lift it. As you sip, the bitters-soaked sugar cube begins to dissolve, adding both sweetness and bitterness. To mitigate the sweetness, an extra-brut champagne is advisable, which can be used to top off the cocktail if the guest requests it. I often serve this over cracked cubes, which chill and dilute the cocktail while you sip it, but an ice sphere is a nice touch if the cognac is diluted with the ice used to chill it instead of being pouring directly from a freezer.

Hacks Depending on the occasion and constraints you're working with, old cognac, VEP Chartreuse, and tête de cuvée champagne can transform this from superlative to sublime.

2 oz. Robert Moncuit Blanc de Blancs champagne

1 oz. Hine H cognac, chilled

0.25 oz. green Chartreuse

1 Demerara sugar cube soaked in Angostura bitters

Garnish: None

Place the bitters-soaked sugar cube in the bottom of the chilled coupe, then place an ice sphere on top of it. Add the cognac then top with the champagne and float the Chartreuse.

FRENCH MAID

Origin I created this for an art gallery opening hosted by John Pellaton of Hine Cognac in the fall of 2007.

Logic This recipe was created to complement my former Pegu Club colleague Sam Ross's Old Maid cocktail, prepared with gin, cucumber, lime, and mint, at Eastside Company Bar in 2005, and a more famous riff served with bourbon called the Kentucky Maid at Milk & Honey. The cocktail world was so small back then that we shared the same guests and served each other's cocktails. Using Sam's trinity of mint, cucumber, and lime as my foundation, and "maid" as the nomenclature to classify it in the name, I embellished the template using ginger wort in place of soda and falernum to add spice and sweetness.

Hacks The French Maid hails from the Old Maid, which descends from the Mojito, itself a relative of the Julep. Be wary of anyone who says they've "created" a cocktail using ingredients that have been around longer than they have. Bartenders improvise on recipes like jazz musicians riff on a musical score, and Sam is one of the best at it.

1.5 oz. Hine H cognac

1 oz. ginger wort (page 393)

0.75 oz. lime juice

0.5 oz. simple syrup (page 391)

0.25 oz. John D. Taylor's Velvet Falernum

3 cucumber wheels

5 to 7 mint leaves (plus 1 for garnish)

Garnish: 1 cucumber spear

Muddle the cucumber wheels, mint, and syrup, then add everything but the garnish. Shake with ice, then fine-strain into a chilled collins glass filled with ice cubes. Garnish with a mint leaf and the cucumber.

JAPANESE COCKTAIL

Origin According to *Imbibe!*, Jerry Thomas created this in 1860 for a delegation of Japanese dignitaries who were staying in the Metropolitan Hotel—right across the street from his bar at 622 Broadway. He included it in *The Bar-Tenders Guide*.

Logic Wondrich distinguishes the Japanese cocktail as one of the only two cocktails Thomas invented in his book (the other being the Blue Blazer), which remained popular until Prohibition. The recipe for orgeat in Christian Schultz's supplement to the 1862 edition of Thomas's book calls for it to be made naturally with blanched almonds, sugar, and orange flower water, so substituting artificially flavored modern almond syrups won't cut it. The added bitters and citrus twist (two were called for in Thomas's recipe) help balance the richness of the nutty orgeat.

Hacks The original recipe calls for the cocktail to be stirred and served on the rocks. In the photo, I chose to serve it with a lemon wheel supporting the sphere for aesthetics in a coupe. If you're going to use more than one twist, try adding an orange twist to round out the nose instead of a second lemon twist.

2 oz. Louis Royer Force 53 cognac

0.5 oz. Small Hand Foods orgeat

½ tsp. Boker's bitters

Garnish: 1 lemon twist

Stir with ice, then strain over a large ice sphere into a chilled rocks glass. Garnish with the lemon twist.

ENGLAND

NETHERLANDS

POLAND

BELGIUM

GERMANY

English Channel

Fécamp ⊙

CZECH REP.

SLOVAKIA

Paris ★

Angers ⊙

Steyr ⊙   Vienna ★

Bay of Biscay

Meursault ⊙   Bern ★

FRANCE

SWITZERLAND   AUSTRIA

HUNGARY

Cognac ⊙

Virieu ⊙

Percoto ⊙

CROATIA

Voiron ⊙   Milan ⊙   Torreglia ⊙

Beaucaire ⊙   Villeneuve ⊙

BOSNIA & HER.

SPAIN

ITALY

Adriatic Sea

Mediterranean Sea

Rome ★

Benevento ⊙

AUSTRIA
⊙ *Steyr*
(Rothman & Winter)

FRANCE
⊙ *Angers*
(Giffard)
(Cointreau)

⊙ *Beaucaire*
(St. Germain)

⊙ *Cognac*
(Pierre Ferrand)
(Grand Marnier)

⊙ *Fécamp*
(Bénédictine)

⊙ *Meursault*
(Domaine Roulot)

⊙ *Villeneuve*
(Cazottes)

⊙ *Virieu*
(Bigallet)

⊙ *Voiron*
(Chartreuse)

ITALY
⊙ *Benevento*
(Strega)

⊙ *Milan*
(Fratelli Branca)

⊙ *Percoto*
(Nonino)

⊙ *Torreglia*
(Luxardo)

SWITZERLAND
★ *Bern*
(Tempus Fugit)

⋮⋮⋮ *Traditional Production Region*   ⊙ *Distillery Site*   ★ *Capital*

LIQUEURS

The earliest known reference to the word *alcohol* appears in the twelfth century, where it refers to the production of perfumes and cosmetics, not to potable spirits. *Alcohol* is derived from the Arabic *al-kuhul*, where *al-* is the definite article "the" and *kuhul* is derived from *kahala*, "to stain or paint." It was an eye powder, refined through vaporizing a metallic base to stain the eyelid. The first distillers of alcohol as we know it were monks who applied herbalism to create medicinal alcoholic elixirs known as liqueurs—from the Latin word *liquifacere* ("to liquefy")—in the Middle Ages.

Working from global trade outposts throughout France and Italy, monks received botanicals from all over the world, which they used to produce liqueurs with medicinal qualities. They documented ingredients such as fennel's ability to relieve menstrual cramps, beet's ability to lower blood pressure, aloe's capacity to regenerate cells, and bitter orange peel's function as a laxative. The monks documented medicinal properties of the leaves, peel, flesh, seeds, flowers, and roots, including the best methods to preserve their healing properties, color, and aroma.

In the sixteenth century, once spices like orange peel, vanilla pods, and ginger root arrived via the ships of powerful global merchants like the Dutch East India Company, distillers across Holland and others who traded with them began creating liqueurs for recreational appreciation. Dutch distillers are famous for orange curaçao and advocaat, but they have also created hundreds of lesser-known formulas to commemorate weddings, birth announcements, and other milestones.

Spirits expert Philip Duff distinguishes French and Italians monastic distillers, who were "artisans, quality-obsessed, and highly skilled" from Dutch distillers, who were primarily "businesspeople that learned industrialized processes from the French and Italians." He adds that while venerable firms such as Bols and DeKyuper have been in business for centuries, they periodically shifted focus from liqueurs, based on market conditions rather than generational leadership. In contrast, French and Italian liqueur producers such as Chartreuse and Campari have weathered fashion's waxing and waning moons.

Today, producers typically use the cheapest, most plentiful local sources for neutral spirit and sugar to produce liqueurs worldwide. In the European Union, where nearly all the classic liqueurs of the world are produced, regulations are specific about sugar and alcohol levels for each style, but flexible on how flavor and color are imparted, which leaves the door open for industrial extracts. All but dairy liqueurs must be a minimum of 15% ABV and contain a minimum of 100 grams of sugar per liter, except gentian-based liqueurs like Suze and cherry-based maraschino liqueur. Crèmes must contain a minimum of 250 grams of sugar per liter, with the exception of cassis, which must contain a minimum of 400 grams.

The most common extraction process to produce traditional liqueurs is maceration—a fancy word for infusion—in which alcohol functions as a solvent. In *Distilled Knowledge*, Brian Hoefling notes that "while aroma compounds tend to not dissolve well in water, they're usually perfectly happy to do so in ethanol . . . which is why the world is full of flavored spirits."

Cointreau Still Room

"If you look at the last three to four hundred years, northern amari such as Jägermeister, Underberg, and Zwack are quite bitter. Southern amari are much sweeter. Why? Because the liqueurs were linked to the ingredients you could find in the area. Northeast Italy was lucky, because we have Venice, one of the top European ports, and access to spices and chocolates from the East.... Many of the ingredients we have in our amari were linked to ingredients we could source."

ELISABETTA NONINO

Master Distiller

Fruit liqueurs are flavored by macerating fresh fruit in neutral alcohol and then sweetening the "tincture" before filtration and bottling. The strength and type of spirit, temperature of the infusion, and duration all factor into the extraction quality and character.

Instead of lengthy macerations, some producers pass the alcohol—either hot, cold, or as a vapor—through botanicals suspended in a percolator—a tall narrow funnel with a stop valve at the bottom—for a more focused extraction. This is how Tempus Fugit extracts coffee beans for crème de moka, tea leaves for crème de thé, and mint leaves for Fernet Angelico. Founder John Troia explains, "If we did a maceration, we'd have bitter, muddy flavors. We pass it through because we just want the aromatic top notes."

Distillation is required to extract the citrus notes of coriander seeds or separate the bitter properties of wormwood from the more desirable herbal notes. Most producers macerate leaves, seeds, citrus peels, roots, barks, and flowers in alcohol of varying proofs in the chamber for up to twenty-four hours before distilling them to isolate the essential oils they're looking for. Low moisture content of meticulously dried botanicals is key to maximizing extraction of essential oils, whose quality and quantity are tested from lot samples sent to the producer's laboratory.

Luxardo Citrus Botanicals

Just because a liqueur is labeled crème de cacao, cassis, or menthe doesn't mean the chocolate, blackcurrant, and mint are the only ingredients in the recipe (with sugar and water). Many classic formulas contain more than a dozen other botanicals—often multiple varieties of the feature ingredient—with complementary botanicals to buttress it. Every herb has its optimum extraction method, so most are processed separately and blended together. Producers typically reserve a two years' supply of each botanical in the event of a bad harvest.

ON MODERNIZATION

"The labor- and time-intensive processes that made exceptional versions of historic crèmes and liqueurs in the nineteenth century have been all but abandoned in favor of using oils, extracts, and even artificial ingredients that are simply added to neutral alcohol and sweetened with sugars made from cane, beets, and corn."

JOHN TROIA

Company Director

Italian amari and French herbal liqueurs are the most complicated liqueurs to produce. For example, the formula for Bénédictine, which dates to the sixteenth century, is a blend of macerated, distilled, and double-distilled components that mature in oak for eight months before they're sweetened with honey, spiced with saffron, heated to 131°F, then rested in oak barrels for another four months before filtration and bottling. The process takes nearly two years, due to the lengthy maceration and aging processes used to harmonize the aroma and taste of twenty-seven botanicals, including angelica, hyssop, and melissa, which were once harvested from cliffs surrounding the abbey.

Bénédictine Still Room

In additional to their medicinal heritage (which is also documented in the aperitifs primer), liqueurs have a longstanding connection to the culinary world, where they've been used in truffles and cakes going back to the eighteenth century—Cointreau made confections before they began making liqueurs. In the nineteenth century, bartenders began using small measures of liqueurs—just like their culinary counterparts—to improve Old-Fashioneds and enhance punch.

In the twentieth century, liqueurs' role expanded from adding complexity in cocktails to taking the place of sugar altogether in formulas like the daisy, which called for curaçao in place of sugar in a sour. This yielded the Sidecar, White Lady, and Margarita and more sophisticated recipes that use multiple liqueurs, like the Aviation and Last Word. When bartenders began preparing their Old-Fashioneds with vermouth (spawning the Martini and Manhattan), both curaçao and maraschino liqueur often accompanied it.

Liqueurs became the lynchpin of strong, sweet, rich drinks called nightcaps, which hail back to the early nineteenth century, when it was common to sip something strong before donning a cap to go to bed on a cold night. In *The Essential Cocktail*, Dale DeGroff describes the Stinger (page 381) as a "nightcap—an adult after-dinner mint—which dates to the 1890s, when it was the final drink of the evening for many high rollers. The only cocktail that can follow a Stinger is another Stinger, but you can't sit around knocking back these things, because they're all liquor—very, very strong—so one is pretty much the limit."

This neatly sums up the purpose, function, and service of "nightcaps," with the distinction that it wasn't just the brandy—Dale insists on VS quality cognac or better—that reserved nightcaps for high rollers; it was the price of liqueurs. Before discreet, well-financed flavor labs like Givaudan, Firmenich, and IFF slashed production costs in the category with "natural" extracts permitted by EU law to substitute for actual fruit, herbs, seeds, spices, and beans, the cost of these ingredients made fine liqueurs among the rarest and most expensive spirits in the world.

While historically liqueurs have functioned as the base or co-base spirit of recipes like the Stinger, Rusty Nail, and Negroni, I typically pour less, so their sweetness isn't overbearing. In this section, in the absence of a substantial number of recipes that revolve around a liqueur as a cocktail's focal flavor, I've split my overview of their types and purpose between the aperitifs and liqueur primers and have rounded up rich recipes that require dairy, winter warmers, and cocktails that I'd be wary of doubling down on because of their strength or sugar content.

COFFEE COCKTAIL

Origin This recipe appears in the posthumous 1887 edition of Jerry Thomas's *The Bar-Tenders Guide* with the annotation, "The name of this drink is a misnomer, as coffee and bitters are not to be found among its ingredients, but it looks like coffee when it has been properly concocted, and hence probably its name."

Logic I "discovered" this recipe in 2005 in a facsimile edition of Thomas's book while tending bar at Gramercy Tavern, which offered half a dozen ports by the glass to pair with a rotating selection of cheeses. I'd never prepared a cocktail with port or a whole egg, and I couldn't believe the combination was potable enough to print, let alone coffee-like. Curiosity got the better of me, so I shook one up and stood dumbfounded at the deliciousness the recipe yielded. The surprisingly balanced cocktail was milkshake-like, with chocolate notes and dark berry fruit. It was nothing like coffee in appearance or character, but it was the perfect nightcap to recommend to diners right around the time they typically order a cup of coffee.

Hacks After experimenting with the ingredients, I've found that fruity ports such as young rubies, or Quinta do Noval Black in particular pair well with VSOP grade cognacs. Twenty-year-old tawny ports, tannic late bottle vintages, and rancio-heavy XO cognacs don't improve the cocktail, so reserve them to savor neat. The aromatic nutmeg helps mask the earthy quality of the egg and accentuates the woody notes in the cognac, but a pinch of freshly ground coffee would work, too.

1.5 oz. Hine H cognac
1.5 oz. Quinta do Noval Black port
0.25 oz. simple syrup (page 391)
1 whole egg
Garnish: Grated nutmeg

Dry shake, then shake with ice and fine-strain into a chilled highball. Garnish with nutmeg.

RUSTY NAIL

Origin David Wondrich traces the first scotch and Drambuie combination (the B.I.F.) back to 1937; it was followed by many others until the recipe became universally recognized as the Rusty Nail in the 1960s. Stan Jones was among the first to list it, in his *Jones' Complete Barguide* in 1977.

Logic In 1746, as a token of gratitude for helping him escape the king's men on the Isle of Skye, Bonnie Prince Charlie gave clan chief John MacKinnon the recipe for his personal elixir. The recipe was passed down to John Ross, who produced and sold it at the Broadford Hotel, where it became known as Drambuie. The aged, Scotch whisky–based liqueur is flavored with a blend of herbs and spices and sweetened with heather honey. The ingredients for the cocktail follow the same logic as Bénédictine and brandy, in which you combine the liqueur's base spirit with it to create a stronger, drier offering. Unless you're serving it for dessert or to a known sweet tooth, mix the Drambuie sparingly to let the scotch shine.

Hacks I pinch an orange twist over the surface to brighten up the nose, and serve it over one large cube—like an Old-Fashioned—to give it gravitas. For special occasions, you could mix Drambuie's fifteen-year-old bottling (which is drier, so up the quantity to 0.75 ounce) with Talisker ten-year to bring them all home to the Isle of Skye.

***

2 oz. Dewar's 12-year blended Scotch whisky

0.5 oz. Drambuie

Garnish: None

Stir with ice, then strain over a large ice cube into a chilled rocks glass.

STINGER

Origin In *Imbibe!*, Wondrich attributes this recipe to a typed supplement in Bill Boothby's *American Bartender* from around 1905. Doudoroff's scholarly *Martin's Index* app attributes the first appearance to Jacques Straub's 1914 *Drinks*.

Logic I wrote off this drink for years until I discovered it was a guilty pleasure of Dale DeGroff and David Wondrich while working as one of their apprentices, producing BarSmarts on behalf of Pernod Ricard. As with other spirituous "duos," as Gary Regan classified them in *The Joy of Mixology*, the key is to pare back the liqueur and choose a base spirit that shines. Before Tempus Fugit released their clear crème de menthe in 2011 and the liqueur lines from Giffard and Marie Brizard were well distributed, most bars only carried a rotgut green crème de menthe for Grasshoppers and made the drink with peppermint schnapps. During those dark days, Dave made me a Stinger with a French crème de menthe brand called Get (pronounced "jet") 27, which isn't imported to the States, and Martell Cordon Bleu cognac, and I was instantly converted.

Hacks In both of his books, Dale, who's the main reason I'm writing about the drink, calls for the Stinger to be shaken and served in a rocks glass filled with crushed ice. In *The Craft of the Cocktail* he calls for two parts cognac and one part crème de menthe; in *The Essential Cocktail* he calls for them in equal parts. I prefer it served up in a smaller coupe with dilution meted out in the bartender's mixing glass, or bottled and served out of the freezer as a nightcap in place of dessert.

---

2 oz. Martell Cordon Bleu cognac

0.25 oz. Tempus Fugit crème de menthe (white)

Garnish: 1 mint leaf

Stir with ice, then strain into a chilled coupe. Garnish with the mint leaf.

GRASSHOPPER

Origin A pousse-café prepared with equal parts crème de cacao and crème de menthe is credited to Harry O'Brien of San Francisco's Palace Hotel in Bill Boothby's 1908 *World Famous Drinks and How to Mix Them*. The modern cream-based version is credited to Philibert Guichet of Tujague's in New Orleans, who began serving it at the bar before Prohibition in 1919.

Logic Tradition compelled me to prepare countless ice cream–based Grasshoppers as a bartender at Paul's Club in Madison, Wisconsin, which was famous for their sundae-like renditions of the Grasshopper and the Pink Squirrel (sub crème de noyaux for crème de menthe). I thought I'd seen the last of this drink, but barman Jeff Morgenthaler brought it back in 2014 when he opened up Pépé le Moko in Portland with a photogenic version served in an ice cream soda glass on a silver platter, with a red-and-white-striped straw and a napkin. The key to my recipe is high-quality vanilla ice cream and Tempus Fugit's superlative crème de menthe, which comes in only a clear formula, so I use a drop of green food coloring. Jeff prepares his with a quiet handheld stick blender instead of revving up a traditional blender behind the bar.

Hacks Part of the allure of Morgenthaler's recipe is the addition of Fernet-Branca Menta, which adds a mentholated bitterness to balance the sweetness. Some view adding an ingredient to enhance a classic recipe as scandalous, but the renown of Morgenthaler's bourbon-spiked Amaretto Sour and fernet-spiked Grasshopper prove that sometimes you've got to look beyond traditional forumulae to enhance a classic.

---

8 oz. Häagen-Dazs vanilla ice cream
1 oz. Tempus Fugit crème de menthe (white)
1 oz. Giffard crème de cacao (white)
1 drop green food coloring
Garnish: 1 mint sprig

Build in a blender cup and blend until creamy. Pour into a chilled ice cream soda glass. Garnish with the mint sprig.

TOM AND JERRY

Origin Jerry Thomas claimed ownership of this recipe, which he became known for, but in *Imbibe!*, David Wondrich dates it back to an article in the *Salem Gazette* published in 1827, three years before Thomas's birth.

Logic I remember preparing eggnog and Tom and Jerry in Wisconsin at the end of the 1990s with cheap brandy, hot water, and a spoonful of gelatinous Connolly's Tom and Jerry batter scooped from a plastic tub. I wrote it off as one of the many peculiarities of Wisconsin culture I grew to love during my time there, until Audrey Saunders reintroduced me (and New York City) to the drink at the Pegu Club. The recipe here is based on hers, which is the best I've ever tasted. I'd whip the eggs with a KitchenAid stand mixer if you have access to one, and store the batter with the milk in a hot water bath to avoid scorching when you heat them for service.

Hacks You could lighten up the recipe by serving it with hot water instead of milk or adjust the proportions for the batter, but there's no way around this drink's richness. If you're looking for spirits substitutions, Jeff Morgenthaler makes a delicious eggnog with añejo tequila and amontillado sherry that stand in nicely for the cognac and rum.

—————

6 oz. whole milk

2 oz. Tom and Jerry batter (page 391)

0.75 oz. Rémy Martin VSOP cognac

0.75 oz. Bacardi 8-year rum

Garnish: Grated nutmeg

Build in a preheated tempered mug, then stir. Garnish with nutmeg.

AFTER NINE

Origin I created this for the PDT cocktail menu in the winter of 2012.

Logic The hot chocolate and Chartreuse *verte chaud* is a classic après ski cocktail in the Alps, where many of the botanicals used to produce the iconic herbal liqueur grow wild. Inspired by the Verte Chaud (whose flavor profile—chocolate and green herbs—resembles the After Eight chocolate thin mints I grew up with and riffed off for the name for the cocktail), I chose lavender mint tea and woodsy gin—to augment the alpine quality of the Chartreuse—and crème de cacao to stand in for the rich hot chocolate. With no layer of cream or lemon to prevent the alcohol from evaporating (which causes the cocktail to smell like pure ethanol), this drink should be served warm instead of hot.

Hacks Hans Reisetbauer's Blue gin, which is distilled an hour away from the Alps, works well in place of Monkey 47 if that's unavailable. I've had great success serving this cold as a punch, but you'll have to rejigger the proportions to balance its strength and sweetness at a lower temperature.

8 oz. brewed lavender mint tisane

1 oz. Monkey 47 gin

0.5 oz. Brizard crème de cacao (white)

0.25 oz. green Chartreuse

Garnish: 1 sprig of lavender

Build in a preheated tempered mug. Garnish with the lavender sprig.

CAFÉ ARROZ

Origin I created this recipe for Gran Centenario tequila (which also works well in this recipe) in the spring of 2008.

Logic Horchata, a rice water–based refresher spiced with cinnamon and often enriched with milk, struck me as the perfect substitute for cream in a tequila-based White Russian variation. The Especial bottling of Kahlúa packs a higher proof than the "original" and more coffee character, making this the perfect ingredient to unify the recipe's Mexican heritage. This recipe is one more example of how "what grows with it goes with it" translates in cocktail form, and shows how helpful visiting a production region is for creative inspiration.

Hacks This recipe was developed for a reposado bottling, but it works well with blanco and añejos as well. You're welcome to tinker with the horchata recipe—traditional horchata has no added milk—and experiment with your tequila and coffee liqueur brands of choice; no sense in overintellectualizing a White Russian variation.

2 oz. horchata (page 390)
1.5 oz. Partida reposado tequila
0.5 oz. Kahlúa Especial
Garnish: Grated cinnamon

Shake with ice, then fine-strain over a large ice cube in a chilled rocks glass. Garnish with cinnamon.

MILK PUNCH

Origin A nearly identical recipe appears in Jerry Thomas's *The Bar-Tenders Guide.*

Logic This is another nineteenth-century gem that's been incubated at restaurants like Brennan's in New Orleans long enough to prevent it from slipping out of the pantheon of mixed drinks. Due to its richness, I have it listed as an after-dinner drink, but it's classically served as a brunch drink in New Orleans! Unless you're looking for a pairing for fresh beignets or French toast, I'd serve this cocktail in place of dessert after dinner. It's unlikely, but be sure to confirm that the guest who's ordered this isn't expecting a punch prepared using a seventeenth-century technique, where milk is deliberately added to a punch, curdled into solids, then strained from the mixture to create a silky texture.

Hacks It's classically made with brandy—stick to fine alembic brandies—as the base, but bourbon is popular and delicious as well. If you go this route, I'd use honey or maple syrup to fill in for the bittersweet quality of the molasses in the Myers's. In my experience, cream is too heavy and 2% milk is too light, so stick to whole milk or half-and-half.

1.5 oz. whole milk

1 oz. Pierre Ferrand ambre cognac

1 oz. Myers's Original dark rum

0.75 oz. simple syrup (page 391)

Garnish: Grated nutmeg

Shake with ice, then fine-strain over one large ice cube in a chilled rocks glass. Garnish with nutmeg.

BLACK FLIP

Origin I created this for the PDT cocktail menu in the winter of 2007.

Logic This cocktail was inspired by the chapter on early eighteenth-century flips in Wayne Curtis's book *And a Bottle of Rum: A History of the New World in Ten Cocktails*, released in the summer of 2007. Later that year, I visited the Cruzan Rum distillery in St. Croix, where I discovered that their Black Strap rum tasted exactly like the rums Curtis described from colonial America. Curtis says that early flips were mixed with strong beer, making Brooklyn Brewery's seasonal black chocolate stout an ideal candidate at 10% ABV. The chocolaty malt pairs perfectly with the burnt caramel notes of the rum in this cake batter–like cocktail; back in the day it would have been heated with a red-hot metal poker called a loggerhead.

Hacks Dave Arnold (see page 73) created a modern loggerhead he calls the "Red Hot Poker." Even though I'd love to taste this after a 1500°F rod is submerged in it, I think I'll pass on that for safety's sake. I've used this formula with different beers, spirits, and sweeteners to create other flips, but you'll need to stick with these products for authenticity.

2 oz. Brooklyn Brewery black chocolate stout

1.5 oz. Cruzan Black Strap rum

0.5 oz. Demerara syrup (page 391)

1 whole egg

Garnish: Grated nutmeg

Add all ingredients to a shaker and swirl to decarbonate the beer. Dry shake, then shake with ice and fine-strain into a chilled wine glass. Garnish with nutmeg.

SUBRECIPES

Horchata

(in Café Arroz)

MAKES 32 OZ.

1 cup white long-grain rice, uncooked

40 oz. filtered water

10 oz. whole milk

½ tsp. bourbon vanilla extract

½ tsp. ground cinnamon

3 tbsp. Demerara sugar

In a blender, combine the rice and water and puree until the rice begins to break up, about 1 minute. Transfer to a nonreactive container and let stand at room temperature for 12 hours. Strain the rice water (approximately 20 oz.) into the blender and discard the rice. Add the milk, vanilla, cinnamon, and sugar and blend until the sugar is dissolved, then refrigerate. Stir before serving.

Tom and Jerry Batter

(in Tom and Jerry)

MAKES 48 OZ.

6 large organic eggs, yolks and
whites separated

1 lb. superfine sugar

1 oz. Bacardi 8-year rum

½ tsp. ground cinnamon

½ tsp. ground allspice

¼ tsp. ground nutmeg

¼ tsp. ground cloves

2 dashes Angostura bitters

1 tbsp. vanilla extract

Whip the egg yolks in a mixing bowl
until they are completely broken up
and smooth, then stir in the sugar, rum,
spices, bitters, and vanilla. In a separate
bowl, whip the egg whites into stiff peaks.
Combine the contents of both bowls and
blend until smooth. Bottle and refrigerate
in between service.

Simple Syrup

(in Pimm's Cup and others)

MAKES 25 OZ.

16 oz. filtered water

2 cups superfine sugar

Simmer the water and sugar in a pot over
medium heat (approximately 160°F) until
the sugar dissolves. Cool and bottle.

Demerara Syrup

(in Toronto and others)

MAKES 33 OZ.

16 oz. filtered water

3⅓ cups Demerara sugar

Simmer the water and sugar in a pot over
medium heat (approximately 180°F) until
the sugar dissolves. Cool and bottle.

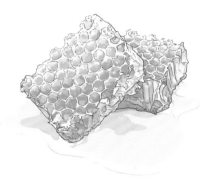

Honey Syrup

(in Airmail and others)

MAKES 32 OZ.

16 oz. filtered water
24 oz. honey

Simmer the water and honey in a pot over medium heat (approximately 180°F) until the honey dissolves. Cool and bottle.

Vanilla Syrup

(in Cocktail Culture)

MAKES 20 OZ.

16 oz. simple syrup (page 391)
4 oz. bourbon vanilla paste

Combine the syrup and vanilla paste in a saucepan and stir over low heat until well integrated. Cool and bottle.

Agave Syrup

(in Tommy's Margarita and others)

MAKES 25 OZ.

13 oz. filtered water
19 oz. agave nectar

Simmer the water and agave in a pot over low heat (approximately 120°F) until the agave nectar dissolves. Cool and bottle.

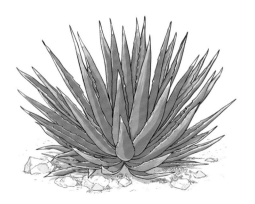

Ginger Wort

(in French Maid, Mezcal Mule, and others)

MAKES 25 OZ.

24 oz. filtered water
1/3 cup minced ginger
2¼ tbsp. light brown sugar
0.75 oz. lime juice

Bring the water to a boil in a pot. Combine with the ginger and sugar in a nonreactive container. Cover for 90 minutes, then strain through a chinois, pressing the ginger to extract as much liquid as possible. Add the lime juice, then bottle and refrigerate.

Lime Cordial

(in Gimlet)

MAKES 24 OZ.

12 limes
24 oz. simple syrup (page 391)

Zest the peel off the limes with a microplane. Combine the lime zest with the simple syrup in a nonreactive container. Steep for 10 minutes, then fine-strain, bottle, and refrigerate.

Whipped Cream

(in Irish Coffee)

3 oz. heavy cream
0.25 oz. simple syrup (page 391)

Whip the cream and syrup in a bowl until soft enough to pour over the surface of the drink.

Cocktail Menu

Entire volumes have been written on the art of menu design and the elements that distinguish great bar and restaurant menus from mere lists. Taschen Books executive editor Jim Heimann and longtime *New York Times* art director Steven Heller's gorgeous four-hundred-page coffee table book *Menu Design in America* (2011) features reproductions of hundreds of museum-worthy examples from 1850 through 1985. It's a visual repository filled with examples of menus with artistic typography and graphic design that still fulfilled their purpose as culinary cue cards for diners and drinkers.

While modern desktop publishing has been great for bars and restaurants that update their menus daily, it has undermined the artistry of menu design. In this chapter, I'll examine how menus function like business plans, helping operators to guide guests through the dining experience. Beyond aesthetics (which are crucial for setting the tone and clearly communicating purpose), a menu serves as the guest's playbill for the drama that is about to unfold.

At Left: Dead Rabbit Menu

The absence of a menu can also be a statement in itself, by signaling to guests that the bartender or waiter is prepared to be flexible—and that the guest is expected to be an active participant.

SPACE AND COST CONSTRAINTS

Before writing a menu, consider the logistics of your bar setup. How much space do you have? This includes countertop space behind and on top of the bar for small bottles and decanters; cold storage for perishable produce, juices, syrups, wines, beers, and other chilled beverages; and undercounter cabinet space for spirits storage. Naturally, the less space you have, the smaller your menu should be, especially if you anticipate a high volume of guests. One way to achieve this is to rein in the variety of base spirits you stock, which will free up the space and inventory budget necessary to stock all the "modifiers" required to prepare the widest variety of cocktails. For example, I love artisanal French brandies such as calvados, armagnac, and marc, but they're typically sipped, not mixed, so I don't stock them year-round at PDT.

Many operators still use pour cost models that predate the modern cocktail renaissance. The previous model was more applicable to fast-casual restaurants, where volume drives profit from low-cost, low-price drink sales. The contemporary model hinges on operators' adopting a fine-dining food cost structure for beverage, with high-cost, high-price drinks served in modest volume, which will generate similar gross profits. Spending more to make the same profit is a challenging ask until you figure in the pride that accompanies serving better products.

At a cocktail bar like PDT, where more than 85 percent of the cocktails ordered are from the menu, it's crucial for the operator to stabilize the cost structure of these items—as opposed to off-menu orders such as classic cocktails, neat spirits, or highballs, which must be variably priced based on cost of goods. You'll never be able to predict with certainty what will sell, but this is one of the best ways to normalize liquor costs (a variable cost in bars

ON THE DRINKS

"At a Connoisseur's Club talk back in Belfast in 2008, Sasha Petraske posed a series of questions to our audience. 'What's a good customer experience in a bar and how do you measure it?' 'What makes a customer go away thinking, *Tonight was a great experience*?' Some suggested service, while others said ambience and drinks. Sasha, whose bars were renowned for cocktails, singled out drinks and told them they were only one element to a great experience. He said, 'I would say if you have ten different metrics you're measuring a bar on, the drinks are only ten percent of what makes a great experience.'"

SEAN MULDOON

Bar Operator

that offer a variety of options) so this item falls in line with fixed costs such as rent, utilities, taxes, and payroll.

Bars such as PDT list a fixed price for all cocktails on their menu; others, such as Teardrop Lounge in Portland, have variable prices based on each cocktail's relative pour cost. There are pluses and minuses to both structures, but ultimately it comes down to the customer's perception of value. At busy bars in larger cities, cocktail menu pricing tends to be commodified into a fixed price, like the cost of a movie ticket or a pack of cigarettes, whereas cocktail bars in smaller markets tend to have to compete for their customer's entertainment budget, so variable prices are posted to project value.

Cocktails aren't the only item on the menu that determines perception of value. By serving $7 hot dogs with $16 cocktails at PDT, instead of more-pricy bar food like cured meats or oysters, we created a counterbalance that lowers the overall check average. Once the hot dogs took off, we recruited local chefs, starting with Momofuku's David Chang, to provide us with toppings that brought our "fast food" in line with our beverage program's artisanal, market-driven philosophy. The chefs provide the toppings in exchange for a bar tab, which helps us fill our seats with industry leaders while passing along their generosity by not charging more for the gourmet hot dogs.

DEVELOPING YOUR CORE MENU

Once you've established your bar's concept (see chapter 2), it's time to write the menu. A balanced cocktail menu includes a core collection of signature recipes that are served year-round, supplemented with warm- and cold-weather seasonal cocktails and recipes with short life spans that cycle on and off the menu based on availability. At PDT, we relist a number of our most popular seasonal cocktails annually, which helps build anticipation for the change of menu throughout the calendar year. We develop limited-edition, short-run cocktails based on hyperseasonal produce or spirits with small allocations; these appeal to adventurous imbibers and the media, who are always looking for novel listings.

While seasonal and limited-edition cocktails diversify the menu, delight the regulars, and reinforce the reputation of your drinks program, the signature recipes your bar is known for must carry the business. Ideally, one particular cocktail, such as the Irish Coffee at the Dead Rabbit in New York, the Daiquiri at El Floridita in Havana, or the barrel-aged Negroni at Clyde Common in Portland, will be the bar's "calling card"—the drink that people know and talk about, that inspires newcomers to visit. The remaining cocktails on the menu should be composed from a variety of base spirits; come from various recipe families, such as sours and fizzes; have varying flavor profiles, alcohol contents, colors, and textures; and be served in every type of glassware you stock in quantity. This approach may seem broad, but the alternative is to haphazardly compile an entire menu, only to realize that it's filled with recipes of the same style because you didn't map everything out before recipe development. I've done this myself.

It would be nice to open a bar with your menu of signature recipes already in place, but it doesn't work that way. Signature cocktails are vetted over time by guests, whose preferences should be tracked and reflected in the menu. Some bars and restaurants, especially those with a seasonal focus, will change the whole menu several times over the course of a year. I'm wary of this, though; you need to give recipes time to "breathe," and a constantly evolving list (even if it helps drum up media interest) pulls the rug out from under patrons. Imagine a guest who has a great experience at your bar, returns to host their friends, and finds that none of the items they enjoyed before are available anymore.

I learned this the hard way, then rejiggered my menus around three core offerings. The foundation is popular cocktails served year-round that don't require ingredients with short growing seasons or spirits produced in limited quantities. I supplement these with secondary seasonal offerings that appeal to guests based on the time of year, such as swizzles when it's hot and toddies when it's cold. The most dynamic component is cocktails prepared with ephemeral produce such as Concord grapes and blood oranges, mixed with limited-edition spirits that cycle on and off the menu for a few weeks at a time.

RECIPE DEVELOPMENT

In most cases, the best place for a cocktail bar to start is by serving classic recipes, plus a few of the best local bartenders' cocktails (with their permission, of course). However, once a bar team has mastered that opening menu, they will be eager to develop their own creations. There are a number of strategies to help guide them. The most elemental way to create "new" cocktails—and I put "new" in quotation marks because it's nearly impossible to create something truly new unless you're working with a newly released ingredient or obscure produce and mixers—is what bartender Phil Ward calls in *Death & Co* the Mr. Potato Head theory of mixing drinks.

Using Mr. Potato Head's interchangeable eyes, ears, nose, and apparel as a model for the structure of a recipe, a bartender can mix and match them as long as they use an ingredient—equivalent to a body part—of the same classification. One example is the classic daisy formula, composed of a spirit, citrus, and a liqueur or cordial. A Sidecar (brandy, lemon, triple sec), Margarita (tequila, lime, triple sec), and White Lady (gin, lemon, triple sec) are all daisies with interchangeable base spirits (brandy, tequila, gin) and citrus.

The key to the theory is classifying each cocktail ingredient correctly. This is straightforward when it comes to switching out primary "body parts," such as the gin in the White Lady or tequila in the Margarita, as they're both dry, 80-proof spirits that are primarily responsible for the alcoholic strength

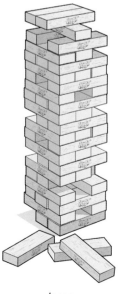

of the cocktail. Using this analogy, substituting lemon juice for tequila in a Margarita would be like putting an ear or arm where the nose belongs.

The sweetness, strength, or acidity of an ingredient—or lack thereof—can complicate the decision-making process. If you swap out a triple sec such as Cointreau, which is both sweet and high proof, for the tequila in a Margarita, you actually have two components (eyes with a pair of glasses, perhaps?) to replace. For this reason, I've chosen the Jenga block-stacking game as another useful analogy, as a cocktail's quality is predicated on balance.

Every time you remove an ingredient in a foundational recipe and replace it with something else, you risk toppling the whole structure. A good example is taking a daisy like the White Lady just mentioned and adding Lillet blanc and absinthe. To pull this off, you need to pare back the gin and triple sec and add only a few dashes of absinthe, which otherwise can overwhelm

Jenga

the delicate balance of the other ingredients. This is the recipe for the classic Corpse Reviver #2 cocktail (page 232), which towers closer to the sky thanks to its carefully balanced ingredients.

Many bartenders approach cocktail development as a chef would, looking to seasonal produce for inspiration (with produce often taking precedence over the spirits they have on hand). Instead of workshopping a new gin cocktail, they bring rhubarb or ramps to the bar, and want their character to play the starring role in the recipe. This is the premise behind fresh fruit "martinis," "daiquiris," and "bellinis," in which vodka, rum, and prosecco provide relatively neutral alcoholic bases for fresh juices to shine through. (I put quotations around these names because there are traditional ingredients for each of these recipes.)

Before proceeding down this path, consider the ideal preparation to bring out an ingredient's most flattering character in a frosty alcoholic format. For berries, stone fruits, and most melons, ripeness is key before you juice, muddle, or mill them. More stubborn ingredients, such as tamarind, require soaking and shelling, while mature coconuts must be opened with a drill and cooked for their cream. Fibrous fruits and vegetables such as rhubarb, celery, and apple should be extracted and mixed within hours before oxidation diminishes their vibrant character. Without a well-equipped kitchen and support staff dedicated to bar prep, working with these ingredients is prohibitively time-consuming.

Consistency is another challenge with farmers' market produce, as ingredients such as peaches, tomatoes, and berries vary in acidity, sweetness, and texture. One week you find perfect fruit; the next, it may be moldy, sour, or unavailable. In the days before refrigeration, modern shipping advances, and greenhouses made many fruits and vegetables available year-round, bartenders preserved fresh fruits with sugar for preserves, vinegar for shrubs, and high-proof spirits for infusions. Many chefs still pickle and can vegetables such as tomatoes and ramps, and make preserves and sorbet from Concord grapes, figs, and the like—and bartenders should do more of the same. Investing in local farm produce is vital to maintain and expand foodways that undermine the hegemony of massive corporate farms.

You must monitor the growing season for ingredients prone to mold and mildew—like raspberries, stone fruits that require weeks of warmth to ripen, and late-harvest fruits like frost-sensitive Concord grapes—if you're

Farmers' Market Berries

considering them for your menu. Instead of substituting genetically modified produce, which looks great but has little flavor, try rotating cocktails prepared with these ingredients on and off the menu in short-run, two- to three-week menu slots. In the United States, we think of the seasons in four quarters—winter, spring, summer, and fall—that rarely reflect the growing seasons of the ingredients we mix with for market menus. Look for the seasons within the seasons, or use other calendars— such as the Japanese Sekki system, which divides the year into twenty-four equal periods—for inspiration.

In spite of any material link to the natural seasons, spirits like cachaça and tequila conjure up warm tropical weather, while armagnac and Islay malt whisky recall cold nights near a hearth. When developing a menu, you can and should harness the transportive power by which these spirits, along with certain beers, wines, and sweeteners, conjure up environmental memories. My warm-weather recipes tend to feature lighter, hydrating, produce-driven cocktails, and my winter recipes tend to be richer and spirit-forward, with dried spices and preserved fruit accents.

When it comes to mixing with seasonal produce, think about pairing flavors—for example, strawberry with rhubarb or cucumber with dill. Karen Page and Andrew Dornenburg's *The Flavor Bible* is an excellent resource for this type of inspiration. Even better, pay close attention when you have the privilege of eating or drinking in the establishment of a talented chef, bartender, barista, or sommelier. I'll never forget a raspberry, rose, and lychee gelée that Gramercy Tavern pastry chef Nancy Olson brought back to me from Pierre Hermé's bakery in Paris in 2006. The flavor combination inspired a cocktail called the R&R, with muddled raspberries, rose water, bourbon, and iced tea.

Chefs and sommeliers often say, "If it grows with it, it goes with it," and the strategy works well with cocktails, too. The R&R employs this strategy: both sweet tea and bourbon are ubiquitous in the American South, and they happen to pair well flavor-wise. This is the logic behind classic recipes like the Cuba Libre, Venetian Spritz (page 167), and Paloma (page 281), and the inspiration for cocktails I've created with horchata and tequila, sorrel and rum, and maté and pisco.

COCKTAIL TITLES

Often, bartenders decide on the title of a recipe after finalizing the proportions, ingredients, glassware, garnish, and logistics to prepare it, after they've all but exhausted their creative energy. I've worked with scores of mixologists who could create cocktails with ease, but couldn't name them, thus missing out on the longevity the recipe might have enjoyed with a catchy title. The title of a cocktail is its marketing plan, and without it, the recipe is destined for anonymity (or, worse, getting attributed to another bartender who merely comes up with a catchy title for it).

Cocktail titles often project a promise: the (fancied) ability to make us feel better (the Penicillin), more debonair (the Cosmopolitan), more worldly (the Old Cuban), or more fun and attractive (the Hanky Panky). What we drink is a reflection of our moods, predicaments, desires, and conceptions of ourselves. The title is a microcosmic marketing plan that uses all these elements to drive interest in the drink.

Hand Mirror

Cocktails that stand the test of time have memorable titles. Some refer to personalities, like the Negroni (named after a famous count), or places, such as the Manhattan and Moscow Mule. Titles with shock value have a long history—from the modern-day Porn Star Martini to the nineteenth-century Bosom Caresser—which proffer false hope your cocktail could raise more than eyebrows. The style of drinks you serve—epitomized by their titles—cue your audience on how they're expected to behave. Personally, I'd rather drink Moscow Mules with counts than Porn Star Martinis with bosom caressers.

One of the most famous brand ambassadors (Michael Jordan) might disagree with me here, but even though you may put your heart and soul into your first few creations, resist the urge to name them after yourself (unless you have Air Jordan's fan base). Other notable newbie mistakes include translating the most obvious title into a foreign language (this will be awkward if the recipe travels there, and likely difficult for your local audience to pronounce) and using Wikipedia as your sole source of inspiration. Most recipe titles catch on because the story behind them is worth telling again and again and again, or because they're obvious.

Meehan Family Crest

One last practical note: Google your recipes' titles and ingredients before finalizing them, as you're probably not the first person to come up with a combination or title. Double-check your spelling, and if your title is based on a historical anecdote, review multiple sources (not everything you read on the Internet is factually correct).

"I was thrown into it. We're a quiet family. We're not out there tooting our horn. . . . I came into the business and did processing, quality control, the bookkeeping, was assistant to the treasurer, and then I moved into sales. I've worked in each area of the company and learned so I know the overall business. I did not want to do sales. I loved production. I wanted to make the product. My father basically said you're the only Laird that can do it. You have to do it. I remember shaking like a leaf and I'm still nervous every time I present. But I've grown to love it. Every time I travel and meet new people, it reinstills how much I love what I do and how much pride I have in the company."

LISA LAIRD

Company Director

GOING GLOBAL

It used to take years for a cocktail to catch on globally, but thanks to social media and the favorable press that many bartenders and cocktails receive, a recipe can travel the world quickly. If you have international ambitions for your cocktails, mix them with well-known spirits with global distribution so you'll rarely have to worry about scarcity or shortages. One thing all classic cocktails share is ingredients that can be sourced all over the world.

If you're fortunate, your recipes will be published, and if they become popular, you'll be asked to prepare them in other cities, at bar shows or guest bar shifts. The more flexibility a recipe has—like the Negroni, which can be prepared with numerous gins, sweet vermouths, and bitters—the more likely you and the recipe will travel well. On the flip side, the more infusions, house-made ingredients, and limited-edition spirits you use in the recipe, the less room you'll have for clothing in your luggage and the less time you'll have for tourist activities after you arrive, so develop your recipes accordingly.

For the majority of bartenders—who are working without a publicist on retainer, and in venues past their prime media cycle—two of the best ways to get new recipes out there is by entering cocktail competitions and mixing with newly released products supported by marketing resources during their launch. Spirits companies are always on the lookout for recipes to market their products, so make sure their representatives are aware of your efforts by tagging them in social media and liaising with marketing and salespeople.

ROUNDING IT OUT

Every element of the beverage program counts. There's no sense in writing a sophisticated cocktail menu, then offering generic beers and wines. What's the point of pouring premium spirits if you're mixing them with pasteurized juices or drowning them out with corn syrup–sweetened soda from a gun? Many bars and restaurants devote all their energy to the wine, spirits, and cocktail program and then, for their guests' final beverage of the evening, serve espresso from a pod or tea brewed with a glued, stapled bag. Should this be their final impression?

Countless hours go into the alcohol-related portion of the menu, but when a designated driver, pregnant mother, guest taking antibiotics, teetotaler, or someone taking the night off the sauce looks at the menu, their options are almost always less compelling. Much the same way chefs pride themselves on their vegetarian tasting menus and being able to accommodate diners with allergies, beverage directors should further devote themselves to nonalcoholic menu options with relish.

THE PRINTED MENU

While cocktail menus have been published by bars for over a century, they're trendy today thanks to pioneers like Dale DeGroff, whose menu at the Rainbow Room was the talk of the town when he launched it in 1987. At that time, most bars didn't offer printed menus—let alone twenty-four cocktails, six champagne drinks, and five nonalcoholic options—impressive even by today's standards.

In spite of the popularity of menus, a handful of bars go menu-free thanks to highly trained servers, who guide their guests through an omakase-like experience. This style of service was best embodied by Sasha Petraske's legendary New York City bar Milk & Honey. Here, the bartenders guided guests through a series of questions to divine the perfect drink for each of them. Their queries included preferred base spirit (such as gin, rum, or tequila) and style of cocktail (such as light and refreshing or boozy and stirred), along with other questions that helped the bartender choose a recipe from the bar's catalog.

Paradoxically, *not* having a menu requires more training and logistics than having a menu. That's not to suggest that creating a printed menu is easy! Operators should devote the same attention to detail to their menu as to their business plan. Many menus, particularly cocktail and wine lists, remain at the table during service, when spills or splatters can stain or permanently damage them, so I recommend protecting individual pages in water-resistant sleeves.

Investing in books or binders with laminates may not be necessary if your menu changes daily and must be scrapped at the end of the night. But whether you intend for your menus to last for days or weeks, you should invest in thoughtful, professional design. Many bars and restaurants invest thousands of dollars in designers who choose fonts, create logos, incorporate imagery, and make typographical choices—ranging from type size to line length, spacing, and color.

My advice is to trust these decisions to a professional, even if you have a good eye or the software to design a menu yourself. A professional designer will anticipate issues such as legibility in low light and clean layouts that will help customers make quick decisions. Investing in good design pays off.

It's worth noting here that some beverage suppliers—including soda, wine, and spirits companies and their distributors—offer menu design and printing services if you agree to list their products on the menu. This option may be tempting, but resist—you lose control over not only the content and appearance of your menu, but also the ability to reprint it when you run out of stock on an item or change the vintage, style, or brand of a particular product.

In some cases, a well-designed menu can become a piece of merchandise that you sell in your bar, like the Dead Rabbit's seasonal menu. Of course, the more "collectible" your menu is, the greater the risk of it being stolen ("collected," if we're being generous). At least one of PDT's leather-bound menus is stolen each week, but wear and tear limit the shelf life of menus in a cocktail bar, so it's a calculated loss.

One way to help curtail theft is to list the retail price of the menu prominently; this signals to customers that it's of material value. If your customers, after a few inhibition-curbing drinks, *still* decide to pocket your menu as a memento, at least you can congratulate yourself for having a good one (after all, someone is willing to take the risk of being caught stealing it).

You'll need to consider the size, heft, and number of pages in a menu in relation to the size of your tables or bar; guests need enough room to browse comfortably without obstructing their view of each other. Consider whether your guests will want to hold on to their wine list or cocktail menu after ordering; if so, make sure there is space for the menu around, on top of, or underneath the table (in a custom cubby).

The last logistical consideration is how many menus to print and have on hand. Determining a menu par (the ideal number of menus) requires planning—and budgeting, if your menus are costly. I find it's best to allocate one menu for every guest, plus an extra that will remain at each table after the order is placed, so that hosts never have to wait to seat tables until more menus are available. Store the bulk of your menus at the host stand, but also build dry, accessible storage space into service hutches and the backbar so servers can easily bring guests a new menu if needed.

PHILOSOPHICAL CONSIDERATIONS

The menu's physical presentation is crucial, but its content is even more so. The French word for "menu" is *carte*, which translates as "map"—and indeed, the best menus help guests navigate through a venue's offerings. A concise selection of options, thoughtfully chosen for their quality and value, is preferable to a lengthy catalog that most guests will find unnavigable.

Good maps have a key; similarly, a menu should have headers and a clear organization that helps guests understand the concept and ethos of the venue, whether it's a New American restaurant, English gastro-pub, or French brasserie. The menu can also help you express a more specific thematic focus—as do the cities that produce cheese along the Tour de France route (per Stockholm's Frantzén/Lindeberg restaurant), or cocktails inspired by the vistas of Route 66 (Manhattan's Pouring Ribbons bar). Other menus explore ingredients and traditional preparation methods that are unique to their region, such as Noma's new Nordic cuisine in Copenhagen, Husk's Low Country cuisine in Charleston, and Cochon's Cajun fare in New Orleans.

Wine lists follow several popular conventions that cocktail menus could emulate, including organizing listings from lightest (in body, flavor, or ABV) to fullest (typically aged, spirit-based cocktails with bitter components, high-proof liqueurs, rich sweeteners, or dairy) or grouping each style of cocktail, just as wine lists are grouped by region, producer, or varietal. While listing wine pairings on a menu is quite standard, cocktail pairings are mostly uncharted territory. I think suggesting pairings is a nice touch, but insisting on them puts the server at risk of a disagreement with a guest.

I'm not a fan of the tasting notes often found on wine lists. It's easy to alienate your audience, and undermine the discovery process, by telling them how something tastes beforehand. I've had guests return items when they didn't taste as they were described, which is unsurprising, given that we all have different palates and perspectives.

One difficult aspect of menu writing is deciding how detailed to make it. More often than not, a guest won't order something if they don't know what it is, so there are obvious advantages to listing the provenance or otherwise defining lesser-known ingredients. Most guests know what grape juice and brandy are, but they don't know that Pineau des Charentes is a combination of the two—known as a mistelle or vin de liqueur—from Cognac, so a sentence or two included below the entry, explaining how it's made, can be the difference between a guest's ordering a drink prepared with it or not. That said, your menu should leave room for the server to build a relationship with their guest through conversation. You can learn a lot from a great menu, but it should never feel didactic—and well-informed staff should be able to answer any questions that an interesting menu inspires.

I prefer to instead think like a journalist when I write my menus: I include who, what, when, where, how, and why, and explain obscure ingredients so servers spend less time answering trivia and more time trying to find the best option for a guest, based on their personal preferences.

The supplementary text annotating menu listings is traditionally written in the first person by the chef, sommelier, or head bartender, or narrated to a manager or other staff member, who transcribes the item in the house style. First-person narrative is more intimate than third person, which tends to arise when consultants or corporate directors who don't work on premise create the menu for a group. Chefs rarely credit the originator of a dish or preparation, as kitchen staffs work collaboratively; however, bartenders tend to work individually with the bar manager, so they should have their recipes attributed on the menu.

LOOKING TO THE FUTURE

While there are restaurants that build their food menu around a library of precious wines, it's far more common for a restaurant's cocktail program to be tailored to the food, a practice I favor. There's more than a century of wisdom on pairing food with wine, but there are no explicit rules for cocktail pairings. The cocktail renaissance was incubated in cocktail lounges, but innovation is being driven in bars owned by chefs such as Grant Achatz (Aviary), Barbara Lynch (Drink), and Daniel Humm (NoMad bar).

Increasingly, the craft of the cocktail is being incorporated into cooking schools' curricula. This means it's possible that cocktail programs will merge into the back of house, as the preparation required for service and execution is similar mentally and physically to working behind a kitchen line. Like a cook, bartenders must prepare an extensive list of perishable juices, syrups, and garnishes and must anticipate the quantities they'll need to get through service to be profitable.

Restaurant menus that list the origin of every single ingredient—and every farm or purveyor used to plate a dish—have become a bit of a punch line in recent years. This is rarely true of cocktail menus, which typically include generic descriptions of their cocktail ingredients. You would never pay a premium for a varietal bottle of wine in a restaurant without knowing the producer, region, and vintage, so it boggles my mind that bartenders of the same caliber withhold spirit brands, as if their guests weren't interested in them.

One of the final frontiers for the craft cocktail movement is more transparency. I'm not saying you need to provide a source for staple ingredients like simple syrup or lime wedges. However, many of the world's top bars are heavily subsidized by spirits companies (where it's not forbidden by law), yet make no efforts to disclose how menu items are selected.

A guest has a right to know that while the chef paid a premium for your venison, and the sommelier begged for the allocation of your red Burgundy, the bar accepted thousands of dollars and free product to list the gin in your aperitif or to be the sole bottled-water supplier. I believe in generating symbiotic business relationships, but I'd rather drink and dine in establishments that choose each component of what I consume based more on quality than on profitability; I'm happy to pay the premium for them on the check myself.

Service

I didn't grow up with Emily Post or finishing school, but my parents taught me the importance of etiquette, and I'd say its fundamental purpose is, perhaps surprisingly, to make people feel comfortable. I recall sitting down for a formal dinner for the first time and seeing a dozen pieces of (real) silverware at my table setting and not knowing how to use them.

Etiquette dictates that you set (and clear) the table with appropriate silverware for each course from the outside in, which is not only easy to follow, but logical. Asking guests if they'd like their coats checked upon entry, pushing in and pulling out chairs when they sit down or get up, and refolding a napkin when they leave the table isn't just pageantry; these gestures acknowledge the importance of your guests' presence and your effort to anticipate their needs.

Seeming formalities such as the presentation of the cork for a bottle of wine were instituted not merely for show but to check for faults and to safeguard against counterfeit wines. Offering to decant a wine that benefits from aeration, serving a highball with the mixer on the side for the guest to add to their taste, or asking whether a guest would like their Margarita with or without salt are all examples of anticipating their wants and needs.

Cleanliness is another way in which we make guests feel comfortable, which is why proper service involves gripping plates from the bottom and side (away from the surface food rests on) or glasses by the stem (away from the rim where guests put their lips). By extension, a spotless uniform, a neat workstation, and a clean bathroom all relate to the environment the food and beverage *should* be prepared in, which is why managers monitor these conditions vigilantly during service.

Every bar and restaurant has a different style of service, but whether you're serving cold bottles of Bud at a dive bar or salt-crusted sole in a fine dining restaurant, there's a cycle of service to be followed. You *can* codify these gestures without service feeling scripted, but please note: I'm not trying to discourage the spontaneity of organic interactions. As with the placement of many pieces of silverware on a formal dining table, my goal is to uncover the logic behind service. None of these suggestions should come as a surprise, as they're all derived from years of careful observation of a storyline that unfolds every night when a patron walks into a restaurant or bar.

WELCOMING YOUR GUESTS

Warm Hand Towels

The two most important points of contact for a guest are when they enter your business and when they leave. Make sure your storefront and sidewalk are swept and scrubbed, with sparkling windows, dust-free lamps, and a clean awning. A warm welcome at the door, conveyed after eye contact is established, and a gracious good-bye, either before or after asking about their experience, are two of the most effective

"The most important service step is the greeting. People need to be recognized when they walk into a room. It could be a maître d' recognizing them, or the manager working the floor, or a bartender or server working in proximity to them. The greeting is the magic touch. It sets the tone for everything. I teach this to all my bartenders: no matter what you're doing—whether you're in the middle of building a cocktail— stop what you're doing, say hello to the guest, give them a menu, and give them a glass of water. I'm a huge fan of the glass of water and menu, as it buys you time to go back to what you're doing, and it makes them feel appreciated and welcomed."

BRIAN BARTELS

Bar Operator

ways to ensure that your guests feel acknowledged and recognized for their patronage. In restaurants, this is typically communicated by the host, who may have been their first point of contact on the phone. But in bars, this may be the doorman, coat checker, or even a bartender, who must be trained to deliver the message graciously as they attend to their other duties.

Mission control for any well-run restaurant is the host stand, where you'll find the host or manager along with the reservation book, phone, menus, business cards, wedges to prop up wobbly tables, coat-check tickets, and a variety of other tools related to service. Whether noted in writing or using a reservations service such as Open Table, valuable data about guests should be collected, recorded, and communicated, including any important notes

Host Stand, Frasca Food and Wine

about the occasion for their visit and meal preferences. The more you know about a guest and the reason for their visit, the more likely you are to meet or exceed their expectations.

Many operators make the mistake of seating the restaurant in its entirety when it opens, which leads to all the orders going in at once, all the food going out at once, all the checks being asked for at the same time, and another tidal wave to follow. The entire service staff should be communicating throughout the night so tables can be turned for another seating or allowed to camp out so the room remains full. Once a dining room empties out, it's hard to restore the energy a roomful of happy people generates to entice new customers to join.

You need to put careful thought into the seating chart, taking into account guest table preferences, servers' abilities, and the look and feel of the business. Most maître d's seat customers near the front at the beginning of the night to generate buzz and later space them out to evenly distribute the workload among servers. This is where intuition comes into play, as some guests will want an intimate experience, while others may be gathered for a boisterous celebration. Putting too many large parties in one section of the room, seating dates next to singles on the prowl at the bar, or reserving a small table for a large party are three examples of seating issues that must be avoided to help ensure a positive guest experience from the outset.

Once the guest has checked in and been seated, the next point of contact is with the bartender or server. I don't think it's necessary for the server to introduce him- or herself by name, but eye contact, a warm greeting, and a menu are essential. The server should first wait for the party's undivided attention, then address the table from a position that's easiest for everyone to see and hear them.

If bottled water is available, it should be offered before tap water is served, when specials or anything off the menu are introduced. Some guests like a few minutes to decompress and catch up with their companions when they sit down, whereas others like to hear about the menu right away, so it's important to follow cues—such as their reading the menu or disregarding it—to gauge how quickly they'd like to discuss their options.

In spite of the server's best attempts to open a dialogue with all the guests, some people are nearly impossible to reach and don't feel obligated to interact. It's just as important to identify these guests and adapt your approach to serving them as it is to open friendly banter with those who do want engagement.

When the bar is busy, the server won't have the luxury of letting their guests set the pace; this is when they must establish that they will be *serving* rather than *waiting on* them. The distinction is subtle, but the point is to motivate the guests to be receptive to the server when they're at the table. This is possible only when the server is thoughtful about when they approach the table to avoid unnecessary disruptions.

Some guests relish their server's attention, but spending too much time at the table with them will cause guests at other tables (and seats at the bar) to wonder why they're not getting the same attention. At the bar, patrons should be served in the order in which they arrive, without exception, and each should be acknowledged with eye contact, a greeting, and a menu.

Chef Jimmy Bradley (see page 442) once explained to me that the server's dialogue at the table (and at the bar) regarding the menu is the art of "the in and the out." Information about food and drink is like an iceberg: display too little and your guest will crash into it, seeking more; display too much of it and they will sail around you, wishing they had never asked. The goal is to field questions, but in a concise way, to get out the order as efficiently as possible.

Briefly explain the organization of the menu, including any unusual service customs such as "family-style" shared portions for the table, or that the kitchen can't make ingredient substitutions. Ask about food allergies and answer any questions about the pronunciation of unusual menu items. Confirm your guests' preferred meat temperature and sides, plus preparation method and garnish for drinks. Remain mindful of stock levels so you don't recommend the last bottle of wine or pour of a spirit, in case the guest might desire a second serving. To support this practice, post a list of low and "86" (out of stock) items where all servers can refer to it and keep it updated.

Take orders for the first round of drinks all together, and serve everyone their drink at the same time; take subsequent drinks orders as each guest finishes their drink. Everyone drinks at a different pace, so don't wait for the whole table to finish their first round. If a guest sits with an empty drink too long without being offered another, they will typically wait for their companions to finish, and you'll lose out on a sale and the opportunity to tailor service timing for each guest at the table. Clear the empty glass onto a tray before you serve the new drink on a fresh napkin or coaster. Replenish bar snacks until guests decline them.

Open-Handed Pour

Once you take the order, leave behind a cocktail menu or wine list (if there's room at or near the table), then promptly enter the order. Return the extra menus to the host. Clear your guests' table of any superfluous items so there's plenty of room for plates, silverware, and glasses in addition to personal items like mobile phones. Discreetly clear soiled or soaked napkins, crumbs, spills, and any refuse from the guest such as gum wrappers. Refill water and wine glasses before they're emptied, unless the guest requests to pour their own. Refill water glasses even after the final drinks are finished and cleared.

Crumber

Instead of worrying about the dated custom that dictates from which side to serve or clear, make sure each guest sees the plate or glass that's being served or cleared to avoid collisions (and spills). If you do have a choice, follow tradition: food and beverages are served from the left side of the table to the right—or clockwise at a round table—with women and children being served first, then men. Every item should be ordered by the server with a position number so whoever delivers the prepared items knows which person to serve without having to ask or "auction" it off to the table. Servers should ask their colleagues for assistance delivering food or drinks to large parties to avoid guests having to wait for their companions to receive their order to begin.

When you place an item on the table or pour into a glass, do it "open handed" so you never show the back of your arm to a guest; this requires serving guests on your left with yout right hand and those on your right with your left. Guests sitting out of your reach should be politely asked to pass their glass and plate when they need to be cleared so you don't need to stretch awkwardly over the table.

Place each plate and glass on the table so the composition of the dish faces the guest as the chef and bartender intended. Affix cocktail garnishes at the two o'clock position of the glass's rim, and place the drink at the seven o'clock position relative to the water glass, which should be placed above the knife on the right side of the plate, if there is one.

Any other glass without a stem—such as old-fashioned and collins glasses and mugs—should be served on a cocktail napkin, placed in front of the guest with any logo or writing facing correctly. You don't need to serve stemmed cocktail and wine glasses on a cocktail napkin, as the stem mitigates condensation. Replace napkins when soaked, but be mindful of unnecessary interruptions and the environmental impact.

If a guest removes a straw or garnish, discreetly clear these. If a guest reorders the same drink, ask whether they'd like the straw or garnish omitted. Left-handed guests tend to shift their drinks over to their left side; follow their lead when serving the second round. If colleagues do any table maintenance, they should let the server know, to avoid unnecessary interruptions.

COMMUNICATION

I would never presume to script the conversation a server has with their guests, but you should avoid inappropriate phrasing, such as "Are you still working on that?" (as if eating were a chore) or "Are you still enjoying that?" Always say "May I?" instead of "Can I?"—and keep in mind that many questions can be communicated nonverbally through eye contact. Stay nearby after serving a plate of food or drink to verify there are no issues, which can be done without interruption in most cases.

If there are any issues with the food or drink, ask what was wrong, relay the information to the bar or kitchen, then promptly replace the dish. If the item was prepared incorrectly, offer to have it remade, or present a menu for the guest to choose something else. The best way to prevent this is before ordering, by asking about their preferences and making suggestions when an item is ordered.

If the guest seems unfamiliar with an ingredient or unlikely to appreciate it, make a judicious inquiry to affirm their interest in ordering it. Avoid explicitly "teaching" the guest; try conveying unknown information with an analogy to another item they're more likely familiar with. Don't offer personal recommendations unless requested, and make every effort to help the guest select items that will suit their tastes.

Whether a drink was prepared correctly or not, the guest has a right to return it once, and the server or bartender should never take this personally. You have no control over how your guests will perceive your food and beverage, but if they feel like you're on their side, they'll be more inclined to appreciate your offerings because they respect and trust your intentions.

BAR SERVICE

Service at the bar, where guests eat and drink an arm's length away from the bartender's workstations, is far more intimate and accessible than table service, where servers work from a distance. While many have always preferred drinking at the bar, dining at the bar has become increasingly popular; this requires bartenders to be more fluent in food service, which is why I've dedicated so much attention to it here.

I could write an entire additional book about the conversations that occur between a guest and a bartender, but for now I'll be concise. Don't inject religion and politics into a conversation, and keep your personal values and beliefs to yourself until it would be inappropriate to remain aloof. A great bartender has the ethics of a judge, the diplomacy skills of an ambassador, and the morals of a minister and should always steer guest interactions toward higher ground.

Your guests want to be listened to more than they want to hear what you have to say, even if it seems otherwise. Be an active listener who encourages them to share more, and use what you learn about them to guide them through the experience you believe they've come to have. Do not ever curse, shout at, disparage, or embarrass your guests or colleagues while behind the bar—even if you think it's all in good fun.

As a bartender, you need to be especially mindful of the cleanliness of your workstation, because it's in full view of your guests. The station should be maintained from the outside in,

Oscar

meaning you should focus first on the cleanliness of the bar top: cleaning and organizing from the guest's area inward toward the workstation. Stow clean wet and dry towels out of guests' view so condensation and spills can be mopped up quickly and discreetly. When in view of the guest, turn your back only if you must, and never eat, use your personal phone, or touch your hair or face with your bare hand. If you need to step away from the bar, excuse yourself from your guests, and if you anticipate any forthcoming requests, let your colleagues know.

Both waiters and bartenders should be mindful to avoid making any disruptive noise while in service. Place empty bottles in the recycling bin so they don't clink. Set plates in bus tubs. Don't pop sparkling wine corks— ease them out. Avoid slamming shaker tins closed on the bar top or clinking them together for a tighter seal. Close refrigerator doors quietly. Keep casual conversations with coworkers to a minimum and never conduct them in front of or within earshot of guests. Televisions (if present) should be set at a reasonable volume. Operate coffee grinders and steam wands where their noise can be muffled. Once the bar or restaurant is filled with people and service is at full tilt, all the sounds compound into a dull roar—which can be mitigated with thoughtful, discreet service.

When the guests have everything they've ordered, pay special attention to how the surrounding environment may affect them. Is the music creating privacy and fostering intimacy, or is it too loud, forcing them to shout? Do they have enough space, or have the neighboring guests angled their own stools, causing them to recoil? Are customers standing behind them trying to communicate through them instead of around them? Is there enough light, or are they reaching for a votive to read the menu? Would they like to check the sweater they just removed with their coat? Does their cell phone need charging? Do they need the Wi-Fi code? Would they benefit from meeting someone nearby who's hoping for an introduction, or should you safeguard their privacy? These are the sorts of questions bartenders should consider as they prepare to intervene, if necessary, with the help of a manager and their coworkers.

PRESENTING THE CHECK

The check should always be kept up-to-date with everything guests have ordered, so a colleague can present it if the server's away from their station when it's requested. As soon as a bill is requested, the host should be alerted so they can be in position to say good-bye at the door and have colleagues ready to reset the table for another party if necessary. If a party is waiting for a reservation slated for the table and the turn time is reasonable, the check can be presented as soon as the guests occupying it confirm they're done eating and drinking.

If the guests fail to produce payment within a reasonable time, offer to have their check transferred to the bar to continue their experience there. In the event there's an argument over who pays the check, avoid choosing sides, unless it's obvious who the host is and they insist upon their right to pay. As soon as cash or a card is produced, the bill should be processed so paying doesn't delay a guest's departure.

Every payment method possible should be accepted, and no one should refuse to allow guests to split a check; why would you work so hard to please a guest, then refuse a payment, making this one of their final impressions? Thank the guests when the bill is dropped, again after the payment is added, a third time once it is returned with change or a credit card slip, and a fourth time when they get up to leave. Make each thank-you to the whole table—not just the person who paid—and help expedite any coat check needs before guests get up.

After the bill is signed or the cash is left, collect it promptly; no need to wait for the guest to leave. This way, if there's a mistake, you can correct it at the table, instead of on the sidewalk—assuming you can catch them before they're gone. If the guests sit long after the bill is paid and there's no party waiting to be seated at their table, offer them another drink or coffee.

As soon as the guests depart, clear and clean the table or spot at the bar, even if it's the end of the night and no one else will be seated there, out of respect for any remaining diners. However, hold off on breaking down the stations and cleaning them as long as possible; then do it discreetly if guests are still present, to prevent their feeling they're not welcome or it's time to go.

Unless the law or well-established closing hours forbid it, never ask guests to leave the bar or restaurant against their wishes—*especially* if they're still eating or drinking. That said, at a certain point the business has every right to ask for seats to be made available if new guests are waiting to be seated at a table where earlier guests have finished eating and drinking and have paid.

RESPECTING PRIVACY

Never violate confidentiality between servers and their guests. Servers shouldn't gossip about their tables during or after work and should never reveal who ate and drank in their restaurant or bar, what they had, or when it happened, unless requested by law enforcement in relation to a crime.

Everyone deserves privacy and confidentiality, including guests who bring different dates on different nights, or business entities that wouldn't be pleased to know about the other parties. Like the doctor's Hippocratic oath to preserve patient's privacy or attorney/client privilege, a server is honor-bound to not divulge guests' secrets to others or judge them for their behavior as long as it doesn't intentionally harm or offend others.

ADDRESSING CONFLICT

If conflicts aren't managed diplomatically, a bartender can lose control of the station. Decorum is the bartender's responsibility, so if you don't say something when someone yells, curses, slams their hand on the bar, gropes their companion or another guest, or says something offensive in earshot of others, the guests will assume this is acceptable behavior. A busy bar takes cues from the bartender, who must remain cool, calm, and collected in the midst of a frenzy of activity.

Make every effort to handle conflicts without losing your temper. An apology should be made to acknowledge and diffuse the frustration of an irate guest before corrective behavior is prescribed in a firm, diplomatic tone. Ideally, this comes from a manager who steps in, or an employee whose station is far away from the guest (think good cop, bad cop).

In a bar or restaurant, the server working within earshot of the offender shouldn't have to deliver the corrective suggestion. No one likes to be told they're misbehaving, so a defensive response should be anticipated and deflected with a compassionate apology to avoid conflict, while holding the line.

I always give the guest some time and space to consider my suggestion. All staff must maintain nonthreatening body language throughout the confrontation so the guest believes there are no hard feelings and the desire is to move on.

In the event the interaction escalates into a conflict with the bartender, a manager or other employee should step in to hear out the guest, who should be asked to step out of earshot of other guests to avoid a scene. These situations tend to happen when a guest has had too much to drink and been refused service, or a conflict at a table is projected toward the server. The key to righting their experience is to listen actively and sympathize with their position, even if you don't agree with it. It's more important to defuse the situation and maintain decorum than to be right, so never let a confrontation get personal.

Another potentially challenging situation is when guests offer to buy a drink for other guests they don't know or members of the staff who are working. Allowing guests to buy servers drinks fosters a false sense of community and misconstrues the reason they're working: for money, not drinks. More often than not, the gesture to another guest is earnest, but it's best to vet it with a manager before asking for the recipient's blessing to avoid an uncomfortable situation facilitated by the bartender.

Most conflicts and issues that occur in a bar or restaurant are complicated—that's why I've always described bar management as "mastering the gray area." I've never written a manual like this, because there's always an exception to any rule in a bar, which is typically populated with guests and employees with an artful rebellious streak. Just as in politics, it takes compromise to get two sides to work together; by exploring this first, both sides may retain their pride after a misunderstanding. Assume the goodness of your guests and colleagues, but don't be surprised when they let you down from time to time. We're all human.

One of the most common methods to smooth issues over is through a "comp" in which the business takes something—for example, a dish that had to be remade—off the check. Many bars and restaurants take a round off an exceptionally large check, which is called a "buyback." The privilege— not right—of giving and receiving comps and buybacks should be instilled through company policy to avoid a misguided sense of entitlement among the customers and staff.

APPLYING THE BRAKES

Above all else, a guest's health and safety—while you're serving them and after they leave—are your most important responsibility. Do not serve more alcohol to a guest who appears intoxicated, no matter how much they implore. Signs included slurred speech, irritability, slow response times, unsteady gait, and disregard for social decorum.

As the evening progresses, you must anticipate that you're not serving someone their first drink, so making small talk about a guest's night can help you gauge how much they've had to drink before they arrived. Age, drinking experience, body mass, and the strength of what's being served should all factor into your assessment.

To mitigate the intoxicating effects of alcohol, serve all drinks with water, recommend food, and slow down service after the third drink. When a guest starts exhibiting the deleterious effects of alcohol, I politely ignore their requests for more drinks as if I didn't hear them or tell them it's coming and never bring it. Chances are they'll catch on and thank you for it later!

I should note that all of this assumes the guest isn't driving. Drinking and driving is illegal, and some states and countries hold the establishment and even the bartender accountable for crimes committed by a guest who left your business intoxicated. If you discover that a guest who's had too much to drink is planning on driving, alert a manager and come up with a plan to prevent it. It could be a matter of life or death.

Car Key

THE FINISHING TOUCHES

Remembering names, faces, visits, and favored drinks will immortalize you in the bar and restaurant business. And forgetting a bad tip, moving past a terse comment, and forgiving a clumsy mistake will keep you from losing your mind in a job that is driven by methodically repetitive work, night after night.

Each link in the chain of events that form an experience in a bar or restaurant is important, but none more so than the ending, which leaves the most indelible mark on a guest's memory.

I'm always disappointed—and surprised—when a great dining and drinking experience is punctuated by an inferior cup of coffee or tea, followed by difficulty getting the waiter's attention to get a check, hassles with payment methods, and a complete lack of hospitality once the transaction is completed.

No matter what happens during your guest's experience, never leave a bad taste in their mouth by slacking off after they've paid the check. Thank them, welcome them to return, and solicit their feedback. In Japan, I've had bartenders and waiters accompany me all the way to the sidewalk, help me get a cab, and then wave until I disappeared from sight. That's service.

Hospitality

While the notion of what constitutes great service can vary based on the type of bar you're patronizing, a server's desire to please guests—hospitality—is an instinct that's either nurtured or repressed long before guests walk through the door. Unlike service, which is a choreographed skill set that can be developed through a training program, hospitality is a sensibility that is cultivated (or neglected) in all of us from childhood onward. Enlightened operators recognize that their most important asset is their staff—and as such, they recruit people who exhibit kindness and hone their hospitality skills.

A server's instinct to please others must be well directed through proper training. This is what separates good operators from the legends, whose bars become institutions. I have covered the nuts and bolts of service; in this chapter, I'll examine ways to foster a hospitable environment—because without hospitality, service rings hollow.

We all have some instinct for hospitality, but it comes more naturally for some people than for others. Steve Olson (see page 461), a mentor of mine

At Left: Don Javier Delgado Corona of La Capilla Bar in Tequila, Mexico

who spent decades working in restaurants before forming his own wine and spirits consulting company, describes people who gravitate toward careers in service as having "a sick need" to make other people happy.

He's referring to the sort of person who gets more enjoyment from giving a gift than receiving one, and who thrives in an environment where there's an open feedback loop, such as a bar or dining room filled with guests. This person is most at home in a festive environment, but prefers working the party to attending. Even on their nights off, they spend their hard-earned money in bars and restaurants because they love food and beverage as much as the circus of service.

In *Setting the Table*, restaurateur Danny Meyer says hospitality "starts with the genuine enjoyment of doing something well for the purpose of bringing pleasure to other people." Whether you're an amateur who prepares food and drinks in your home or a professional who serves them for a living, the goal of your efforts must be pleasing people. I remind my staff and other bartenders that we don't serve drinks to people; we serve people drinks. It's a subtle distinction: even though we love making drinks, we're there to serve our guest's interests, not to venerate the platonic ideals of mixology.

Years before I fully grasped this concept, a guest at a table I was serving asked me to return their plate, which was prepared as requested, to be remade on a busy brunch shift. On the way to the kitchen, I told the general manager how nervous I was to ask the chef-owner of the restaurant to remake the food. The chef was a brilliant, hard-nosed, old-school taskmaster who berated the staff for their mistakes. Even though I hadn't made one, I knew I was going to get an earful for returning the plate. The GM asked me who my boss was. When I stammered, he told me the guest was my boss, so return the plate.

As a stubborn young bartender, I too was reluctant to remake cocktails sent back to me. I wish I had understood and accepted the fact that we all have different palates and preferences, and that it was nothing personal. If anything, the guest's bold request was an opportunity for dialogue. If I'd used the drink they sent back to narrow down my options, I'd have had a better chance of winning them back with a cocktail tailored to their palate.

"The espresso-to-go movement was started by Ninth Street Espresso. We were the first shop to say no espresso to go and then we were the first shop to go back and serve espresso to go. You know why? That little 4-ounce paper cup is sitting on the counter. So who the fuck am I to say no to a customer that walked past three other shops for my coffee? That's beyond bad service, but it took me a long time to get that. I came onto the scene with a lot of publicity for being the ornery guy that said no and then realized that had its time and place and it doesn't anymore."

KEN NYE

Coffee Shop Operator

WHY WE DINE OUT

The key to hospitality is understanding why guests choose to dine out in the first place. In *Setting the Table,* Danny Meyer writes, "The number-one reason guests cite for wanting to return to a restaurant is that when they go there, they feel seen and recognized." It took me years to realize that we aren't in the food and drink business; we're in the people and relationship business. We dine out because we want to be part of something, not just because we're hungry or thirsty. Great servers make their guests feel like they belong in their bar or restaurant, that they are part of a revolving community of diners and drinkers whose values are validated by the business's ethos.

Given the limited amount of time and money most patrons have for entertainment, a night out at restaurant or bar needs to deliver more than what appears on the check. Instead of going to a movie, sporting event, or the theater, many guests choose to visit your bar or restaurant, so the experience should be remarkable enough to share with their friends and family. Running into friends or making new ones, being introduced to a new ingredient or product, or discovering the best version of an iconic drink or dish are the sorts of experiences they make a point of sharing with others the next day.

Hospitality isn't one-size-fits-all; it must be adapted based on cues from the guests. Sometimes great hospitality means giving a table space and privacy; other times it requires a high-touch, personal experience with frequent communication. Look for physical items guests bring along—such as a briefcase, a wrapped present, or a suitcase—to better understand where they are coming from or going. When there's time for chitchat, try to find common interests such as sports, music, food, or literature, then connect that guest with other servers or regulars at the bar who share the interest. In this sense, a bartender works like a bee pollinating flowers. Bartenders don't just mix drinks; they mix people, too.

MANAGEMENT

The business of cultivating and nurturing relationships in the bar starts from the top down with owners setting the tone. When I'm a guest in a bar, before passing judgment on an inhospitable bartender, I often question what their manager must be like, how their colleagues treat each other, and how they're all enabled or affected by the way the operators run the business.

Bullying runs rampant in the bar and restaurant business and has a devastating effect on the demeanor of those on the front line of the abuse. Great service starts with the way people treat and speak to each other behind the scenes, and it radiates out to the guests.

A successful bar or restaurant has a culture of accountability: every stakeholder, from dishwashers to the general manager, can trust that every coworker will take care of his or her responsibilities. This means that each staff member's responsibilities are clear—and this takes us back to management.

As a manager, the first thing I always ask myself when one of my colleagues doesn't do what I expect of them is, *Did they know that I expect them to do this?* The second is, *Were they trained to do it the way they're supposed to?* No one wants to fail, and, in most cases, staff members make mistakes because they weren't trained or managed properly. I always give the benefit of the doubt on the first infraction—unless it's outright theft or another crime—and follow up with a written warning that gives an employee control of their fate.

Calculator

Ultimately, whatever goes wrong in a bar or a restaurant is the operator's responsibility. And when things go right, it's because the staff met or exceeded the expectations and training of their managers. When my star began to rise in the industry, I accepted credit for what went right in the bars I worked in, so people paid closer attention to my work. I failed to recognize that the spotlight my good work attracted cast a dark shadow on my colleagues around me, who began to resent me in spite of my earnest intentions.

Since then, I've made a point of diverting attention to the people who make my success possible so they receive the credit they deserve. Great leadership should be invisible unless there's an issue that needs to be addressed.

One of the most valuable insights related to problem solving I've gleaned over the years emerged during a conversation with Danny Meyer while I was still working at Gramercy Tavern. He clarified that the restaurant's goal wasn't perfection; rather, it was excellence. In *Setting the Table* he writes, "Perfection is impossible in business. As a company policy, the notion of perfection can be dangerous, and the folly of pursuing it can stunt your team's willingness to take intelligent risks." People make mistakes when they step outside their comfort zone, but if they're punished for this, they'll stop trying. Better to help people when they stumble instead of being cross with them.

BUILDING A TEAM

You can teach all the technical skills necessary to do a job, but you can't train someone to care, be conscientious, behave with integrity, and be kind to others. In my experience, the best way to recruit new staff is through your existing staff, who can vouch for the value of the position (if you're holding up your end of the bargain) and can act as a surrogate manager to expedite their candidate's integration into the team.

When you're opening a place, you should seek out candidates who are interested in building a business's reputation and learning along the way. Once you've solidified your reputation, you need to supplement the first group with a second wave of employees who will help you sustain and grow your business.

Your opening staff are sprinters: the equivalent of high-risk/high-reward stocks; they are looking for a promotion and an opportunity to learn, and they are willing to work through the chaos of opening a restaurant to achieve those goals. The second group of hires are marathoners: the equivalent of blue chip stocks; they value a steady paycheck and job security over the topsy-turvy period before a restaurant finds its footing.

In most cases, the team that gets you where you want to be won't be the team that keeps you there. In spite of this, I've tried to hold on to as many of the opening staff members of bars I've managed as possible, which helps keep each successive generation of employees rooted in tradition.

It's humbling to work with colleagues who have skills you lack or are better at certain areas of the business than you are. The best managers are keenly aware of their strengths and weaknesses and hire to complement them accordingly. For example, I value bilingual employees (as I speak only English), rely on

ON NEGATIVITY

"I don't want negative people in this bar, and that goes for the guests and staff. You come to a bar to find positivity. You're not coming here to get more negative. There are different styles of management within the bar world. There are 'me' people and 'you' or 'team' people. As soon as I walk into a bar I can feel whether there's negativity. Obviously, the first thing is, is this bar good? Do the operators care about it? But from there, you can also sense the operator's attitude. Are they an optimistic or positive person? You'll quickly see that trait mirrored in their staff."

JACK MCGARRY

Bartender

colleagues who are computer-savvy for tech issues, and keep a handyman on retainer for weekly maintenance issues ranging from plumbing to electric to wear and tear on the barroom.

In addition to recruiting team members with unique, complementary skills, I strive to maintain cultural diversity to attract the widest possible range of patrons to the business. If you have any doubt that this is important, start paying closer attention to the relationship between the staff and patrons of bars.

Clubs hire attractive staff and attract a similar clientele; bars where fights are common hire antagonistic bouncers to work the door; and cocktail bars hire

"My reputation is for being brutally honest. There's no bullshit; I'm going to tell you exactly what I think. With staff, it's not to make them feel bad; it's always to help the big picture."

JULIE REINER

Bar Operator

mixology devotees, who attract like-minded customers. To attract a diverse audience (assuming your bar is located in a diverse locale), you should make sure that diverse ages, races, genders, and sexual orientations are represented.

When your leadership finds its footing and the business gains a respected identity, suddenly you'll discover that new recruits go from wanting to work *with* you to wanting to work *for* you. There's a huge difference between hiring the best person for the job, who's interested in finding the best job they can get, and hiring someone who's taken the time to visit your bar, see how you work, taste what you serve, and get to know your team and guests. You can train the person who's looking for a job, but you can't mentor them unless they desire to learn more about the way you and your team do things—and why.

COMPANY CULTURE

The legendary hotelier César Ritz famously said, "We are ladies and gentlemen serving ladies and gentlemen," which I interpret as, "If you want people to behave like ladies and gentlemen, you must both treat them accordingly and endeavor to be one yourself." The staff sets the tone in a bar or restaurant by embodying the behavior they'd like their guests to manifest. Dress your staff formally if you want people to feel comfortable coming straight from work, or dress them informally to attract patrons who don't wear a suit or dress to work.

When the guests don't follow your lead, be the change you want to see in your bar. If you surround yourself with a diverse group, chances are there's someone on your staff with the temperament, approach, and communication skills to smooth over nearly every situation. For this reason, I like to cross-train my staff on as many positions as possible, so bartenders work the floor some nights, waiters sometimes work behind the bar, and everyone hosts occasionally. This helps deter mental and physical burnout, fosters empathy and awareness of your coworkers' challenges, and increases the chances that a guest's questions can be answered with expertise.

Training is another key to hospitality, and there are a variety of approaches that work depending on the style and concept of your business. Your staff will thrive in an environment where they know what to do and how to do it—and your guests will surely appreciate it, too—but I've become leery of rigorous training and too many policies over the years.

Consistency is vital, and everyone should know what to do and why, but technique offers staff members an opportunity to express themselves, so codifying it too rigidly stymies both personal expression and the chance of someone discovering a better way to do things because they were encouraged to experiment. I spend less time training the whole staff and more time working with underachievers and those who actively seek out supplementary training.

What's the point of hiring a diverse staff and expecting them all to conform to the same methodologies? When managers helicopter over the staff to nitpick, step in whenever there's an issue with a guest, and spend too much time making sure no one does something they're not supposed to, mistakes inevitably follow. If you're always there to clean up your staff's mess, they fail to develop problem-solving skills. If you treat people like children or thieves, you run the risk that your behavior will be a self-fulfilling prophecy. Most bar and restaurant employees have an artistic, rebellious streak in them; it's best not to aggravate that through heavy-handed management.

I've found that with the right group of people—such as my team at PDT—the best course of action for me as a manager is to sleep on whatever I feel the need to say or do, and see whether I still think it's important to communicate the next morning. I've stopped calling staff meetings to talk about issues that pertain to only a handful of colleagues; instead, I spend more one-on-one time with them. Instead of viewing my staff through my own eyes, I evaluate their work through the opinions of our regulars and their coworkers, who appreciate me soliciting their point of view, which is just as integral to the success of the business as my own.

STAFF TURNOVER

Though you'll want to do everything you can to retain your best staff members, at some point you'll have given them all you have, and they'll want to go work for someone else to realize their full potential. I ask my employees to give me a minimum of one year to train and mentor them, followed by a second year for them to pay it back, and at that point I tell them we're even. Often they'll take a second job in their third year to broaden their skills and for a change of scene that provides perspective for them and frees shifts for eager staff members waiting in the wings for new opportunities.

I encourage staff members not only to help find their replacement when they're ready to leave, but also to train them before departing. The old sports maxim of finishing strong is something I preach as they work out their last

ON BEING RIGHT

"I demand from people who choose
to work with me that they abandon
the need to be right at all costs.
Because 'I need to be right' is the
root of all problems in our world,
from the smallest to the biggest.
In the workplace it's incredibly
poisonous. Instead, I tell people,
pure and simple, to focus on the
results. The results will give you all
the information you need to know
about how successful you were. Once
you abandon the need to be right,
you get creative, and your pathway
to the results isn't usually a straight
line. I use the results to tell me what
I need to work on."

JIMMY YEAGER

Restaurateur

shifts, as this is where the baton is passed or dropped, with lasting effects for
both parties in the race.

SELF- AND STAFF-CARE

You're probably wondering when I will talk about how this all plays out
for the guest. For me, hospitality starts long before the guest enters the
equation. Putting your own wants and needs aside for six to eight hours so
you can focus entirely on the needs of others requires a great deal of personal
and collective effort. Do you recall the part in the safety demonstration on a

Airplane Oxygen Mask

commercial airplane where they instruct you to put your oxygen mask on before helping others, with the image of the mother putting her own mask on first, then her child's? Well, that's the approach you need to do to be successful in the hospitality industry.

When I started bartending in the 1990s, most people who worked in bars did so only until they were in their mid-twenties at the latest, then got a "real job." But I fell in love with the industry and decided to make a career of it a few years before the modern cocktail renaissance transformed what many had thought to be a questionable decision into a "smart" choice. Twenty years later, working in the bar business is seen as a legitimate career move. However, this means that bartenders are turning what used to be a part-time job into a decades-long career—and if you don't want to burn out, you need to take the long view.

In *Cocktail Technique*, lifelong Japanese bartender Kazuo Uyeda writes, "Sickness prevents you from applying your mind. Therefore remember: Don't drink too much and stay in control of your health." Truer words have never been spoken about bartending—for some, being in the festive environment of the bar can blur the boundaries between work and play, and when that happens, "sickness" in the form of alcohol or drug abuse can prevent bartenders from realizing their potential. After working in both bars that permitted and encouraged drinking behind the bar and those that didn't, I would strongly urge operators and bartenders to refrain from drinking during their shifts.

The easiest way for bartenders to maintain balance is to cut out alcohol consumption in other parts of their life. For me, this means eliminating

"I knew if I wanted to be great, I had to be disciplined. I come from an athletic background . . . Running has been the cornerstone of my sommelier career. That's how I got through my Master Sommelier program. I think about things when I run. A lot of practices we've established at the restaurant have come from my runs. Monday night menus came from a run. Guest chef series came from a run. [As for drinking on the job], I like catching a buzz as much as anyone else, but it's going to affect what you're trying to do. So more nights than not, I have only one beer on a shift. Or just one glass of wine at dinner. That's enough—and all of a sudden everything starts clicking into place."

BOBBY STUCKEY

Sommelier

shots, watery beer on my day off, and drinking at home—not to mention drinking with the aim of getting intoxicated. If you're drinking to get drunk, chances are you need to reevaluate your choice of the alcohol business for your career.

Given that most servers work during traditional mealtime hours and late into the night, it's challenging for them to maintain a healthful diet. Shamefully, most bars and restaurants that pride themselves on the quality of their cuisine don't provide a balanced meal for their staff before and after service. Servers should invest in healthful snacks to fuel them during their shifts, and avoid alcohol and grazing on junk food after their shifts, when the numbness

ON TEAM BUILDING

"Do I want my team to be homogenous or dynamic? There's no right or wrong answer, but I want mine to be broad. When I'm building my team, do I just do what I want to do, or do I share it? And if I share, am I just sharing it with the other coaches and managers or with the whole team? Do I allow the team to have a voice in what's going to happen? That's the most difficult form of management and that's the form I've chosen. It's also the closest one to democracy. I want my people to feel like they're critical to the success of the team."

JIMMY BRADLEY

Chef

of a night of work dulls their discipline. It's far from glamorous, but the best thing you can do after a shift is hydrate with plenty of water, stretch, then prop your feet up against the wall to give your body a chance to recover.

"Our bodies prefer to use alcohol as a fuel source, so if you eat high-fat foods while drinking, the fat in these foods is directed to 'storage' as opposed to being used," says health and fitness consultant Georgia van Tiel (see page 463). In addition to paying closer attention to diet and exercise, Georgia recommends that bartenders be disciplined about getting a full night's sleep and mitigating stress—which is exacerbated by alcohol, caffeine, and drugs—with meditation, music, nutritional supplements such as magnesium and omega-3s, and sex. I concur.

Like an athlete before a big game, I begin each day before work visualizing my evening in service, to prepare mentally, physically, and emotionally for the challenges that lie ahead. In addition to picturing everything going as planned throughout the evening, I imagine resolving any challenging interactions with guests and colleagues. As I've said, great managers anticipate problems, and after running scenarios through my mind before service as a bartender, I find it easier to chart the correct course of action during service.

Medicine Ball

The effectiveness of these preparations is enhanced if you show up to work on time; this allows you to make all the necessary preparations before service, so you can focus on being in the moment. Of course, your advance preparation is undermined if you *don't* show up to work on time.

Blowing off steam with a few drinks after work is fun and builds camaraderie, but late-night drinks lead to late-night meals, romantic affairs with coworkers, and encounters with cocaine and other stimulants that keep the party going. The way you behave on both sides of the bar will affect the way your colleagues perceive you, so I always tell my staff that their actions on and off the clock are a reflection of me and our bar.

One of the surest ways to avoid this path is to cultivate a life outside of the industry with family, friends, or even a pet, all of which give you good reasons to wake up in the morning with a clear head to accomplish something that motivates you to grow as a person. For me, this is my family; for others, it could be exercise, religion, school, another career, or a creative

Time Clock

hobby such as writing, painting, or music. When you have a life outside your work, you'll be less likely to take questionable risks that could jeopardize it.

Hospitality is an instinct fostered by empathetic, self-conscious operators with the magnetism to attract a like-minded staff. As I reflect upon what's driven my success and failure as a member of this industry over the past two decades, I've found there's no way to separate personal development from professional growth; the lessons I've learned have helped me become a better father, son, husband, friend, and businessman.

Family

ON INSECURITY

"Part of our success is we never want to fail and always want to be great, and we're always very insecure, because we feel like we don't know what we're doing, so we question absolutely everything all the time. And that allows us to be very accepting of change. When there's no change, and everything's set and there's no chaos, you miss the world of chaos. For us, change is normal. When things are going well, we think we're failing or being complacent."

LEO ROBITSCHEK

Bar Operator

Beyond Bars

Today, talented bartenders have more career options beyond bartending than ever before. They don't have to choose between burning out and leaving the industry entirely. Those who've moved on are supporting bartenders though insightful journalism; as educators, training bartenders and consumers on how to prepare cocktails and evaluate spirits; and as consultants, bringing more sophisticated bar concepts (that employ and train bartenders) to venues that a decade ago wouldn't even have considered using fresh juice. Cocktail bars are more popular than ever, with owners, operators, and bartenders reaping the benefits.

This wasn't the case when I started working in the business in Madison, Wisconsin, in 1995. Most of my colleagues back then were part-time students who chose the profession for the flexible hours, which allowed them to attend classes during the day, or part-timers from other fields looking to supplement their income from traditional 9-to-5 jobs.

At Left: Moore & Giles Meehan Bag

Many found the alternative hours and high hourly wage (where tipping is practiced) hard to relinquish for full-time entry-level jobs in their field of expertise, but most eventually left anyway. In spite of the pay cut involved in the employment transition, there was cultural pressure to move on, as many consider working in the bar business an alternative vocation for those who can't hack a career in "the real world."

Imagine the baffled stares I received when I told friends and family I was going to continue bartending after I graduated from college with two degrees in 2001. I knew, and they knew, it would be a difficult path. Being a career bartender means working during mealtimes and holidays, and late into the night, and it takes its toll on significant others, kids, and bartenders themselves. But my plan wasn't to stay behind the bar forever; I had worked for numerous independent operators who structured their hours around their personal life, and I wanted to follow their lead. My plan was to open my own bar, with the help of investors, by the time I was thirty.

Of course, my twenty-year-old self didn't fully grasp the financial challenges faced by operators who don't own their building, such as costly build-outs that need to pay off over relatively short-term leases, with few protections. Ultimately, I decided to transition into management and consultancy, which give me the sense of accomplishment of operations without the responsibilities (and unforeseeable catastrophes) of ownership. In addition to working with bars, I supplement my income by writing for magazines (that English degree came in handy after all), spirits and cocktail consulting, and receiving royalties from products I helped create, ranging from a bar bag to a spice line.

Anyone who says that moving away from full-time bartending into management or some similar role is "selling out" is wrong—and probably lacks the creativity and confidence to take on new challenges. There are incredible, inspiring lifelong bartenders—such as Seattle's Murray Stenson, San Francisco's Marco Dionysos, Paris's Colin Field, Munich's Charles Schumann, and Tokyo's Kazuo Uyeda—but these people are exceptional, gifted outliers. We mere mortals should not plan to match their longevity.

Like athletes, most bartenders peak in their early thirties and decline when the physical and emotional demands of the job accumulate. The repetitive motions of shaking, stirring, bending down to scoop ice, and all the hours standing wreak havoc on joints and lead to repetitive-stress injuries. There's also the psychological wear and tear: most bartenders are still subjected to dozens of indignities each night by guests who have little regard for the vulnerability that great service demands.

HOMEWORK

While there is no shortcut to mastering the craft, there are many new resources that may expedite the journey. Helpful as these are, they are not a bonus, but a real necessity; today's bartenders must extend their apprenticeship beyond the fundamentals to become adept at skills outside the confines of the bar to gain a following for their work behind it. Reputable bars train their staff in how to operate within their system, but the bartender who seeks a career in the industry must pursue ongoing professional development, ranging from product education to technique refinement.

Notebook

My generation learned about cocktails from books such as Gary Regan's *The Joy of Mixology*, Ted Haigh's *Vintage Spirits and Forgotten Cocktails*, and Dale DeGroff's *The Craft of the Cocktail* long before spirit companies began investing in education programs such as BarSmarts, and trade organizations such as the United States Bartender's Guild (USBG) began training and certifying bartenders as mixologists.

Nowadays, most of the young bartenders I meet in the United States and abroad are learning about the craft through online videos on YouTube long before they read books like my first bar guide, *The PDT Cocktail Book*.

Whether they research online or in print, modern bartenders have two to three times as much to study as the previous generation, as the sheer volume of content throughout many media has grown.

To stay on top of it all, I scan through *Grub Street*, *Eater*, *Punch*, *Tasting Table*, and *Difford's Guide* online for food- and beverage-related content and read the *New York Times* food section on Wednesday. In the past, there'd be one or two cocktail or spirits books released a year, but that number has tripled, with new titles focusing on drink through the lens of history, culture, economics, and politics in addition to house cocktail books and single-spirit category overviews. I devour beverage-focused quarterlies like *Imbibe!* and *The Cocktail Lovers*; page through food magazines such as *Food & Wine*, *Bon Appétit*, and *Saveur*; and take a peek at lifestyle magazines like *Vogue*, *Marie Claire*, *GQ*, *Playboy*, and *Esquire* to see what my guests are learning about cocktails and spirits.

U.S.B.G. Lapel Pin

Familiarize yourself with the products out there and learn more than just the names and shapes of the bottles. Attend lectures and trainings by distillers and spirits brand ambassadors like Simon Ford and Charlotte Voisey, who, in their previous roles with Plymouth and Hendrick's gins, respectively, educated bartenders on the history of the entire gin category, not just their brands, and how each style could be applied in classic and modern cocktails.

BRAND AMBASSADORS

Ford and Voisey have been promoted and now oversee larger portfolios of spirits within their respective companies; however, their innovative educational campaigns have set a new standard in the industry. Their success as marketers has encouraged producers, importers, and distributors to hire bartender "ambassadors" for part- and full-time work that relies

ON DIPLOMACY

"All of a sudden, the term 'brand ambassador' became interesting and press-worthy, so people began calling brand reps 'ambassadors' in the hopes that success would follow the label. Of course, we know that calling someone an 'ambassador,' is like calling yourself a 'master mixologist,' doesn't mean that you are. Being an 'ambassador' requires diplomacy: it's how you interact with people. It's the sweet spot between 'what's our agenda' versus 'what does our audience need.' The very word has always rung true to me."

CHARLOTTE VOISEY

Portfolio Ambassador

on their insights for package design, new spirit development, marketing strategy, public relations, education, sales, and more.

With their diverse responsibilities, brand ambassadors are the spirits industry's "Swiss Army knife," as all these roles tend to fall under the marketing budget, despite responsibilities in other realms. While most brands hire well-known, respected bartenders with loyal followings for brand ambassador roles, some prefer candidates with formal marketing, sales, and PR training and experience.

Swiss Army Knife

AUDREY SAUNDERS

Bartender

ON PRESENCE

"I found strength in the work and research. To have forums like Drink Boy and eGullet was huge because the people online were like-minded thinkers. It wasn't overly important how they perceived me: it was important how they perceived my work. Being on an online forum is protective: you're allowed to do what you set out to because you're not dealing with a room full of people and worrying about what they think. I don't want people to know I'm in the room from seeing me. I want them to know I'm in the room through my drinks."

COCKTAIL MEDIA

National newspapers and magazines have started employing bartenders and enthusiasts to cover spirits and cocktails, and consulting work now trickles down beyond cocktail "luminaries" to their protégés.

One of the rewards for remaining on top of it all—and getting ahead of it from time to time—is being quoted as an industry source for a feature in a media outlet. To secure this opportunity, the secret is simple: be available via phone or email at all times and respond to media requests immediately. Most writers are nearly late for the deadline by the time they reach out to potential sources, and their publishers don't always allocate the budget to send a photographer, so the best way to ensure that your work is included is to always be fully prepared to respond, with neatly organized recipes, background text, and a professional-quality photo.

The word will soon spread among drink writers that you're a reliable and responsive source. Many magazines and newspapers are embedding videos with their stories online, so being asked to clear an afternoon to shoot supplemental content for stories requires bartenders to become more comfortable in front of the camera. Years ago, I teased actors who'd become bartenders; now I wish I shared their skills and training!

For bartenders without corporate publicists pitching their work, who have much more to say about subjects not covered by traditional media outlets, self-publishing is a great way to get your voice out there. Online forums such as eGullet, blogs such as *Jeffrey Morgenthaler*, podcasts such as *The Steve Schneider Show*, radio programs such as Damon Boelte's *The Speakeasy* on Heritage Radio Network, and *Jamie Oliver's Drinks Tube* on YouTube have expanded the channels on which bartenders and consumers learn about spirits and cocktails and made their hosts barroom icons.

Social media such as Twitter, Facebook, Instagram, and Snapchat are key, too; each bartender and bar has its own personality, so you can capture yours via the social medium that fits best (pontificate on Facebook, make pithy quips on Twitter, take gorgeous photographs on Instagram, or bring people into your universe via video on Snapchat). Many bartenders and experts such as David Wondrich, Joerg Meyer, Bobby Heugel, and Giuseppe González have built their reputation through their commitment to social media channels and their followers.

Newspaper Stand

NETWORKING

As information technology continues to unite the industry as a global community, travel becomes more important to build and maintain relationships abroad. While following your favorite bars and bartenders on social media helps keep you up-to-date with their offerings and events, there's nothing like face-to-face contact and time spent experiencing their hospitality.

Suitcase

Most bartenders offset the cost of these visits by arranging guest bar shifts, master classes, and pop ups underwritten by hotel groups or spirit companies, who fly them in and put them up in return for their patronage. You can learn a lot by sitting at a great bar if you're vigilant, but there's no substitute for working with the world's best bartenders if they'll host you. Our guests are traveling more, too, which makes well-traveled bartenders who can double as a concierge a more valuable asset for their employers.

Besides visiting well-known bars and bartenders when I'm traveling for inspiration, I make reservations at reputable restaurants to see how chefs are shaping the culinary landscape. During the days, I check out farmers' markets, wine and spirits shops, and specialty stores. Depending on where you travel, there are iconic vessels, tools, spirits, and cocktail accessories that are unique to each region, that make excellent souvenirs to decorate your bar and gift in thanks to coworkers who covered your shifts.

Wherever possible, I set up appointments at distilleries, breweries, and wineries to expand my knowledge of production and deepen my bonds with purveyors. When it's appropriate, I document my favorite experiences on social media to thank the people and places that welcomed me and encourage others to visit.

"You need to make money at what you do to pay your bills and your taxes and take care of your family, but I swear to God, if you look at life, it's about the experiences you have and the time you get to spend with people. It always ends up being beneficial."

JULIO BERMEJO

Bar Operator

CONVENTIONS, SEMINARS, AND COMPETITIONS

The emergence of international cocktail conventions such as Tales of the Cocktail in New Orleans, Bar Convent Berlin, and London Cocktail Week has paved the way for a handful of cocktailians to build their reputation on an actual stage instead of behind the bar. The pioneers include the Oxford-educated son of a legendary author (Angus Winchester, see page 3); Irishman Phil Duff, who moonlighted in Amsterdam for over a decade before moving to New York, where he overseas seminar selections for Tales of the Cocktail; and New Zealander Jacob Briars (see page 118), who tended bar through law school, then chose the spirits business over the chamber. Each has channeled their skills as gifted public speakers, insightful advisors, and crafty marketers into careers in the industry that other brainy bartenders are gravitating toward today.

Besides seminars, guest bartending shifts, and networking opportunities with colleagues and enthusiasts, bar shows host awards ceremonies that raise the profile of bars and bartenders to the public. Some awards, such as those given

Bar Show Credential

out at Bar Convent Berlin, are geared toward local markets, while others, such as Tales of the Cocktail in New Orleans and London Cocktail Week, recognize bartenders and bars all over the world at the prestigious Spirited Awards and the World's 50 Best Bars ceremonies.

Because the industry lacks a Michelin-like brigade of independent judges, the voting process that determines the finalists reflects popularity more than empirical excellence, but the very existence of these spectacles and the attention they garner have raised awareness among consumers. In 2012, the James Beard Foundation, whose awards ceremony dates back to 1990, began recognizing an Outstanding Bar Program each year, which has helped validate cocktails as a culinary art.

The interest and acclaim that bar shows and awards have generated has built a consumer base that helps many bartenders secure funding to take a step beyond education, marketing, or sales into entrepreneurship. The pioneers who made this step possible before awards made minor celebrities out of bartenders include David Nepove, who began producing and selling Mr. Mojito muddlers in 2002; Gary Regan, who launched his orange bitters in partnership with Sazerac in 2005; Ryan Magarian, who launched Aviation Gin with House Spirits in 2006; and Jen Colliau, who founded Small Hand Foods in 2008.

ON COMMUNITY

"I tried to bring people together to push our industry forward, with education being the key. I brought bartenders from America to England to meet each other, but it didn't have to be that way. I could have just taken bartenders on a trip to Plymouth to show them the distillery. But that would have defeated the objective of everyone meeting, sharing ideas, building a friendship, and developing a network of like-minded people to push the industry forward. I was constantly trying to champion the industry through these decisions."

SIMON FORD

Portfolio Ambassador

Each saw an opportunity to create products that bartenders wanted and to capitalize on their reputation. Thanks to the success of these endeavors, former bartenders such as Dushan Zaric and Jason Kosmas have their own spirits line (The 86 Co.), Brooks Reitz has his own line of cordials (Jack Rudy), Erik Lorincz has his own Japanese bar tools (Birdy), and Sean Hoard and Daniel Shoemaker have their own FDA-approved fresh juice delivery service (The Commissary).

Cocktail competitions are another opportunity for young bartenders who don't work at a high-profile bar in a major metropolis to make a name for themselves. Bartenders and cocktails have been judged and awarded prizes

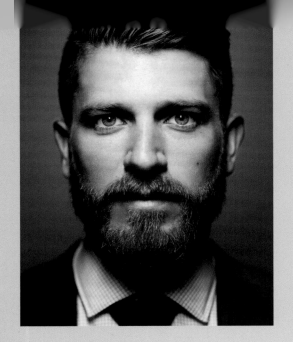

ON COCKTAIL COMPETITIONS

"I see a lot of bartenders signing up for competitions because they want to be made. It can expedite things, but it's not going to take you to the next level unless you work with it. Competitions are a moving sidewalk. You can stand on the moving sidewalk and still have people sprint past you in the concourse. A lot of bartenders coast through because they think they're on the fast track."

JEFF BELL

Bartender

for more than a century, as you can see by the portraits of all the medalists in Charles Mahoney's *The Hoffman House Bartender's Guide* (1905), but the bartending world has never seen the likes of multimillion-dollar marketing extravaganzas put on by Diageo and Bacardi, which recognize the best bartender (World Class) and cocktail (Legacy), respectively.

While bartending is a team sport and the most prestigious competitions test individuals, the rigor of the challenges and fanfare for the winners have been transformative for the careers of bartenders like London's Erik Lorincz, New York's Shingo Gokan, and Chicago's Charles Joly and led to unique opportunities for each of them to prosper beyond the bar.

In 2011, New York bartenders Ivy Mix and Lynnette Marrero founded a cocktail competition called Speed Rack, which they developed to raise both awareness for underrepresented female bartenders in the cocktail industry and, in the process, money for breast cancer research and prevention. In 2010, Josh Harris and Scott Baird's San Francisco–based consulting firm, the Bon Vivants, established a charity event called Swig & Swine, which raises money for charter schools where the bartenders who produce the event volunteer the day before. These are two examples of cocktail-oriented charity initiatives that give bartenders a platform to showcase their talents and build alliances among guests, chefs, the media, purveyors, and restaurateurs throughout the city, while improving the lives of others in the process.

Competition Trophy

When they're not raising awareness through charity or overseeing their own operations at Trick Dog in San Francisco, the Bon Vivants work with clients on and off premise to design bar programs, co-develop spirits brands, and engage the trade through education and events. A similar bartender-founded agency, Proof & Co. of Singapore, not regulated by laws that prevent spirits distributors from operating their own bars, takes their involvement with spirits brands a step further by serving as their importer and distributor, in addition to running their own world-famous bars, including 28 Hong Kong Street.

Proof & Co. recently opened a liquor store with a demonstration bar that can be used for educational seminars and as a cocktail development lab by company bartenders who use it to create new cocktails for their accounts. All over the world today, bartenders are sharing what they've learned behind the bar with spirits brands and other operators to improve the industry, which is helping bartenders raise their profile and earn a living in new ways.

JUMPING THE LINE

Many of those who have witnessed or participated in the industry's sea change are concerned that bartenders spend less time mastering their craft before moving on to related opportunities such as brand advocacy or consultancy. They gripe about certain bartenders becoming "startenders" without paying their dues, and about the way spirit companies pluck talent away from bars that have invested in training and mentoring them.

As an operator who tended bar for more than a decade before people stopped asking me what my "real job" was, I share these concerns. That said, these

Rolodex

new opportunities have attracted a whole new pool of educated, personable, self-motivated candidates to the industry who weren't interested in bartending when I entered the trade.

As I look back on my career, I would say that the most important asset I've accumulated consists of the relationships I've cultivated along the way. After I had a tumultuous experience training for one of my first restaurant jobs, a sous chef who saw me struggling pulled me aside and insisted that however I decided to handle the situation, I shouldn't burn any bridges. It's the best advice I've ever been given, and while I've flirted with fire and reluctantly burned a few since, I'll pass it along: *Do everything within reason to avoid compromising relationships with colleagues and guests.* If, like me, you're passionate and vocal about what you do, you'll find yourself in hot water from time to time; this means you should be more self-aware and ready to apologize when you let your emotions get in the way of sound judgment.

Thanks to more talented applicants entering the industry, guests have a larger variety of bars and servers to visit. Given a choice between

ON TEACHING

"I look for the twinkle in your eye
when I see that you got it. When I
see that light go on, and you get it, for
me, I've done my job. I live for that
moment. I was a service animal and
loved being on the floor. People
say, 'Don't you miss that?' I say,
'I did, but I don't anymore.' Because
I realized I can reach even more
people. So instead of reaching a six
top, or twenty people in my station,
or one hundred fifty people in my
restaurant, I can reach thousands
by doing lectures and TV and radio.
I can reach more people and help
them learn to make their own
decisions by empowering them
with information. I love sharing."

STEVE OLSON

Teacher

two bartenders with similar talents, they'll choose the one they prefer
interacting with nearly every time. The bartenders who get promoted to
management, move on to sales or ambassadorship, or embark on their own
as entrepreneurs aren't always the highest achievers; rather, they're the ones
who nurture relationships with guests and colleagues.

While I now retain staff for longer tenures in my bars than I did in my earlier
days as a manager, many still move on to other careers. As they depart, I
couldn't be more proud of the customer service, teamwork, and conflict-
management skills they've learned along the way. I agree with the old adage
"everyone should work in the service industry at least once in their life." I'd
go even further and argue that being a bartender is the best possible training

for any number of careers. Bartenders are both craftspeople and salespeople: they make something, and then sell it to you. No surprise, then, that so many go on to become entrepreneurs.

Imagine your favorite bartender behind the window at the post office, seated at the rental car–agency desk, or checking you in for your flight at the airport; now, can you honestly tell me there aren't dozens of other service and sales-driven occupations that would benefit from the sense of urgency, diplomacy, and tireless work ethic of great bartenders? Great bartenders—and former bartenders—have a preternatural ability to be fully present with the customer, while also staying fully conscious of their responsibility to move on to serve others.

Years after my last scheduled shift, I nostalgically fill in "bartender" on forms as my occupation, as I've never stopped thinking or behaving like one, and it's hard to explain what I "do" to those who aren't familiar with the industry. While I don't tend bar regularly anymore, I still create and serve cocktails, entertain guests in bars, and spend most of my nonfamily time with colleagues from the bar business.

For me, working in the bar and restaurant business is a call to service that's just as noble as the work of other public servants because it puts me in a position to improve the lives of others. When the opportunity to serve my community beyond the bar was presented to me, I eagerly accepted it and have never looked back. It's also made me grateful for every opportunity I'm given to tend bar again today.

ON HAPPINESS

"Don't forget about happiness. When you're on the road, chances are you're full of energy, because you're out there doing the thing you love to do. Quality of life is really important. You talk to a lot of people who work in the hospitality industry, and you ask them on a scale of 1 to 10, how happy are you? And a lot of them will be pushing up to 8. You flip that to someone who is corporate or has a desk job and it's below 6. There's something really important about happiness. Sleep, routine, and having a semblance of a normal life are important, but normalcy isn't as important as happiness."

GEORGIA VAN TIEL

Health and Fitness Consultant

BIBLIOGRAPHY

Arnold, Dave. *Liquid Intelligence: The Art and Science of the Perfect Cocktail.* New York: W. W. Norton & Co., 2014.

Baiocchi, Talia. *Sherry: A Modern Guide to the Wine World's Best-Kept Secret, with Cocktails and Recipes.* Berkeley: Ten Speed Press, 2014.

Baiocchi, Talia, and Leslie Pariseau. *Spritz: Italy's Most Iconic Aperitivo Cocktail, with Recipes.* Berkeley: Ten Speed Press, 2016.

Baker, Charles H., Jr. *The Gentleman's Companion: Being an Exotic Drinking Book, or Around the World with Jigger, Beaker, and Flask.* New York: Crown, 1946.

Bava, Roberto. *Futurist Mixology: Polibibite, The Autarkic Italian Answer to the Cocktails of the 1930s.* Mappano, Italy: Cocchi Books, 2014.

Bebe, Lucius. *The Stork Club Bar Book.* New York: Rinehart & Co., 1946.

Bergeron, Victor Jules. *Trader Vic's Bartender's Guide: Over 1000 Recipes for the Newest Drinks and Most Popular Stand-Bys, Including 143 Trader Vic Original Exotic Mixed Drinks.* rev. ed. Garden City, NY: Doubleday & Co., [1947] 1972.

Berry, Jeff. *Beachbum Berry's Potions of the Caribbean: 500 Years of Tropical Drinks and the People Behind Them.* New York: Cocktail Kingdom, 2013.

Beverage Alcohol Resource LLC. *BarSmarts Workbook 6.0.* Purchase, NY: Pernod Ricard USA, 2011.

Boothby, William T. *The World's Drinks and How to Mix Them.* San Francisco: Boothby's World Drinks Co., [1908] 1934.

Broom, Dave. *Gin: The Manual.* London: Mitchell Beazley, 2015.

———. *Rum: The Manual.* London: Mitchell Beazley, 2017.

———. *Whiskey: The Manual.* London: Mitchell Beazley, 2014.

Bullock, Tom. *The Ideal Bartender.* St. Louis: Buxton & Skinner Printing & Stationery Co., 1917.

Byron, O. H. *The Modern Bartenders' Guide.* New York: Excelsior, 1884.

Cate, Martin, and Rebecca Cate. *Smuggler's Cove: Exotic Cocktails, Rum, and the Cult of Tiki.* Berkeley: Ten Speed Press, 2016.

Craddock, Harry. *The Savoy Cocktail Book.* London: Constable & Co. Ltd., 1930.

Curtis, Wayne. *And a Bottle of Rum: A History of the New World in Ten Cocktails.* New York: Broadway Books, 2007.

DeGroff, Dale. *The Craft of the Cocktail: Everything You Need to Know to Be a Master Bartender, with 500 Recipes.* New York: Clarkson Potter, 2002.

——. *The Essential Cocktail: The Art of Mixing Perfect Drinks.* New York: Clarkson Potter, 2008.

Difford, Simon. "Difford's Guide for Discerning Drinkers." Odd Firm of Sin, Ltd. www.diffordsguide.com

Doudoroff, Martin. "Martin's Index of Cocktails." Mixology Tech, Version 1.2 (2016). mixologytech.com/martinsindex

——. "Vermouth 101." Vermouth 101. N.p., 2011. Web. 14 Mar. 2017. www.vermouth101.com

Duffy, Patrick Gavin. *The Official Mixer's Manual.* New York: Long & Smith, 1934.

Edmunds, Lowell. *Martini, Straight Up: The Classic American Cocktail.* Baltimore: Johns Hopkins University Press, 1998.

Embury, David A. *The Fine Art of Mixing Drinks.* Garden City, NY: Doubleday & Co., [1948] 1958.

Ensslin, Hugo R. *Recipes for Mixed Drinks.* New York: self-published, 1917.

Gale, Hyman, and Gerald F. Marco. *The How and When.* Chicago: Lincoln Printing Co., 1937.

Gjelten, Tom. *Bacardi and the Long Fight for Cuba: The Biography of a Cause.* New York: Viking, 2008.

Greene, Philip. *To Have and Have Another: A Hemingway Cocktail Companion.* New York: Perigee Books, 2012.

Grimes, William. "'The Hour,' Famous Cocktail Guide, Is Reissued. *New York Times*, 8 June 2010.

——. *Straight Up or On the Rocks: A Cultural History of American Drink.* New York: Simon & Schuster, 1993.

Grohusko, Jack. *Jack's Manual.* New York: printed privately, 1910.

Grossman, Harold J. *Grossman's Guide to Wines, Spirits, and Beers.* New York: Scribner's, 1964.

Gross, Matt. "Crystal Clear: A Guide to Real Schnaps," *Saveur.* (December 2010): 49.

Haigh, Ted. *Vintage Spirits and Forgotten Cocktails: From the Alamagoozlum to the Zombie and Beyond.* Gloucester, MA: Rockport Publishers, 2004.

Harrington, Paul, and Laura Moorhead. *Cocktail: The Drinks Bible for the 21st Century*. New York: Viking, 1998.

Heimann, Jim (ed), Steven Heller, and John Mariani. *Menu Design in America*. Cologne: Taschen Books, 2011.

Hemingway, Ernest. *Islands in the Stream*. New York: Scribner's, 1970.

Herlihy, Patricia. *Vodka: A Global History*. Chicago: University of Chicago Press, 2012.

Hess, Robert, and Anistatia Miller (eds). *The Museum of the American Cocktail Pocket Recipe Guide*. London: Mixellany Limited, 2006.

Hoefling, Brian D. *Distilled Knowledge: The Science Behind Drinking's Greatest Myths, Legends, and Unanswered Questions*. New York: Abbeville Press, 2016.

Hosanksy, Eugene A. "The Current Scene: Film Posters." *Print*, 19, no. 4 (1965): 20.

Huff, Marisa. *Aperitivo: The Cocktail Culture of Italy*. New York: Rizzoli, 2016.

Hutson, Lucinda. *Viva Tequila! Cocktails, Cooking, and Other Agave Adventures*. Austin: University of Texas Press, 2013.

Lasa, Juan A. *Libro de Cocktail*. N.p., 1929.

Johnson, Harry. *Bartenders' Manual*. New York: self-published, 1900.

Jones, Stan. *Jones' Complete Barguide*. Los Angeles: Barguide Enterprises, 1977.

Judge Jr. *Here's How!* New York: John Day Co., 1927.

Kaplan, David, Nick Fauchald, and Alex Day. *Death & Co: Modern Classic Cocktails*. Berkeley: Ten Speed Press, 2014.

Ledesma, S. E. *Nuevo Manual de Cocina a la Criolla*. Lima: Ledesma, 1903.

Mahoney, Charles S. *The Hoffman House Bartender's Guide: How to Open a Saloon and Make It Pay*. New York: Richard K. Fox Publishing Co., 1912.

Mario, Thomas. *Playboy's Host & Bar Book*. Chicago: Playboy Press, 1971.

Martineau, Chantal. *How the Gringos Stole Tequila: The Modern Age of Mexico's Most Traditional Spirit*. Chicago: Chicago Review Press, 2015.

Matus, Victorino. *Vodka: How a Colorless, Odorless, Flavorless Spirit Conquered America*. Guilford, CT: Lyons Press, 2014.

McDonnell, Duggan. *Drinking the Devil's Acre: A Love Letter from San Francisco and Her Cocktails*. San Francisco: Chronicle Books, 2015.

McElhone, Harry. *ABC of Mixing Cocktails*. London: Odhams Press, 1922.

——. *Barflies and Cocktails*. Paris: Lecram Press, 1927.

Mies van der Rohe, Ludwig. Inaugural Address as new head of the Department of Architecture, Illinois Institute of Technology, Chicago, IL, 20 November 1938.

Meier, Frank. *The Artistry of Mixing Drinks*. Paris: Fryam Press, 1936.

Meyer, Danny. *Setting the Table: The Transforming Power of Hospitality in Business*. New York: HarperCollins, 2006.

Miller, Anistatia, and Jared Brown. *Cuban Cocktails: Drinks and the Cantineros behind Them, from Cuba's Golden Age*. London: Mixellany Limited, 2012.

Miller, Anistatia, Jared Brown, and Miranda Dickson. *My Absolut: What the Bartender Saw*. London: The Absolut Company, 2010.

Morgenthaler, Jeffrey, and Martha Holmberg. *The Bar Book: Elements of Cocktail Technique*. San Francisco: Chronicle Books, 2014.

Moss, Robert F. *Southern Spirits: Four Hundred Years of Drinking in the South, with Recipes*. Berkeley: Ten Speed Press, 2016.

Neal, Charles. *Calvados: The Spirit of Normandy*. San Francisco: Flame Grape Press, 2011.

Newman, Frank P. *American Bar: Recettes des Boissons Anglaises et Américaines*. Paris: Société Française D'imprimerie et de Librairie, 1904.

Picchi, Luca. *Negroni Cocktail: An Italian Legend*. Florence: Giunti Gruppo Editoriale, 2015.

Proulx, Theodore. *The Bartender's Manual*. Chicago: J.M.W. Jones Stationery & Printing Co., 1888.

Rams, Dieter. "Design by Vitsœ." Presentation at Jack Lenor Larsen's showroom, New York, NY, December 1976.

Regan, Gary. *The Bartender's Bible: 1001 Mixed Drinks and Everything You Need to Know to Set Up Your Bar*. New York: HarperCollins, 1991.

———. *The Joy of Mixology: The Consummate Guide to the Bartender's Craft*. New York: Clarkson Potter, 2003.

———. *The Negroni: Drinking to La Dolce Vita, with Recipes & Lore*. Berkeley: Ten Speed Press, 2015.

Ridgewell, Mark. *Spirits Explained*. London: Mixellany Limited, 2012.

Rogers, Adam. *Proof: The Science of Booze*. Boston: Houghton Mifflin Harcourt, 2014.

Saldaña Oyarzábal, Iván. The Anatomy of Mezcal. Milton, DE: Expresslt Media, 2013.

Saucier, Ted. *Bottoms Up*. New York: Greystone Press, 1951.

Schmidt, William. *The Flowing Bowl: What and When to Drink*. New York: Charles L. Webster & Co., 1891.

Schultz, Christian. *A Manual for the Manufacture of Cordials, Liquors, Fancy Syrups, Etc.* New York: Dick & Fitzgerald, 1862.

Seutter, Carl A. *Der Mixologist*. Leipzig, Germany: P. M. Blühers Verlag, 1909.

Stewart, Amy. *The Drunken Botanist: The Plants That Create the World's Greatest Drinks*. Chapel Hill, NC: Algonquin Books, 2013.

Straub, Jacques. *Drinks*. Chicago: Hotel Monthly Press, 1914.

Tarling, W. J. *Café Royal Cocktail Book*. London: Pall Mall, Ltd., 1937.

Terrington, William. *Cooling Cups and Dainty Drinks*. London: George Routledge & Sons, 1869.

Thomas, Jerry. *The Bar-Tenders' Guide*. New York: Dick & Fitzgerald, [1876] 1887.

——. *How to Mix Drinks or The Bon-Vivant's Companion*. New York: Dick & Fitzgerald, 1862.

Tiano, Jack. *The American Bartenders School Guide to Drinks*. New York: Rutledge Press, 1981.

Toye, Nina, and A. H. Adair. *Drinks—Long & Short*. London: William Heinemann, 1925.

Uyeda, Kazuo. *Cocktail Techniques*. New York: Mud Puddle Books, 2010.

Van Eycken, Stefan. *Whisky Rising: The Definitive Guide to the Finest Whiskies and Distillers of Japan*. Kennebunkport: Cider Mill Press, 2017.

Vermeire, Robert. *Cocktails: How to Mix Them*. London: Herbert Jenkins, Ltd., 1922.

Whitfield, W. C. (ed). *Here's How*. Asheville, NC: Three Mountaineers, Inc., 1941.

Wondrich, David. *Esquire Drinks: An Opinionated & Irreverent Guide to Drinking, with 250 Drink Recipes*. New York: Hearst Books, 2004.

——. *Imbibe! Updated and Revised Edition: From Absinthe Cocktail to Whiskey Smash, a Salute in Stories and Drinks to "Professor" Jerry Thomas, Pioneer of the American Bar*. New York: Perigee Books, 2015.

——. *Killer Cocktails: An Intoxicating Guide to Sophisticated Drinking*. New York: HarperCollins, 2005.

——. *Punch: The Delights (and Dangers) of the Flowing Bowl*. New York: Perigee Books, 2010.

ACKNOWLEDGMENTS

I've mentioned as many of the people who helped me reach the finish line as I could within the text of the book, but there isn't enough room to acknowledge everyone, so please give me a hard time if I've left you out. Most of you were planning on it anyhow.

First and foremost, I'd like to thank those who took the time for an interview and portrait. These friends, colleagues, and mentors of mine answered countless emails, phone calls, and texts about information most consider proprietary.

This book wouldn't exist if it wasn't for my brother Peter, who suggested I meet with Emily Takoudes to discuss cocktail books at Phaidon. While we didn't end up working together, I'm grateful she recognized the merits of this book before anyone else.

Ultimately, Kim Witherspoon led me to Aaron Wehner, whose peerless team and commitment to publishing the world's best cocktail books sealed the deal. For three years, Kim and Aaron helped maintain the project's momentum and for this, I am deeply grateful.

Emily Timberlake validated my decision: structuring a free-flowing narrative into a book, making me a better writer and person in the process. William Callahan helped me wade through her edits, motivating me to keep my chin up and head down.

Betsy Stromberg transformed a stack of old car manuals and vintage cocktail books into a gorgeous manuscript, integrating hundreds of images with thousands of words. Emma Campion weighed in along the way and Jane Chinn handled the heavy lifting with the printer.

Kristi Hein and Doug Ogan made judicious textual changes to clarify my intentions and Jeff Bell, Dave Broom, Wayne Curtis, Sean Hoard, and David Wondrich fact- and gut-checked my writing and research. Special thanks to H James Lucas for polishing the final draft.

Allison Renzulli, Erin Welke and Windy Dorresteyn helped me produce a package and tell a story that readers will remark upon for years to come.

I'm blessed and forever in debt to Doron Gild (assisted by Don Lee) and Gianmarco Magnani, whose timeless artwork carry this project in ways my words cannot. Their commitment to this book was as uncompromising as mine.

Special thanks to Brian Shebairo and our team at PDT, Liz Kohansedgh of American Express, and my colleagues at Banks Rums and Moore & Giles for keeping the lights on while I wrote this.

To Tatiana Martushev, Chris Metro, Erin Stoneburner, and Katie Fuller, who put my body back together after I left New York; Bill Dailey, who lifted me up when my spirit was heavy; and Brad Parsons, who is my friend and literary shrink.

To the Simis and Meehans: especially our parents, who instilled the values I've attempted to infuse into this text. And to all our friends in Portland, especially Sean Hoard and Hannah Scott, who welcomed us to our new home.

Finally, to my wife Valerie and our daughter Olivia, who put their lives on pause for nearly three years: I couldn't have done this without your support. And lastly to our son, who's due to enter the world the week the book is released.

Doron Gild: I dedicate my efforts to the love of my life, Ana Jovancicevic. Thank you for your unyielding support and patience: this wouldn't be possible without you. To Chris Polinsky, Mete Ozeren, and David Miao for your help finishing the images: your hard work was integral to capture all the colors. And to Dale DeGroff, Philip M. Dobard, Jyl Benson, and Jennie Merrill of the SoFAB in New Orleans for letting us use your space.

Gianmarco Magnani: I would like to thank Jim for giving me the opportunity to illustrate this book, for his confidence and his professionalism across these years working together, and especially I would like to thank Daniella, for believing in me, for supporting me in every decision and for always pushing me towards it.

• • •

Most of the book's illustrations were drawn from snapshots of my personal possessions or tools and machinery I encountered during my research. Thank you to my friends and colleagues for supplying the following images: Daniel Krieger and Andy Seymour for images of me; Catherine Laraia, Catherine Shotick, and the Driehaus Museum for *Tiffany Roman Punch Bowl*; Jason Crawley for *Imperial Shaker*; Toby Cecchini for the image of himself; Julio Bermejo for *Tommy's Menu Board*; be-pôles for *NoMad Library*; Stonehill and Taylor, Jacobs, Doland, Beer Design, and Sydell Group for *NoMad Floorplan*; Andrew Kist for *The Dead Rabbit Taproom*; Neel Munthe-Brun for *Likdoeb*; Lacy Landre for *Bryant's Cocktail Lounge*; Eric Mackey for *Bryant's Floorplan*; Jan Holzer for *Drink*; Ezra Star, Sean Frederick, Jeffrey and Cheryl Katz, and Jordan Bissett for *Drink Floorplan*; Bo Hagood for *Hoke Home Bar Schematic*; Louis Anderman for *Scale*; Shintaro Okamoto for *Clinebell Ice Machine*; Dave Smith for *St. George Mixing Tank*; Robin Robinson for *Compass Box Tasting Room*; Gilles de Beauchêne for *Noilly Prat Salle des Secrets*; Myriam Hendrickx for *Rutte Genever Recipe*; Jade Oliver for *Bundaberg Molasses Well*; Jeff Grdinich for *Santa Catarina Minas Horno*; Paul O'Connor for *Fausto Vasquez and Assistant*; Megan Meloche for *Grain Harvester*; Bruno Delessard for *Maison Ferrand Paradis*; Thierry Desouches for *Cointreau Still Room*; Matteo Luxardo for *Luxardo Citrus Botanicals*; Sean Muldoon for *Dead Rabbit Menu*; Erin Pommer and Alexander Joyce for *Frasca Host Stand* and *Open-Handed Pour*; Ryan Huber and Sam Parker for *Medicine Ball*; Ryan Portnoy for *Moore & Giles Sidecar* and *Meehan Bag*; Jennifer Mitchell for *Bar Show Credential*.

I owe a debt of gratitude for numerous other contributions to: Camper English of the website Alcademics; Liz Brusca, Karl duHoffmann, Georgiana Green, Alan Kropf, Liz Staino, and Bill Zhen of Anchor; Wilkin Cabrera and Jenny Sze of Baccarat; Colin Appiah, Carlos Argamasilla, Cristiana Fanciotto, Giuseppe Gallo, Manuel Greco and Ian McLaren of Bacardi; Diego Loret De Mola of Barsol; Dan Cohen, Gardner Dunn, Adam Harris, Takahiro Itoga, Kate Kenny, Jamie MacKenzie, Pamela Pincow, Dave Pudlo, and Daisuke Tsukahara of Beam Suntory; Chris Dauenhauer, Joanna Glass, and Mayur Subbarao of Blueprint; May Matta-Aliah of B.N.I.A.; Eric Hay of Breakthru; Becky Codd, Simon Coughlin, Allan Logan, Lynne McEwan, and Carl Reavey of Bruichladdich; Elizabeth Colton, Caitlin Crisan, and Dave Karraker of Campari; Tremaine Atkinson of CH; Debbie Burke-Smith and Kerrin Egalka of Compass Box; Peter Connell and Rob Cooper (R.I.P.) of Cooper Spirits; John Deragon; Catherine Ahn, Tracy Gilbert, Jess Slevin, and Melissa Woodbury of Diageo; Kevin Law-Smith of East Imperial; Kate Krader and Suzie Myers of *Food & Wine*; Tim Master of Frederick Wildman; Megan Hurtuk of Gemini; Jackie Patterson Brenner and Kaj Hackinen of Giffard; Robert Bohr and Danielle Harris of Grand Cru; David Hughes and Eric Seed of Haus Alpenz; Laura Bruce, Dave Mitton, Ryan Powell, and Rama Zuniga of Hiram Walker; Sebastian Beckwith of In Pursuit of Tea; Máire Coffey and Brian Nation of Irish Distillers; Christian Glyche of Karlsson's; Lior Sercarz of La Boîte; Nancy McCarthy of Laird's; Steve Luttman and Whitney Peak of Leblon; Melanie Asher and Elizabeth Datrindade of Machu Pisco; Oliver Matter of Matter Distillery; Liz Barrett, Kanchan Kinkade, Antonella Nonino, Bonito Nonino, Giannola Nonino, and Marina Vernon of Nonino; Shawn Kelley and Lora Piazza of Pernod Ricard; Benjamin Galais, Guillaume Lamy, and Manuela Savona of Pierre Ferrand; Andreas Mühlböck of Reisetbauer; Nathan Burdette, Alfred Cointreau, Kyle Ford, Richard Lambert, and Johanna Marchena of Remy-Cointreau; Anthony Basso of Rhum Clément; Ben Carlotto, Albert De Heer, Marc de Kuyper, and Mark de Witte of Rutte; John Bick and Adam Schuman of Skurnik; John Monetta of Small Hand Foods; Katie Cavenee and Ellie Winters of St. George; Kate Laufer Gorenstein of Sydney Frank; Michelle Dunnick and Ann Tuennerman of Tales of the Cocktail; Alex Michas of Vintus; Asema Bektemessova and Jennifer Vallejo of Żubrówka.

INDEX

A

Abou-Ganim, Tony, 25
absinthe, 150, 154
    Absinthe Drip, 161
    Corpse Reviver
        #2, 232
    For Peat's Sake, 339
    fountains, 89
    Sazerac, 331
Ace Hotel, 37
Achatz, Grant, 411
Adair, A. H., 361
After Nine, 386
agave syrup, 392
Airmail, 265
Albemarle, 37
Alperin, Eric, 26–27
Andrews Sisters, 19
Angel's Share, 27
aperitifs, 150–59. *See also individual aperitifs*
aperitivos, 153
Aperol, 150, 153
    Venetian Spritz, 167
apple brandy, 348–49
    Jack Rose, 359
    Newark, 363
    See also calvados
applejack, 344, 349, 350, 359
Arnold, Dave, 73, 81, 100, 101, 105, 389
Ashley, James, 11, 12
Asplund, Krister, 182
Astor, Vincent, 193
Attaboy, 27, 75, 76
Augier, Philippe, 344
Aviary, 411
Aviation, 223
awards, 456

B

Bacardí Massó, Facundo, 243
Bailey, Preston, 53
Baiocchi, Talia, 167
Baird, Scott, 459
Baker, Charles H., 1, 17, 113, 249, 365
Ballymaloe, 53
Bamboo, 175
Bank Exchange Saloon, 355
Banks, Joseph, 266
Bar Agricole, 350
bar design
    branding, 40–41, 44
    concept, 29, 35–37
    décor, 50–53
    environment, 53–55
    evolution of, 29–30
    examples of, 38–39, 42–43, 48–49, 58–59, 62–63, 68–69
    home bar, 66–69
    interior design, 44–47, 50
    location, 30–34
    physical bar, 56–57, 60–61, 64–65
Bar High Five, 234
Bar La Florida, 251, 261
barrel maturation, 136–37
Barrymore, John, 225
barspoons, 87–88
Bartels, Brian, 5, 415
bartenders
    awards for, 456
    career options for, 447–62
    competitions for, 457–59
    conflicts and, 424–26
    media and, 452–53
    networking and, 454
    professional development for, 449–50
    self-care and, 439–44
    self-expression and, 121
    service vs. point, 91
    splitting orders between, 91–92
    well-rounded, 118
Batida, 245
Baum, Joe, 24
Beach, Donn, 20
Beau, Paul, 346
Beebe, Lucius, 19, 173, 189, 234
beer, 156
    Black Flip, 389
    Czechmate, 199
    Michelada, 111, 177
    pouring, 111
    tap troubleshooting, 112
Bell, Jeff, 5, 253, 339, 458
Bellagio, 25
Bendavid, Roberta, 53
Bénédictine, 368, 373, 374
    Bobby Burns, 323
Bergeron, Victor. *See Trader Vic*
Bermejo, Julio, 283, 455
Berry, Halle, 249
Berry, Jeff, 20, 21, 257, 259
Besant, Henry, 42, 283
Betts, Richard, 278, 291
Biltmore Hotel, 290
bitters, 153
    decanters, 95
Blackbird, 26
Black Flip, 389
Blanc, Jacques, 344
blenders, 90
blending, 137–38
Blood and Sand, 317
Bloody Mary, 79, 104–5, 193
Blue Hill Stone Barns, 53
Bobby Burns, 323
Boccato, Richard, 27
Boehm, Greg, 2, 9, 287, 290
Boelte, Damon, 453
Bohrer, Andrew, 255
Bols, Lucas, 204
Bonfanti, Gabe, 129
Bon Vivants, 459
Boothby, Bill, 175, 381, 383
bottling, 139–40
Boudreau, Jamie, 227, 231, 335, 341
Boulaabi, Atef, 229
Boulevardier, 329
bourbon, 136–37, 296, 301–2, 305
    Brown Derby, 313
    Manhattan, 327
    Mint Julep, 315
    Purple Rain, 337
    Stone Fence, 311
Bradley, Jimmy, 5, 418, 442
Bradsell, Dick, 198, 311
brand ambassadors, 450–51, 457
branding, 40–41, 44
brandy, 342–49, 350. *See also* apple brandy; calvados; cognac; pisco
Breaux, Ted, 154
Brennan's, 388
Briars, Jacob, 115, 176, 181, 455–56
Broadford Hotel, 379
Brock, Sean, 337
Brooklyn, 325
Broom, Dave, 125, 203, 295
Brosnan, Pierce, 249
Brown Bomber, 336
Brown Derby, 313
Bruman, Henry J., 269
Bryant's Cocktail Lounge, 58
Buena Vista Café, 108, 321
Buichet, Philibert, 383
Bullock, Tom, 15
buybacks, 426
Buzza, George, 313
Byron, O. H., 231, 327

C

cachaça, 239, 245
    Batida, 245
    Caipirinha, 245, 255
Café Arroz, 387
Caffè Camparino, 169
Caffè Casoni, 235
Caipirinha, 245, 255

calvados, 126, 343, 345, 348–49, 350
Camerena, Don Felipe, 271
Cameron's Kick, 338
Campari, 150, 153, 369
    Boulevardier, 329
    East India Negroni, 266
    Negroni, 235
    Old Friend, 233
    Rosita, 287
Campari, Gaspare, 153
Canadian whisky, 296–97, 303
    Toronto, 335
Canlis, Mackenzie, 38
Caribe Hilton, 21, 257
Carpano, Antonio Benedetto, 151, 153
Casey, Ryan, 337
Castellon, Fernando, 261, 353
Cate, Martin, 147, 264
Cecchini, Toby, 24, 25, 201
champagne, 114, 155
    Airmail, 265
    Champagne Cocktail, 163
    French 75, 221
    Hans Solo, 236
    Jimmie Roosevelt, 365
    Rosy Cheeks, 309
Champs-Élysées, 361
Chang, David, 398
Chartreuse, 369
    After Nine, 386
    Champs-Élysées, 361
    For Peat's Sake, 339
    Jimmie Roosevelt, 365
    Last Word, 227
Chatham Bar, 364
check, presenting, 423
Chef's Club, 233
cherry liqueur
    Blood and Sand, 317
Cipriani Group, 24
City Hotel, 12
Clarke, Paul, 227
cleaning, 107, 423–24
Clyde Common, 398
Coale, Ainsley, 345

cobblers, 171
Cock 'n Bull, 189
Cocktail Culture, 200
cocktails
    future of, 410–11
    with global popularity, 405–6
    history of, 7–27
    media and, 452–53
    pairing food and, 398, 409, 410–11
    recipe development for, 399–403
    titles of, 403–4
    See also menus; individual cocktails
coffee, 108
    Irish Coffee, 321
Coffee Cocktail, 377
Coffey, Aeneas, 297
cognac, 342, 343, 344–45, 346–47, 350
    Champs-Élysées, 361
    Coffee Cocktail, 377
    French Maid, 366
    Japanese Cocktail, 367
    Jimmie Roosevelt, 365
    Milk Punch, 388
    Sidecar, 357
    Stinger, 381
    Tom and Jerry, 385
Cointreau, 368, 370, 374
    Corpse Reviver #2, 232
    Cosmopolitan, 201
    Margarita, 285
    Sidecar, 357
    White Lady, 234
Coleman, Ada, 237
Colliau, Jen, 74, 191, 217, 355, 456
Collins, John, 11
Collins, Wayne, 336
competitions, 457–59
comps, 426
conflicts, addressing, 424–26
Connaught, 121
Connery, Sean, 19
conventions, 455–56
Cooper, Ron, 129, 272, 277, 279, 291, 341

Corby, Henry, 296
Corpse Reviver #2, 232, 401
Cosmopolitan, 24, 26, 183, 201
Craddock, Harry, 3, 5, 16, 223, 225, 232, 234, 313, 317, 335, 361
crème de cacao
    After Nine, 386
    Grasshopper, 383
    Rosy Cheeks, 309
    20th Century, 225
    21st Century, 288
crème de cassis
    El Diablo, 290
    Kir, 165
crème de menthe
    Grasshopper, 383
    Stinger, 381
crème de violette
    Aviation, 223
Crème Yvette
    Purple Rain, 337
Crosby, Bing, 271
Crow, James, 296
Crowley, Martin, 272
C3, 25
Cuervo, José Maria Guadalupe de, 270
curaçao
    El Presidente, 261
    Mai Tai, 264
Curtis, Wayne, 16, 18, 19, 389
Czechmate, 199

D
Dabney, John, 12
Daiquiri, 262
    Hemingway Daiquiri, 251
Davis, Greg, 132
Dead Rabbit, 37, 40, 41, 42–43, 74, 109, 398, 408
Death & Co, 272
deBary, John, 253
décor, 50–53
DeGroff, Dale, 5, 11, 13, 18, 23, 24, 25, 26, 120, 221, 313, 323, 375, 381, 407, 449
DeGroff, Jill, 24

DeJoria, John Paul Jones, 272
Delaplane, Stanton, 321
Delgado Corona, Don Javier, 281
Delmonico's, 37
de Mandelslo, Johan Albert, 10
Demerara syrup, 391
Denton, Bob, 271–72
Deragon, John, 363
Detroit Athletic Club, 227
DeVoto, Bernard, 207–8
Dewar, John, 297
Dickson, Miranda, 181, 185
dilution, 101
Dionysos, Marco, 448
distillation, 133–34
distillery tours, 123–24, 143, 454
Doh, Sullivan, 350
Don the Beachcomber, 20
Dornenburg, Andrew, 402
Doudoroff, Martin, 361, 381
Drambuie, 379
    Rusty Nail, 379
Dreyfuss, Henry, 225
Drink, 61, 62–63, 411
Dubonnet, Joseph, 152
Dubonnet Rouge
    DuBoudreau Cocktail, 341
Duff, Philip, 206, 369, 455
Duffy, Patrick Gavin, 17
Dutch Kills, 27

E
Eames, Charles, 45
East India Negroni, 266
Eaton, Alfred, 296
eau de vie, 142, 342, 343, 344, 349–50
    Rose, 364
egg whites, 98
El Diablo, 290
El Floridita, 398
Eliot, T. S., 147–48, 149
Ellison, Brian, 139
El Presidente, 8, 261
Embury, David, 1, 9, 307, 323, 335

Employees Only, 25, 327
Ensslin, Hugo, 223, 335, 361
Eppinger, Louis, 175
Errico, Enzo, 325
Escalante, John B., 261

F

Farber, Dan, 147, 345, 346, 347
Farrell, Frank, 227
Faviken, 53
Fedroff, Susan, 35
fermentation, 133
Fernet-Branca
    DuBoudreau
        Cocktail, 341
    Hanky Panky, 237
    Newark, 363
    Toronto, 335
Ferrand, Pierre, 346
filtration, 138–39
Five Island
        Flamingo, 263
Five Points, 53
Flatiron Lounge, 25
Fleming, Ian, 153, 184, 187
floating, 116–17
Ford, Simon, 208–9, 450, 457
For Peat's Sake, 339
French Maid, 366
French 75, 221

G

Gabriel, Alexandre, 244
Gaja, Angelo, 52
Gantt, Ernest Raymond
        Beaumont. *See*
        Beach, Donn
Garcia, Ricardo, 257
Garcia Vasquez,
        Faustino and
        Maximino, 124,
        129, 279
garnishes, 79–80,
        114–20
Garvey, Hugh, 309
genever, 202–4, 206,
        209–10
Gertsen, John, 61
Gimlet, 219
Gimlette, Thomas, 219

gin, 202–13
    After Nine, 386
    Aviation, 223
    Corpse Reviver
        #2, 232
    French 75, 221
    Gimlet, 219
    Gin and Tonic, 217
    Hanky Panky, 237
    Hans Solo, 236
    Last Word, 227
    Martinez, 231
    Martini, 215
    Negroni, 235
    Old Friend, 233
    Ramos Gin
        Fizz, 229
    20th Century, 225
    Vesper, 187
    White Lady, 234
ginger wort, 393
Glaser, John, 32, 141
glassware
    holding, 99
    icing, 99
    placement of,
        419–20
    rims, applying
        spice to, 93
    selecting, 51, 82–83
    storing, 83
Gokan, Shingo, 458
Gold Coast, 197
Gonzales, Giuseppe, 453
Gramercy Tavern, 52,
        53, 191, 217, 287,
        361, 377, 403, 433
Grand Hotel
        (Yokahama), 175
Grant, William, 208
Grasshopper, 8, 383
Greene, Philip, 219, 251
Green Tea Punch, 247
Green Thumb, 253
Grimes, William, 17,
        208, 217
Grohusko, Jack, 325
Guidara, Will, 36–37
Gwynne, Erskine, 329

H

Hagood, Bo, 64, 67
Haigh, Ted, 17, 225, 325,
        359, 364, 449

Hamilton, Ed, 242, 259
Handy, Thomas H., 331
Hanky Panky, 237
Hans Solo, 236
Harrington,
        Paul, 223
Harris, Josh, 459
harvesting, 127
Hawtrey, Charles, 237
Hearn, Lafcadio, 259
Heimann, Jim, 395
Heller, Steven, 395
Hemingway, Ernest,
        219, 251
Hemingway Bar, 199
Hemingway
        Daiquiri, 251
Hendrickx, Myriam, 205
Hennessy, Richard, 345
Herman, Thomas, 195
Hermé, Pierre, 403
Hess, Robert, 227
Heugel, Bobby, 453
Highball, 307
Hine, Thomas, 345
Hoard, Sean, 74, 457
Hoefling, Brian, 370
Hoffman House,
        13, 15, 37
Hoke, John, 51, 67, 68
home bar, 66–69
honey syrup, 392
horchata, 390
        Café Arroz, 387
hospitality
    company culture
        and, 437–38
    instinct for,
        429–30, 444
    key to, 431–32
    management and,
        432–34
    self-care and,
        439–44
    service vs., 429
    staff and, 434–42
    See also service
Hot Whiskey, 319
Huff, Marisa, 151
Humm, Daniel,
        36–37, 411
Huston, Lucinda, 269
Hyman, Gale, 290

I

ice, 12, 81–82, 99–101, 112
Imperial Cabinet
        Saloon, 229
Irish whiskey, 136–37,
        294, 297, 298, 299
    Cameron's Kick, 338
    Hot Whiskey, 319
    Irish Coffee,
        108–9, 321
    Rosy Cheeks, 309

J

Jack Rose, 359
James Beard
        Foundation, 456
Jannuzzi, Felipe, 255
Japanese Cocktail, 367
Japanese whisky, 298,
        302, 303–4
    Highball, 307
jiggers, 88–89, 96–97
Jimenez Vizcarra,
        Miguel
        Claudio, 269
Jimmie Roosevelt, 365
Johnson, Harry, 4
Joly, Charles, 458
Jones, Ben, 241, 242
Jones, Stan, 23, 379
Jordan, Michael, 404
Judge Jr., 15, 221, 313
juice, fresh, 77–79
juleps, 12–13, 315

K

Kahlúa
        Café Arroz, 387
Kalkofen, Misty, 293
Karakasevic, Marko, 191
Katz, Allen, 126
Katz, Cheryl and Jef-
        frey, 62
Keller, Thomas, 217
Kina L'Aéro d'Or,
        150, 153
    Corpse Reviver
        #2, 232
King Cole Bar, 193
Kipling, Rudyard, 355
Kir, 165
Klein, Michael, 340
Kosmas, Jason, 24,
        25, 457

Krieger, Daniel, 55
Krogstad, Christian, 135

L

La Capilla Bar, 281, 429
Laird, Lisa, 359, 405
Langlais, Bernadette, 149
Lasa, Juan A., 249
Last Word, 227
Ledesma, S. E., 353
Lee, Don, 5, 117, 229
Leopold, Todd,
        136, 147–48
Le Syndicat, 350
Lidkoeb, 46, 48–49
lighting, 54, 55
Lillet blanc, 187
        Brown Bomber, 336
        Peaches and
                Cream, 195
        20th Century, 225
        Vesper, 187
lime cordial, 393
liqueurs, 368–75. *See
        also individual
        liqueurs*
Little Branch, 26
Livermore, Don, 305
Lombard, Carole, 225
Lomborg, Rasmus,
        46, 47
Lorincz, Erik, 87,
        457, 458
Lovell, Henrietta, 96
Lynch, Barbara, 411

M

MacKinnon, John, 379
madeira, 156, 158
        Hans Solo, 236
        Purple Rain, 337
Magarian, Ryan, 456
Mahoney, Charles, 4,
        15, 458
Mai Tai, 20, 264
management, 432–34
Manhattan, 327
maraschino liqueur, 370
        Aviation, 223
        Brooklyn, 325
        For Peat's Sake, 339
        Hemingway
                Daiquiri, 251

Last Word, 227
Martinez, 231
Newark, 363
Marco, Gerald, 290
Margarita, 270–71, 285
        Tommy's
                Margarita, 283
Mario, Thomas, 21
Marrero, Lynnette, 459
Martell, Jean, 345
Martin, Jean-Marie, 241
Martin, John G., 189
Martineau, Chantal, 275
Martinez, 8, 231
Martini, 215
mash, 130
Masso, Dre, 283
Mayahuel, 272
McCarthy, Steve, 345
McCrady's, 337
McDonnell, Duggan, 355
McElhone, Harry, 16,
        219, 234, 329,
        338, 364
McGarry, Jack, 37,
        41, 435
McIlroy, Michael, 27
McSorley's Old Ale
        House, 41
measuring, 88–89,
        94–97
Mechuga, 293
Meehan, Peter, vii–ix, 5
Meier, Frank, 193
Mencken, H. L., 17
menus
        absence of, 407, 408
        contents of, 409–10
        cost constraints and,
                396–98
        developing core,
                398–99
        as maps, 409
        nonalcoholic options
                on, 406
        printed, 407–8
        role of, 395
        space constraints
                and, 396
        theft of, 408
Merchant Hotel, 37
Meyer, Danny, 430,
        431, 433
Meyer, Joerg, 453

mezcal, 142, 268–69,
        272–73, 275–79
        Mechuga, 293
        Mezcal Mule, 291
Michelada, 79, 111,
        145–46, 177
Michener, James, 20
Mies van der Rohe,
        Ludwig, 37, 139
Milk & Honey, 26, 27, 80,
        325, 366, 407
Milk Punch, 388
milling, 129
Mint Julep, 12, 110, 315
mise en place, 84–86
Mitta, Johnny, 364
Mix, Ivy, 459
mixing glasses, 87
Miyamoto, Mike, 131,
        134, 302
Mizaga, Ludovic, 176
Mojito, 249
Molson, Thomas, 296
Momofuku, 398
Morgan, Jack, 189
Morgenthaler, Jeffrey,
        8, 76, 81, 98, 383,
        385, 453
Morris, Chris, 133
Morris, Victor, 353
Moscow Mule, 8, 19,
        180, 189
Moss, Robert, 12, 313
muddling, 97
Muldoon, Sean, 37, 397
Murray, Charles
        Augustus, 13
Museum of the
        American
        Cocktail, 24
music, 54, 422
Musso, Beppe, 5, 159, 169

N

Napoleon House, 173
Negroni, 119–20, 235
        East India
                Negroni, 266
Negroni, Count
        Camillo, 235
Nepove, David, 456
networking, 454
Newark, 363
Newman, Frank, 16, 215

Nichol, Tom, 135, 207
Nicol, Duncan, 355
Nightjar, 119
Nimb Hotel, 195
NoMad, 36–37, 38–39,
        40, 56, 84, 411
Nonino, Elisabetta, 371
Nurse, 176
Nye, Ken, 431

O

O'Brien, Harry, 383
Odeon, 201
Okamoto, Shintaro, 82
Old-Fashioned
        Old-Fashioned
                Whiskey
                Cocktail, 333
        Plátanos en Mole
                Old-Fashioned, 267
Old Friend, 233
Oliver, Garrett, 52
Oliver, Jaimie, 453
Olson, Nancy, 403
Olson, Steve, 127, 157,
        429–30, 461
Ordinaire, Pierre, 154
Osius, Frederick, 18

P

Pace, 167
Page, Karen, 402
Painturaud, Guillon, 346
Palace Hotel, 383
Palazzi, Nicolas, 340
Paloma, 281
Pariseau, Leslie, 167
Park Hyatt New York
        Bar, 253
Parkside Fizz, 191
Paul's Club, 383
Payne, Desmond, 213
PDT, 44, 74, 147, 195,
        236, 253, 289, 336,
        339, 340, 341, 363,
        386, 389, 396–98,
        408, 438
Peaches and Cream, 195
Pegu Club, 1, 75, 76, 209,
        287, 288, 359, 365,
        366, 385
Pelczer, Éva, 343
Pellaton, John, 366
Pépé le Moko, 383

Per Se, 217
Petiot, Fernand, 193
Petraske, Sasha, 24,
    26–27, 80, 397, 407
Piccadilly Hotel, 225
Picchi, Luca, 235
Pimm, James, 173
Pimm's #1 Cup, 41
    Pimm's Cup, 19, 173
Piña Colada, 21, 119, 257
pisco, 343, 348, 350
    Pisco Punch, 355
    Pisco Sour, 353
Plátanos en Mole Old-
    Fashioned, 267
port, 126, 156, 158–59
    Coffee Cocktail, 377
Pouring Ribbons, 409
pour spouts, 85, 96
Pravda, 25
prep order, deciding,
    92–93
privacy, respecting, 424
Prohibition, 15–17, 298
Proof & Co., 459
Proulx, Theodore, 333
Pub Royale, 173
punches, 10–12, 247
    Green Tea Punch, 247
    Milk Punch, 388
    Pisco Punch, 355
    Rosy Cheeks, 309
    Rum Punch, 7–8
    Ti' Punch, 242, 259
Purple Rain, 337
Pŭta, Aleš, 199

Q

quinquinas, 152–53

R

Rainbow Room, 24,
    323, 407
Ramos, Henry Charles
    "Carl," 229
Ramos Gin Fizz, 229
Rams, Dieter, 30
Reed, Ben, 199
Regan, Gary, 103, 287,
    381, 449, 456
Reiner, Julie, 24, 25, 436
Reisetbauer, Hans, 5,
    127, 147, 236, 349,
    350, 351, 364, 386

Reitz, Brooks, 74, 217, 457
rhum agricole, 239,
    241–42
    Mai Tai, 264
    Ti' Punch, 242, 259
Ribalaigua,
    Constantino,
    251, 261
Richter, Tom, 217
Ridgwell, Mark, 343
Ritz, César, 437
Ritz Hotel, 193
Roberts, Lewes, 344
Robin, Hubert
    Germain, 345
Robitschek, Leo, 445
rolling, 105
Rose, 364
Rose, Lauchlin, 219
Rosita, 287
Ross, John, 379
Ross, Sam, 18, 27, 366
Rosy Cheeks, 309
Roulot, Jean-Marc, 236
rum, 19, 238–41, 243–44
    Airmail, 265
    Black Flip, 389
    Daiquiri, 262
    East India
        Negroni, 266
    El Presidente, 261
    Five Island
        Flamingo, 263
    Green Tea Punch, 247
    Green Thumb, 253
    Hemingway
        Daiquiri, 251
    Mai Tai, 264
    Milk Punch, 388
    Mojito, 249
    Piña Colada, 257
    Plátanos en Mole
        Old-Fashioned, 267
    Rum Punch, 7–8
    Tom and Jerry, 385
    See also cachaça;
        rhum agricole
Russell, Jimmy, 132
Rusty Nail, 379
rye whiskey, 301, 302, 303
    Boulevardier, 329
    Brooklyn, 325
    DuBoudreau
        Cocktail, 341

    Old-Fashioned
        Whiskey
        Cocktail, 333
    Sazerac, 331
    Toronto, 335

S

St-Germain
    DuBoudreau
        Cocktail, 341
    Green Thumb, 253
    Old Friend, 233
Salcito, Jordan, 155, 157,
    165, 221
Saldaña, César, 127
Samuels, Bill, 305
San Miguel, 292
Saucier, Ted, 227
Saunders, Audrey,
    1–2, 5, 24, 26,
    209, 288, 359,
    365, 385, 452
Sauza, Don Cenobio, 270
Savoy Hotel, 237
Sazerac, 331
Sazerac House Bar, 331
Scarselli, Fosco, 235
Schaf, Peter, 161
Schmidt, Ozaline, 189
Schmidt, William, 15
Schneider, Steve, 453
Schultz, Christian, 367
Schwartz, Joseph, 26
Scotch, 25, 136, 294, 297,
    298, 300
    Blood and Sand, 317
    Bobby Burns, 323
    Cameron's Kick, 338
    For Peat's Sake, 339
    Rusty Nail, 379
Seagram, Joseph, 296
Seed, Eric, 153, 231
Seestedt, Tad, 139
seminars, 455–56
service
    bar, 421–22
    check presentation
        and, 423
    communication and,
        417–18, 420–21
    conflicts and, 424–26
    finishing touches
        for, 427
    hospitality vs., 429

    importance of, 413–14
    noise and, 422
    placement of glasses,
        419–20
    position numbers
        and, 120–21
    privacy and, 424
    safety and, 426–27
    setting up for, 74–83
    side for, 419
    timing and, 120, 418
    welcoming guests,
        414–17
    See also hospitality
Seutter, Carl, 16
Seymour, Andy, 157
shaking, 86–87,
    101–3, 107
Sheridan, Joe, 321
sherry, 156–58
    Bamboo, 175
    East India
        Negroni, 266
    Mechuga, 293
    Peaches and
        Cream, 195
    Sherry Cobbler, 171
Shoemaker, Daniel, 74,
    75, 457
Sidecar, 357
simple syrup, 76, 391
sloe gin
    Rosy Cheeks, 309
Slotnick, Bonnie, 2
Smith, Marilyn, 271–72
social media, 453
Sombra, 291
speed pourers, 85, 96
staff
    care for, 440–42
    hiring, 434–36
    training, 437–38
    turnover, 438–39
Stag Saloon, 229
Starck, Philippe, 50
Starlight Room, 25
Stein, James, 205
Stein, Robert, 206, 297
Stenson, Murray,
    227, 448
Stinger, 375, 381
stirring, 105–6
Stone Fence, 311

straining, 88, 103–4, 106, 107–8
Straub, Jacques, 262, 325, 359, 381
straws, 116
Strega
    Witch's Kiss, 289
Stuart, Charles Edward (Bonnie Prince Charlie), 379
Stuckey, Bobby, 441
Suze, 150, 370
    Brown Bomber, 336
Swedish Punsch
    Gold Coast, 197
swizzling, 110

T

Taketsuru, Masataka, 298
Tarling, W. J., 225, 285
tasting, 98–99, 140–41
Tatanka, 198
Taylor, Will, 16
tea, 96
    After Nine, 386
    Green Tea Punch, 247
Teacher, William, 297
Teardrop Lounge, 397
Teeling, John, 299
tequila, 142, 268–75
    Café Arroz, 387
    El Diablo, 290
    Margarita, 270–71, 285
    Paloma, 281
    Rosita, 287
    San Miguel, 292
    Tequila Sunrise, 270–71
    Tommy's Margarita, 283
    21st Century, 288
    Witch's Kiss, 289
Terrington, William, 16
terroir, 146–47, 244
T.G.I. Fridays, 22
Thomas, Jerry, 1, 4, 14–15, 17, 163, 171, 311, 315, 319, 367, 377, 385, 388
throwing, 104–5
Tiano, Jack, 22
tiki bars, 20–21

Ti' Punch, 242, 259
Tom and Jerry, 385, 391
Tommy's Margarita, 283
Tommy's Mexican Restaurant, 31, 283
Tonutti, Ivano, 169
Torii, Shinjiro, 298
Torino Torino, 169
Toronto, 335
Toye, Nina, 361
Trader Vic, 18, 20, 21, 264, 290
tradition, honoring, 113
transportation, 128
travel, 454–55
Trick Dog, 459
Troia, John, 371, 373
Trou Normand, 350
Tuck, C. A., 225, 288
Tudor, Frederic, 12
Tujague, 383
20th Century, 225
21st Century, 288

U

Ueno, Hidetsugu, 118, 234
uniforms, 51–52
Usher, Andrew, 297
Uyeda, Kazuo, 113, 440, 448

V

Valentino, Rudolph, 317
Van Eycken, Stefan, 304
Van Flandern, Brian, 217
vanilla syrup, 392
van Maerlant, Jacob, 203
van Tiel, Georgia, 442, 463
Varnish, 26
Vendôme Club, 313
Venetian Spritz, 167
Vermeire, Robert, 221, 335, 357
vermouth, 150, 151–52
    Bamboo, 175
    Blood and Sand, 317
    Bobby Burns, 323
    Boulevardier, 329
    Brooklyn, 325
    El Presidente, 261
    Hanky Panky, 237
    Manhattan, 327
    Martinez, 231

Martini, 215
Negroni, 235
Newark, 363
Nurse, 176
Rose, 364
Rosita, 287
Torino Torino, 169
Vernon, Edward, 240–41
Vesper, 145–46, 153, 187
Vic's, 53
vodka, 19, 24, 178–85, 208
    Bloody Mary, 193
    Cocktail Culture, 200
    Cosmopolitan, 24, 26, 183, 201
    Czechmate, 199
    Gold Coast, 197
    Moscow Mule, 8, 19, 180, 189
    Parkside Fizz, 191
    Peaches and Cream, 195
    Tatanka, 198
    Vesper, 187
Vogler, Thad, 350
Voisey, Charlotte, 209, 450, 451
Von, 26

W

Walker, Hiram, 296, 305
Walker, John, 297
Ward, Phil, 272–73, 279, 400
water, 130–31, 417
whipped cream, 393
whisk(e)y, 18–19, 25, 136–37, 294–305
    Boulevardier, 329
    Brooklyn, 325
    Brown Bomber, 336
    DuBoudreau Cocktail, 341
    George Washington, 340
    Highball, 307
    Old-Fashioned Whiskey Cocktail, 333
    Sazerac, 331
    Toronto, 335
    See also bourbon; Scotch

White Lady, 234
Whitfield, W. C., 265
Wilkinson, William H., 331
Willard, Orasmus, 12–13
Winchester, Angus, 3, 195, 455
wine
    fortified, 156–59
    Kir, 165
    sparkling, 155
    still, 156
    Venetian Spritz, 167
    See also champagne; madeira; port; sherry
Winters, Lance, 124, 137–38, 191, 345
Witch's Kiss, 289
Woelke, Eddie, 16, 261
Wondrich, David, 2, 5, 8, 10, 12, 13, 14, 171, 175, 204, 206, 223, 227, 231, 247, 261, 265, 270, 281, 311, 333, 353, 355, 361, 367, 379, 381, 453
Woon, Basil, 17
wort, 130

Y

Yeager, Jimmy, 439
yeast, 132

Z

Zaric, Dushan, 24, 25, 457
Zig Zag Café, 227

Published in the United States by Ten Speed Press, an imprint of the Crown
Publishing Group, a division of Penguin Random House LLC, New York.
www.crownpublishing.com
www.tenspeed.com

Ten Speed Press and the Ten Speed Press colophon are registered trademarks of
Penguin Random House LLC.

Library of Congress Cataloging-in-Publication Data

Names: Meehan, Jim, 1976– author.
Title: Meehan's bartender manual / Jim Meehan ; illustrations by M ;
  photography by Doron Gild.
Description: First edition. | California : Ten Speed Press, 2017. | Includes
  bibliographical references and index.
Identifiers: LCCN 2017024758
Subjects: LCSH: Cocktails. | Bartending. | BISAC: Cooking / Beverages /
  Bartending. | COOKING / Beverages /Wine & Spirits.
Classification: LCC TX951.M355 2017 | DDC 641.87/4--dc23
LC record available at https://lccn.loc.gov/2017024758

Hardcover ISBN: 978-1-60774-862-5
eBook ISBN: 978-1-60774-863-2

Printed in China

Design by Betsy Stromberg

10 9 8 7 6 5